CORPORATE
LEADERSHIP

CORPORATE LEADERSHIP

LEADERSHIP

BOARDS, DIRECTORS, AND STRATEGY

Stanley C. Vance
University of Tennessee

McGraw-Hill Book Company

New York   St. Louis   San Francisco   Auckland   Bogotá
Hamburg   Johannesburg   London   Madrid   Mexico   Montreal   New Delhi
Panama   Paris   São Paulo   Singapore   Sydney   Tokyo   Toronto

This book was set in Optima by Black Dot, Inc. (ECU).
The editors were Kathi A. Benson and Jonathan Palace;
the production supervisor was Diane Renda.
The cover was designed by Infield, D'Astolfo Associates.
R. R. Donnelley & Sons Company was printer and binder.

CORPORATE LEADERSHIP

Boards, Directors, and Strategy

ISBN 0-07-066873-6 HC

ISBN 0-07-066872-8 SC

Library of Congress Cataloging in Publication Data

Vance, Stanley C.
    Corporate leadership.

    (McGraw-Hill series in management)
    Includes bibliographical references and indexes.
    1. Directors of corporations—United States.
I. Title. II. Series.
HD2745.V33 1983   658.4'22   82-10040
ISBN 0-07-066873-6
ISBN 0-07-066872-8 (pbk.)

CONTENTS

FOREWORD

Many years ago, Bishop Gore of Oxford, whose life had been dedicated to education, was asked to make some generalizations about students. He said the most striking and unexpected discovery he had made was that, although the natural gifts of people varied enormously, such differences in talent were of little or no value compared with how a person used the talent he or she possessed.

The effectiveness of a corporate leader without strong individual determination and a full use of existing talents is likely to be determined by the organization or by the environment in which the institution finds itself. The challenge of corporate leadership is to reverse this determination. An underlying, if implicit, postulate to Dr. Stanley Vance's *Corporate Leadership* is that a leader must influence a corporation more than it influences him or her. Certainly this activist perspective for directors and top management is the core issue and a challenge for all corporate leaders in the future.

The corporate leaders of tomorrow need to initiate and better maintain corporate structure and expect interaction with their own organizations, constituents, and the public. This is the true meaning of corporate leadership.

In order to do this, it is necessary to have an understanding of the concepts, dynamics, maturation, and interaction of governance and management processes and structures. Dr. Vance understands these and provides us with an intelligent, comfortable clustering of various notions and distinctions, including the abstract roots and driving forces at work in the field of corporate leadership. While focused mainly on corporate leaders in the United States, the case examples and roundup of evolving trends and experimentation in Japan, Sweden, Germany, France, Peru, the United Kingdom, and other nations provide a rich backdrop. This book is an update of issues and innovations of contemporary boards and directors in the corporate business world. The rather complete inventory of conventional concepts about corporate governance is provided in the first seven chapters. The author thus offers a readable source book which should be especially valuable for those who wish to bring their understanding of the state of the art of corporate leadership into current focus. The author's occasional flashbacks to the historical roots, canons, articles of faith, traditions, legal framework, and philosophical underpinnings of the overworld of corporate governance make the text a sprightly as well as pragmatic guide and think book.

Dr. Vance's ordered interpretation of past boardroom experiences, corporate lamentations, legal challenges, governmental intrusions, public concerns, and internal and external forces at work on corporations provides a balanced perspective of the issues of corporate leadership for the 1980s. This is a timely contribution to the literature on corporate governance.

The perturbation of corporations around the world by mostly uncontrollable economic, social, legal, technological, and political forces is at least twice as great now than it was a mere decade ago. The relatively steady-state environment in which corporations existed in the past no longer prevails. Corporation leaders find themselves facing disequilibrium, instability, turbulence, discontinuities, and an unusual degree of uncertainty in external situations when governing and managing corporations.

In these unstable, uncertain days the effective development of boards and individual directors in order to provide better leadership for our corporations is like playing Chinese baseball. Chinese baseball is played almost like American baseball: there are the same number of players, the same field, the same bats and balls, the same methods of keeping score, and so on. The batter stands in the batter's box, and the pitcher stands on the mound, as usual. The pitcher winds up in normal fashion and zips the ball toward the batter's box. There is one and only one difference: after the ball leaves the pitcher's hand, as long as the ball is in the air, anyone can move any of the bases anywhere. The result is that the game is continuously changing. Uncertainty, some confusion, and some errors occur on the playing field. The analogy in the field of corporate governance is that disconcerting environmental, competitive, political, social, economic, cultural, military, and technological changes are occurring frequently in the board of directors' "game." The symmetry of past states of relative equilibrium is dissipating. Traditional board perspectives, structure, and processes are no longer sufficient to prepare directors to effectively carry out their conventional roles.

Dr. Vance provides a clear understanding of where the conflicts, problems, issues, and areas for improvement lie in corporate leadership. In addition, he provides us with some innovative thinking: experiments for the domain of corporate governance, directors as intangible assets on the balance sheet, and the hypothesis that board structure has some meaning for industrial productivity are all novel concepts worth pondering.

As the introduction to this foreword observed, leadership must influence an institution more than it influences the leaders. In corporate governance this calls for a somewhat detached view of the conceptual framework. This task is especially difficult given the plight that corporations and their leaders find themselves in, as reflected in diminishing public esteem, trust, and confidence. The situation tends to shape corporate cultures to that of an enclave with status quo orientation. Preserving those conditions and dynamics of which the leaders are certain become prime objectives. However, this fails to provide the drive and means for more effective corporate leadership.

The attitude of corporate leaders must thus undergo transformation to be able to adapt and adjust to the conditions under which boards of directors must now govern. This transformation will be reflected in changes in the role and nature of boards; the boundary or compass of board concern, board structure, and board processes; and board continuity, renewal, and development.

For the most part, these transformations will be evolutionary. Changes are often subtle. More boards are experimenting very carefully with respect to their activities. Preserving the past nature of corporate governance is no longer the prime governance issue; facilitating transformation of the board is the new issue. Dr. Vance goes a long way in helping us understand the limitations and this new leadership issue. The following seldom-cited limitations of corporate governance are a few conceptual curbstones which currently inhibit that enclave known as the boardroom.

Boardroom Boundaries: Boards of directors tend to draw boundaries around their domain with more certainty than experience or good conduct warrants. Boards tend to perform mostly as a closed system similar to the command-and-control, closed-system characteristics of a conventionally structured, orderly management system.

Boards should be conceptualized as open systems allowing information, beliefs, intuition, attitudes, aspirations, value systems, need hierarchies, and psychic forces of morality and ethics to continuously relate to the board's role in monitoring, auditing, strategic thinking, and direction in a complex environment.

Board Nature: Many boards do not explicitly allow for ambiguity in choice situations faced in corporate governance. Ambiguity may be an asset in certain instances where interpersonal relationships, political considerations, or tolerance of conflicting attitudes are important for focusing on multiple causation rather than on single causes. Dr. Vance illustrates this limitation in many of the case examples which supplement the individual chapters. Chapter 8 discusses this limitation.

Board Life Cycles: All boards have a life cycle of their own, and the stage in the life cycle represented by the board's condition may not be congruent with the life cycle(s) of the corporation served or the strategic business units involved in a diversified enterprise.

The life cycle of the board depends upon the nature and composition of its members, their respective maturity, and the group's experience in working together. This relationship is either a social, intellectual, or emotional contract, or a mix of these. As a consequence, directors are bound together by sharing the same fate of directing an institution as stewards, trustees, or fiduciaries. Chapter 3 describes in detail the implications of life cycles of boardroom incumbents which are incongruent with cycles of the enterprise being governed.

Board Renewal: Renewal, succession, and continuity for a board of directors are as vital as that for key management. Director recruitment, education, development, evaluation, separation, and succession are frequently neglected processes.

Board Process: Governance processes do not necessarily match those most effective in the management realm. The latter are hierarchically oriented, judicial and directive in nature with allocation of power and accountability. Corporate governance, in contrast, is achieved in a nonhierarchical forum. Political processes and peer processes are at work. Concensus is strived for. Differences in opinion are (or should be) encouraged. The separation of governance from management with a distinct role for the board is yet to be universally and realistically accepted in many firms. This is particularly true of closely held corporations—small- and medium-sized companies—where stakeholder or commonweal interests may not be fully acknowledged. Dr. Vance orients us on this subtle distinction between governance and management.

The Temporal Dimension: Boards tend to be occupied with the present or short-term future. Many tend to confirm the status quo. Chapter 7 is a good treatment of this common limitation of corporate governance.

Board Score: Dynamic criteria and standards are usually neither adequately established nor recognized for rating an individual's board worthiness or an entire board's effectiveness. Dr. Vance devotes his final Chapter 9, one of the most important chapters in the book, to the subject of board evaluation and its challenges.

Learning: Directors' personal mechanisms of perception and cognition basically operate to limit sensory input so that the individual can make sense of a data-rich world. A learning process is involved as the organizing framework is modified to account for repeated exposure to experience not in accord with the original tenets of an individual director. *Corporate*

Leadership provides us with a readable, scholarly framework for studying and understanding governance and management.

Strangely, because of the prior limitations cited, boards are inclined to behave in ways that inhibit the learning process. To some extent, this makes individual directors immobile, i.e., incapable of grasping (let alone grappling with) anything that is not forced on them by dramatic external events and pressures.

Undoubtedly, there are other limitations in the current trends and transformation of boards as they address the issues of the 1980s. The heartening aspect is that the level of consciousness about the need for changes in corporate governance is increasing rapidly. Dr. Vance's contributions in this book will not only raise the level of consciousness about the need for more effective corporate leadership but also provide us with a base station from which we can educate ourselves, and conduct experimentation in the way Bishop Gore suggested. This means utilizing the latent talent that currently exists in those persons in corporate leadership positions.

Robert K. Mueller
Chairman of the Board
Arthur D. Little, Inc.

PREFACE

Every year an average of 10,000 businesses (and an estimated 24,000 in 1982) make the corporate obituary list—death due to mediocre management and lackluster leadership. This phenomenally high corporate mortality takes its toll, not only in millions of wasted investment dollars but also in heartaches and shattered dreams of so many venturing entrepreneurs.

While some would say chronic bankruptcy and liquidation loss are unavoidable—a price we pay for freedom and competition—this claim is only partially true. We have an encouraging parallel in the area of health care. Even though illness and death are inevitable, medical science has learned how to restrain unconquerable diseases. If the corporate sector is to restrain its ills, it must start with the organization's executives and directors, for an organization is only as healthy as its leaders.

Since no competent medical technician would venture a diagnosis without having some knowledge of the patient's medical past, so, too, the following appraisal of boards of directors will take a look into the past. "Boardroom Roots: The Early American Experience" (Chapter 1) shows that many of today's governance problems are several centuries old and could even be congenital. Recognizing them could help in finding cures.

Following in sequence are three basic concepts—"Board Purpose," "Board Characteristics," and "Board Structure" (Chapters 2 to 4, respectively). They set the corporate health parameters and discuss what a board is supposed to do and what specific characteristics condition goal setting, strategy selection, and effective performance. Organization structures might be viewed as either cause or effect; yet structure invariably is a paramount consideration.

While these initial chapters suggest "how-to" prescriptions to a degree, they are intentionally kept general and broad in scope. Consider in our enterprise system the wide latitude in company size, product mix, financial structure, geographic setting, congenital traits, leadership styles, and a dozen other vitally differentiating factors. In these few pages it would seem foolhardy to venture comprehensive "how to" advice that would lead only to management nostrums, not to logical directorate diagnoses.

In sequence, the analyst must get a proper index of the subject's "Internal Constraints" (Chapter 5). Here lies a near-infinity of possibilities. More complicating is the increasing array of external factors—government regulatory bodies, professional associations, public interest groups, and others. As one's health becomes affected by extraneous agents, so, too, a corporation's well-being is increasingly conditioned by "External Constraints" (Chapter 6) such as inflation, gold-price gyrations, OPEC oil perturbations, and reverberations of military adventures 10,000 miles away.

The next topic, "Evolution through Precedents" (Chapter 7), presupposes that as unpatterned legal problems arise, they tend to be settled individually in duly constituted legal settings. The decisions that follow then set a precedent in the manner of evolving common law. A sample series of narratives, ranging from the "phases of the moon" through the Texas Gulf, Penn Central, and more recent J. P. Stevens and Gulf Oil episodes, show how logic and common law in corporate governance are slowly yet inexorably evolving.

It should be noted that most of the case illustrations describe experiences of large corporations. This is inevitable. It is the bigger, public corporation that tends to get in the limelight. There is considerable documentation in the media, and the interested reader can identify the firm and corroborate. Episodes based on small-company experience are often extremely difficult to find and to verify. Moreover, in corporate governance, as in virtually every business practice or fad, it is the bigger companies that set the pace. Smaller firms invariably follow the leaders.

Up to this point the study is basically diagnostic—a viewing of symptoms and suggestions for improvement. The next chapter, "New/Innovative Designs for Boards" (Chapter 8), is more prognostic, suggesting a number of innovations. Here we have a glimpse of what the future may have in store for board structures, directors and boardroom practices, policies, and philosophies. Shared authority, codetermination, and ESOPs are among the innovations considered.

The final topic, "Board Evaluation" (Chapter 9), is an even bigger step in the direction of prognosis. Each of the topics discussed is controversial and guaranteed to raise the hackles of some readers. Yet these are issues that must be faced. "Director Dimensions," for example, is concerned with using reason in staffing a board. What particular attributes does a specific board need? How do we determine what candidates possess the needed attributes and in what quantities? How do we measure?

Another subject is director certification. Among professionals, directors stand out as being the only group without rigid entrance requirements. There are no professional designations such as the CPA or CLU. Yet the formal education level continues to rise: half of all executives under age forty hold M.B.A. degrees, compared to only one in six for the age-fifty group. As the percentage increases, it is highly likely that an M.B.A. will become a prerequisite, not only for hiring but for eventual certification at the directorate level.

There is also the irritating issue of how much "sunshine" should be allowed to penetrate the boardroom. Thirty years ago, in trying to find out how one macrocorporation's board functioned, this author was bluntly told: "It's none of your goddamned business what goes on in the boardroom!" Directorate illumination, a generation ago, was intentionally kept at a low level, just as artificial lighting in the workshop averaged a mere 7 footcandles. Today, well-lighted plant work areas receive up to 100 footcandles of illumination, and areas of very fine work get up to 200 footcandles. Unfortunately, the area where the most delicate corporate decisions are made—the boardroom—has not risen much above a mere 7-footcandle power.

Other open-ended issues arise, such as corporate constituency, productivity, and *entelechy,* the last being the ultimate in motivation. Boards of directors have very little by way of constituencies, even though 33 million Americans are directly owners of common stock, and every other citizen is indirectly an owner.

In regard to productivity, is the economic slump of the past decade related to the significant increase in outside directors? Logic could support this inference. What we seemingly need are fewer "independent" or detached directors and more who are inextricably meshed with the affairs and future of the firm. In particular, we need boards that equate to composite entrepreneurs.

Then there is *entelechy,* the Aristotelian and fundamental motivator which translates into "I have my goal within." Although every healer recognizes the importance of prescribing the right curative, a more important force is the drive from within, the patient's indomitable will to survive. A board of directors with real entelechy, a board that has powerful goals within, where self-actualization and self-motivation have definite meaning, is a board immune to most management maladies.

There is some urgency in this corporate boardroom "call to arms." Productivity, competition, and our very way of life are at stake, and the effectiveness of our enterprise system depends upon diligent and competent corporate directors. This becomes even more apparent as the scale of enterprise expands. Presently there are 315 industrial corporations with sales volume over the $1 billion level; this number is almost doubled when nonindustrial companies are counted. There are an additional 433 foreign industrials, and a near-equal number of other foreign firms, in this billion-dollar sales "club." Unfortunately, in this book, only a casual consideration could be given to foreign enterprises.

Although we now total about 15,600,000 domestic corporations, partnerships, and sole proprietorships, for reasons of expediency this study has been limited to the large publicly owned macrocorporations—less than 1 percent of the total. It is here that the real governance action is visible, chronicled, and diagnosed by the media. The public reads about the doings of these trendsetters and forms opinions.

Obviously, these corporate pacesetters are not doing their best to influence the attitudes of the public or even of their own shareowners. The most recent Opinion Research Corporation poll (March 1982) rated large companies fourth from the bottom, and their boards of directors second from the bottom, on the basis of public trust and confidence. Of nineteen occupations ranked by ethical and moral practices, corporate board members were ranked seventeenth, barely beating out the bottom-rung labor leaders and federal government officials.

But even as the public rated corporations and their directors extremely low on public trust and confidence and on ethical and moral practices, it recognized the preeminence of these institutions. A *U.S. News & World Report* survey conducted in May 1982 ranked large business as the second most influential institution out of thirty—only the White House placed ahead (television was third and the U.S. Senate was fourth). Conversely, small business ranked next to the bottom, just ahead of cinema, the least influential.

There is an obvious dichotomy here: a yin/yang, love/hate sort of ambivalence evidenced periodically in the many thousands of business attritions and the more than compensating new ventures. The challenge for big business—and for boards of directors—is to continue as a leading institutional influence, and to build public trust and confidence by improved ethical and moral practices. Part of the problem is in corporate and directorate turnover, a consequence of minimally informed, poorly motivated, and unqualified directors who are unwittingly pushed into corporate leadership roles.

This year, as a half million new enterprises (mostly sole proprietorships) come upon the business scene, and as many as 3000 neophyte directors fill seats on at least 400 new public corporations, serious governance and leadership needs will continue to be apparent. Nevertheless, we should strive not to repeat mistakes of years past, which resulted in approximately 24,000 corporate closures in 1982 and probably exacerbated the low public trust and confidence in corporate leadership. While dynamism and innovation must be encouraged with new entries, boardroom turnover costs might be reduced and director stature might be heightened if we had better-informed, dedicated, and effective directors.

However, there is no rigid prescription for universal boardroom effectiveness. In the words of Chairman Mao Tse-tung, "Let a hundred flowers bloom, let a hundred schools of thought contend." In our enterprise world, the flowers (firms) that bloom can literally be counted, not in the hundreds but in the millions, and there are thousands of different and even divergent schools of thought.

In a unique way, these many and varied enterprises, with different structures, technologies, policies, and philosophies, coalesce into a remarkable economic mechanism. This mechanism continues to give us a veritable corporate cornucopia of material blessings, along with the best in education, health care, social welfare, and freedom in all sectors, unmatched anywhere in history. This bountiful cornucopia deserves to be appreciated and perpetuated.

ACKNOWLEDGMENTS

On a recent adventure to the land of Marianne, I had a number of opportunities to observe how France has contributed to governance theory. Seldom if ever mentioned is the saga of the Norman invasion of Britain by William the Conqueror. This conquest, in 1066, centralized the fragmented Anglo-Saxon principalities. Its effect led to the revolt of the barons and the signing of the Magna Carta at Runnymede two centuries later. This was the real beginning of modern checks-and-balances governance and, one could say, of boards of directors.

This saga is depicted in the famous Bayeux Tapestry, a 230-foot worsted embroidery, sequentially showing the genesis of the invasion and conquest. While some of its scenes might seem to be out of order or appear to be inconsequential, and the authenticity of some scenes could be disputed, in its composite the Bayeux Tapestry does record an epic "the way it was." It is not only William the Conqueror's story but also the story of a host of participants—thousands of footmen and boatmen, archers, artillery and horsemen, and many bystanders.

Similarly, the vignettes in this book offer a portrayal of corporate governance, the way it was and the way it is. None of the scenes or episodes can stand alone; all are intertwined and woven into an endless sequencing, a kaleidoscopic tableaux. Though many individuals and organizations have contributed to the designing and fashioning of this corporate governance tapestry, only those directly quoted in specific references have been properly acknowledged. Many participants contributed less to the "quotable" and more to the "inspirational." Some are unaware that they provided the substance and encouragement I needed during my years of interest in corporate governance. I am especially grateful to:

Armstrong World Industries (formerly Armstrong Cork), for giving me the first opportunity to get acquainted with an optimal board during the summer of 1950.

Business Week, for printing an analysis of my earliest research on boards of directors—in a November 1955 issue—thereby sparking within me a growing enthusiasm for continued research on the subject.

Bernard "Barnie" Kilgore, eminent former editor of *The Wall Street Journal,* who set off a conflagration within me when he editorialized on the inside director–outside director controversy researched in my study, *Boards of Directors: Structure and Performance* (Eugene, Oregon: University of Oregon Press, 1964).

John O. Larsen, former corporate secretary at Standard Oil Company (N.J.), now Exxon, for making a sixteen-month research opportunity possible in 1967. Through Fred Lindsley, John's associate, numerous boardroom doors were open to me.

In addition, I would like to acknowledge Dr. Keith Davis, professor emeritus, Arizona State University, long-time consultant to McGraw-Hill's Series in Management, long-time author and scholar, and long-time friend, who in the course of dinner and a margarita at a San Antonio meeting dreamed up the idea of putting my pet research into book form.

Dr. Alexandra Reed, editor of *Directors & Boards,* and John Nash, executive director of The National Association of Corporate Directors, who took time out from their demanding schedules to read and critique this manuscript.

From the academic world, I wish to thank those who read my manuscript in various stages: John D. Blackburn, The Ohio State University; Robert Corley, The University of Georgia; Jon Goodman, University of Houston; Fred Luthans, The University of Nebraska-Lincoln; Curt Stiles, University of Southern California; and John L. Ward, Loyola University of Chicago.

And finally, I owe much to Regina ("Gene"), my wife and perennial teammate, who for many years has worked on all my manuscripts: this too has been a labor of love. We hope our "invasion" into the insularly secure corporate boardroom—during the summer of 1981—will be as successful as the invasion depicted in the tapestry at Bayeux.

Stanley C. Vance

CORPORATE LEADERSHIP

CHAPTER 1

BOARDROOM ROOTS: THE EARLY AMERICAN EXPERIENCE

Boardroom roots go as deep as the very foundation of our nation. The American colonies, for example, were products of two British merchant adventurer associations: the Virginia Company of London and the Virginia Company of Plymouth, the latter subsequently succeeded by the Massachusetts Bay Company. Established in 1606 by royal charter, the Virginia societies secured two settlement grants. Each grant, with 100 miles of coastal frontage and extending inland from "sea to sea," was to be governed by a local council, an on-the-scene group of colonists (an inside board of directors). However, a higher council residing in England (an outside board), and answering directly to the sovereign, had the final say on all policy matters.

This vesting of authority in councils of peers was unique to British governance, a derivation from the Magna Carta (1215). In sharp contrast, the more conventional colonization at that time, as practiced, for example, by Spain, was to endow a favored nobleman, frequently a conquistador, with a land grant. Britain's chartering of societies of adventurers put governance of an enterprise into the hands of groups of peers. While the higher councils (or boards) in the home country were invariably of the gentility, political peers, those composing the governance group in the colonies, soon evolved into enterpriser peers. In every instance, however, authority devolved from the sovereign.

Historically, there are a number of governance parallels between yesterday's Virginia Company and today's macrocorporation. Both were and are

1

"fictitious entities created by state fiat." Even though it was not until 1819 that Chief Justice John Marshall rendered the classic Dartmouth College decision, stating that "the corporation is an artificial being, invisible, intangible and existing only in the contemplation of the law," his was not really a pioneering decision. The Chief Justice was simply reiterating the three-century-old Elizabethan notion that an association of merchant adventurers, the corporation, was "an artificial entity created by legal fiat." Herein lies a caution for all of us concerned about the corporation and its board of directors: What the state can create by fiat, it can take away by fiat. Consequently, much of the current debate over business regulation is not a matter of whether the government *can* impose business parameters, but rather to what extent the political *should* regulate the commercial. And since this is a matter of political and corporate constituencies, each pulling in the governance tug-of-war, the side with the greatest weight and muscle will have the greatest pull.

Among other similarities, the Founding Fathers also had to wrestle with the inside/outside dilemma. Ultimate authority presumably rested with the sovereign and his designated council in the homeland. While this group of directors included some absentee owners, basically it was an outside directorate similar to what we presently refer to as an "oversight" board. In the long run both the Virginia and Plymouth enterprises outgrew this two-tier governance mechanism.

Early evidence that on-the-scene authority was replacing absentee outside director control was manifest in Captain John Smith's classic mandate —"Those who do not work shall not eat"—and also in the Mayflower Compact. In the latter, the Pilgrims, while pledging allegiance to the king, nevertheless selected their own government and "officer-directors" by the will of the majority. The ultimate in this inside-director/outside-director dichotomy came in 1776 when even the figment of allegiance to an absentee authority gave way to on-the-scene authority.

For very obvious reasons, the wider use of boards of directors had to wait for the growth in the number and scale of industrial enterprises. One of the very first colonial "corporations," The Philadelphia Contributionship for the Insurance of Houses from Loss by Fire, was founded by Benjamin Franklin in 1752. This early joint venture was actually a superpartnership, very similar to the Elizabethan merchant adventurers. Interestingly, the Contributionship continues to function to this day. Its board is the epitome of the SEC's "ideal board"; all outsiders but one, the chief executive officer (CEO). Significantly, the Contributionship, even after 230 years, makes minimal impact on the insurance field. It has less than twenty employees, and its insurance in force is less than one-thousandth of such leaders as Prudential or Metropolitan. Yet the board of directors of this less-than-minuscule firm has relatively more Philadelphia Main Line blue blood and Ivy League encrustations per share than any comparable U.S. entity. Election to its board is equivalent to getting an engraved invitation from the Keeper of the Pearly Gates!

Equal credit should also be given to another great pioneer father, Alexander Hamilton, who organized our young nation's first real industrial corporation. In 1791 he completed his "Report on Manufactures," which was our nation's first business and manufacturing census. His list of seventeen manufacturing lines of endeavor set the precedent for today's Standard Industrial Classification Index, with its nearly 1400 SIC code numbers.

Evidently Hamilton's entrepreneurial zest was sparked by his census, and he decided to venture. On November 28, 1791, the New Jersey Legislature gave life to Hamilton's "The Society for Establishing Useful Manufactures," authorizing it to produce paper, linens for sails, women's shoes, brass and ironware, carpets, and print cloth. More than a century and a half before we even dreamed of conglomerates, Hamilton had structured one. But Hamilton's conglomerate lasted less than five years. It fell apart not only because it lacked competent workers and skillful managers, but also because the absentee outside directors failed to involve themselves in the affairs of the enterprise.

Hamilton's Society, sometimes referred to by its initials—SUM— employed some modern boardroom functions; for example, long before we were concerned about audit committees, Hamilton included a truly independent Committee of Inspectors, consisting of five stockholders who were not directors. These vigilantes were chosen from among defeated directorship candidates, generally the five who came closest to winning. Or the stockholders, if they saw fit, could simply elect any five stockholders, but nondirectors, to serve as inspectors. These had the right of access to all the books of the company and of examination into all its affairs.

Among other modernizations, Hamilton included a profit-sharing incentive for top managers of 5 percent of the preinterest profits. He recognized the serious limitation of our present one-share, one-vote proxy mechanism. He also shied away from a strictly equalitarian one-stockholder, one-vote concept, and recommended—not for SUM, but for our National Bank, which he also helped organize—that voting rights be scaled as follows:

Owners of 1 or 2 shares get 1 vote per share
Owners of 3 to 10 shares get 1 vote per 2 shares
Owners of 11 to 30 shares get 1 vote per 4 shares
Owners of 31 to 60 shares get 1 vote per 6 shares
Owners of 61 to 100 shares get 1 vote per 8 shares
Owners of 101 or more shares get 1 vote per 10 shares

Hamilton recognized that lifetime or longtime directorship appointments entailed weaknesses, and advocated a rotation whereby no more than three-fourths of the board could be renominated. Even more radical, SUM was authorized to run a lottery for up to $100,000 a year for five years. It also received exemption from real estate taxes for ten years, and from personal property taxes forever.

Interestingly, Hamilton and his eminent contemporary, Jefferson, also anticipated today's inside-director/outside-director dichotomy. Although both were elitists and aristocrats, Jefferson leaned toward the little guy, states' rights, agriculture, decentralization, and the individual entrepreneur. Hamilton, in contrast, believed that the wealth-generating process was in itself a natural selection process and that the Lord had destined successful bankers, merchants, esquires, and politicians to serve as outside directors.

As previously mentioned, Hamilton's SUM was given legal life by the New Jersey Legislature in 1791. Although several states, as early as 1776, had begun to charter corporations, there was no great chartering crush. For example, the Pennsylvania Society for the Encouragement of Manufactures and the Useful Arts was formed in 1787 but was defeated in the legislature by one vote. By 1800 there were less than 300 chartered firms, of which only eight were manufacturing ventures.

At the turn of the century, two equally momentous happenings occurred: J. P. Morgan midwifed our first billion-dollar corporation, United States Steel Corporation, and Henry Ford gave birth to the Model T prototype. Significantly, these firms had completely different directorate mechanisms. At U.S. Steel, Morgan pooled an amalgam of 300 iron and steel makers, merchants, and financiers into a giant capitalized at $1322 million. This was somewhat of a miracle because the pool included the five most powerful and ferociously antagonistic forces in that field. Morgan employed the same technique some of today's experts on mergers think they have invented, namely, cash and stock sweeteners of 40 percent or better.

From its inception, U.S. Steel was the epitome of outside-director control. It provided both a structural and a functional design for thousands of boardroom emulators. Among its obvious features, it was an amalgam, but certainly not a fragmentation. It epitomized the strong-leader syndrome, the heavy hand of Pierpontifex Maximus, as Morgan was sometimes called. Critics, on the other hand, point to this very same heavy-handedness, this directorate dictatorship, as the basic reason for U.S. Steel's slow but steady decline—from over two-thirds of the market at its founding, to a current one-fifth.

At the same time that J. P. Morgan and his cohorts were building U.S. Steel and shaping the ideal outside-director type of board (1901–1902), Henry Ford came into action. Henry, whom *The Wall Street Journal* once referred to as "The Ace," to differentiate him from his grandson, Henry "The Deuce," epitomized the classical entrepreneur.

The very organization of the Ford Motor Company in 1903 shows how boards of owner-founder firms could make decisions with speed and dispatch. For example, a year earlier, Ford had formed a partnership with an ice merchant named Malcolmson. Their initial success led to the need for more capital, and so the partnership was expanded to an even dozen. At the organizational meeting there was a Dr. Frederick Zumstein who had been invited to join and had $500 in his pocket to pay for five shares. But Henry counted his prospective board—it came to an unlucky thirteen, and so Zumstein was vetoed. His intended five shares were picked up by another director who subsequently sold them for $1.75 million. This episode stresses how strong-willed, unidirectional entrepreneurs can guide not only their own destinies but also those of others.

In *We Never Called Him Henry,* written in 1951 by Harry Bennett, longtime personnel director and confidant of Henry Ford, Bennett gives some insight into how the old-style owner-founder inside board operated. Titles, for example, were virtually nonexistent. From 1918 when Ford appointed his son, Edsel, as president, until 1943 when he resumed the presidency after Edsel's death, Ford was without title. During most of his tenure, there were no vice presidents. And this was the pattern set forth for most inside-director companies—few titles, lean, fast-acting. With few titles and levels of organization, there was no complex chain of command; command was instantaneous. At one meeting of his board, Ford turned to Bennett and boomed, "Come on, Harry, let's get the hell out of here. We'll probably change everything they do anyway."

It should be emphasized that the tough, dominant, or even dictatorial CEO was not exclusively the hallmark of founder-owner firms. J. P. Morgan, for instance, hired as U.S. Steel's first CEO a production genius, Charles Schwab, and paid him a salary said to have been over $1 million. Then just a year later, he arbitrarily fired him.

POSTSCRIPT

It is known that the past is prelude to the future; but where does the past end and the future get its beginning? For instance, the Prospectus of the Society for Establishing Useful Manufactures, the first real American corporation established by Alexander Hamilton in 1791, had an up-to-date sounding statement of directorate purpose. *Note:* "The affairs of the company [are] to be under the management of thirteen directors." Two centuries later we are still using similar phrasing, and many directorships continue according to the Hamiltonian mandate that boards of directors are *to manage and to control the affairs of the corporation.* Recently, however, others have viewed this precept differently, namely, that the affairs of the firm are *to be managed by or under the direction of the board.* Engaging in this use of semantics will be discussed in Chapter 2 and will reappear frequently thereafter—it is a paramount issue.

It is apparent that in structuring our first large-scale public corporate governance mechanism, Alexander Hamilton anticipated today's differences of opinion about what is best for the board and its enterprise. In his sage observations, Hamilton differentiated enterprisers from employees, and directors who manage on the scene versus those who operate from a distance. He stated: "In the establishment proposed we must in the first place have as many faithful and enlightened directors as there are different branches, then a number of managers each capable of following the branch entrusted to him with the eye of a real and intelligent manufacturer, without which it will be necessary to depend absolutely on the head workmen, who, even if they should be all honest, can never be stimulated by that interest which animates those who work for themselves."[1]

In this capsule paragraph, Alexander Hamilton, progenitor of a two-century-long line of American enterprisers, laid down the precepts for corporate leadership. Directors must be loyal and competent and imbued with a special faith. The vital force for effective enterprise is enlightened self-interest. That was the entrepreneurial scenario in 1791. Will it be the same in 1991?

[1]Arthur Harrison Cole, ed., *Industrial and Commercial Correspondence of Alexander Hamilton Anticipating His Report on Manufactures* (New York: A. M. Kelley, Publishers, 1968), p. 201.

CHAPTER 2

BOARD PURPOSE

CORPORATE GOVERNANCE: A DEFINITION

"Corporate Governance ensures that long-term strategic objectives and plans are established and that the proper management structure (organization, systems, and people) is in place to achieve those objectives, while at the same time making sure that the structure functions to maintain the corporation's integrity, reputation, and responsibility to its various consituencies."[1]

This is a rather complex definition, perhaps because it is a blend of views held by the Advisory Board of the National Association of Corporate Directors (NACD). The eighteen advisers-directors, most practicing experts, some basically theoretician, worked several months before the consensus definition was agreed upon. Considering the stature of these eighteen experts, the outstanding work of the NACD, and the eminence of its parent, the American Management Associations (AMA), this is probably the most authoritative definition we will have for quite a few years to come.

BOARD TYPES

The NACD definition is purposely broad in scope because it must cover a great variety of boards, most of which change and adapt over time. To

---

[1]*The Advisory Board Minutes of the National Association of Corporate Directors Meeting,* AMA Headquarters, New York, April 5, 1981.

illustrate this variety, the NACD groups all boards into four functional categories:

1 *Minimum boards* meet only to fulfill statutory requirements.

2 *Cosmetic boards* serve as rubber stamps to management prerogatives.

3 *Oversight boards* function primarily to review programs, policies, proposals reports, and performance of managers.

4 *Decision-making boards* are involved in setting corporate policy, determining management objectives, and authorizing their implementation.[2]

From a slightly different perspective, following an evolutionary progression, corporate directorates can be viewed as:

1 Constitutional boards
2 Consultive boards
3 Collegial boards
4 Communal boards[3]

This classification considers the locus of power and the increasing significance of directors in the corporate governance mechanism:

1 *Constitutional boards* are akin to minimum boards. The major difference is that the constitutional board emphasizes the legal mandate each corporation receives from its creator, the authorizing state. As previously mentioned, every corporation, from the minute to the gargantuan American Telephone and Telegraph, gets its right to legal life from the sovereign, who technically has the power not only to create a corporation but also to dissolve it. In the act of creation, the state issues a corporate charter which generally includes a proviso that the new entity have a board of at least three directors. Thus the corporate "constitution" prescribes the board. Unfortunately, while they fulfill the legal mandate, most constitutional boards do little else. The directors tend to be unobtrusive and let all authority gravitate to the CEO. This characteristic is most prominent in small, new, low-technology, closely owned firms, particularly if the founding enterprisers are still on the scene.

Constitutional boards also carry other hereditary traits, depending upon their inception from proprietary or syndical parentage. *Proprietary,* in this instance, refers to founder-owner-managers who run the enterprise as a satrapy, and only when necessary do they relinquish a measure of boardroom control to key executives who then serve as officers or inside directors. *Syndical* refers to ownership and power being concentrated in a group of

---

[2]"Evolution in the Boardroom," *NACD Corporate Director's Special Report Series,* vol. 1, August 1978, p. 5.

[3]Stanley C. Vance, *The Corporate Director: A Critical Evaluation* (Homewood, Ill.: Dow Jones-Irwin, Inc., 1968), pp. 211–229.

financial entrepreneurs who do not attempt to run the firm actively. Instead, even while serving on the board, they give nearly unqualified control to a strong CEO. Over time the syndicate members relinquish their boardroom seats to outside directors who, in earlier days, served passively as cosmetic boards. United States Steel Corporation, discussed earlier, was a good example of the syndical constitutional type of board. In distinct contrast, the Ford Motor Company, under its founder, epitomized the proprietary constitutional form.

2 *Consultive boards* are the products of evolutionary progression. With growth in scale and complexity of endeavor, the dominant CEO finds it more difficult to act as the unquestioned helmsman. He needs either technical assistance, buyer-seller contacts, or legal, financial, or political advice. The logical source of aid is the board. If the CEO adds lawyers, bankers, or other business people, he fabricates an *outside* board of directors. If he leans on his key executives and gives them titles as directors, it then becomes an *inside* board. In either case, over a period of time, the directors become better educated, better qualified, and as ownership tends to be more diffused, more independent. Also, as operations become more complex and global, and as its customers, suppliers, government, and the general public take a keener interest in the firm, the CEO must consult more seriously with his board. Currently, the great majority of American boards are consultive in function.

3 *Collegial boards* are the next logical stage in the governance progression. Broadly diffused public ownership is an absolute prerequisite for collegial boards. There must also be strong countervailing power coalitions within the board and the corporation. These power coalitions serve to minimize the prospects of one-man rule. Sometimes a benevolent despotic CEO will try to convey the image of collegiality, but real collegiality needs more of a permanent checks-and-balances, coalition structuring.

Collegial meetings are characterized by discussion, debate, and disagreement. Differences of opinion are resolved by a vote, a majority vote prevailing. Of special significance is the fact that disagreement with the majority or with the CEO does not mean dismissal from the board.

Collegial boards meet more frequently than constitutional boards (usually quarterly) or consultive boards (from ten to twelve times a year). This characteristic, meeting as frequently as needed, means that all directors must be available at all times; otherwise power gravitates into the hands of those present. Moreover, if a director is to perform in meaningful collegial fashion, he or she must be a technically proficient professional manager.

At this stage in the evolution of the American boardroom, only a mere handful of our large publicly owned corporations have even the semblance of collegial boards. The era of the collegial board is still in the distant future, and its eventuality is not guaranteed. The most serious obstacles to widespread use of collegial boards in business are the slowness and indecisiveness of such group actions. Petty jealousies, preconceptions, and vested positions tend to slow down the collegial decision-making process. All the imperfections and inefficiencies associated with committee action are typified in collegial boards.

4 *Communal boards,* in one context, are public boards. Their membership closely parallels the composition of the political authority. Note, for example, how the three-person board of the Tennessee Valley Authority (TVA) adapts to Republican/Democratic shifts in the White House. A subsequent section on representative boards will illustrate another kind of communal board. The current stress on "public" directors might also propel our system into the wider use of political types, including ex-government officials as directors. The concept of *Mitbestimmung* (detailed in Chapter 8) is distinctly a move in this direction even though the communal element here is the union or worker representative. Yugoslavia's work councils are just one other communal board form. This is not necessarily the ultimate in the evolutionary progression. The important consideration is that if boards of directors, constitutional, consultive, or collegial, lose their vigor and fail to satisfy society's needs, then communal boards will become more likely prospects.

The prime objection to any form of communal control in our governance mechanism is its supersystematization; all pertinent components are rigidly fixed within the infrastructure; all responses are automatic, predictable, and compliant. Conformity and regimentation prevail. This is the domain of the bureaucrat. While there are many benefits which follow from bureaucratization, the cost in terms of curtailed freedom, reduced motivation, and stifled initiative is high.

Table 2-1 summarizes and contrasts the four basic board types (constitutional, consultive, collegial, and communal) on four norms: (1) the reason for the board, (2) its authority form, (3) who is the decision maker, and (4) the board's decision-making role.

Note that there are some very significant differences. The particular board type which will be used will depend upon the prevailing milieu, that is, the composite of socio-politico-economic forces which shape a given society at a given time. The important consideration is that every milieu reflects the aspirations and accomplishments of its members. A society that recognizes the need for enterprise, innovation, and equity will sanction, gestate, and perpetuate appropriate governance mechanisms.

BOARD INCORPORATION

A corporation, described as a legal entity, gets life and continued existence from its political sovereign. In the United States there are fifty corporation-begetting sovereigns, namely, the individual states. As should be expected, some states are more prolific, begetting corporations at a faster rate than others. Although New Jersey initially set precedent in this respect, Delaware, parent to more than 80,000 corporations, is currently the most prolific corporation-begetter. Nearly half of our 1000 largest corporations are legally domiciled in Delaware. Even though most of these do not have major facilities in the state, they nevertheless schedule annual meetings in Wilmington or Dover. Nearly one-fourth of Delaware's entire annual revenue comes from corporate franchise and business income taxes.

The reason why corporations "pick their parents" (notably Delaware and secondly New Jersey and Nevada) is because of the wide range in state incorporation and performance restrictions, and in fees and business taxes. Delaware, for example, minimizes the tax onus and imposes no "blue sky" law. But the really big attraction is the relative freedom Delaware allows management. "Stockholders are interested in management that can move quickly. There is no other state that is as 'liberal.' What they mean by 'liberal' is that management can do no wrong. . . . As one New York attorney says, tongue in cheek, 'It used to be said colloquially, the greatest thing about Delaware corporate law was that it was written by New York lawyers.' "[4]

If Delaware continues in this permissiveness, it is possible that other states will go even further in relaxing incorporation requirements. And, ultimately, if the states do make a mockery of the incorporation process, the threat of federal chartering will become a reality.

[4]"Why Companies Love Delaware," *Business Week,* June 8, 1968, p. 140.

TABLE 2-1
RATIONALE TYPICAL OF BASIC TYPES OF BOARDS

	Constitutional	Consultive	Collegial	Communal
Reason for board	Legal	Economic	Socioeconomic	Political
Authority form	Autocratic	Oligarchic	Technocratic	Bureaucratic
Decision maker	Chief executive	CEO plus key executives	The board	Central planning agency
Board's decision-making role	Acceptive	Advisory	Definitive	Adaptive

Source: Stanley C. Vance, *The Corporate Director: A Critical Evaluation* (Homewood, Ill.: Dow Jones-Irwin, 1968), p. 233.

Even more serious are the tax-shelter opportunities presented by an increasing number of revenue-hungry mininations, particularly the tax-haven islands of the Caribbean. Likewise, Panama and Liberia are classic as petroleum-shipping "flag of convenience" incorporators. But the principality of Liechtenstein sets the international pace. Before some tightening up of legal curbs in 1980, "mailbox companies" helped give Liechtenstein one of the very few balanced national budgets. Some of these "mailbox companies" actually consist of only a nameplate and a letterbox and are recognized fronts for shady dealing. With more than 40,000 incorporated firms, each paying at least $600 per year, Liechtenstein holds the title of international incorporator.

Although Delaware permits considerable latitude in what corporations and their managements can do, it, and every other sovereign state, follows a basic corporate-begetting and breeding format. For instance. persons or groups wishing to become more than an individual enterprise or partnership must abide by a rigidly prescribed incorporation procedure. In addition to getting three or more incorporators, applicants must specify their broad intentions as to lines of endeavor, source of capitalization, and similar information as required by the particular sovereign state. Each corporation, for example, must have specific authorization to exist, namely, a state-granted charter. Also, there is a certificate of incorporation, analogous to a corporate birth certificate. In its charter every corporation is given the right to enact bylaws—prescriptions for self-governance and for running the enterprise.

At the very outset of the bylaws, Article I invariably is captioned "Stockholders" and deals with the rights and actions of stockholders, for example, in regard to annual meetings, and the voting process. It is logical that Article I should deal with the stockholders since they are entrusted, in the first instance, with specific rights and duties by the creating sovereign, the state.

Next in sequence, Article II of the bylaws carries the heading "Boards of Directors." Despite the near-infinite variety in corporate size, history, purpose, and experience, there is remarkable unanimity as to what constitutes the board's basic functions. Virtually every bylaw in its Article II, Section 1, clearly states that the "business and property of the corporation shall be managed and controlled by the board of directors." Occasionally there are some variances such as "all of the authority of a corporation shall be exercised by its directors." While the former states the tenor of the New York Business Corporation Law and the latter the Ohio Code, there is, nevertheless, an unequivocal mandate in the corporate birth certificates issued by all fifty states: that the board of directors manage and control the affairs of the corporation.

Historically the verb *to manage* has meant "to direct or to control the

course of affairs by one's own actions" and "to succeed in accomplishing."
In turn, the verb *to control* has meant and continues to mean "to exercise
authority over, to check or verify, to regulate or to exercise restraint or
direction upon free actions."

As is obvious, these definitions are rather broad and permit semantic
variance. Quite recently, as a concomitant of the increased focus on outside
directors, there has been a shift in the corporate governance mandate of "to
manage and to control." The 1974 revision of the Delaware Code provides
that "the business and affairs of every corporation organized under this
chapter shall be managed by or under the direction of a board of directors."
Subsequently, the Model Business Corporation Act (MBCA), adopted in
substance by twenty-five states, accepted the "under the direction of"
phraseology, reflecting the fact that boards do not manage day-to-day
operations.[5] Actually, such a change in wording is really more of a reversion
than a progression. In what was probably the first attempt at corporate
chartering in this country and, moreover, a federal chartering proposal, the
Report on a National Bank, communicated to the House of Representatives,
December 14, 1790, states: "The affairs of the bank shall be under the
management of twenty-five directors. . . ." If "under the management of"
is synonymous with "under the direction of," then nothing new has been
added.

An unfortunate aspect of the current rephrasing which, as demonstrated,
is really almost two centuries old, is that some assume it absolves the board
of directors from ultimate responsibility for the operating of the firm.
Regardless of the phrasing, ultimate responsibility for corporate performance is squarely in the hands and on the shoulders of the board of directors:
final responsibility cannot be delegated.

This fine distinction in semantics gives concern to forward-viewing
enterprises. For example, in *Exxon News* (December 1981), the corporation
explains to its stockholders that broad policy guidance for the entire Exxon
family of companies is provided by corporate headquarters, under the
general direction of Exxon's board of directors. Day-to-day management of
the corporation is the responsibility of the chief executive officer, assisted by
a management committee composed of senior executives. The newsletter
then tries to explain how these executives oversee management performance, especially monitoring long-range investment plans, capital budgets,
operating results, and executive recruitment.

A number of legal experts, intent on justifying the concept of oversight
boards, argue that "under the direction" means simple monitoring, while
"managed and controlled by" implies day-to-day supervision. Surely these

---

[5]William E. Knepper, *Liability of Corporate Officers and Directors,* 3d ed. (Indianapolis:
Allen Smith Company, 1978), p. 6.

redefiners are attempting to make allowances for outside or independent directors' lack of competency, time, and interest in the affairs of the corporation on whose board they serve. Obviously, such legal stress on nuances raises some serious implications. If the board of directors does not manage and control, then who does? At this point a reading of definitions seems to be in order.

The Society for Advancement of Management (SAM), an articulate proponent of sound and scientific management since the society's founding in 1912, almost eighty years later found it necessary to restate what managers and the managed all the while have taken for granted. The new definition is a consensus of a committee including three businessmen, three academics, and three SAM officials.

> Managing is designing and maintaining an environment for effective and efficient use of resources and performance of individuals working together in groups toward accomplishment of preselected missions and objectives.
>
> Management is both a science and an art. As a science, it is organized knowledge—concepts, theory, principles, and techniques—underlying the practice of managing; as an art, it is application of the organized knowledge to realities in a situation, usually with blend or compromise, to obtain desired practical results.[6]

But even as SAM's blue-ribbon committee hammered out a seeming consensus, one of its members expressed a rational reservation: "While I agree with the definitions, this is somewhat of a futile project. As has happened with comparable studies, we could have agreement on terms in 1981, and by 1991 a new generation of practitioners and scholars would be using a new set of terms, thus demonstrating their creativity. Only medicine and law seem to have benefited by constant terms for education and practice."[7]

Following this observation, it seems judicious to skip further frustrating semantics and to consider how both the management and governance concepts interrelate. This comparison can be effected by discussing the duties of the director. If these duties encompass activities normally considered part of the managing function, then contrary to what any legal experts might postulate, directors do manage. If, on the other hand, the duties as described are performed by someone other than the board and only "under the direction of the board," then the directors are more monitors and less managers.

[6]*Report of the Professional Management Designation Feasibility Study Committee,* Society for Advancement of Management, March 5, 1981, p. 6.

[7]John F. Mee, Mead Johnson Professor Emeritus and Dean of Fellows of the Academy of Management (personal letter), March 9, 1981.

BOARD DUTIES

The best approach to learning what a board does, and what it should do, would be to survey the field of practitioners and authorities and synthesize their varied responses. Over an extended period of time the author, as described in the section "Director Dimensions" in Chapter 9, has made a number of surveys that include the responses of several hundred chairmen, presidents, and other directors. The cooperating individuals indicated a tremendously wide spectrum as to the duties and activities of a director. The following is a list of what seemed to be the most frequently mentioned functions expected of a board of directors. These functions are not set forth in any sequence of importance but are grouped into four related categories:

1 Management: control and oversight
2 Legal prescriptions
3 Stakeholder interests
4 Stockholder rights

In the first category, *control over management,* directors must:

a Select the chief executive officer
b Sanction the CEO's team
c Provide the CEO with a forum
d Assure managerial competency
e Evaluate management's performance
f Set management salary levels, including fringe benefits
g Guarantee managerial integrity through continuous auditing
h Chart the corporate course
i Devise and revise policies to be implemented by management

The second broad category, *adhering to legal prescriptions,* means more than simply following the incorporation procedure. Directors should:

a Keep abreast of new laws
b Ensure that the entire organization fulfills every pertinent legal prescription
c Pass bylaws and related resolutions
d Select new directors
e Approve capital budgets
f Authorize borrowings, new stock issues, bonds, etc.

The third category, *consideration of stakeholders' interests,* has gained significance in recent years. The term "stakeholder" refers to all persons or agencies which have even an implied "stake" in the corporation and its activities. Obviously, this includes almost everyone who comes into contact with the corporation: employees, customers, suppliers, and the community. Specifically, directors are expected to:

a Monitor product quality
b Facilitate upward progression in employee quality of work life (QWL)
c Review labor policies and practices
d Improve the customer "climate"
e Keep community relations at the highest level
f Use influence to better governmental, professional association, and educational contacts
g Maintain a good public image

The fourth category, *advancement of stockholder rights,* is paramount but with the realization that these rights must mesh with stakeholders' interests, with the legal constraints, and with management's competencies and aspirations. The board should:

a Preserve the stockholders' equity
b Stimulate corporate growth so that the firm will survive and flourish
c Guard against equity dilution
d Provide articulate and equitable stockholder representation
e Inform the stockholders, through letters, reports, meetings
f Declare proper dividends
g Guarantee corporate survival

Obviously, these twenty-nine duties could suggest a job description for directors. Note that each statement's initial word implies *action*. Judging from this context, it would seem that "the board of directors should manage and control the affairs of the company." This is a more dynamic and responsible charge than saying "the affairs of the corporation should be managed under the direction of a board of directors."

The controversy will certainly not be resolved by this or any other listing of duties, or by the focus upon any particular director's job description, as long as subjectivity prevails. The following episodes illustrate the wide range of meaning attached even to some commonly assumed director duties.

ILLUSTRATION: Who's Watching the Store?

Every successful CEO eventually is faced with the dilemma of whether to get involved in sociopolitical affairs, doing good for the public, or to concentrate on corporate functions and "stay home and mind the store." Herbert E. Strawbridge, chairman and CEO of Higbee Company, Cleveland, was condemned by critics for spending too much time nursing the city of Cleveland's very frail health and attending too little to the operation of Higbee's stores. Strawbridge's tactic had been to take a hyperactive role in civic affairs, concentrating on stimulating Cleveland's growth, and Higbee's, in the process. "His biography lists 31 pursuits outside Higbee—a list so long that each item is footnoted as a 'primary, secondary or tertiary interest'. . . ."[8]

While this dedicated and hyperactive CEO spread his talents in so many directions, his firm had a series of negative cash flow years where only heavy borrowing avoided financial embarrassment. One competitor commented that Higbee is a company "that has confused its civic responsibilities with those it owes to its shareholders."[9]

The same precept for both CEOs and directors was limelighted in a *Time* article when, after thirty-two years of distinguished service at Chase Manhattan Bank, Chairman David Rockefeller relinquished his post. Despite a glamorous and successful career, critics pointed to Chase Manhattan's being outpaced by its leading rival, Citibank, now New York's largest bank. In 1961, when Rockefeller became president, Chase Manhattan held that honor. Says one Wall Street analyst, " 'He ran Chase like an exclusive club. Bank officers tended to worry more about how many oils from the Chase art collection they had on their walls than about profits.' Insiders complained that top managers seemed to be chosen for their tailoring or the virile timbre of their voices rather than for their administrative skills or financial savvy. Rockefeller appeared to be off frequently, polishing his reputation as a world statesman by visiting Yugoslavia's late President Josip Broz or the Shah of Iran."[10]

The results reflected on the management. Return on assets slumped to a miserable 33 cents per $100. In 1975 the comptroller of the currency described the state of the Chase back-office operations, like check-clearing services, as "horrendous." In 1976, when W. T. Grant went bankrupt, Chase lost $50 million in that failure. That year alone, the bank's bad loans reached a staggering $1.9 billion.

These two episodes have emphasized that no matter how compelling or uplifting service to the community and society might be, a chief executive's and every director's prime responsibility is to tend to company affairs: to manage and to control. The next illustration shows how confusing this managing function can become when the interests of the company and those of clients become inextricably intertwined.

ILLUSTRATION: The "Chinese Wall" Defense

The concept of the "Chinese Wall" defense has been used in the field of banking for many years in order to protect against the abuse of confidential information. All directors, but especially bankers, must be tight-lipped; nothing of consequence should ever be leaked even to intimates. The Chinese Wall defense is a hypothetical

---

[8]"Perils of Not Minding the Store," *Business Week,* January 15, 1979, p. 56.
[9]Ibid.
[10]"The Change at David's Bank," *Time,* September 1, 1980.

process whereby inside information needed for some investment banking and corporate investment advisory functions is ordered sealed off from employees in brokerage, research, or other market functions such as trading and arbitrage. Supposedly there is an unbreachable wall separating the several banking functions and their respective functionaries. Without such "walling off" the bank might use high-priority information for its own illegal or unethical benefit.

For example, late in 1978 Morgan Stanley and Company, one of our most reputable investment bankers, seemed to be violating an investment confidence by turning over internal earnings projections of one of its clients, Olinkraft,[11] to another of its clients, Johns-Manville. Meanwhile, the bank assembled a hefty 149,200-share arbitrage holding of Olinkraft's stock. Keep in mind that instant and internal information can give the arbitrager, working simultaneously in two or more different markets, big advantages over the uninformed competitor.

There was a spontaneous reaction to the presumed penetration of Morgan Stanley's Chinese Wall. Analysts and even competing bankers reacted with barely concealed glee at Morgan Stanley's embarrassment. They were delighted to see the giant made the target of an Olinkraft stockholder suit, the object of a Securities and Exchange Commission trading inquiry, and the subject of a harsh cover story in the monthly trade magazine *Institutional Investor*.

But the flagellators' zest suddenly waned when they realized that the bad publicity and the court action could lead to industrywide tightened regulations. This would impinge on their own operating freedom and curtail the fat profits reaped through arbitraging whenever merger transactions were contemplated. If the issue became more aggravated, this single presumed breaching of Morgan Stanley's Chinese Wall could result in a figurative razing of all such antiquated protective devices. In an age when electronic espionage and silicon-chip-tapping are so easy for the unscrupulous, Chinese Walls probably have little defensive value.

And how does this episode relate to director duties? Keep in mind that under either definition, "the board of directors should manage and control the affairs of the company," or "the affairs of the corporation should be managed and under the direction of boards of directors," the Chinese Walls exist only because directors see the need and approve their building. Once established, directors should see that no breaching occurs. The onus is theirs.

ILLUSTRATION: Codes of Ethics

A century ago most corporate codes existed for the employees' edification; none was for corporate governance guidance. As one example of this bias, consider some excerpts from "dos and don'ts," posted by the proprietor of a carriage and wagon works. The source and authorship, unfortunately, cannot be identified.

    1 Office employees will daily sweep the floors, dust the furniture, shelves and showcases.

---

[11]Tim Metz, "Morgan Stanley's Rivals Lose Their Smirks over Olinkraft as Fear of Crackdown Dawns," *The Wall Street Journal*, April 5, 1979, p. 31.

2 Each clerk will bring a bucket of water and a scuttle of coal for the day's business.

3 Clerks will each day fill lamps, clean chimneys, trim wicks. Wash the windows once a week.

4 This office will open at 7 a.m. and close at 8 p.m. daily except on the Sabbath, on which day it will remain closed.

5 Men employees will be given an evening off each week for courting purposes, or two evenings a week, if they go regularly to church.

6 Any employee who smokes Spanish cigars, uses liquor in any form, gets shaved at a barber shop, or frequents pool or public halls, will give me a good reason to suspect his worth, intentions, integrity, and honesty.

Anticipation of the Foreign Corrupt Practices Act (FCPA) of 1977 brought on a big surge in corporate conduct codes. In a recent survey, 97 percent of the major corporations responded affirmatively to the question "Does your company have an employee code of ethics?" By contrast, one study of the 1960s reported that three-fifths of the cooperating companies had not issued general written statements of ethical principles to guide employees in the conduct of the business.[12]

The White and Montgomery analysis, product of a survey sent to the chief financial officers of 2000 leading American corporations, revealed other interesting information. The study tabulated the subjects addressed in the various codes. At least thirty-seven different subjects were identified, with conflict of interest (73 percent), acceptance of gifts (77 percent), political contributions (67 percent), payments to government officials (63 percent), and inside information (63 percent) heading the list. The rationale for this focus is evident; yet only 17 percent of the respondents actually mentioned the Foreign Corrupt Practices Act of 1977.

The authors conclude that most corporate codes are simply a pragmatic "must." A formal code, even though superficial, points to the firm's good faith and desire to be a good citizen. In the event of litigation, this could become an important defensive measure. But "if codes of conduct are to serve more than documentary window dressing and play a constructive role in encouraging ethical practices by corporate employees, much remains to be learned about designing and administering them."[13]

Another study stated that "while the data received did not indicate that boards of directors and executive committees took a completely hands-off attitude toward the formulation and application of standards, it did indicate that they show an aloofness relative to the participation of chief executive officers. Given the nature of boards, this is somewhat understandable, but this situation should be corrected. Active and vigorous participation of

[12]Bernard J. White and B. Ruth Montgomery, "Corporate Codes of Conduct," *California Management Review,* Winter 1980, p. 80.

[13]Ibid., p. 86.

boards and executive committees in the area of standards of conduct sets an emulative example to all company personnel. Boards should be apprised of the results of compliance checks and the violations and penalties which occur within their companies."[14]

Still another analysis, by Robert N. Holt, notes that the Opinion Research Center reported in 1979 that more than half of current corporate codes of ethics had been formulated in the past five years. The only real stimulus was Public Law 95-213, or the Foreign Corrupt Practices Act of 1977. The author emphasizes that the majority of the codes reviewed had not been significantly revised since 1976.[15] This leads to the inference that most codes are matters of expediency—they are largely gloss and little substance.

While directors have recently been concerned with detailed corporate codes of ethics, they have given little, if any, consideration to building codes for themselves and their peers. Yet virtually every corporate scandal, including those which were FCPA-related, can be imputed to the respective boards of directors. Some standard of ethics and conduct for boardrooms seems to be long overdue.

While the following Director's Decalogue is proposed with tongue in cheek, note that by simply dropping the word *not,* you will have a set of positive precepts; certainly not the ultimate, but a good start.

Director's Decalogue

1 Thou shalt not ask questions.
2 Thou shalt not dissent seriously.
3 Thou shalt not rock the boat.
4 Thou shalt not blow whistles.
5 Thou shalt not demand liability insurance coverage.
6 Thou shalt not call for recorded votes.
7 Thou shalt not investigate issues.
8 Thou shalt not strive for perfect attendance.
9 Thou shalt not mind the shareholders.
10 Thou shalt not study the meeting agenda.

POSTSCRIPT

As stated in the Preface, the American enterprise system does foster the blooming of many flowers (firms) and lets a hundred schools of thought

---

[14]Paul M. Hammaker, Alexander B. Hornimar, and Louise Rader, *Standards of Conduct in Business* (Charlottesville: Colgate Darden Graduate School of Business Administration, University of Virginia, 1977), pp. 35–36.

[15]Robert N. Holt, "A Sampling of Twenty-Five Codes of Corporate Conduct: Call for a Renascence," *Directors and Boards,* Summer 1980, p. 7.

contend. This is evident in the variety of board types, procedures for incorporation, board duties, and even codes of conduct. Yet even though all boards are given considerable latitude, and no two boardroom value systems are identical, there is one area of agreement. All boards and directors are surrogates—they act as fiduciaries for the owners, the shareholders.

For generations it was universally agreed that the board's basic function was *to manage and to control* the business and property of the corporation. This charge has been set forth in virtually every state's corporation code. As was pointed out, semanticists recently have sought to rephrase this legal and ethical prescription, to say that the business and affairs of the firm shall *be managed by or under the direction* of the board.

While this interpretation might seem innocuous, it does portend a major change that would lift the onus of ultimate operating responsibility from the directors, who would then deal only with broad, ephemeral policy and strategy. Some will question whether policy and management can be so neatly cleaved; others will justify it, arguing that today's corporations are so complex that directors cannot possibly be versed in all the business and technical facets.

However, much lies behind the simple semantics of switching verbs from the active "to manage and control" to the passive "to be managed and under the control of" the board. Such a shift cannot be made without affecting the very purpose of the board. It will also impact on board characteristics and board structure.

CHAPTER 3

BOARD CHARACTERISTICS

DIRECTOR ATTRIBUTES

The preceding illustrations emphasized the vagueness of director responsibilities. In each case it was the chief executive officer who, as the chief enunciator, would be singled out for praise or blame. Yet in every instance, it was the board of directors who bore the ultimate operational responsibility. These examples, plus a review of the twenty-nine specific duties listed in Chapter 2, while not definitive, nevertheless provide a good summary. But what kind of person will most effectively fulfill these duties? What attributes are conducive to effective directorate performance?

Although many listings of directorate attributes have been recorded, one easily comprehended summary holds that directors must be:

1 Conversant with operational and policy matters
2 Fully informed
3 Available
4 Motivated
5 Accepted
6 Accountable

Another equally concise but more graphic six-point program portrays the directorate as being structured on six stately and solid pillars:

1 Involvement or participation
2 Prudence

3 Competence
4 Loyalty
5 Accountability
6 Integrity

These are not set forth in any order of importance, for like any edifice that is supported by six pillars, if one weakens, the structure itself is in danger. *Involvement* assumed new proportions in the late 1960s as activists questioned the very necessity for boards of directors. It was during this tumultuous era that the respected publisher-editor, Malcolm S. Forbes, editorially questioned: "Directors: Who Needs'Em?"[1] Forbes, echoing sentiments heard far beyond social activist camps, argued that if boards were really cosmetic or rubber stamps, then our enterprise system was in jeopardy. Directors simply had to take a more active role, through participation, through involvement.

Prudence has long been a legal stipulation. In a well-known precedent-setting Massachusetts case, *Harvard College v. Amory,* an old common-law mandate was articulated by the court. A trustee or director must observe how men and women of prudence, discretion, and intelligence manage their own affairs, not in regard to speculation, but in regard to the permanent disposition of their funds, considering the probable income as well as the probable safety of the capital to be invested. Kampner elaborates by quoting Professor Scott, a Harvard law professor, on a clarification of what constitutes prudence. Scott states that a prudent man is one who exercises care, skill, and caution in carrying out his activities. *Care* means careful investigation; *skill* means a recognized ability to deal with pertinent issues; and *caution* stresses safety.[2]

Competence, implied in the prudent-person attribute of skill, was, in the past, more honored in the breach than in performance. Even today, after a generation of hard focus on director attributes and performance, there are no competency tests for directorate candidates. More pathetically (as will be explored subsequently), there are no standard performance evaluation norms. In most boardrooms, the adequacy of a given director continues to be a matter of opinion—either of the chief executive officer's or of the dominant peer-group coalition.

Loyalty, in an exaggerated sense, can be interpreted, rightly or wrongly, as follows: There must be no violation of the boardroom oath of silence. This line of thinking has effectively concealed that which transpires behind the closed boardroom door. In a more meaningful sense, loyalty means dedication to the interests of the corporation and its owners. Setting one's

---

[1]Malcolm S. Forbes, "Directors—Who Needs 'Em?" *Forbes,* November 15, 1965, p. 11.
[2]Paul I. Kampner, "When Is a Prudent Man Prudent?" *Management Review,* June 1976, p. 37.

own gain ahead of the corporate commonweal constitutes disloyalty. This and the related "whistle blowing" will be discussed subsequently.

Accountability, in the past, was limited to the extent of the individual director's stockholding investment. This has been dramatically redefined so that directors, exposed to an increasing array of responsibilities, now find liability insurance imperative.

Integrity means more than the precepts "know thyself" and "to thine own self be true." It implies an identity first with a basic moral code, then with one's societal standard, and next with corporate aspirations and activities.

These six pillars, obviously, carry generic or global prescriptions, subject far too much to varying individual interpretation. However, coupled with the twenty-nine previously listed director duties, the composite could provide a meaningful mandate for effective corporate governance.

BOARD PERFORMANCE: ATTENDANCE

A record of attendance at regular, committee, or annual meetings is one of the best measures of director participation and involvement. The Gilbert brothers, Lewis and John, often characterized as corporate meeting gadflies, for almost half a century have focused upon directors' poor meeting attendance records (among other things). For years they have tried to get stockholder resolutions passed so that nominees for the board would be ineligible for reelection if they failed to attend two successive statutory meetings. Of course, this ruling would be mitigated if the errant director submitted an acceptable written excuse.

Despite the blatant abuses, industry did little to rectify this situation. Then, late in 1978, the Securities and Exchange Commission, in a restatement of its proxy requirements, initiated a request that the names of all directors who attended 75 percent or less of all meetings be publicized. This was still trivial punishment for a serious misdemeanor, a shirking of duty. Reflecting facetiously on this subject, the SEC could have helped boost attendance to a near-perfect mark by requiring that absent directors have their annual retainers reduced proportionately. Corporate governance annals have as yet few, if any, recorded instances of high-minded outside directors refunding their unearned stipends. While many boards do refuse to renominate chronic absentees, such procedure has not been formalized by most corporate boards and generally is not known publicly.

Assuming a director is striving to earn a perfect attendance gold star, how many meetings must he attend? As with so many aspects of our corporate governance mechanism, there is no set figure. The SEC, in its attempts to systematize and democratize the proxy mechanism, tabulated boardroom meeting frequency. While the overall average was seven meetings, there was considerable variance. Scale of company operations seems to be the prime reason for this variance. The smallest firms, those with assets under $50 million, averaged four or fewer meetings. The biggest companies, those with $150 million in assets, averaged eight or more meetings, with an increasing number meeting thirteen times or more per year.

While presumably lackadaisical attendance attitudes have plagued some firms, corroboration is impossible because record keeping has been fragmentary and it is assumed to be strictly a board matter. Annual meeting attendance, however, is more readily verifiable. But some insist that these are meetings of stockholders, and even though most directors are also stockholders, director attendance need not be mandatory. There have been some instances where directors, usually outsiders, ignore the annual meeting. Even an outstanding corporation such as General Electric Company for years has rarely had any outside directors attend its annual meeting. GE, of course, contends that although the outside directors do not attend the annual meeting, they do attend a shareholders' information meeting in the fall. And it can be disconcerting to find officer-directors on the platform and only a scant two or three of the sixteen to eighteen outside directors in attendance. While GE's pattern is not typical, there are still far too many corporations which rationalize the absence of directors at annual meetings.

Admittedly, some of the aversion to attending annual meetings stems from the excessive length and boring content of too many meetings. Of particular irritation are the meetings "turned into circuses" by chronic disrupters, initially only a handful of "gadflies" but now a more numerous and vociferous breed. While some of the gadfly antics are theatrical and some downright disruptive, these challengers to management's prerogatives and privileges have done considerable good. They have raised, in a systematic fashion, dozens of pertinent issues which later became acceptable to industry. Director attendance at annual meetings has been a corporate gadfly issue which has forced many a board to tone down such abuses.

Yet staying away from an annual meeting simply to avoid gadfly confrontation is not the only excuse; outside directors have other excuses. Some complain that the meetings are too long, and others feel their meetings are so brief that it is a waste of time and money to attend. At Cook Industries' 1978 meeting, for example, the chairman won two $1 wagers: one that the meeting would last a mere ten minutes; the other that there would be no questions. It should be pointed out that the company's proxy statement prominently showed that the chairman had a controlling interest, thus indicating the business of the meeting was precluded. Cook Industries' ten-minute break, however, does not set the record for brevity. A few years earlier, Hanna Mining Company completed its business in seven minutes and four seconds; included were thirty seconds of silence in memory of its longtime CEO, George M. Humphrey. In 1972 Fuqua Industries' annual meeting lasted all of one minute and fifty seconds, no doubt setting an all-time record for brevity.

Sometimes when a corporation calls a meeting almost no one shows. This was the case at Tensor Corporation's 1981 meeting when only one stockholder and no outside directors came. The same situation occurred at the 1978 meeting of Technical Tape, Incorporated, where only five people were present: two corporate officers, the firm's lawyer, a reporter, and one stockholder, the perennial champion of corporate democracy, Lewis Gilbert. The company's chairman and CEO was not present even though he was up for reelection.

While it is a rarity for chairmen to skip their company annual meetings, a record of sorts has been set by William Black, chairman of Chock Full O'Nuts Corporation. Annoyed at stockholders' questions, Black, in 1970, stormed out of a meeting and has refused to attend any since. " 'I'd be very glad to attend our annual stockholders' meetings if something were done about changing the rules so that a few gadflies who have no experience in our line of business, but have a 20/20 hindsight, aren't permitted to make a shambles of our meetings,' Mr. Black says. His remarks came in the company proxy statement after a holder offered a bylaw amendment that would, in affect, force Mr. Black to show up."[3]

If the *primus inter pares* of directors, the CEO, disdains to attend stockholders' meetings, it is no wonder that ordinary directors sometimes feel a lessened obligation. Fortunately, there are very few CEOs or directors with such extremely negative views. Yet there have been concerted campaigns such as that of J. F. Fuqua, who sought approval from his stockholders to abolish Fuqua Industries' annual meetings. Technically, this became possible in 1971 when the state of Delaware amended its laws so that a physical get-together of stockholders is no longer necessary. Instead, Delaware permits an alternative called a "consent meeting," which is an annual meeting conducted entirely by mail. Fuqua's attempt to utilize the "consent meeting" failed when the New York Stock Exchange threatened to delist the company stock.

This focus on annual meetings has a point. It is the directors who are responsible for tolerating any and all abuses. Derelict directors not only do themselves and their corporations a disservice but also invite corrective legislation. This is so for governance not only in corporations but in all organizations. Most university campuses face this problem in all their governing bodies. Several years ago, the University of Tennessee Student Senate voted 9 to 8 in an unusual roll call. It asked that the student *Daily*

---

[3]Bill Abrams, "Chairman Eschews Annual Meetings, Chock Full o' Barbs," *The Wall Street Journal*, December 2, 1978, p. 10.

Beacon publish the previous quarter's attendance record of each senator at the beginning of each quarter. The senate president commented that "only four or five out of 16 senators have bad attendance records. All the others are very good." The opposition senators claimed the publicity would reflect poorly on the senate as a whole. "We'd become the laughing stock of the school. Everybody would think that student government isn't doing anything." One senator firmly rebutted, "'If it makes us look bad, it's because we're doing bad.'"[4]

ILLUSTRATION: Sokaiya

The Japanese, in a unique modification of the American corporate "gadfly" annual meeting, have devised the attention-getting *sokaiya*. These are, by their own definition, consultants who loudly proclaim their clients' interests. At other times, as stated by an official of Rondan Doyukai Company, probably the biggest sokaiya, "they serve as a checking organization for the sound operation of enterprises. So sometimes we behave as lawyers, sometimes as prosecutors and sometimes as journalists."[5] Rondan publishes books and ten newspapers, mostly monthlies.

By other accounts, they are boorish thugs who disrupt Japanese annual meetings, but only when the stockholders threaten to give management a rough time. As such they are distinct opposites of our "gadflies," who disrupt management; the sokaiya disrupt the would-be disrupters. Currently, the sokaiya practice costs Japanese corporations a total equivalent to $500 million annually. In one sense this is protection money. The sokaiya ruffians have been extremely successful in shouting stockholders into silence and occasionally roughing up the more courageous but foolhardy ones. As a consequence, most Japanese corporate annual meetings seldom run beyond thirty minutes.

Presumably because of its success, Rondan Doyukai, with 500 major Japanese companies as clients, claims it is going to invade the United States and use its disruptive but effective tactics. In corroboration, it states it has made token investments, totaling over a quarter-million dollars, in twelve American firms listed on the Tokyo Stock Exchange. The stock purchasing strategy is used to gain admittance to corporate annual meetings in the United States to observe our meeting formats, their strengths and limitations.

While there is no immediate threat that this Japanese invasion will regiment our domestic annual meetings into ten-minute coffee breaks, we cannot cavalierly dismiss the sokaiya. We have already suffered dozens of casualties as a result of our inattention to Japanese potential in electronics, steel, shipbuilding, television, automobile, and other industries. Where should this potential sokaiya threat be monitored, and by whom? Very obviously, by every American board of directors.

[4]"Senate Votes to Publicize Attendance," *The Daily Beacon*, University of Tennessee, January 10, 1979, p. 1.
[5]"Japan Exports Way to Quiet Stockholders," *The Wall Street Journal*, April 16, 1981, p. 29.

AGE FACTOR

Two very tough questions every board nominating committee has to consider periodically are: (1) When is a candidate old enough to become a director? (2) When is a candidate too old to direct? Of course, these are moot questions when other factors such as competency or extent of ownership are unknowns. On the youth side of the age continuum, we have a steady flow of talent eager to assume boardroom seats. (There is even a Young Presidents Association which sets a low age ceiling.) Age is a pertinent issue, not only in industrial corporations, but in all institutions. The First Pennsylvania Bank and Trust provided a classic example where a young person was appointed to the board specifically to force the board to recognize the existence of a younger generation. Many universities have student representatives on their boards of trustees. At the University of Tennessee, for instance, there is a rotational system whereby the several geographical sectors of the university, such as Knoxville (UTK) and Chatta-nooga (UTC), get their turn to nominate a student to the board.

Concern over the degree of youthfulness—in the young—is not really a problem. It is a problem with the elderly. In an era of "gray-panther" activism, the concern lies with director superannuation. Specifically, how can you determine when a director's savvy turns to senility? Even more perturbing, how do you tell a mature director, who has served long and effectively, that he or she is to be put out into the boardroom pasture?

The issue of a director's value and utility must be wrestled with. A director is a corporate investment. Before a firm turns its director capital investment into incidental scrap value, the decision makers must determine if they have obtained the maximum value out of their aging director. Consider the horrible waste of director talent when officer-directors, at age sixty-five, are universally ejected from the boardroom. Ironically, these same individuals are allowed to serve other corporations as outside directors, in areas where they have probably had much less meaningful experience. If we are really sincere in our lamentations about executive talent and directorate acumen being our scarcest strategic factor of production, then how can our firms be so profligate?

To continue using director talent beyond the customary age (sixty-five for officer-directors and seventy-two for outsiders), one must consider the vast differences among directors in physical age as contrasted with chronological age. Some individuals burn out in their youth, and some become managerial Methuselahs. Among some notable record-setting directors was Robert S. McLaughlin, who served on General Motors' board until the age of ninety-five. Even after his retirement from the parent GM, he continued serving as chairman of General Motors of Canada until his death at age one hundred. He spent several hours every day in his office at the Canadian main plant. Keep in mind that GM's really great days coincided with

McLaughlin's service as a director beyond the usual sixty-five-year retirement age.

During its halcyon days General Motors had several other "antiquarians" on its board, among them the nonagenarian Charles Stewart Mott. At age ninety-six Mott ran once more for reelection to GM's board, serving a total of almost sixty years. "Come hell or high water, I will be at Cobe Hall [for the annual meeting] May 19—if I am alive I'll be there,"[6] he emphasized upon being nominated.

Another example of courage and determination is Robert Winship Woodruff, the ninety-one-year-old patriarch of Coca-Cola, who is credited with making Coke the most widely known product in the world. In 1981 he relinquished his chairmanship of the powerful Finance Committee without giving a reason, although he is nearly blind and deaf and has been almost crippled by a stroke. He continues to serve as a director, having been reelected to another three-year term at the 1981 annual meeting. As for attendance—he was present at twelve of eighteen board and committee meetings in 1980.

There are other examples of how boardroom service is conducive to longevity, and in return, longevity seems to be associated with successful corporate performance:

Nicholas H. Noyes, named to Eli Lilly and Company's board in 1913, served sixty-four years. Until his death at age ninety-three, he attended board meetings faithfully.

Cyrus S. Eaton, at ninety-four, retired as a director from the Chessie Systems Railroad, the holding company of the predecessor Chesapeake and Ohio Railway and Baltimore & Ohio Railroad. He had served as a director for thirty-five years, including nineteen years as chairman. After his retirement, he continued as chairman emeritus and honorary director.

Armand Hammer, long synonymous with Occidental Petroleum, has continued to celebrate his birthdays by chairing the company's annual meetings every May 21st. On the occasion of his eightieth birthday in 1978, "The question of Dr. Hammer's age and possible retirement was brought up several times by holders who urged him to stay on. They gave him a standing ovation when he agreed to do so: 'When Occidental stock hits 100, then I'll leave it to the board to decide on retirement' . . . (The stock ranged around $25 at that time)."[7] In 1981 a minor stockholder managed to raise a proxy issue, suggesting that the annual meeting date be changed so as not to coincide with the "doctor's" birthday. Note that this spoilsport resolution fell far short of even suggesting that Dr. Hammer retire.

Without doubt, an entire thesis could be written showing a positive

[6]*The Oregonian,* March 7, 1972, p. 19.
[7]Stephen Sansweet, "Occidental Petroleum Holders Applaud Hammer," *The Wall Street Journal,* May 22, 1978, p. 19.

correlation between board maturity—agewise—and company perform-ance. Du Pont prospered as long as approximately one-third of its board consisted of mature, over sixty-five directors. It did not do as well when the age balance shifted.

Genesco prospered under the guidance of the Senior Jarman (Maxey) and then almost disintegrated when the Junior Jarman (Franklin) usurped his father's chairmanship. Great Atlantic and Pacific Tea Company, likewise, prospered under the aging Hartford Brothers but began to totter when maturity gave way to a younger succession.

Note also the ramifications of the "sixty-and-out" or "step-down-at-sixty" policies, notably at Westinghouse Electric and IBM. As will be stressed in a following section, this arbitrary sacrifice of top talent—of both executives and directors—has not been conducive to outstanding perform-ance at either of these companies. To the contrary, the great entrepreneurial merchandisers (and their merchandising marts), like old wine, seemed to get better as they aged. J. C. Penney, at age ninety-five, was still active on the board of the company he founded and guided; Sebastian Kresge, likewise, performed through his ninety-eighth year; and so it was with W. T. Grant, at ninety-six, and Morton May, a "junior" eighty-five. Not surpris-ingly, the firms on whose board they served did very well under the guidance of these near-centenarians. When trouble erupted, it was general-ly after the aged founder-director's demise.

Of course, there are some contrary views, as evidenced by the perennial "dump-the-elders" campaigns. For example, in the early 1970s, Detroit Edison Company's Walter L. Cisler, the productive and dedicated CEO, annually extended his chairmanship despite the policy of mandatory retirement at age sixty-five for all company employees. Resentment among young executives, who felt their promotional opportunities were being stymied by Cisler's overstay, led to acrimony at the utility's annual meeting. The disgruntled stressed that two directors were above age eighty and a total of five were beyond age seventy-three. Somehow it was assumed that "dumping" these elders would open up hundreds of executive slots.[8]

Ironically, the aggrieved ones were oblivious to the fact that, at best, only a few promotions would result from a wholesale dismissal of aged directors. As in virtually all public utilities, there are very few officer-directors. Consequently, except for Cisler's CEO post, all the boardroom replace-ments would most likely come from the outside. The young manager mavericks would have done themselves a service if, instead, they had argued for more officer-directors on the board. In so doing, they would have given their more deserving colleagues opportunities to advance from the

---

[8]"Dump-the-Elders Plan of a Detroit Edison Holder Gets Dumped," *The Wall Street Journal,* April 20, 1971, p. 12.

executive to the directorate. If the boardroom is truly an Olympus, then for the ambitious and qualified executive, there is no greater challenge than to climb this mountain.

BOARD SIZE

One usually assumes that as a corporation grows, so does its board of directors. If two heads are better than one, then surely a dozen heads are better than six—this is a logical conclusion. As a firm expands its scale of endeavor, its problems compound geometrically, and supposedly it would need more, rather than less, heads in its boardroom. But this is not entirely so. To date there have been no reputable studies which show that size of board increases proportionately to size of capital, net assets, or even sales. In view of this, how big should the board of directors be?

Giovanni Agnelli, grandfather of the two brothers heading Italy's huge Turin-based Fiat conglomerate, and founder of that firm, had a pithy comment on the subject. "He was reported to have once said, 'Only an odd number of directors can run a company, and three is too many.' "[9] Signor Agnelli's grandsons did not heed this advice—they expanded Fiat's board and paid a price. In the past decade, Fiat has seen its share of the Western European market drop, from about 20 percent to less than 10 percent. Along with board expansion came corporate decentralization and unforeseen political trouble. "Fiat makes cars with one hand and fights a guerrilla war with the other." Indeed since 1975, three Fiat executives have been killed and seventeen other employees wounded by terrorists.[10]

As one consequence, Agnelli's heirs decided to revert to a more centralized management style, in sharp contrast to the policy of management devolution recently practiced. " 'The company must tackle a whole series of painful and unpopular problems and these responsibilities should fall on the shoulders of a few,' according to the Fiat chief executive."[11] Consequently, the firm is seriously embarking on a return to some of the corporate governance practices set by its founder.

Of course, the Fiat founder's philosophy of authoritarian and centralized control—by a very small board of directors—is still effective in closely held firms. It is also comparably effective in bankruptcy situations, where a court-appointed referee or trustee is given extraordinary authority. Penn Central was eventually extricated by a small team of trustees, after almost eight years of court-imposed control (Section 77, Bankruptcy Act).

Minimal-size boards, one day, might characterize most government-

[9]Paul Betts, "Heads Begin to Roll at Fiat," *Financial Times* (Paris), June 18, 1980, p. 18.
[10]Ibid.
[11]Ibid.

owned utilities. Since its inception, the Tennessee Valley Authority has successfully relied on a three-member board. However, every occupancy change in the White House does cause periodic friction, but this usually passes as the board adapts to the political party in power. After the 1980 election, Republican restiveness with the three Democrats on the board led to several proposals to neutralize their control by adding Republicans. The proposals were set aside when a new chairman, a Republican, was named and approved.

Boards range in size, from the very small to thirty or more. A few years ago, W. R. Grace and Company expanded its board to thirty-six members. Du Pont has long been run by a board numbering approximately thirty directors. Very few banks use boards with less than twenty-five directors. But real records for size are set in nonbusiness organizations—the National Education Association, for instance, has an eighty-one-member board of directors.

Industrial boards tend to reach maximum size after successful large-scale mergers. This follows the very obvious tactic of trying to make both merging parties feel they have won. When Champion Paper merged with United States Plywood, ten directors from Champion and ten directors from U.S. Plywood were designated to the new board. This was to be a marriage of equals. Yet, within a few years, the dominant Champion coalition took over the new firm, and slowly but deliberately ousted its merger partner from the firm, subsequently renamed Champion International. When, in 1980, Kraft, Incorporated, joined with Dart Industries in a $9 billion combination, the new Dart & Kraft, Inc., board was expanded to twenty-three members. Of these, Kraft contributed thirteen members and Dart, ten. It is still too soon to tell if one of the merging parties will eventually displace the other.

Sometimes a board is squeezed to minimal size to keep obstreperous interests from seizing control. Dillingham Corporation, Hawaii's biggest, voted to reduce its number of directors from fifteen to three, in a move to prevent Honolulu investor Harry Weinberg from winning representation on the board. In order to placate the twelve former directors, they were constituted as an advisory adjunct to the board. Usually, drastic changes of this sort are politically motivated. Yet, on occasion, as at National Broadcasting Company, the action is prompted by managerial considerations. In 1979, ten NBC insiders resigned directorships, leaving a majority of five outsiders on the new nine-member board. The reason stated was that, over the years, so many insiders had been added to the NBC board that it had become unwieldy. Also, this cutback supposedly reduced the board size to parallel the structure of RCA's other subsidiary boards. A more likely reason was to establish the preeminence of the outside directors at NBC—a concomitant of the increasing power of the institutional investors.

There definitely is no optimal-size board; specific circumstances, and especially history, condition the structuring. A chairman–chief executive officer, with expertise in handling relatively wide spans of control, might be comfortable with a twenty-member board. Conversely, the one-to-one type of CEO would probably prefer working with a smaller board. But the trend seems to be toward larger boards because of the representation issue—the adding of women, blacks, academics, foreigners, and others. Even Exxon responded to these and other growth pressures when it switched from a completely inside board of fifteen members to a mixed board with nineteen members. Its current board includes three educators (one a woman, another a black) plus two foreign representatives. This ecumenism tends to inflate the board.

Similarly, as boards embark on more meaningful oversight functions, and institute more committees of the board, they need more directors. Typically, a board with the five now-conventional committees—executive, audit, nominating, compensation, and finance—needs at least eight outside directors. This presupposes that no director can effectively serve on more than two committees of the board.

On the overall, board size has remained remarkably the same during the past half century. The Gordon study,[12] probably the first of its kind, showed that in 1935 the boards of the 155 largest corporations had an arithmetic mean of 13.5. A dozen years later, the *Conference Board* found that the 101 biggest companies averaged 12.3 directors. More recently, Korn and Fery as well as Heidrick and Struggles, Incorporated, leading consultants in board-room matters, found similar results. The former's survey showed boards for the larger corporations averaged fourteen members; the latter's findings indicated thirteen.

What really matters is not so much that the number for board size be thirteen or three; it is the long-run results that count. Reflecting again on Signor Agnelli's sage observation, while only an odd number of directors can run a company, three could be too many.

THE ANNUAL REPORT

Nowhere is there a better testimony of free enterprise at work than in the spectacular parade of annual reports. They start with one-page multilithed sheets—from small unlisted firms—and occasionally will cover close to ninety pages. When Distillers Corporation–Seagram asked its eighty-year-old president and founder, Samuel Bronfman, to submit a history of the company as part of an annual report, he obligingly increased the report to eighty-four pages.

[12]R. A. Gordon, "Business Leadership in the Large Corporation," *Brookings Institution,* 1945, pp. 117–118.

Reports vary in dimension and detail. Some are very plain, almost austere; others are spectacular in their colorful displays and professional presentation. It almost seems as though a new school of art is developing with the corporate annual report. By the late 1960s, the more dramatic of the annual reports were being entered in an annual award competition, staged by *Financial World*. Strategically, the parade of annual reports invariably comes just before the company's annual meeting—in addition to being informative, annual reports are also considered to be conditioning. Since only a handful of shareholders attend annual meetings, the annual report is the best way for a corporation to communicate with its owners, with financial analysts, and with the general public.

Indirectly, annual reports are the province of the board of directors. They are rarely prescribed by corporate charter or in the bylaws, but could be considered as communications between management and shareholders. Since management reports to the board, then at least seemingly, the board gives tacit approval to the annual report. This approval is supported by the report's letter of transmittal, where the chief executive addresses the shareowners in the name of both management and the board of directors.

As with so many of our enterprise system's innovations, the present generation assumes we have always had this colorful periodic parade of annual reports. Actually, before the 1900s, annual reports appeared only at the inclination of the chief executive. Yet, as early as 1836, the Baltimore and Ohio Railroad published a ninety-two-page annual report—a marvel for its time.

The New York Stock Exchange (NYSE) issued a ruling, in 1899, that each listed company must publish each year a properly detailed statement of its income and expenditures and a balance sheet giving an accurate statement of the condition of the company at the end of its fiscal year. This broad requirement led to varied interpretations and great variety in compliance. Yet not until the early 1950s did a few apperceptive chief executives recognize, in the NYSE's annual reporting requirement, a real public relations opportunity. IBM was among the first of the more imaginative corporations to upgrade the prosaic NYSE requirement. Its 1955 annual report, for example, appeared in a glamorous magazine-styled, twenty-page publication, picturing and promoting IBM's newest computers and typewriters. The idea was contagious.

But not all annual reports have been cast in the IBM salespitch mode. Electronics Corporation of America has used the same format for twenty-five years. Year after year it features on its cover the same picture, "a moody photograph of its headquarters building in Cambridge, Mass.—'rather than change it to something confusing' like various electronics products."[13]

---

[13]*The Wall Street Journal,* March 29, 1979, p. 1.

Armstrong World Industries, formerly Armstrong Cork, publishes a special report, aimed at high school and college students. The special issue includes a series of colored inserts that describe production and financial terms such as amortization, LIFO, and the like, included in the regular report. In addition, the special report explains why annual reports are issued, how and where the company operates, how it is governed, and how it fits into our business system. "The Lancaster, Pennsylvania, interior furnishings manufacturer will distribute some 20,000 copies of its annotated report this year to students, educators and others interested in using it as an educational aid to explain how a corporation reports on its activities. . . . The company also would be pleased if other companies pick up the idea as a means to help promote a better understanding of business and the American free enterprise system."[14]

The educational potential of annual reports seems to be gaining recognition among boardroom policy makers. A good example of a theme issue was General Electric's 1978 report, emphasizing corporate governance. By going off on the governance tangent, GE set forth a logical thesis that business people, not government bureaucrats, are best equipped to manage corporations for shareholder and public good.

During the social unrest of the early 1970s, most annual reports by major corporations placed emphasis on what the corporation was doing. In 1972, for example, about two-thirds of the annual reports showed concern for corporate social responsibility. A year later, however, social issues were prominent in only about one-fifth of the same annual reports. Energy conservation had now become the fad.

Meanwhile, other innovations appeared. Because so many firms got on the conglomerate bandwagon, it became progressively more difficult, and even impossible, for investors to recognize which products were profitable. This led to a demand for differentiation by lines of business. Surprisingly, a large number of companies refused to comply, arguing that it would give competitors vital information. Yet much of this information was already given to the SEC in 10-K reports—publicly held companies have been required to file detailed 10-K reports since 1941. Also, since 1970, the SEC has required a profit breakdown by lines of business, on registrations for stock and bond sales.

In the product-line inclusion of the annual report, it should be pointed out that a number of firms, such as W. R. Grace and Textron, have followed this practice since the early 1960s. Presently, only a handful of holdouts remain, and most of these conceal the fact by using subterfuge, that is, indicating that their thousands of products are all in one product line— chemicals, automotive equipment, or food products.

[14]"The Annual Report as a Best Seller," *Management Review*, September 1977, p. 42.

Sometimes an innovation in an annual report has a really short span. On December 28, 1972, and without any prior publicity, Fuqua Industries, Incorporated, issued a preliminary and unaudited report for 1972, together with a forecast of 1973 earnings. This was really a first. The board's chairman prefaced the report with, "This is the first time you have ever received an annual report on the last day of the corporate fiscal year. It is even more unique to include detailed forecasts for the following year's operations."[15] Soon a dozen or more imitators took up the fad, and there were rumors that the commission might even make forecasting mandatory— earlier the SEC had dropped its longstanding policy against forecasting. Then, inflation, high interest rates, international tensions, tepid stock market prices, and other uncontrollables put this fad to rest within two years.

One radical innovation, which must await the next social-responsibility outbreak, is the "counterreport." At the 1972 Continental Oil annual meeting, the attending shareholders were surprised to get two different annual reports as they entered the meeting room. The "counterreport" was aimed at Conoco's subsidiary, Consolidation Coal Company, the country's largest coal producer. The regular report contained the conventional glowing commentary about energy targets and profit expectations. It had four-color pictures of sweeping landscapes with Consol's mining equipment esthetically, and almost unobtrusively, in the background. "The other report was a stinging indictment of the social ills allegedly wrought by Consol. . . . The 20-page 'counter-report,' the cover of which carries the names of 78 men who died in a Consol mine accident in 1968, is as inflammatory as Conoco's is bland. . . . It represents a new weapon in the arsenal of the social activists who are trying to force corporations to be more responsible."[16] In distinct contrast to Conoco's pretty pictures, the counter-report showed grimy coal towns and grim-faced coal miners, and revealed the hard fact that in the past five years, 178 Consol employees were killed in their mines. Fortunately for corporations, the high cost of publishing counterreports makes their wider use impractical. But even this single edition did show up a seamy side that intelligent directors cannot ignore.

Perhaps overextended emphasis on bland, nonconsequential, unabashed huckstering—to the near-exclusion of really significant facts and issues—is why the SEC initiated a move to integrate into the annual report the 10-K report. Coincidentally, the SEC pushed the proposal to have a majority of the directors sign the 10-K report. This raised the hackles of many outside directors. Whatever reasons the objecting outside directors might have, they are probably incidental and will not stop this phase of the corporate

[15]Quoted in John K. Shank and John B. Calfee, Jr., "Case of the Fuqua Forecast," *Harvard Business Review*, November–December 1973, p. 34.
[16]"Dissenters Compose an Annual Report," *Business Week*, May 6, 1972, p. 25.

governance evolution. It is significant that directors—officers and outsiders —*all* sign the annual report and *all* become conversant with the document.

Boardroom involvement in the preparation, dissemination, and interpretation of annual reports will become imperative as the board takes a more active role in corporate governance. Board duties will also assume greater proportions as shareholders and the general public become better acquainted with annual reports. Consider the impact of Gulf & Western's $5 million advertisement: inserted in the February 5 issue of *Time* was its entire 1978 annual report. Clorax began publishing a separate report for its employees, shorter and easier to read than the regular report. Wheelabrator-Frye even publishes an *Annual Report for Young People,* geared to readability and comprehension.

But of even greater significance is the potential of mass audiences. International Paper proposed to present its 1980 annual report in a half-hour program, through 1600 cable television stations. While other companies have produced video versions of their annual reports, International Paper was the first offered nationally to the general public.

The annual report is, by far, the corporation's best medium for stating its policies and philosophy; however, both are the province of the board of directors. By default, the board has given free reign to its surrogate, the chief executive officer, to express basically his views, policies, and philosophy. It is time that every board of directors states its own views, policies, and philosophy. "A corporation's philosophy and personality do count, and few documents provide this kind of unstatistical but important information as effectively as the annual report—as this year's report from Greif Bros., an Ohio-based paper-products manufacturer illustrates. Any shareholders searching for clues to the character of the company's top management will find one on the back cover. It's a photograph of the corporate boardroom, on whose wall is a large portrait of Jesus Christ. The cover carries a caption: 'Beneath this portrait and at this conference table for the last thirty-two years have been made the major decisions of the corporation.' "[17]

HEADQUARTERS

Since locating headquarters is a boardroom function or duty, rather than a characteristic, this section might have seemed more appropriate in Chapter 2. It was placed here, however, to stress the significance of headquarters' location as an environmental characteristic, determining to a large degree how a board will be structured, and even how it will tend to perform. In a way it sets a hereditary parameter.

[17]Herbert E. Meyer, "Annual Reports Get an Editor in Washington," *Fortune,* May 7, 1979, p. 222.

Unquestionably, there is a propinquity factor in the boardroom selection process, particularly for the small- and medium-sized firms. Just as college students tend to have a high mating rate with students at their respective institutions, so, too, directors tend to select individuals with whom they have frequent and friendly contact. Consequently, it is quite logical to assume that locating company headquarters in New York will mean that an overproportionate number of the firm's directors will be domiciled in the New York area. Moreover, inside or officer-directors, still approximately 40 percent of the total, invariably are selected from among the key personnel at headquarters.

These inferences do not overlook the relative ease with which directors—particularly of larger corporations—can commute, even cross-country, to board meetings. It does recognize the hardships imposed on cross-country commuting directors who usually dedicate an extra two or three days to the getting-to-the-meeting process.

As stated earlier, corporate boardrooms are usually located at corporate headquarters. Once established, corporate headquarters tend to be set until some compelling reason forces the board to make a move. Initially, in the one-plant days, there was no choice—the plant was headquarters—and this is the reason for the present location of a large percentage of our corporate headquarters. Even after the single plant has expanded into many plants, headquarters remains where it always has been. This accounts for the corporate headquarters of Armstrong World Industries being in Lancaster, Pennsylvania, Caterpillar Tractor in Peoria, Illinois, and Hershey Foods in Hershey, Pennsylvania, and the same holds for perhaps a quarter of all our enterprises.

A second reason accounting for headquarters and boardroom location is the centripetal force of financial centers. This has particularly been the case with large firms that are rapidly expanding, building through borrowing or through merger. Since large sums are needed to effect large-scale expansion, headquarters tends to move toward the source of funds. Financial leveraging has been, and will continue to be, an important factor in locating corporate headquarters. This is why New York City, with its high concentration of macro-financial institutions, continues to be a corporate capital-producing capitol, and hence the home for many corporations.

During the 1960s, New York City's long-accepted dominance—as well as other influential centers of corporate control—was challenged by the sun belt. There were various reasons for the subsequent migration from the snow belt to the sun belt. Urban decay, crime, congestion, confiscatory taxes (among them) prompted a southern and westward migration of plants, people, and corporate headquarters. This exodus, having now slowed to an orderly migration, continues. Note the following contrasts in the corporate headquarters' experience of two cities that have been the biggest losers and two which have been among the biggest winners, on the basis of "Fortune 500" data:

HEADQUARTERS

	1955	1975	1980
Losers			
New York City	141	90	81
Chicago	49	30	26
Winners			
Houston	1	11	12
Dallas	6	6	11

The trends are obvious. However, a conditioning factor must be mentioned. For example, New York City, during the 1956–1980 period, lost sixty major corporate headquarters of "Fortune 500" firms, but these firms did not necessarily move to the sun belt. A number simply moved a few miles northeast, to Westchester County, New York, or to Fairfield County, Connecticut, and a lesser number moved southwest to New Jersey. In 1955, Connecticut had only seven large-industrial headquarters; by 1980, its number had grown to thirty-six. New Jersey's headquarters also grew from eight in 1955 to nineteen in 1980.

Although the board of directors—at least in principle—makes the momentous decision on whether to move or not to move headquarters, in practice, few boards have any meaningful input in such decision making. In virtually every instance when a corporation talks about making a headquarters move, it is the chief executive officer or one of his vice presidents who does all the public discoursing. When, in 1976, Union Carbide announced plans to move its staff of 3500 from Park Avenue, New York City, to a 144-acre site near Danbury, Connecticut, Governor Hugh Carey made appeals to Union Carbide's top executives; he did not, however, appeal directly to Union Carbide's board of directors.

Again, when Diamond Shamrock Corporation decided to abandon Cleveland, Ohio, in 1979, and move its headquarters to Dallas, Texas, a pro-con dialogue was conducted between Shamrock's CEO and Cleveland's Mayor Dennis J. Kucinich. Similarly, when American Airlines said it would move its headquarters (with 1300 employees) to the Dallas–Fort Worth area, its chairman and CEO, Albert Casey, made the announcement. One inference, therefore, can strongly be drawn: in decisions relating to where the company's principal offices should be located, boards of directors invariably let the CEO do the deciding. Unfortunately, abdication of this very important prerogative is frequently justified by comments such as: the move was engineered by the CEO for personal benefits or lower taxes; because of proximity of executive playgrounds, golf links, ski slopes, yacht basins; or for the opportunity for baronial living.

The Wall Street Journal focused on allegations relating to Greyhound Corporation's move from Chicago to Phoenix in 1971.[18] It mentioned specifics about the Greyhound board, apparently being inclined to go along with the CEO's wishes rather than question or even stop faraway moves.

Shortly after his third marriage, in 1965, Gerald H. Trautman moved to Phoenix, Arizona. For years he continued to commute from Phoenix every week to work in Greyhound's headquarters, then based in Chicago. Before his decision to move Greyhound out of Chicago, Trautman engaged Fantus Company, a reputable consulting firm, specializing in location problems. Fantus reportedly recommended the move, and Trautman had his board of directors approve it. But several former executives disagreed. They pointed out that the public reason was that the move would bring the recently merged Armour Company and Greyhound together in a neutral corner. Also, they said, Trautman hoped the move would help reduce the staff with the resignations of some unwanted executives.

Executives and outside directors concurred that the subject of moving headquarters was not a debatable item since it was the strong preference of the chief executive, supported by his key executives. Since a number of these executives sometimes attended board meetings and were privy to inside information, their impression was that this was a "rubber stamp" board. This uncomplimentary characteristic, it should be said, was not a function of executive obsequiousness—Greyhound's board consisted of ten outsiders and only three insiders.

" 'The numbers are really deceiving,' says one former director. 'The board is full of Trautman's hand-picked candidates who get at least $20,000 a year for a total of four meetings that maybe last an hour and a half each. Every August meeting is really a free vacation with spouses in some spot like Hawaii, Scotland or a resort in Canada.' "[19]

Most knowledgeable persons stressed that the board meetings were very brief and went "like clockwork. The directors ask only the most mundane questions, and they pretty much do what Trautman asks of them. John M. Martin, retired chairman of Hercules, Inc. and a director for five years, calls the board: 'excellent and fully aware of what's going on.' However, Mr. Martin says he can't ever recall one negative vote cast on any issue. 'We do things by consensus.' "[20]

There are numerous similar episodes, all underscoring the pressure

[18]Stephen J. Sansweet, "Chairman Trautman Finds Greyhound Post Remains a Hot Seat," The Wall Street Journal, November 20, 1980, p. 1.
[19]Ibid., p. 24.
[20]Ibid.

exerted by chief executive officers when making the momentous decision to move corporate headquarters. Regardless of the motivation for these decisions, whether prompted by commendable bottom-line considerations or condemnable CEO personal reasons, there is one ingredient lacking. Rarely, if ever, do the respective boards get involved in researching, analyzing, discussing, or the real decision making.

CEO HIRING AND FIRING

Although collectively the board of directors is considered to be the "helmsman," it is important that there be at the helm only one person—not a committee—to guide the corporate vessel. This individual is the chief executive officer. Every corporate charter bestows upon the board of directors the right and duty to appoint the CEO and such other officers as it deems necessary for the proper conduct of the business of the company. A parallel right is also conferred to remove at any time any officers it has elected or appointed. The specific officers to be designated, and their functions, are then further detailed in the corporate bylaws, usually in Article IV.

It is almost universally agreed that the chief executive officer, in the manner of a captain at sea, has full authority. But there are some obstructions to the full exercise of this authority, as when a majority owner and retired CEO refuses to release the hand on the tiller. An example of this occurred when Henry Ford gave the presidency of his company to his son, Edsel, but never relinquished control. Twenty-five years later when Edsel died of cancer in 1943, "A newspaperman assigned to write an obituary complained that Edsel's longest statement to the press had been, 'See Father.' "[21]

Actually, the ex-helmsman who refuses to be sidelined does not have to be a majority owner to cause serious problems for the new CEO. When Harold Geneen finally relinquished the CEO post at International Telephone and Telegraph Corporation, after extending his stay beyond the mandated retirement age, he still held on to the chairmanship of ITT's board. Within eighteen months after his installation as Geneen's successor, Lyman Hamilton, Jr., was relieved of his post by ITT's twenty-member board. While he "resigned over policy differences," the unanimous opinion of insiders is that he dared to differ over a divestiture program with his predecessor and chairman, Harold Geneen.

What Hamilton failed to consider was the fact that ITT's board of directors was made up of Geneen's close outside associates and hand-picked officers. Subsequently, Hamilton's successor, Rand V. Araskog, was

[21]"The Outspoken Ford Remains a Mystery," *Business Week,* February 23, 1981, p. 13.

described as following the identical divestiture plan which presumably got Hamilton in trouble. But according to some, he was more discreet. "Araskog confers regularly on the phone and in person with Geneen and he strongly defends this as proper. 'Harold Geneen to me is a very respected and friendly person.' Araskog stressed that 'this company is mine to run.' And, that contact between the two happens 'very much on my initiative,' although Geneen adds to that remark: 'But if I have any ideas I don't hesitate to call Rand.' "[22] Araskog continues to hold all three top positions at ITT—chairman, president, and chief executive.

The Ford and ITT examples are not exceptions. In fact, there are far too many instances where owners or former top executives could not resist calling the signals from the sidelines. According to SEC and stockholders' expectations, the entire board should participate in the CEO search. The nominating committee can be useful, but it must not take over what is the board's most important function.

Not only is CEO selection an important directorate duty, but at one time it was assumed to be the only duty. The ideal board, according to yesterday's corporate governance authorities, was one that went into hibernation after it selected and anointed the CEO. Directors were expected to come out four or five times a year for short breathers, but were only to become really activated when a new CEO was needed. Of course, this was and still is a warped kind of thinking, contrary to law, logic, and the interests of the corporation and its shareholders.

Today, however, directors' duties (listed earlier) show an expanding array of functions. In addition to hiring the CEO, a less pronounced but equally important duty is the firing of an unwanted CEO. Rejection can stem from a variety of causes: personality differences, competency decline, or inability to stimulate. For example, a moribund board might simply refuse to respond to an executive dynamo—one who might want to take the corporation to loftier levels—and the CEO ends up in dismissal. Nevertheless, for whatever reasons, valid or only perceived, it is the duty of the board, at an appropriate time, to "lower the boom."

Fortune graphically portrayed how one very respected business leader, Roy L. Ash, was "axed" without warning. Ash was cofounder of the very successful Litton Industries, and subsequently became director of the U.S. Office of Management and Budget. After his tour of public service ended, Ash accepted the headship of AM International, formerly known as Addressograph-Multigraph. But even before he assumed his post, AM's mismanagement and unending problems had already caused financial pundits to dub it Addressogrief-Multigrief. Although initially Roy Ash seemed to have mesmerized his associates with his talk about turning AM

---

[22]"ITT: Groping for a New Strategy," *Business Week*, December 15, 1980, p. 66.

around, his downfall ultimately was caused by his inordinate propensity for looking into the not-so-near future. "He preferred to talk about where AM would be in five years rather than where it was at the moment. Everyday problems bored Ash—even as they multiplied. When a problem arose, Ash liked to dissect, scrutinize and analyze—exhaustively. Declared a former AM executive: 'Sometimes I wanted to damn near grab Roy by the collar and say, there are three alternatives we can take—one, two or three. Let's do it instead of talking about it.' "[23]

AM's outside auditor, Price Waterhouse, released a rather uncomplimentary annual report in 1980—calling the firm's operating controls sloppy. It also criticized AM's abnormally high employee turnover; for instance, the key duplicator division had four different presidents in the short span of three years.

Sadly, while many around him sensed what was coming, even weeks before his firing, Ash seemed oblivious. Actually, even the conspirators seemed satisfied with him until just four weeks before a special (February 1981) board meeting. The prime conspirator, John Birkelund, chairman of New Court Securities, the New York private investment firm of the Rothschilds, initiated a dump-Ash campaign even though he had, four years earlier, recruited him. The behind-the-scenes boardroom conniving was harsh and embarrassing. Ash, presumably unaware of this portentous plot, made a three-hour presentation, but there was no changing the course—a motion was made that he resign—and he did.

The sequel to this story was bittersweet. "It was a humiliating exit. . . . The stock market compounded the insult, as news of his departure led to a $4-per-share jump in AM stock—boosting the value of his 300,000 shares by $1.2 million."[24] In spite of the windfall profit, the whole affair was more bitter than sweet—an illustrious corporate commander-in-chief had succumbed under his counselors' coup.

Within the past fifteen years, we have had a heavy incidence of deposed CEOs. Also, presidents in charge, but without CEO designation, are particularly vulnerable. Some examples: Metrocare, Incorporated, a Clearwater, Florida, developer of retirement communities, went through three presidents in four months. Falstaff Brewery had two presidents resign within nine months—the second resignation came less than two months after installation. National Tea had three presidents in eight months. Over a longer period, Kaiser Steel had eight presidents in seven years.

Sometimes CEOs expire naturally, and it becomes the unpleasant duty of the board to step in immediately upon the death. This can be a traumatic experience for the board especially when death is instant. A tragic incident

---

[23]Susie Gharib Nazem, "How Roy Ash Got Burned," *Fortune,* April 6, 1981, p. 71.
[24]Ibid.

took place in 1979 when Northwest Bancorp's 51-year-old president-CEO, while walking his dog near his home after a severe storm, stepped on a fallen power line and was electrocuted. Within hours the bank's directors were alerted and activated a contingency plan, fortunately prepared earlier by the CEO.

The board's hiring and firing functions encompass a variety of related chores which too often suffer from inattention. One of these is to support all CEO-related actions with facts. In selection, for instance, more than just the job specifications are needed; each candidate should be ranked objectively. Yet often the hiring of a CEO is based on emotion, not a systematic or scientific analysis. Even bathing beauty contest judges do not justify their choices on emotion alone. More appalling is the fact that dismissals are universally based on unsupported allegations. The rationale for these dismissals could hardly stand up in court cross-examination and adjudication. The following is an example.

A sensational dethroning occurred at RCA Corporation when Edgar H. Griffiths, forced to resign as chairman and CEO, became chairman of the finance committee, a newly created position. Griffiths had succeeded Anthony L. Conrad who was ousted because of the national scandal he created—it was revealed that he had failed to file his income tax returns for the previous five years. Conrad's predecessor, Robert W. Sarnoff, also was ousted as chief executive because of a series of financial blunders.

The recent RCA sequence of CEO terminations would make a beautiful libretto, filled with intrigue and malediction. Griffiths himself was not averse to using the stiletto. He recently had brutally deposed two of his key executives—Maurice R. Valente, whom he hand-picked for president five months earlier, and then Jane Cahill Pfeiffer, from the chairmanship of RCA's National Broadcasting Company. In spite of charges and counter-charges, in neither of these executive assassinations did there appear to be adequate cause for such harsh treatment. Griffiths behaved in a brutal manner when he refused to buy out Ms. Pfeiffer's contract. He was subsequently rebuked by the board, which in its embarrassment, voted her an $800,000 severance package. Unbelievably, Griffiths, in his resignation, accepted a $2,250,000 deal, payable as salary over the next five years, for services as a "consultant" to the corporation.

It is said that Griffiths was peeved because he was being criticized and second-guessed by his board. He had spent a lifetime at RCA and knew it intimately. He "resented what he often considered vacuous advice. On at least one occasion he remarked that he didn't feel he should have to waste valuable time 'teaching the business to board members.' "[25] His reluctance

[25]John E. Cooney, "Griffiths's Resignation at RCA Follows Year of Turmoil, Criticism," *The Wall Street Journal,* January 26, 1981, p. 1.

to play nursemaid and tutor to the uninformed outside directors irked them. They charged him with refusing to consult and failing to heed anyone's advice but his own. His successor, Thornton Bradshaw, former president of Atlantic Richfield Company, very likely will not be accused of being a reluctant tutor or a poor listener. Unlike Griffiths, who spent a lifetime at RCA and knew every facet of the business, Bradshaw's broadcasting experience has been limited to nine years of service on RCA's board plus a recent sailing trip with Walter Cronkite.

INSIDE AND OUTSIDE DIRECTORS

During the past several decades we have heard much discussion about the relative merits of inside directors versus outside directors. Insiders are board members who are on the company payroll and head a geographical division, product line, or staff function such as sales, production, or finance. Consequently, they are sometimes referred to as "functional," "employee," "management," or "officer" directors—they are also known as "full-time," "active," or "working" directors. Since they are full-time employees, inside directors are usually available for all board meetings, both regular and special. As a rule, inside directors do not receive any additional compensation for board or board committee services. Except for retired CEOs, their tenure usually ceases when they leave the company's employment. A question now arises about the relatively few ex-officer-directors (usually former CEOs) who do continue to serve after retirement: Are they still insiders, or have they been transformed into outside directors? Common sense suggests that these ex-employees should retain insider status for at least several years—their grooming, competency, allegiance, and perspective do not instantaneously disappear upon retirement.

Another category of inside director (and at one time the most important) is the owner-director, his designee, or his close relative. Generally in our older, large-scale enterprises (as Berle and Means[26] wrote more than a half century ago), corporate control has been divorced from ownership, and owner-directors are a breed of the past. Even in our so-called family firms—Ford Motor Company, E. I. du Pont, for example—individuals with ownership of more than 4 percent of the common stock are a rarity. Yet, in several hundred thousand first-generation owner-entrepreneur firms (especially in smaller firms), stock ownership is the prime factor in structuring the board.

Historically, inside directors are the legacy of strong company owner-founders who elevated the top executive group from "hired-hands" status to

---

[26]Adolphe A. Berle, Jr., and Gardiner C. Means, *The Modern Corporation and Private Property* (New York: The Macmillan Company, 1933).

that of policy makers. Their long tenure and dedication to specific chores give them an unparalleled competency plus a high loyalty quotient. In capsule, inside directors tend to have:

1 Superior pertinent technical backgrounds
2 Demonstrated leadership ability through long service in the company
3 Immediate availability for both routine and emergency sessions
4 Complete dedication to the organization
5 A keener comprehension of the wants and attitudes of the company's rank and file, the stockholders, the customers, and their management colleagues

At the other end of a confusing continuum are the outside directors—also known as "nonmanagement," "nonemployee," "part-time," "honorific," "independent," or "professional" directors. It is assumed that their separation from the company and its routine problems gives them a measure of superiority. Among the more frequently listed advantages of outside directors are that they:

1 Provide independent assessments
2 Have broader backgrounds
3 Are more representative of stockholders and society
4 Are stockholder-oriented
5 Give the best in checks and balances

An increasing number of retiring company top executives, public figures, government officials, and university presidents now seek postretirement careers as outside or professional directors. Note that the designation "professional" is used in a wide variety of senses, but generally it refers to an outside director who makes a living by serving on a number of boards. Obviously, the living-off of directorate fees can be quite comfortable. A commonly quoted statement is Lord Boothby's sentiments on his own "eight or nine" directorships—explaining what he and his British peers serving as outside directors do in adding prestige to corporate letterheads: "No effort of any kind is called for. You go to a meeting once a month in a car supplied by the company. You look both grave and sage, and on two occasions say 'I agree,' say 'I don't think so' once, and if all goes well, you get $1,440 a year. If you have five of them, it is total heaven, like having a permanent hot bath."[27] That was twenty years ago. Today, with U.S. major public corporations paying $40,000 or more, including committee stipends, five such sinecures can certainly provide the professional director with a heavenly feeling.

Industrial elitism in the form of "old boy" networks is not exclusively a

[27]*Time,* October 5, 1962.

British phenomenon. After World War II, when the German aristocracy was displaced, there arose a new hierarchical top-level *Geldaristokratie,* the industrial plutocracy. Thousands of blue bloods now found a new sinecure. "The boards of big industrial companies are liberally studded with noble names. The names are particularly in demand as public relations men. 'I do like snobs' exclaims one princely P.R. man. 'They are all so kind to one. . . . All you need to get ahead in industry is reasonably good looks, self-assurance and organizational talent.' This the nobility had, and now the young ones are all fat people in their firms."[28]

In the United States, "old boy" networks are not so much a function of aristocracy as they are of plutocracy—control by monied interests. Yet there is a congenital propensity among successful businessmen to found dynasties. One dynasty, that of the Boston Brahmin Cabots, is typified in a classic "poem":

> Here's to good old Boston
> Land of the bean and the cod.
> Where the Lowells talk only to the Cabots
> And the Cabots talk only to God.[29]

The Cabot name is perdurable. Last year, Boston's Cabot Corporation (with several Cabots on its board) made news when it paid its president, Robert A. Charpie, a grand total of $4,706,206—the third highest salary paid in the United States.

The Lowells, likewise, continue to be visible. For many years before his recent demise, Ralph Lowell, former chairman of Boston Safe Deposit Trust Company, was a front-runner in the outside-director race, holding forty-two positions as officer, director, or trustee. A close second was George E. Allen, an intimate of several U.S. presidents, who held a record of thirty-two positions, twenty-six with corporation boards.[30]

Among the list of multiseated outside directors, the name of Hulett Clinton Merritt stands out. During his lifetime, Merritt acquired a grand total of 138 company directorates. Just trying to remember the names of so many companies would be a feat for any director. Moreover, attending a hundred or more board meetings annually would require instant transport and computerlike acquaintance with the many different agenda, the profusion of problems, and the volumes of related facts and figures.

There have been other outstanding examples of outsiders being in many places at the same time. Probably the best-known and most widely

[28]"An Eclipse of Princes," *Time,* April 26, 1963, p. 32.

[29]Quoted by William M. Bulkeley, "Lacking an Aristocracy, Americans Confer Role on Clans like Cabots," *The Wall Street Journal,* May 7, 1979, p. 1.

[30]See "Inside vs. Outside Directors," *NACD Corporate Director's Special Report Series,* vol. IV, 1979, p. 4.

respected professional director was Sidney J. Weinberg. In addition to his full-time job as senior partner at the investment firm of Goldman, Sachs, Weinberg served on thirty-five different boards. Eventually he curtailed his directorships to eleven, which included seats on the boards of Ford Motor Company, General Electric, General Foods, General Cigar, National Dairy Products, Continental Can, B. F. Goodrich, Champion Paper and Fiber, Van Raalte, McKesson & Robbins, and Cluett Peabody. Incidentally, most of these "Goldman, Sachs board seats" had been occupied much earlier (1929) by Waddill Catchings, a predecessor of Sidney Weinberg. Upon Weinberg's death, as a sort of patrimony, several of these same seats were "bequeathed" to his son, John L. Weinberg.

Interestingly, there is no evidence to show that corporate boards cluttered with prestigious personages have been particularly effective. In fact, some negative relationships might come about because these prominent outsiders have other more pressing demands. "In the past some directors—particularly notables 'who look good on the roster,' according to one businessman—often skipped meetings. Ellsworth Bunker, the U.S. Ambassador to South Vietnam, has been a director of Curtis Publishing Company since 1963. But he has attended only one board meeting in the past two years, a Curtis spokesman says."[31] Ellsworth Bunker's tenure as a Curtis Publishing director correlates perfectly with the decline of the once-eminent publisher of the *Saturday Evening Post* and other magazines. Likewise, Asa Spaulding's tenure as a W. T. Grant director (also the first U.S. black director) did not prevent that merchandiser's demise.

Howard Butcher III, senior partner of Philadelphia's financial firm Butcher and Sherrerd, was accused of conflict of interest. Using secret information, gleaned as a Penn Central director, he sold out his substantial Penn Central holdings just before the railroad's collapse. The SEC investigated and penalized the firm and six of its partners, charging that Butcher and Sherrerd violated antifraud provisions of federal securities laws by providing certain customers with trading recommendations on Penn Central stock—just before the company's railroad subsidiary met financial disaster. Butcher's response (see the Penn Central Company illustration, Chapter 7) was to "quit all his outside directorships in close to 70 firms."[32] Nevertheless, Penn Central folded soon afterward.

These few examples of association with grandiose business failures certainly are not atypical—outside directors are definitely not a guarantee of success. Yet the American Institute of Management has persistently lauded the superiority of outside directors over inside directors. In one of its earlier

[31]*The Wall Street Journal,* March 13, 1969, p. 1.
[32]"Executives: Crying on the Inside," *Time,* October 18, 1968, p. 100.

issues of the *Manual of Excellent Managements,* the AIM makes a profession of faith. "One of the fundamental tenets of the Institute is that the majority of the members of any board should be drawn from outside the company. This is, the Institute is convinced, the only means whereby objectivity in approach and clear-cut decisions on corporate problems can be assured. Companies which are rated excellent in this category, but who do not fulfill this requirement, are excellent *despite* the condition."[33]

Such unmitigated bias would raise the blood pressure of any statistician; such an imagined conclusion needs study to corroborate or refute. In this instance, it did inspire the first analytical studies of inside- and outside-director worth. In a pioneer study of 200 major industrial corporations between 1925 and 1950, the composite firms with distinctly inside boards unquestionably outperformed those with predominantly outside boards, while the companies with mixed or "hybrid" boards had an intermediate performance record.[34]

A second updated study, to 1963, is detailed in Chapter 9, "Boardroom Evaluation." Again, the inside- or officer-director boards were found to be superior. This follow-up study did, however, show that the ratio of inside to outside directors had begun to shift somewhat in favor of outsiders.[35]

A common misconception in regard to inside and outside directors is that, in the early days of the economy, when individual enterprise was at its heyday, inside directorates predominated. This is not so. The era of trusts and the first great merger waves put the focus on outside directors. In some industries such as banking and textiles, boards of directors were over-whelmingly outside. This was the case here and abroad. For example, Robert Owen, the renowned utopian and founder of New Lanark Mills, had his start as an apprentice to an individual named Drinkwater. Owen was so proficient that the absentee directors promoted him to plant manager and hired-hand director. This was the typical textile industry corporate govern-ance structure, namely, all absentee or outside directors except for the hired-hand production manager. The hired hand ultimately had his fill of absentee directors and formed his own company, and New Lanark Mills came into being. This governance pattern was typical not only in Great Britain, but also in the United States.

Inside directorships came into being with the turn of the century's rapid industrialization. The dramatic success of many individual entrepreneurs and the consequent increase in family firms accelerated the need for

---

[33]*Manual of Excellent Managements,* American Institute of Management, New York, 1955.
[34]Stanley C. Vance, "Functional Directors and Corporate Performance," reviewed in *Business Week,* November 26, 1955, pp. 128–130.
[35]Stanley C. Vance, *Boards of Directors: Structure and Performance* (Eugene, Oregon: University of Oregon Press, 1964).

technically competent officers to serve as directors. By 1925, as the Vance study shows, out of a sample of 1296 directors, 56.2 percent were insiders, while the comparable figure in 1963 was 59.3 percent.[36]

A profound change occurred in the late 1960s. Coincidentally, Keith Funston, president of the New York Stock Exchange, arbitrarily set forth a stipulation that, henceforth, only companies with a minimum of two outsiders on their boards could apply for listing on the NYSE. Around the same time, the sociopolitical activists launched their concerted efforts against officer-director managements. Despite their superlative past performance records, companies with historically all-insider boards—such as Standard Oil (N.J) (now Exxon), Bethlehem Steel, American Tobacco (now American Brands), E. I. du Pont, Dow Chemical, and Monsanto—reacted in a near stampede to obey the NYSE mandate, even though they could all have availed themselves of the "grandfather clause."

Other forces accelerated the preference for outsiders. Increasing mergers, during this period, put the focus on suppliers of funds rather than upon the marketing and production processes. Then in the 1970s, when more than 400 leading corporations were individually accused of a variety of transgressions, particularly bribery, the trend toward outside directors accelerated even further. Yet there was no evidence at all to correlate or link the alleged crimes and abuses to inside directors. Actually, a preponderance of outside-dominated boards—Gulf Oil, Lockheed, Textron, Northrup—were prominent among the transgressing 400.

The pro-outside-director bias was further supported by the chairman of the Securities and Exchange Commission, Harold M. Williams, who went to an extreme in proposing that all boards have all outside directors, with the possible exception of the chairman-CEO. This radical proposal was quickly scuttled because of loud and indignant outcries from the business community.[37]

Probably the most significant factor accentuating the use of outside directors was the proliferation of committees of the board. As will be discussed in Chapter 4, all the newer committees consist almost entirely of outside directors. As a consequence, the inside-outside ratio has been reversed, and today approximately 60 percent of directors in our larger corporations are outsiders.

Board structure estimates vary depending upon the survey—its sample, respondents, time period, and definitions used. For example, a late-1980 tabulation by the executive-search consulting firm of Heidrick and Struggles showed 87.6 percent of boards with outsiders as a majority—up from 70

---

[36]Vance, *Boards of Directors*, pp. 18–21.
[37]*Director's Monthly*, National Association of Corporate Directors, vol. 2, nos. 9 and 10, September/October 1978.

percent in 1978. Considering the precipitous percentage rise in a two-year period, some statistical cautions should be applied. For example, although 1300 firms were surveyed, only 486 responded. So low a response rate must be questioned. Moreover, the same survey indicated that only 55 percent of the respondents had majorities of "independent" outside directors, namely, those with no family business or other ties with the company. As a compromise, it seems reasonable to assume that presently about 60 percent of all directors serving the 1000 largest industrials are outsiders. The percentage probably rises to 75 percent for nonindustrials, but drops to 45 percent for smaller enterprises.

These figures will change as director liability, work onus, compensation, and technical background are increased. Obviously, the inside/outside directorate controversy is far from ended.

PROFESSIONAL DIRECTORS

The typical professional directorship is likened to Lord Boothby's "permanent hot bath." (See "Inside and Outside Directors.") It is a sinecure which provides superlative pay in return for a few hours spent in the boardroom. Boothby's American counterpart, who serves on five to nine boards, can earn close to a quarter-million dollars for approximately 300 boardroom hours. This is a very comfortable "permanent hot bath."

Contrary to various articles on the dearth of director candidates, there actually is a surplus of individuals, eager to get immersed in the professional director "permanent hot bath." Even the increasing threat of liability suits is no deterrent, for how many of the 100,000 or more directors on SEC-regulated boards have been personally penalized by liability suits? Company-paid directors and officers (D&O) liability insurance is the professional (outside) director's safe harbor.

But what is a professional director? The term "professional" implies a rigorous specified schooling, serious entrance hurdles such as the bar exam, apprenticeship, regular technical updating, self policing, an identifiable code of responsibility, and periodic peer association. In this sphere, the only criterion faithfully fulfilled by most directors is "periodic peer association." Board meetings are not peer associations in the lawyer/doctor/professor sense. These associations are generally on the golf links, at the yacht club, on ski slopes, or at the bar. Surely, it would be very difficult to say that there are many truly professional directors.

A generation ago, as senior partner at Goldman, Sachs, Sidney Weinberg epitomized the professional director. (See "Inside and Outside Directors.") Yet even as he served on a total of thirty-five boards, the courts began to question the legitimacy of financiers serving as professional directors. As a result, Weinberg, in 1953, was ordered by a court to choose between board seats on Goodrich or Sears, Roebuck. He chose Goodrich but also tried to maintain his position as one of three trustees of the Sears Fund, which controlled more than 20 million shares of Sears, Roebuck stock. Five years later, another court order forced Weinberg to abandon his Sears Fund trusteeship. The motive behind Weinberg's acting as a presumed professional director was to serve Goldman, Sachs clients and enhance the financial house's position.

Presently, there is a new breed of pseudo-professional directors—former politicians who feel they are too young for passive elder statesmen roles. Periodically, as Washington and state capitols move from one party's control to another's, a wholesale exodus of politicians occurs. A very high percentage of top-ranking nonelected former officials and their appointees must find new employment. After the Reagan landslide, hundreds of bureaucrats and politicians moved into made-to-order boardroom seats. Keep in mind that this new breed of director has few hallmarks of the professional; they actually are pseudo-professional directors.

The paragon of this new version of professional director is the thirty-eighth President of the United States, Gerald R. Ford. When he failed to secure the 1980 nomination, Ford decided he wanted to become a part of the business system he had championed for so long. Influential friends on corporate boards helped open doors to a large number of boardrooms. Within a year, Gerald Ford was elected to the boards of Amax, GK Technologies, Santa Fe International, Shearson Loeb Rhoades, Tiger International, Pebble Beach Corporation (a Twentieth Century-Fox subsidiary), and subsequently to the Twentieth Century-Fox board. In this latter seat, he serves as the first outside director—Fox, a month earlier, had switched from public to private ownership. Marvin Davis, a Denver oil millionaire, and a longtime Ford friend, purchased Fox.

"Ford gets a typical director's fee of about $20,000 from each of these companies. But since he's hardly a typical director, some of them have also retained him as a consultant, at annual fees ranging from $35,000 (GK Technologies) to $100,000 (Shearson). . . . In announcing Ford's election to their boards several companies have cited such attributes as his experience in national and international affairs and his unique and comprehensive perspective."[38]

Keeping active has been financially rewarding for Gerald Ford. His nongovernment income in 1980 topped $800,000:

Board retainers and fees, $125,000
Business consulting, $325,000

[38]"Gerald Ford, Corporate Director," *Fortune,* February 9, 1981, p. 19.

Public appearances, $300,000
Other ventures, $50,000

Indeed, ex-President Ford has comfortably immersed himself in one of Lord Boothby's "permanent hot baths." However, he is not alone; sharing with him at Fox Film is his former Secretary of State, Henry Kissinger, who later joined the "team."

But hot baths are not always so soothing. For example, late in 1981, Sante Fe International was the object of a Kuwaiti buy-out. Sheikh Ali Khalifa offered to pay $51 a share, in cash, to Santa Fe—more than double its market price at that time. The buyer, actually the state-owned Kuwait Petroleum Corporation (with revenues in the $5 billion category), would pay over $2.5 billion in the deal.

While the arrangement was distinctly legitimate, it did pose ethical and political problems for the board. It is claimed that former President Gerald Ford and Roderick Hills, former SEC chairman—both members of the Santa Fe board—were enthusiastically in favor of the sale. The dilemma for politicians turned corporate directors is how to mix chauvinism and cash. Political commentators were quick to point out that this Kuwaiti "invasion" would give the OPEC cartel a strong position in our domestic petroleum industry and, therefore, lessen our ability to compete. One congressman stated that such permissiveness goes beyond the scary; it actually becomes self-destructive.

The situation became more sensitive when it was disclosed that a Santa Fe subsidiary, C. F. Braun, was intimately connected with the Department of Energy's Hanford nuclear works. Also, Congress became concerned when one of the three best companies for building nuclear processing plants was being sold to a foreign government. Transactions of this nature cast shadows on boardroom patriotism even when former national leaders are involved.

High-ranking Republican politicians are not the only ones congenitally suited for this new version of professional director. Former Defense Secretary Harold Brown was paid over $100,000 by Amax in 1981. Former Vice President Walter F. Mondale and Robert S. Strauss (a "factotum" in the Carter White House) have joined the board of Columbia Pictures Industries, Incorporated. " 'It's the government in exile,' cracks one Wall Street wit. 'They are friends of Herbert A. Allen, president of Allen and Company and a Columbia shareholder. Their appointment reflects the influence of Allen who becomes Columbia's chairman on July 1.' "[39]

On the list also is Robert S. McNamara, former Secretary of Defense and

[39]"In Exile at Columbia," *U.S. News & World Report,* May 11, 1981, p. 123.

president (retired) of the World Bank, who was elected a director of Corning Glass. At the same time, Harold Brown, former Secretary of Defense, was elected to the board of CBS, Incorporated, and then later to International Business Machine's board. Joining him at IBM was Patricia Roberts Harris, former Secretary of Health and Human Services. However, both had served on IBM's board before their brief stints in government. Even "second-stringers" such as Martin E. Gouldner, former Deputy Assistant Secretary of Defense (under Harold Brown), was elected a director of Fingermatrix, a developer of electronic fingerprint identification systems.

Although most deposed politicians and bureaucrats seek only outside directorships, occasionally—as with former SEC Chairman Roderick Hills—they do venture forth as inside directors. Hills took over as chairman and chief executive officer of Peabody Coal Company, after its court-ordered divestiture from Kennecott Corporation. Upon assuming his new posts, Hills "confessed that he didn't know much about the business. Last month Hills resigned."[40] Hills tried to run St. Louis-based Peabody Coal while commuting from Washington where his wife, Carla Hills, was then Secretary for Housing and Urban Development. Hills's comment: "The burden of commuting was outrageous."[41]

There are, of course, other pretenders to the professional director title. Since educators are assumed to be knowledgeable and above suspicion, an increasing number of university presidents, college of business administration deans, and even professors are being invited to sit on boards. For some, the pattern set by Donald Kirk David, dean of Harvard's Graduate School of Business Administration (from 1942 to 1955), is most appealing. David moved to the Ford Foundation and then proceeded to acquire directorships at Aluminum Company of America, Ford Motor Company, Great Atlantic and Pacific Tea Company, Sinclair Oil Corporation, Pan American World Airways, R. H. Macy and Company, City Investing Company, and others. In his day, Dean David was probably the closest thing to being the real professional director. In addition to his academic and education administration experience, David also had a lengthy industrial apprenticeship, working up to the presidency of American Maize Products Company before becoming a dean at Harvard.

Another fertile area that is gestating an abundance of would-be professional directors is the rapidly expanding field of management consulting, where frequently there is a high level of technical competency. Another field with great potential is the big labor union hierarchy. While there has not been a great stampede to join Douglas Fraser (union representative) on boards of directors, the potential cannot be ignored. As pension funds

[40]"Commuting Out," *Fortune,* July 17, 1978, p. 16.
[41]Ibid.

expand beyond the half-trillion-dollar level, and as conventional outside-director boards continue to enact more of the Penn Central–W. T. Grant–Chrysler types of dramas, there will be calls for further changes. Unions, if for no other reason than to protect members' pensions, will demand boardroom seats. Most likely their logical choices will be union presidents, who might be reasonably effective as representatives, rather than professional directors.

PUBLIC DIRECTORS

A decade ago two outstanding corporate governance experts almost simultaneously propounded the concept of the public director—Robert Townsend, former president of Avis, probably better known as author of the best-seller *Up the Organization,* and Arthur Goldberg, former Secretary of Labor, Supreme Court justice, and ambassador to the United Nations. They both emphasized that what they were not proposing was the commonly accepted notion that an outside director was automatically a public director. Goldberg, in fact, was emphatic in his opposition to the run-of-the-mill outsider. "It would be preferable in my view, not to have any outside directors at all, rather than delude the public into believing that the outside directors are really monitoring the affairs of a company. Making all the directors 'inside' directors who manage the company and focusing all responsibility on them, may be preferable to maintaining the myth on the part of the public that there is actual and meaningful overseeing by outside directors which, in fact, there is not—and cannot be under the present system."[42]

Goldberg's suggestions for meaningful public directors is to equip them with a small staff of consultants who have access to the meaningful sources of information. He also believes that directors should be adequately compensated so that they could spend sufficient time in fulfilling their fiduciary duties; meetings, preferably, should be monthly but never less than quarterly; public directors should be selected by their fellow directors and not by management.

As Goldberg set forth his definition, it seemed to be more a matter of what the public director is not. For example, he excludes lawyers, accountants, and bankers who have business dealings with the company; also, all customers and suppliers. Most of these affiliated types of directors have also been recommended for exclusion by the SEC. But Goldberg goes one step further by suggesting that "management officials of corporations in active service should not serve on the boards of companies other than their

---

[42]Paul London, "Arthur Goldberg on Public Directors," *Business and Society Review,* vol. 1, no. 1, Spring 1972, p. 37.

own."[43] It is this last exclusion which could toss corporate governance into chaos, since presently about one-third of all outside directors are top executives in other corporations. Generally they have a higher level of experience and technical and governance know-how than do those more readily classified as public directors. Yet Arthur Goldberg is right—it is bad practice for an executive of one corporation to serve on the boards of other companies. These split-personality outside directors try to serve more than one master. Invariably, Goldberg believes, they do a poor job. They cannot be in two or more places at the same time; neither can they consider the corporate governance matters of more than one firm at a time.

Robert Townsend structures an even more detailed and complex public director. He believes that the average outside director spends less than forty hours a year on his outside directorate duties, including meetings. "And the meetings sound like those at the Augusta National Golf Club: name-dropping, discussion of salmon fishing in Norway, some superficial talk about the state of the economy and the goddamned unproductivity of labor; and then they adjourn with two $100 bills or more in everyone's pocket. The directors don't really know what's going on, who the players are, what attitudes, relationships, and problems govern the company's actions. How can they, in forty hours a year?"[44]

Townsend proceeds to detail his plan, starting with its span of coverage. All manufacturing companies with assets of more than a billion dollars would be required to have public directors. Townsend points out that, in 1972, this would have applied to only 110 industrial-sector companies; however, a decade later, the figure was closer to 300. Logically, if giant utilities (AT&T with more than $150 billion in assets), major merchandisers, banks, insurers, transportation companies, and other macrofirms were included, the number would approach 500.

The next significant suggestion is budgetary: each corporation would be required to provide each public director with $1 million. Of this sum, a maximum of, perhaps, $50,000 would be the director's pay. The rest would be for discretionary spending: staff, supplies, surveys, and legal and accounting services. Very obviously, since inflation has cut the value of the dollar in half (within the decade), Townsend's original budgeting suggestion would now have to be doubled to $2 million annually, including $100,000 for salaries. Even this proposed inflation-adjusted salary is low considering what corporations presently pay their "in-and-out" directors. These "in-

[43]Arthur J. Goldberg, from First Annual Manuel F. Cohen Memorial Lecture, reprinted in *Director's Monthly,* National Association of Corporate Directors, vol. 4, no. 3, March 1980, p. 4.

[44]Robert Townsend, "Let's Install Public Directors," *Business and Society Review,* vol. 1, no. 1, Spring 1972, p. 69.

and-outs" might also be called "two-percenters" since 2 percent of a full work year is just about all any director gives to his or her outside seat.

There are some interesting procedural considerations in Townsend's plan. The public director would have an office in the company's headquarters. He would receive notices of all meetings held anywhere in the company and would automatically be invited to attend, or to send a proxy from his staff. Likewise, he and his staff would have access to all company records.

On the public director's part, he would be expected to hold at least two press conferences each year where he would report his views of the company's progress, or lack of progress, on issues of public interest.

Townsend also sets forth some stringent prescriptions for selection purposes. He advocates developing a pool of candidates who meet a minimum of four criteria: "They must be (1) knowledgeable about large corporation behavior, with at least ten-years' experience—some of it in line jobs as opposed to staff or expert jobs; (2) wealthy enough and/or disinterested enough in corporate power to be utterly uncorruptible; (3) energetic; and (4) reasonably intelligent.

"Once a pool of eligible directors is created, specific directors should be chosen by blind draw and assigned to corporations at random. They should be rotated every four years to mitigate against corruption and co-option and be reviewed prior to reassignment by the congressional committee to see whether they've taken the shilling or lost their energy."[45]

The reference to the "congressional committee" is disturbing. Townsend proposes setting up an ad hoc committee to examine and approve candidates for the public director pool. He would form this committee from senators and representatives who have occupied at least vice presidential offices in nonfamily-owned businesses. This committee would put—as federal meatpacking inspectors do—the blue stamp of approval on those who meet standards.

Others who advocate the use of public directors go along with the full-time, well-staffed notions. Christopher D. Stone, a law professor at the University of Southern California, sees these "limited public directors" serving as in-house probation officers, especially helping corporations face social issues such as pollution, plant closings, and occupational health hazards. He also suggests that these public directors be court-appointed, perhaps being nominated by federal regulatory agencies. While he admits his structuring could result in an occasional "factionalist brawl," he argues that a measure of factionalism would be preferable to the present degree of clubbiness.

[45]Ibid.

There are other soft spots in these and similar schemes. Initially, there would be only one public director, working full-time and getting full-time pay. Under this scheme it is hard to imagine that other outsiders would be willing to remain as part-timers or second-class boardroom citizens. Eventually, all or most of the outsiders would have to be reclassified as public directors, thus creating compensation complexities. By the end of this decade (assuming inflation persists), Townsend's public directors would demand at least $3 million for each office. Assuming that fifteen outside directors are now converted to public directors, this would mean a grand expenditure of $45 million.

OTHER DIRECTOR DESIGNATIONS

There is wide latitude for designating special kinds of directors. The honorary and the emeritus director titles are self-descriptive and are generally bestowed upon the firm's retired founder or upon a superdignitary. Another designation, "working director," first used about thirty years ago, was never really accepted; perhaps because of the reciprocal connotation that the other directors did no work.

In the British tradition another designation, "whole-time directors," has some limited use. Lipton Tea (India), for example, has three "whole-time" directors on its board of six. These directors are concerned only with the job of directing, leaving operations to the general managers.

The Federal Reserve Bank of New York has Class A and Class B directors who are elected by member banks. The Class A and B terminology is confusing in that some corporations have Class A common shares and Class B common shares. For example, Times Company, a component of New York Times Company, has 803,100 shares of Class B common which elects 70 percent of the board; the 11.2 million Class A common shares control only 30 percent of the board selections.

A number of organizations are using rotating directors. At Wm. Wrigley and Company, there is a one-year rotating director seat, presumably to let key executives share equitably in the policy-making process. W. R. Grace and Company, which has one of the largest boards in the industrial sector (thirty-six members), has several rotating directorships for a group of its key executives. Generally there are five officer-directors who serve limited terms. In another context, some conglomerates use a rotating directorship whereby the more important subsidiaries can be periodically represented on the board.

The rotation concept is more widely used in a different context. For instance, in order to avoid having all the directors come up for reelection at the same time, their terms are staggered. Most frequently there are three groups of directors with election or reelection spaced over three years, but any combination is possible. What is lacking in all these different designations is the certified public director. This void will be discussed in the section "Director Certification" in Chapter 9.

POSTSCRIPT

If the preceding coverage of board and director characteristics seemed to be wanting, that is intentional. It is impossible to identify, describe, and measure *all* the characteristics that fit corporate governance needs. Nor can boardroom traits be neatly listed and classified in the manner of a periodic table for basic elements. Moreover, prescribing board and director characteristics in precise formulas would be misleading, if not downright foolishness.

Consider the case of television producer Ed Friendly, who, after one month, resigned from the boards of Caesars World Inc. and Caesars New Jersey Inc. The New Jersey Casino Control Commission presented Mr. Friendly with Personal History Form No. 1, a 65-page questionnaire. Among the questions were requests for a listing of all sixteen of his great-grandparents and all his landlords and employers from the time he was a teenager. The commission termed Friendly uncooperative when he declared this inquisition a violation of his Fourth Amendment rights.

The commission's deep concern with traits and backgrounds of gambling-enterprise directors is certainly warranted. Nevertheless, when any regulatory body sets up inconsequentials as important characteristics and attributes prerequisite for membership on a casino's board of directors, it is overstepping its bounds. Checking a candidate's parentage three or four generations back, and employers and landlords over a lifetime, can certainly hobble a board and hurt decent candidates. Although this episode verges on the ridiculous, it is serious in that the Casino Control Commission was not only infringing on Friendly's constitutional rights, but also usurping shareholders' prerogatives.

CHAPTER 4

BOARD STRUCTURE

COMMITTEES

Committees are universally used and are universally abused. Commenting on committees in his company, Henry Ford is reputed to have said, "I'm convinced you can't run a company by taking votes."

Someone once described a camel as a horse designed by a committee. Obviously, this remark was not complimentary to committees in view of the camel's nonesthetic design, ungainly gait, and other shortcomings. But in spite of the ridicule committees receive time after time, they do serve a purpose and are an integral part of all corporate governance mechanisms.

There is considerable variance in the design and function of board committees. Some of this variance is due to state laws, which are far from being uniform. New York, for example, has no specific statutes on the subject; consequently, the kinds of committees, and what they do, must be defined entirely by the courts. Other states are more specific; for example, Delaware, New Jersey, and Pennsylvania permit boards, by statute, to delegate all their powers in the management of the business and affairs of the corporation. Other states add a proviso that the designation of such a committee, and the delegation to it of authority, shall not operate to relieve the board of directors, or any individual director, of any responsibility imposed upon the board or the individual member by law. This is the essence of the Model Business Corporation Act. When committees are given delegated authority, the courts have held that the delegation is restricted to what are called "ministerial" or day-to-day routine business matters. Where the corporation statutes indicate that the full board is to use its discretion in declaring dividends, issuing stock, or dealing with matters that fundamentally affect the corporation, delegating to a committee is obviously an abridgement.

California excepts the power to declare dividends and to adopt, amend, or repeal the bylaws. Wisconsin adds limitations in the election of officers and the filling of board or committee vacancies. Among the most comprehensive statutes is that of Illinois, which gives a board the power to delegate all of its authority except to amend the corporate charter or bylaws; to merge with another company; to recommend dissolution; to declare dividends; to change the membership of the executive committee; or to fix the compensation of members of the executive committee.

In addition, most states expressly provide that the delegation of authority to committees of a board is permissible only to the extent that such delegation is authorized in that corporation's charter or bylaws. Consequently, tremendous variance exists, as befits a pluralistic and free corporate society. A measure of the wide range in committee designation is evident in Table 4-1, which considers only a random selection of sixteen major corporations assumed to be typical. In this group, there are at least a dozen different committee titles, with a tremendous variety of functions and considerable difference in what their members receive as compensation.

On the subject of committee pay, some companies put emphasis on the annual retainer, but the great majority add a sum generally comparable to the additional pay received for attending each board meeting. Chairmen of committees tend to receive an extra fee, sometimes, as at Exxon, a generous $5000. At Du Pont, there is no extra pay for attending either regular board meetings or meetings of board committees. However, the regular retainer for outside members serving on the Audit Committee is $28,800—the chairman receives $34,200. Members of the Finance Committee are paid $40,200—the chairman gets a whopping $132,000. This probably sets the ceiling for board committee compensation. However, Du Pont's Finance Committee is very much a working component, meeting twice each month.

As is evident from the minisample of sixteen typical firms, presented in Table 4-2, salary patterns vary as much as do titles, function, number and length of meetings, inherent authority, or even size of committees. The term "salary patterns" is used intentionally, in contrast to the more commonly used terms: "retainers," fees," "stipends," and, most frequently, "compensation." The intent is to stress that a devolution in value systems is taking place. A generation ago, a majority of outside directorships received minimal pay—terms such as "honorary," "honorific," "honorarium," "nominal," "token," or even "eleemosynary" were applicable. Even today, most directors in foreign industries get very little compensation for their services. In Israel, for example, outside directors typically get no

TABLE 4-1
COMMITTEES OF THE BOARD IN A SAMPLE OF SIXTEEN COMPANIES

Company	Audit	Compensation	Executive	Finance	Nominating	Public policy	Other
Allied Chemical	X	X	X		X	X	XX
American Airlines	X	X	X	X	X		
AT&T	X	X	X	X	X	X	XX
Armstrong World	X	X	X				X
Bethlehem Steel	X	X	X				
Boeing	X	X		X	X		
Champion Intern.	X	X	X				XXX
Dow Jones	X	X	X				
Du Pont	X	X	X	X			
Eastern Air	X	X	X				X
Exxon	X	X	X		X		X
Mobil	X	X	X		X	X	X
Pan Am	X	X	X	X	X	X	
Textron	X	X	X		X		
UAL	X	X	X				
Union Carbide	X	X	X	X	X	X	X

TABLE 4-2
DIRECTOR COMPENSATION, 1982, IN A SAMPLE OF SIXTEEN COMPANIES

	Retainer	Board meeting fee	Committee meeting fee	Committee chairman	Other
Allied Chemical	15,000	500	500		
American Airlines	9,000	400	400		1250 for members
AT&T	17,000	600	600	4,000 (audit) 2,000 (others)	
Armstrong World	7,500	500	400		
Bethlehem Steel	22,500	400	400		
Boeing	18,000	1000	1000		
Champion Intern.	22,500	—	500	2,500	
Dow Jones	15,000	300	500	2,500	
Du Pont	—	—	—	34,200 to 132,000	Members from 28,800 to 40,200
Eastern Air	9,000	300	300		
Exxon	18,000	500	500	5,000	2,500 for members
Mobil	18,000	500	500	3,000 to 5,000	
Pan Am	10,000	300	300		
Textron	18,000	—	500		6,000 for executive committee members
UAL	10,000	350	350	2,500	
Union Carbide	18,000	750	600	2,000	

retainers, and only between $100 and $200 per meeting; those serving on public boards get nothing beyond direct travel expenses, which might amount to a few shekels for bus or taxi fare.

That industry has intensified its focus on director pay is evident in the dramatic skyrocketing within the past generation, from a high of $5000 in 1950 to a current package of almost $100,000. Comparably, the median for "Fortune's 1300" (the top 1000 industrials plus 50 banks, etc.) is in the $20,000 to $30,000 range. Even at the lower end of the compensation continuum, $5000 retainers plus $300-per-meeting fees are the rule and not the exception. In calculating total outside director costs, the retainer-plus-fees sum should be doubled to reflect related expenditures: travel, secretarial, advisory, and other "overhead."

A number of perplexing questions go along with the issue of director pay. Two of the most baffling are: (1) Why is there so much variation in what different boards pay their directors? (2) Why does each board pay all its members the same sum? This presupposes that, on a given board, not only are all directors of equal stature, but they all perform equally. This has to be an impossible assumption.

Corollary to this thinking is the phenomenon of an almost unbroken upward spiral in outside director pay. Yet corporations do have bad years and, logically, should cut outside director stipends. When this happens, it is really newsworthy, as was the case with Pan American World Airways. In the midst of record-setting losses, Pan Am called for a 50 percent reduction in directors' fees, together with a 10 percent cut in all employees' salaries and wages. Obviously, Pan Am's employees had not done well productivity- and profit-wise, and this was their penalty. But then neither had the board of directors performed even up to par, and theirs was the ultimate responsibility.

Differences among committee members are also evident in the size of the working group and frequency of meetings. There is really no prescribed or preferred pattern. As befits the corporate cornerstone of our pluralistic society, there is an amazing diversity in virtually all boardroom and board committee dimensions. This diversity will be more evident in the following descriptions of the currently more visible committees.

THE EXECUTIVE COMMITTEE

As early as 1882, the Trustees of Standard Oil Company (N.J.)—now Exxon Corporation—designated eight top managers and trustees to act as the Executive Committee, for the day-to-day management of the Standard Oil group of companies. While the Executive Committee included several nontrustees, it was distinctly an extension of the trustees, and served to represent them in the periods between board meetings. Within a few years, adjunct committees were specified for manufacturing, export trade, lubricating oil, cooperage, and others. The more important of these committees had at least one trustee as a member; this practice led to Standard Oil's classic and extremely effective "contact director" concept. A contact director was a member of the board, with special expertise in a functional area or geographical sector. His special expertise gave him a unique stature among his peers.

This historical note provides us with several pertinent observations which have some current meaning. A century ago, even as the Founding Fathers of Standard Oil were relinquishing boardroom seats to successors, "the entrepreneurial function was diffused throughout the organization. Though final approval of action resided in the top echelon, ideas originated all along the chain of command and were so modified in committees that the identity of the actual parents was usually forever lost. . . . Although a few decisions appear to have been made from lower echelons, by far the majority of directoral acts resulted from specific recommendations by field men, committees and staff. Approval was virtually automatic."[1]

Of all the committees at Standard Oil, its Executive Committee was the corporate powerhouse, and was referred to by subordinates as "the gentlemen upstairs" or "the men in Room 1400"—they were all officer-directors. Nonetheless, the Executive Committee went into disuse after a radical restructuring of Exxon's board, in the 1970s. Presently on the board itself, eleven outside directors outnumber eight officer-directors; while of the current Executive Committee's five members, three are nonemployees. Although presumably the committee has very broad powers, in practice, it meets infrequently—only about twice a year—to take formal action on a specific matter when it would be impractical to call a meeting of the board.

While Exxon has downplayed its once strategic Executive Committee, its competitor, Mobil Corporation, continues to use its committee effectively. Mobil's Executive Committee is authorized by Delaware law to exercise all the powers of the board of directors when the board is not in session. There are some exceptions, which include electing officers or directors, amending bylaws, declaring dividends, and taking any other action specifically reserved for the full board. This active and important committee consists of directors who are all employees of Mobil or its subsidiaries. Generally, it meets twice a month.

Likewise, at Du Pont, the Executive Committee is the policy-making and supervisory board for all the company's operations. It varies in size, generally having six to eight ranking officer-directors, and meets at least once a week. In addition to reviewing departmental proposals, in terms of

[1]Ralph Hidy and Muriel Hidy, *History of Standard Oil Company (NJ)* (New York: Harper & Brothers, 1955), p. 332.

overall corporate objectives, it considers the likelihood of success when significant appropriations are requested. It also monitors the activities of the company that relate to social concerns—the environment, health and safety, community needs, education, and equal opportunity—and it administers awards under the Special Compensation Plan. This truly is a working and important committee; even the president has no other power than that derived from this committee, and on it he has one vote.

The salient feature of this committee, since it is an extension of the board, is its constant presence near the corporate control center. The committee acts for the board in the interim between board meetings. It is both a check on the CEO and also a council of peers, always available to assist him—this availability follows from the fact that, until recently, almost all executive committee members were officer-directors. Its members tend to be experienced and are dedicated to the company. If the members consist of officer-directors, the executive committee can provide an excellent arena for testing competencies and worth. This is essential for effective promotion from within—to the ultimate, the CEO spot. If more of our executive committees become enervated or even terminated, there will be an increased incidence of CEO successions from the outside, and "headhunters" will be happy. But CEOs from the outside are unknown quantities, and there is very little evidence to prove they are any better than in-house talent.

With all the obvious limitations of part-time outside directors—their lack of pertinent expertise, relatively high cost, nonavailability, pseudo loyalty, and other shortcomings—it is difficult to accept the near-universal praise for them. Too often it is assumed that they are there to watch over the CEO. But how can these governors (in the technical sense), who are on the scene perhaps ten to fifteen days a year, act as checks and balances? More likely, they perform as chaperones at a fraternity party.

THE AUDIT COMMITTEE

A *Conference Board* study, as recently as 1972, revealed that in a sample of 753 companies, 45 percent of the surveyed firms had audit committees. A similar survey of 855 companies, in 1967, indicated only a 19 percent usage factor.[2] Today, however, the audit committee is a near-universal phenomenon. Actually, since June 30, 1978, audit committees have been mandated by the New York Stock Exchange (NYSE) as a prerequisite for listing for its almost 1600 members.

This is a remarkable advancement, considering that only two decades ago, even firms with audit committees generally put a minimum amount of

---

[2]*Corporate Directorship Practices: The Audit Committee,* The Conference Board, Report No. 766, 1979, p. 1.

work on members. According to the *Conference Board,* "At one time, as an executive put it in an interview, the audit committee—if there even was one—was apt to be comprised of directors who were not considered competent enough for more vital committee assignments. It was a committee whose routine responsibilities could be met without difficulty and it required few meetings."[3] Yet there are contrary sentiments. An ex-director of National Telephone Company which went into court-appointed receivership reflected, "If I had my life to live over, the audit committee would have met regularly and forced the auditors to go over the books."[4] Unfortunately, National Telephone's audit committee never met.

By definition, the audit committee of the board consists of at least three directors, a majority of whom are not present or past officers of the company. There is no agreement about how often they meet or about precise functions, but in general, audit committees should[5]:

1 Be responsible for the nomination and appointment, subject to stockholder approval, of independent accountants and auditors.

2 Select the outside auditors and set the range of audit and nonaudit fees.

3 Approve each professional service provided by the outside auditors before such services are performed and monitor the independent auditing.

4 Review management responses to important internal control recommendations by both independent accountants and internal auditors.

5 Review the annual financial statements and, when feasible, other financial reports before issuance.

6 Assist the full board in the better comprehension of the company's accounting policies, internal controls, financial reporting practices, and business ethics policies.

7 Maintain clear and comprehensive lines of communication between the directors and the independent accountants, internal auditors, and financial management.

Actually, the audit committee serves as an intracompany checks-and-balances guarantee that the affairs of the company are being handled competently and ethically. As such, the audit committee is just one other mechanism in the increasing array of checks and balances imposed upon today's management. Other control devices include government regulatory bodies, foremost among which is the ever-vigilant Securities and Exchange

---

[3] Ibid.

[4] "Corporate Directors Scored for Lax Scrutiny of Management Acts," *The Wall Street Journal,* April 10, 1978, p. 1.

[5] See "The Audit Committee," Price Waterhouse and Company, 1980; and Lawrence J. Trautman and James H. Hammond, Jr., "Role of the Audit Committee: Update and Implementation," National Association of Corporate Directors, Board Practices Monograph No. 13, November 1980.

Commission. Then there are the several regulatory bodies of the stock exchanges, notably those of the New York Stock Exchange. Professional associations, such as the American Institute of Certified Public Accountants (AICPA), are increasingly "minding the business" of corporations—the AICPA has even set up a Special Committee on Audit Committees.

But the need for accurate keeping of books is not entirely a twentieth-century phenomenon. Record keeping became essential in the thirteenth century as trade associations evolved into continuing enterprises. One might date the boardroom accounting and auditing function back to a Franciscan monk's invention of double-entry bookkeeping—Fra Luca Pacioli's publication, *Summa Arithmetica* (1494), was lauded by Leonardo da Vinci. Goethe and Oswald Spengler ranked it in importance with the discovery of the New World. Figuratively, Pacioli did open up new economic worlds of infinite dimensions and profound consequences.

In today's context, the first meaningful expression of a real need for audit committees came from the SEC, in the wake of the 1938 McKesson & Robbins scandal. Top-management fraud on a grand scale, conceived and executed by McKesson & Robbins' management, led to a major SEC investigation. Among recommendations made by the SEC in its 1940 report was the establishment of an audit committee of nonofficer directors. Shortly before the SEC report was made public, the NYSE made a comparable recommendation. But as the McKesson & Robbins scandal faded from headlines, interest in audit committees, likewise, paled.

Almost thirty years later, the landmark BarChris decision revived the audit committee issue. In the *E. Scott v. BarChris Construction Corporation* (1968) case, the court stressed that directors be liable for misleading or inaccurate financial statements. Not only were the five inside directors blamed, but also were the four outside directors—for failure to exercise "due diligence." This decision set a precedent in that, previously, outside directors were exonerated if they were not spoon-fed pertinent information. BarChris's outside directors were found guilty for their failure to oversee the affairs of the company competently and prudently. Of the four outside directors who had signed the flawed document, not one had made a reasonable investigation. A tangible result from this was the reinforcement of the AICPA's 1967 recommendation that publicly owned corporations establish audit committees consisting entirely of outside directors.

The decade of the 1970s saw an increased awareness of the need for continued surveillance of the auditing function by nonmanagement directors. The SEC, NYSE, AICPA, corporate activists, and various congressional subcommittees issued numerous exhortations. But the real impetus came when public sentiment was aroused over bribery, kickbacks, illegal contributions, and other unethical practices by American corporations. During that period over 400 American firms abjectly confessed to a variety of transgressions, peccadilloes, crimes, or mere insinuations of wrongdoing. As these charges of chicanery festered, they also fostered yet another law, the Foreign Corrupt Practices Act of 1977.

The basic provisions, as set forth in the FCPA, enunciate Section 13(b)(2) of the Securities Exchange Act of 1934. This required publicly held companies to "make and keep books, records and accounts, which, in reasonable detail, accurately and fairly reflect the transactions and dispositions of the assets of the issuer; and to devise and maintain a system of internal accounting controls sufficient to provide reasonable assurances . . . that management is in control of corporate operations, that corporate records permit the proper preparation of financial reports and properly account for corporate assets, and that access to assets is only as authorized by management. Section 13(b)(2) deals with matters essential to the maintenance of corporate accountability and for which both the audit committee of the board of directors and the internal auditor have significant responsibilities."[6] Soon after enactment of the FCPA, the New York Stock Exchange made a momentous ruling: after June 30, 1978, all of the nearly 1600 firms listed on the Exchange had to have audit committees with a majority of outside directors.

However, the increased role of the audit committee did not mean a diminishing of the internal auditor's importance. For example, a lengthy *Wall Street Journal* article discussed the continuing responsibilities of internal accounting at General Electric Company, whose corporate audit staff has been operating since 1910. The firm's 117 auditors are headed by Charles J. Vaughn, who is quoted, "We're not climbing on the bandwagon. We've been the bandwagon for years."[7] Significantly, the audit staff at GE is a creation of the board of directors rather than of management. This is an integral feature of many of today's audit committees, with more than a third of internal audit managers now reporting to boards of directors instead of to controllers. While the chief auditor at GE is subjected to a once-a-year quizzing by the external auditor, no one tells him what he can and can't audit. This precious autonomy, however, might even now be tempered by the increased vigilance of audit committees. This might be a case of "watchdogging the watchdogs."[8] *The Wall Street Journal* also raised a question—quoting the Roman poet Juvenal—"But who is to guard the guards themselves?" The audit committee might be its answer.

---

[6]John R. Evans (Commissioner, Securities and Exchange Commission), "The Audit Committee Interface with the Internal Auditor," National Association of Corporate Directors, 1980, p. 52.
[7]"More Firms Now Stress In-House Auditing, but It's Old Hat at GE," *The Wall Street Journal,* August 22, 1977, p. 1.
[8]Ibid.

Criticism of this new top-level checks-and-balances technique has been mild, with most serious doubts relating to:

1 The lack of technically trained, willing and able outside directors to serve on such committees. As a consequence, good audit committee talent tends to be overworked. For example, Arjay Miller, former president of Ford Motor Company, and ex-dean of Stanford's Graduate School of Business, is an outside director on seven boards and chairman of three audit committees.

2 The inordinate amount of time required to make frequent and thorough analyses of pertinent records.

3 The unsettled questions arising out of differential liability. Are directors on the audit committee more guilty when flaws go undetected because they presumably are better informed?

4 The effect expanded activity by audit committees will have. Will this make the independent outside CPAs obsolete? Or is the audit committee simply another case of bureaucratic duplication of work?

5 The awkward position of the internal auditor, who would be responsible to two bosses—the CEO and the board's audit committee. This seems to violate a number of basic management principles, particularly unity of command. It also calls to mind Frederick W. Taylor's "functional foreman," proposed nearly three-quarters of a century ago. Taylor's suggestion that every worker report to several foremen (up to seven) was never widely accepted.

6 The fact that one management component is forced to "blow whistles" on management. This in itself seems discriminatory. Why not subject production managers, quality control supervisors, purchasing agents, and all other functional heads to comparable inquisitorial treatment?

7 The newness of the technique. The biggest uncertainty follows from the very newness, with its resultant confusion, inadvertence, and meandering by boards and their audit committees. The concept needs testing. The real test will come when the first outside director is sent to prison for his or her failure to do the job as an audit committee member.

A number of these limitations were typified in the 1980 experience at California Life Corporation, whose board was stunned to learn the company had failed to file its 1978 annual financial report, as required with the Securities and Exchange Commission. Even though there were some extenuating factors, The Wall Street Journal, nevertheless, asked: "Where was the audit committee during all this conflict? Apparently, it was largely missing in action."[9] In 1978, and the early part of 1979, the committee had

[9]"Fuss at Cal. Life Shows Audit Committee Role is Crucial," The Wall Street Journal, March 17, 1980, p. 1.

only two rather perfunctory meetings with another being canceled. While some recommendations were made, they were pushed half-heartedly. The board had almost no communications with the auditors and seemed confused about what it should do.

One of the audit committee members raised a critical question: "Who has the supreme wisdom to say he's smarter than the guys who are in there every day? Who would have the omnipotence to tell the managers they are incompetent?"[10] Directors, understandably, are reluctant to be assertive, fearing this might "upset the genial relationship with management that they find comfortable and necessary to keep the corporate gears well-oiled."[11]

The situation at Cal Life was exacerbated by the inexperience of the committee's newly appointed chairman. He had never served on such a committee before, and even though he tried to learn through reading and seminars what his committee should do, his efforts were too little and too late. Discounting audit committee difficulties, an AICPA spokesperson points to the positive, stressing that diligent members of an audit committee can do the job. "If they're aggressive and take their responsibilities seriously they can be effective. They don't need to know what's going on in the bowels of the company."[12]

With the tremendous growth in board audit committees, some analysts fear that these committees might be grabbing too much power; others view the same situations and praise audit committees for their diligence. This ambivalence was humorously yet seriously headlined, late in 1980, when Playboy Enterprises, once again, was spotlighted. Its chairman and chief executive officer, Hugh Hefner, however, might have said it was unfairly jacklighted, providing a tempting target for investigative potshots. Although Hefner was quite accustomed to being shotgunned by legal agencies, this time the shooting was from an unexpected direction—from his own audit committee. "Earlier this year Playboy's Hefner was ordered to repay about $800,000 which the audit committee said its Boss Bunny had paid for expenses that were more personal than business.

"Then in mid-August the Securities and Exchange Commission took Mr. Hefner to task on the same issue, charging that Hefner and other company officials failed to make adequate disclosures on about $2 million in corporate carrots they allegedly pilfered."[13] Both the SEC and Playboy Enterprises' audit committee singled out the misuse of palatial bunny

[10]Ibid.
[11]Ibid.
[12]Ibid.
[13]"Playboy and Hefner Draw SEC Charges Involving Expenses," *The Wall Street Journal*, August 14, 1980, p. 4.

hutches in Chicago and Los Angeles, questionable entertainment expenses, and high flying in the sumptuously outfitted company plane, the *Big Bunny*.

The significant point in the settlement of these allegations was the agreement, as stated by a Playboy spokesbunny, to add a new outside director to its board and to maintain its compensation and audit committees as part of its structure. While Hefner and his fellow hares pleaded nolo contendere to the alleged leporine cavortings, they certainly were not alone in their administrative aberrations. For instance, in July 1980, Rusco Industries, Incorporated, signed a consent decree with the SEC in which the company and its chairman-president consented to an injunction against further violations of the antifraud, reporting, and proxy provisions of the Securities and Exchange Act of 1934. As with Playboy, the SEC required that Rusco reorganize so that the majority of the board and the entire audit committee be composed of independent directors satisfactory to the staff of the commission. A special counsel, approved by the commission, was also appointed to supervise an audit committee investigation. Along with the consent decree, Rusco announced the appointment of three new outside directors who were approved by the SEC.

Critics have a point in asking if such powers should be exercised by federal courts and federal regulatory bodies. By definition, the structuring of every board of directors is a prerogative of the company's stockholders, even though delegated to the directors. Other qualms include the prospect of skyrocketing auditing and liability insurance costs. Many firms, recognizing the extra time constraints and responsibilities put on audit committee members—particularly on the chairperson of the committee—have increased stipends for these services, and there is a growing sentiment for still more increased audit committee expenditures.

Although Townsend, Goldberg, and others have proposed full-time outside directors, with adequate staff to perform audit committee functions, to date not a single corporation has accepted such a suggestion. Perhaps this is due to the feeling that outside directors should not undermine the corporate staff by employing technicians who report solely to the board. Quoting Arjay Miller: "Although creation of a separate board staff has a certain superficial appeal, I believe it would turn out to be divisive and counterproductive. Direct reporting responsibility is not necessary to establish the proper relationship between the board and corporate employees; all that is required is unrestricted access. This access should work in both directions."[14] All parties would benefit from what Miller describes as his TV test. He recommends: "Don't do anything you wouldn't be willing to

---

[14]Arjay Miller, "A Director's Questions," *The Wall Street Journal,* August 8, 1980, p. 10.

explain on TV. Most of the actions business is being criticized for would not have occurred if those responsible thought that their actions would one day become public."[15] If we had widespread TV-type dissemination of *all* business doings, there certainly would be no need for audit committees of the board.

THE COMPENSATION COMMITTEE

If, according to the old saying, "you get what you pay for," why is it that, in view of the generous salaries paid corporate top executives, many ordinary citizens feel they are not getting their money's worth. Whom do we have to blame for this? Without any doubt, the answer is the board of directors. Every corporation is charged by its charter and bylaws to set the CEO's salary and those of other key executives. The Securities and Exchange Commission, in its Proxy Statement Disclosure Monitoring Program, indicates that almost all our major corporations have compensation committees, whose number-one function is to recommend compensation for senior management. A second and very closely related function is to adopt compensation plans for the company's officers. About half of the SEC sample firms indicated this as a function. A third activity, considered important by about 40 percent of the companies, is the administration of stock option plans.

Increasing citizens' concern over the balance between executive compensation cost and the presumed benefits prompted the Securities and Exchange Commission to make corporations spell out compensation packages so that they "tell it like it is." As a first step, the SEC required that all remuneration information for the firm's five highest-paid officers—including stock options and other long-term incentives—be set forth in a single table. For many years, all compensation information was considered private; even when some firms did reveal executive pay structures, they tended to confuse with the use of small-print footnotes. Pressure to tell who received what, led first to voluntary disclosure. *Business Week* initiated such a listing, in the early 1950s, with its "Annual Survey of Executive Compensation," which, incidentally, continues to date. Other comparable corporate executive compensation analyses are provided by Hay Group Associates, in their "Annual Survey of Directors' Compensation"; *Dun's Review; U.S. News & World Report;* and the periodic publications of the consulting firm Towers, Perrin, Forster, and Crosby. Previously, all such data were provided voluntarily by the respective corporations. Mandatory publication of this type of data is more recent and, undoubtedly, will become more detailed.

[15]Ibid.

Even now the SEC has decided that basic compensation should be separated from compensation which is conditioned on future events and not necessarily paid out in the year reported. Consequently, the SEC asks that the information for the five highest-paid executives be set in four separate tabular presentations, showing basic compensation, options, stock appreciation rights (SARS), and pensions.

There is ample reason for public concern over the rapidly escalating executive salary structure. In 1957, for example, only thirteen executives nationwide passed the $400,000 mark in total awards—nine of these came from Bethlehem Steel, three from General Motors, and one from Chrysler. Interestingly, a quarter of a century later, the median salary for large-scale corporations topped the $400,000 level, and more surprisingly, seventy-one of our key executives were now in the million-dollar bracket. By 1980, a dozen were earning more than $2 million, surpassing the salary once paid to Charles Schwab—at U.S. Steel—over three-quarters of a century ago. And suddenly there were several real breakthroughs—Frank E. Rosenfelt, president and CEO of Metro-Goldwyn-Mayer, received $5.1 million, and Rawleigh Warner, Jr., chairman of Mobil Corporation, was paid $4.3 million. In each of these cases, it was long-term income that projected their salaries sky-high.

Of course, it could be argued that these salaries were just matching the $5 million earned, during that same period, by each of the television personalities—Carroll O'Connor, Alan Alda, and Johnny Carson. That same year the New York Yankees signed a ten-year contract with an outfielder for more than $20 million. While salaries of the top 500 corporate executives averaged about $500,000, major league baseball players approached a $250,000 average. In fact, in 1982 thirteen players received in excess of $1 million each. One gets a better understanding of the runaway corporate executive salary structure when contrasted with top union pay, which averaged only $94,000—about the level of a corporate staff vice president.

Concern over the stratospheric salaries is heightened by lack of any meaningful overall correlation between specific executive compensation and individual contribution to the good of the corporation and its stockholders. A case at hand was Archie R. McCardell's receiving "forgiveness" of a $1.8 million loan by International Harvester Company. The loan was part of an employment agreement Harvester made with McCardell, presumably to entice him from Xerox Corporation. It was used to purchase 60,000 shares of Harvester stock and was to be "forgiven" if, in the next two years, Harvester either met or exceeded the average of selected financial ratios of its top competitors. The company, unfortunately, had rough going during McCardell's first years—including a 5½-month strike. Neither did the company do well on most of the meaningful ratios, when compared with its prime competitors; Caterpillar Tractor and John Deere. Actually, in 1980,

Harvester lost an estimated $400 million and followed with a loss of $636 million in 1981. Nevertheless, the board of directors saw only the positive; they rewarded the chairman-CEO for "spectacular performance" by the generous forgiveness of the $1.8 million debt.

"Wall Street's reaction to forgiveness of the loan was largely one of dismay. In addition to its heavy losses, Harvester's debt soared to three billion dollars, sharply higher than the $1.9 billion a year earlier. . . . 'It seems kind of stupid when they've got that kind of debt. They need every dime they can get,' said John McGinty, an analyst with First Boston Corporation. 'But a contract is a contract.' "[16]

Interestingly, the forgiveness issue was decided by Harvester's Committee on Organization, a five-member group of outside directors, all leading industrialists, who viewed the forgiveness as a contractual obligation. One director felt that McCardell gave up a lot when he left Xerox, and in a sense, he did. He had received a similar deal to purchase Xerox stock, but during his tenure the stock plummeted and its forced sale, at the time of his resignation, resulted in a great loss to McCardell.

This episode provides us with some provocative thoughts about corporate governance. For one thing, International Harvester has a predominantly outside-director board. Yet generally it is assumed that only boards dominated by officer-directors are excessively generous in setting their own executive pay. In essence, this charge was correct when it was levied at Bethlehem Steel Corporation's board in the late 1950s. Bethlehem Steel's all-officer-director board was then most magnanimous in setting its own salaries. As evidence, twelve of the nation's thirty-three highest-paid executives, in 1956, were Bethlehem's officer-directors. This charge, though substantiated, tends to overlook some facts. For instance, the high salaries resulted from a long-established bonus or profit-sharing plan whereby the officers, as a group, shared a sum equal to 4.5 percent of the aggregate cash dividend. The formula would yield high salaries only if the corporation was consistent in boosting productivity, profits, and dividends. The high wage and salary philosophy was a heritage of Bethlehem Steel's founder, Charles Schwab, who, before going to Bethlehem Steel, had been instrumental in the founding of United States Steel Corporation. While at U.S. Steel, Schwab received a munificent salary of $2 million per year. Back at the turn of the century, this was an unheard of salary; actually it remained unmatched in U.S. executive compensation history until the late 1970s.

Schwab then lost his sinecure after a quarrel with J. P. Morgan, the major financier at U.S. Steel. Undaunted, he went into business for himself and

[16]"Harvester Forgives Loan of $1.8 Million Made to Chairman," *The Wall Street Journal*, November 3, 1980, p. 12.

acquired the puny and bankrupt Bethlehem Iron Company, rapidly building it into U.S. Steel's most formidable competitor. Significantly, he brought the high-executive-pay philosophy to Bethlehem Steel. His hand-picked lieutenant and ultimate successor, Eugene Grace, was soon the highest paid U.S. executive; in 1929 he earned $1.6 million. Undeniably, Schwab's high-pay policy worked wonders—the tiny Bethlehem Iron Company became the giant Bethlehem Steel Corporation, our fifth biggest company in 1929. Initially with almost no share of the market, the bankrupt firm was transformed into number two in the industry. Originally, U.S. Steel held almost two-thirds of the market. Gradually, by the end of the 1950s, Bethlehem increased its share of the market from near zero to about 17 percent, while U.S. Steel's share dropped from above 60 to below 30 percent.

The significance of Bethlehem Steel's bonus plan should not be overlooked. It was an attractive and attainable "carrot." During one period (just before the plan was dropped), each of Bethlehem's top twelve executives received compensation higher than U.S. Steel's chairman, Roger Blough. The difference was in the fundamental pay philosophy. U.S. Steel paid its top three executives a base salary averaging $250,000 plus a $9,000 bonus. Bethlehem Steel, in distinct contrast, paid less than half as much salary—$120,000—but gave its top three executives bonuses averaging $460,000. The combined salary and bonus at Bethlehem totaled $580,000, more than twice the amount paid by U.S. Steel. In both cases, it was the board of directors' decision. In Bethlehem Steel's case, it was the board's good judgment that led to the company's growth and prosperity.

But somehow the company's good fortune took a turn—a stockholders' suit prompted Bethlehem Steel to modify its magic formula. Bonuses were replaced by higher salaries and a "dividend unit" credit, based on net income, stock price, and the amount of dividend. This plan was modified periodically, most recently in 1981. But the goose that laid those wonderful steel eggs had exhausted its potential—under the modified incentive plan, Bethlehem's progress, while yielding respectable results, has been nowhere near as phenomenal.

The sequel to this story is that, because of a slump in our nation's industrial productivity, an ingenious plan for motivation and executive compensation has recently been reinvented: the "new carrot" mechanism is called "performance shares." The first performance-share plan was introduced, in 1973, by Columbia Broadcasting System. Performance shares are premised upon each division's or component's contribution to corporate net profit. Authorization must first be secured from the company's stockholders. The compensation committee then awards a specified number of performance-share units to the company executives as a group. The compensation committee then, through an informal job evaluation or merit rating, allocates these performance shares to each executive. The committee also sets time parameters and decides how the premium should be allocated—in cash, stock, or a combination of both.

The time periods tend to vary from two to six years. When a time period is up, the percentages are calculated on the basis of target achieved. The value of each unit is equal to the market price of the company's common stock at the time of the payment. In the first distribution of performance shares, for example, directors and officers at CBS were allocated 130,000 contingent units, valued at $50 each. Thus, in this first experiment, CBS executives received a bonus totaling $6.5 million. One drawback to performance sharing is that recipients get no capital-gains advantages and, therefore, pay taxes on what is treated as ordinary income.

President Robert A. Charpie of Boston's Cabot Corporation, one of the early companies to opt for a performance-share plan states: "We think that performance shares are a dandy way to reconcile the interests of management and the shareholders."[17] Mr. Charpie could be no more than right: in 1980, his $3,300,000 total Cabot compensation put him in the number-one spot of our highest-paid executives. Charpie's performance shares accounted for $2,531,000 of his total pay. Without this bonus, Charpie would have ranked just slightly above the median for the top 500 executives. Two of Charpie's associates also made the list of twenty-five highest-paid executives, with total compensation of $1,613,000 and $1,551,000, respectively. On the basis of Cabot Corporation's achievement, in 1980 alone, performance shares inevitably will require a bit more scrutiny.

Performance norms can vary considerably. "Champion International Corporation measures its managers by comparing the company's earnings per share growth with fifteen competitors in the forest products industry. It's an all-or-nothing program. If Champion International beats the industry average, 12 senior executives receive an award equal to one-fourth of their total regular bonuses over the four-year term. If earnings-per-share growth falls below the average they get nothing."[18]

While use of the performance-share mechanism is new, the basic idea certainly is not. Its aim is to find a way to improve productivity by rewarding those who are responsible. Bethlehem Steel, of course, implemented this system almost three-quarters of a century ago.

Very often performance sharing "jumps the gun." For example, when Burlington Northern, Incorporated, recently hired a new president and chief executive, it "enticed" him with an "expectations" performance-share

---

[17]John C. Perham, "Performance Shares: New Style in Executive Pay," *Dun's Review*, January 1973, p. 34.
[18]John Curley, "More Executive Bonus Plans Tied to Company Earnings, Sales Goals," *The Wall Street Journal*, November 20, 1980, p. 29.

bonus of 25,000 company shares, at 10 cents per share, or a purchase price of $2500. Since the stock was then selling at $40.70 per share, the executive, Richard M. Bressler, made a neat unearned profit of more than a million dollars. (Recall the Archie McCardell incident at International Harvester.) Moreover, Mr. Bressler received a $450,000 interest-free unsecured loan from the company, payable on demand, presumably to cover the $2500 stock-purchase commitment.

But among contingent performance-share examples, probably the most intriguing appeared in *Fortune:* "Effective July 1, 1973, the company entered into a five-year employment contract with an executive and director providing for a salary of $25 per day for each day worked during the term thereof and additional compensation equivalent to 16½ percent of the operating income from the game of poker."[19] This quote is from a prospectus issued by the Golden Nugget, Incorporated, a Nevada casino.

Compensation committees go even further—their granting of perquisites (perks) is an even more sensitive and questionable practice. There have been scores of exposés where chief executives and others have bled their corporations, invariably with the tacit approval of the board and its compensation committee. Even while Braniff International was suffering excruciating financial embarrassment, its flamboyant CEO, Harding L. Lawrence, continued leasing a luxurious villa in Acapulco for $173,000. " 'When you're losing over $50 million a year, you're expected to cut costs— at all levels,' snaps an executive of a major lender at Braniff."[20] Of course, perks are a recognized fact—from the cop on the beat who helps himself to an apple from a cart, to Congress, where legislators get free parking, cut-price meals, free haircuts, shopping privileges, and other inconceivables.

ILLUSTRATION: Mesa Petroleum

The question of executive compensation periodically confronts every corporate board. Generally, the board will try to peg the CEO's salary, bonuses, and long-term awards to some rather vague but upward floating average. Despite this central tendency, there are pay pacesetters and follow-the-leader patterns in our largest corporations. However, the macrofirms rarely head the pay parade since they are too visible and subjected to public pressure. It is usually the medium-sized firm, with more than average ownership concentration, that dares to be most generous in rewarding its leaders.

In 1980, for example, the commodity trader Philbro Corporation paid a total of

[19]*Fortune,* November 20, 1978, p. 36.
[20]"How Braniff's Lenders and Directors Forced Chairman to Resign," *The Wall Street Journal,* January 6, 1981, p. 1.

$8,705,000 in salaries plus bonuses to its top five executives. Of the five, the top executive received $1.82 million; the lowest, $1.63 million. As a consequence, a stockholder sued twenty-five directors and officers for granting grossly excessive salaries and wasting company assets. The suit contended that the compensation was a gift and a gratuity beyond reasonable services rendered. Consider that in 1980 the top pay at General Motors was $400,000; IBM's was $871,000; AT&T's was $716,000; and our number-2 bank, Citicorp, paid its CEO $483,000. That same year, however, a number of smaller firms took even bigger Paul Bunyan-salary strides. Cabot Corporation paid its CEO a total compensation of $3.33 million, its chairman $1.61 million, and its senior vice president $1.55 million.

But Mesa Petroleum, with sales of approximately $400 million, and ranking 560 in *Fortune's* 1980 listing, outpaced the pacesetters. In 1979, the shareholders approved stock options of 1.5 million shares—at $46 a share—for its founder, chairman, and president, T. Boone Pickens. The predominantly outside-director board felt that this special incentive was needed to induce Pickens to remain with Mesa Petroleum. What they did not disclose was the fact that Pickens was already under contract to stay and work with Mesa until 1989. Moreover, his base pay had recently been boosted from $165,000 to $365,000—better than 120 percent.

There was one extenuating circumstance. For some reason, when Mesa went public in 1964, Pickens did not (as is customary) keep any founders shares for himself. Prompting the board's generosity was the fact that Pickens then held options to buy only about 2 percent of Mesa's outstanding shares. "This pales besides the likes of George Mitchell, founder, chairman, president and chief executive officer of Mitchell Energy and Development Corporation. Mr. Mitchell owns 62% or about 29.7 million of that company's 47.9 million shares, valued at more than $1 billion."[21]

Pickens was in luck—after the 1979 stock-option grant, his board declared two stock splits, each on a two-for-one basis. Thus, he was entitled to purchase 6 million shares at $11.50 a share. With the New York Stock Exchange price of Mesa Pete exceeding $30 per share, this meant that the shares owned by Pickens were worth more than $180 million and his profit exceeded $110 million.

Graef S. Crystal, a leading authority on compensation methods, "finds it 'unfathomable that Mesa would grant one executive 9% of its 33.6 million shares outstanding, even over an extended period. The top 100 companies on the "Fortune 500" list in 1980 reserved about 3% of their total shares for all executives over periods of 5 to 10 years. . . . Compared with what everybody else is paid in a company that size, I'd say the guy is getting about 10 times the average on an annualized basis. I realize we're dealing with the age-old question of somebody's worth, but this company may run out of oxygen in its generosity.' "[22]

In justification, one expert commented: " 'I don't know if anyone is worth that big an option, but he is if anyone is. He was one of the first to see the value in offshore acquisitions and to realize the importance of onshore reserves and acreage.'

---

[21]Lynda Schuster, "As Bosses Go, Mesa Pete's T. Boone Pickens Is Doing Very Well—Too Well, Some Say," *The Wall Street Journal,* April 14, 1981, p. 33.
[22]Ibid.

Another supporter states: 'Most executives are only interested in protecting their behinds. But Boone Pickens isn't afraid to take bold steps.' . . . But Mr. Crystal thinks it pretty poor management to remedy 25 years of service at one crack.''[23]

This and the previous examples show that boards of directors are now sanctioning ratios of CEO salaries to workers' median wages of 50 to 1 and even up to 150 to 1. Meanwhile abroad, as in Japan, comparable ratios are closer to 15 to 1.

"Takanori Mizuno, economist in New York for Tokyo's Fuji Bank, estimates that even including generous fringe benefits at Japanese firms, the pay of a top Japanese executive is 'far closer to what a Japanese worker gets than is the case in America.' He notes that the chairman of a top Japanese auto maker receives in the neighborhood of $150,000 yearly, while his counterpart in Detroit hauls home several times that amount.''[24]

THE NOMINATING COMMITTEE

The three most visible committees of the board (not to mention the strong silent executive committee) are audit, compensation, and nominating. In order of popularity, nominating lags far behind the other two. While virtually all corporations listed under NYSE and AMEX have audit committees, and almost 80 percent use compensation committees, the use of nominating committees drops to less than 50 percent for NYSE firms and below 20 percent for AMEX listings. NASDAQ companies approximate AMEX listings in their use of all three committees.[25] Before considering the incidence, structure, and functioning of nominating committees, a glance backward would be helpful.

Boards of directors co-optate; that is, they perpetuate themselves. This might suggest that directors are at odds with corporate statutes, which place the power to elect the board in the shareholders. Until late in 1978, when the SEC promulgated the new requirements for proxy statement disclosure, except for crises or takeover proxy battles, there was very little shareholder input in the director nomination's process. It has long been a practice for legally elected boards to reconstitute themselves periodically, either by renominating current members or by seeking replacements. In theory, at least, co-optation gives the board quasi independence; at most it needs only a pro forma ratification by the shareholders. In practice, this independence is often abridged by the chief executive, who usurps his board's preroga-

[23]Ibid.

[24]Alfred L. Malabre, Jr., "Factory Labor Costs Soar in U.S. but Hardly Budge in Japan," *The Wall Street Journal,* October 15, 1980, p. 52.

[25]*Analysis of Results of 1980 Proxy Statement Disclosure,* Securities and Exchange Commission, Release No. 34-17518, February 5, 1981.

tives. Several instances of this usurpation (Greyhound, Genesco) are detailed in other sections.

Many of our co-optation practices are the consequence of our British corporate governance heritage. Despite some improvement, corporate governance in British business is still characterized by social status. Eton, the Guards, and hereditary peerage are faultless qualifications. References to the "old boy" network still prevail; however, this is slowly changing. "Relentless competition for worldwide markets is making British companies turn away from the Old Boy tradition. There is a lot to turn away from. No fewer than 37 peers and 45 baronets and knights are shared by the boards of the five biggest banks, and a Labour Party study found that 35 out of 107 directors of London's top financial houses were all Old Etonians as were 46 out of 149 directors of the large insurance firms. 'The Chairman of one board I sat on rang me up,' complains one top British industralist, 'and told me: We're thinking of putting up so-and-so. I asked if he knew anything about the business. The answer was: No, but he's an awfully nice chap and married to so-and-so, you know.' "[26]

But criticism of British boardroom elitism does not exonerate us from similar imperfections. By coincidence, a study was being made in the United States just about the time of Britain's Labour Party's analysis of "old boys," and similar inferences were made.[27] Using one index, higher education, the study indicated that, at that time, there was a statistical dependence between the specific academic background of an individual and his chances for becoming a director of one of our 500 largest business enterprises. On the basis of the data, a graduate of the big-three Ivy League schools—Harvard, Yale, and Princeton—had 1 chance in 49 to become a director of one of our bigger corporations. Graduates of the other Ivy League institutions, together with those of a dozen other prestigious schools, had 1 chance in 456; graduates of ten big public universitites, prominent in turning out director talent, had 1 chance in 818. At the lower probability end, graduates of the smaller public universities had only 1 chance in 18,750 to make the directorate grade.

In other words, Harvard, Yale, and Princeton, combined, accounted for 36 percent of all directors in our bigger banks, insurance companies, and industrial enterprises. All told, the Ivy League and a handful of other prestigious institutions (Stanford, MIT) generated 56 percent of all directorate talent. The top ten state universities, despite their disproportionate enrollments, contributed only 14 percent of the total. Yet education is only one biasing factor. Add race, religion, national origin, or social, sports, and

[26]"Shaking the Old Boy Network," *Time*, May 22, 1964.
[27]Stanley C. Vance, "Higher Education for the Executive Elite," *California Management Review*, Summer 1966, p. 23.

political affiliations, and we, too, have an equivalent "old boy" system. There is ample evidence of a chief executive–exclusive club complex in the club rosters of Union, Metropolitan, Links, Brook, Racquet and Tennis, Knickerbocker, River, and New York Yacht (New York City); Philadelphia Club and Union League (Philadelphia); Laurel Valley (Pittsburgh); Bohemian and Pacific Union (San Francisco); and Somerset (Boston).

Since biases do play an important part in director selection, an effort is being made to correct these abuses. In particular, the best prospects seem to be in the universal adoption of nominating committees. Significantly, these committees have sprung up because of a recognized need and because of a government mandate. Basically, as indicated by its name, a nominating committee is supposed to locate competent and available candidates for the board. As a corollary responsibility, the nominating committee is also frequently asked to review the board's total composition, structure, and membership.

The Conference Board believes the responsibilities of the nominating committee are to select and/or evaluate:

1 Qualified candidates as directors
2 Members of board committees
3 Management directors as well as outside directors
4 Top corporate officers, including the chairman and president
5 Candidates for vacancies, as well as slates of candidates for annual elections
6 Candidates for subsidiary boards
7 Incumbent directors[28]

The Security and Exchange Commission in its Proxy Statement Disclosure Monitoring Program, authorized December 1978, agrees in its findings that the nominating committee should recommend directorate candidates. Of course, designating candidates is the prerogative of the total board, and the ratification is a shareholder decision, generally executed at the annual meeting. The second most important function of the nominating committee is the considering of shareholder recommendations. Even though this is now being done, the SEC, nevertheless, is studying the need for and feasibility of issuing a new rule concerning nominating procedures. But even a casual consideration of costs, and the near-impossibility in communicating with thousands of widely scattered shareholders, presents a dilemma. Then, in contrast to political "plums," winning a seat on a board guarantees no sinecure. As for making nominations from the floor at annual meetings, this

[28]Conference Board Listing, quoted in "The Chief Executive Officer and the Nominating Committee," *Director's Monthly*, National Association of Corporate Directors, April 1981, vol. 5, no. 4, p. 2.

procedure probably would be used exclusively by attention-getters and malcontents, and thus would not guarantee the democratic process.

Eastern Airlines deserves plaudits for including in its 1981 proxy the name of Charles Bryan, president of District 100 International Association of Machinists, representing one-third of Eastern's employees. Bryan nominated himself. While Eastern did not print Bryan's name and aspirations on the regular ballot, it did include in the same mailing a leaflet explaining Bryan's intentions, together with a separate ballot. This is commendable.

The first worker elected to any American major corporation board, Douglas Fraser, at Chrysler, was actually union-nominated since he negotiated important concessions to help bail Chrysler out of its financial dilemma. Of course, he was then formally nominated by Chrysler's management. Similarly, at American Motors Corporation, the nomination of a worker to AMC's board is an internal union matter. Suggestions or actual designations by any nominating committee of the board would be resented.

At the 1981 annual meeting of ailing Braniff International, restive shareholders nominated five employees as candidates for the board. Among the comments prompting this unprecedented action: "I'm not proud of our board. They've done a miserable job," and "We want honest representation on our board."

Another possible voting procedure could be that used by TIAA/CREF, the multibillion-dollar pension-investing fund for teachers. Annually, each member of both TIAA and CREF receives a mailing which details pertinent background information on each candidate. Significantly, the "proxy" material generally lists two or more candidates vying for each opening. Thus the voters get a choice and not a management mandate. Nor are the candidates hand-picked by the current board or the CEO; instead, a nominating committee, democratically elected by TIAA/CREF shareholders, does the selecting. This procedure seems to work and is basic to an increasing number of not-for-profit organizations.

There are, however, some negative considerations. A completely free and open shareholders' nominating process could open up a Pandora's ballot box. In the 1978 election at International Controls Corporation, the base once used by Robert L. Vesco for his audacious schemes, there were fifty-four candidates for ten board seats. The company, during the previous six years, had been run by a board of four court-appointed directors. Now the stockholders were being challenged with an ample choice: There was a slate of ten "management" candidates nominated by the court's board; a second slate was designated by a group of disgruntled stockholders, annoyed at the way the court-appointed directors allegedly delayed calling a meeting; and a third slate consisted of the business associates of an individual seeking to gain control of the firm. The remaining twenty-four eligible nominees ran as individuals. In addition to the fifty-four candidates, there were twenty disqualified nominees and three dropouts. If there was a nominating committee at International Controls, certainly it was not doing its job.

Perhaps a preview of what is to come was the unexpected defeat of both the incumbent chairman and vice chairman at a recent Peat, Marwick, Mitchell & Co. annual meeting election. Under a new ruling, unusual among big accounting firms, Peat, Marwick's 1044 partners can nominate an alternative slate of candidates if they do not like top management's nominees. The first time this exercise of true partnership was tested, the firm's top managers, in office since 1965, were unexpectedly ousted. "In the Great Hall of the opulent Boca Raton resort hotel in Florida, there was an audible gasp, then cheers and finally a thirty-second standing ovation when the 1000-odd partners at Peat, Marwick, Mitchell & Co. heard the results of the secret ballot."[29]

These examples are destined to multiply within the next few years, particularly if corporations and entire industries continue to experience hard times in the auto, steel, rail transportation, and other hard-pressed industries. Out of an increased incidence of shareholders, insisting on a more representative director nominating process, major changes in the current practice of co-optation and cloning of directors will become more likely.

Perhaps now is the time to turn back the pages of American corporate history, to the governance innovations suggested by Alexander Hamilton. If the crux of today's voting problem initiates from a disproportionate institutional investor weight, then, obviously, this weight must be trimmed. As was detailed in the brief historical introduction, "Boardroom Roots: The Early American Experience," Hamilton not only founded our first corporation, The Society for Useful Manufactures, but also drew corporate governance blueprints for our National Bank. For the latter he suggested a rational scaling down of voting rights commensurate with increased ownership. Modifying Hamilton's plan, for example, the owner of 100 shares would still have 100 voting rights, but the million-share owner would, hypothetically, be allowed only 1000 votes.

This raises the specter of employing street names, nominees, and other subterfuges: this practice could be eliminated by taking away all voting rights from corporate and institutional owners, and granting ownership Class B or nonvoting common stock. Naturally, this would shake Wall Street's very foundations. However, coupled with a reasonable ceiling on individual voting rights, this would awaken the proprietary instinct in our shareholders, who would feel that their votes really do count. Nominating committees of the board, and even those of dissidents, would then reflect the will of the owners.

[29]"The Battle of Boca Raton," *Fortune*, November 5, 1979, p. 25.

ILLUSTRATION: The Kleroterion: A Study in Leadership

In the reconstructed Stoa of Attalus, now a beautiful Athenian museum, there is an archeological treasure known as the Kleroterion, an ingenious election device used by the early Athenians (Atticans) in a truly democratic selection of leaders. In early post-Dorian invasion days (after 1104 B.C.), there were four tribes in Attica, and each of these was divided into three phratries, or brotherhoods. Each of these twelve subtribes, in turn, had thirty clans consisting of kinsmen with common domicile and interests.

At election time, with the chief of the leading subtribe serving as election supervisor, new chieftans were selected for each of the phratries in a most ingenious manner. Fifty leading candidates were selected in each phratry. These fifty names, engraved on clay nameplates or potsherds, were then affixed aside symetrically cut holes or slots on the Kleroterion tablet or board. Then forty-nine black balls and one white ball were randomly mixed and rolled into the first column of the Kleroterion. A black ball falling into the first slot indicated that the individual whose name was attached to that slot was not elected. The process continued until the sole white ball came to rest in the winner's slot. This individual was then designated chief of that particular subtribe until the next election. Similarly, each of the subtribes elected its chief in this random and democratic fashion.

Here in ancient Athens—almost 3000 years before statisticians invented random numbers—ancient Greeks were putting the random numbers theory to a most practical use. The Kleroterion was an excellent safeguard against demagoguery and chicanery—so evident in modern-day politics. The random roll of fifty balls served as protection against family succession, favoritism, and wheeling-dealing; it also discouraged superperformers and high achievers who were striving for top billing.

Adjacent to the Athenian Stoa, with somewhat of a peripheral relationship, is the famous water clock, used to limit Athenian public figures to maximum six-minute orations. Several hundred feet from the Stoa is the Pnyx, an elevated rocky spot that served as ancient Greece's Hyde Park and New England town meeting house. Here, as in all democracies, overt measures such as fines, public reprimands, and jail sentences had to be invoked to get citizens to participate in the democratic process. The political practice of ostracism was given birth at the Pnyx when red clay tablets or potsherds, with names inscribed, were cast to exile public leaders who were deemed too ambitious, too dangerous, or too nefarious for the welfare of the state.

Nearby at the Areopagus, on the Hill of Aries, was the seat of the Tribunal, the Athenian supreme court or board of directors. This was the final recourse for those accused of crimes or ambitions against the state. Athenians had a congenital aversion for all tyrants, and they would sooner wrongly punish the innocent than tolerate even an incipient threat to their freedom. Socrates and his cup of hemlock is a classic example.

But hemlock, ostracism, the Pnyx, and water clock were all latter-day additions to the Attican-Athenian chief-executive selection process. They followed by several centuries the far less sophisticated Kleroterion. As Athens flourished under its unique leadership, it prospered, expanded, and then abandoned its very simple leadership-designation process. By the time of Pericles, Athens needed all the safeguards it could invent to preserve its "director" and "CEO-nomination" process. Complex checks and balances, nefarious conniving, politicking, alliances, and elaborate search committees replaced the random rolling of balls, and the Kleroterion was laid to rest.

Let us now parallel this ancient example with our modern-day corporation. Leadership in the initial stages of a firm is easily determined—the major investor or his or her designee becomes the CEO. There is no question as to who constitutes the board of directors. But as a firm succeeds, prospers, expands, it too—like ancient Athens—must seek other methods for designating new leaders. In addition to the usual coalitions and connivings of top executives and directors, recourse to outside talent headhunters, and other involved searching, there are more increasing complications. Some of these—codetermination, government-mandated directors, and the degree of director independence—are detailed in other sections. Since director and executive selection is bound to become even more complex, we can only hope that someone, someday, will be able to simplify the process, perhaps even by reinventing the Kleroterion. With 3000 years of technological progress, instead of using clay potsherds and balls, tomorrow's Kleroterion could use silicon chips.

THE PUBLIC POLICY COMMITTEE

As gathered from Table 4-1, there is a rapidly expanding list of committees of the board. A very interesting newcomer is the public policy (or issues) committee. General Motors created such a committee in 1970. American Telephone and Telegraph's Corporate Public Policy Committee, composed of eight directors, meets about five or six times a year to monitor the corporation's responsibility on major public issues, and to provide guidance and perspective to management on these issues and policies. Mobil's Public Issues Committee, likewise, meets about six times a year to review and make recommendations regarding trends in the political and social environment, as they may affect the operations of the corporation. This committee also considers general policy regarding support of business, charitable, and educational organizations.

The popularity of the public policy committee is evident in its rapid growth, from a mere handful of users a decade ago, to approximately 48 in 1976 and about 150 today. Among its proponents—in addition to those already mentioned—are Bank of America, Chrysler, Continental Group, Dow Chemical, General Electric, Gulf Oil, International Harvester, Metropolitan Life, and Union Carbide.

As with so many innovations that sound terrific at inception, the public policy committee needs acid testing to prove its worth. If it does pass the test, corporate governance will witness profound permanent changes.

POSTSCRIPT

Although there is more to structuring a board of directors than simply naming and staffing a few committees, this chapter purposely dwelt on this theme because committees seem to be the overriding current concern of boardroom architects. Some of these architects have a ready response to the increasing size and complexity of the corporate family: as the family expands, simply add another room; in this case, another committee.

The phenomenon of boards fragmented into committees is a concomitant of the oversight board. If we continue to expand "oversighting," the typical board will evolve into a committee on committees—a real powerhouse in the assignment of functions, resources, membership, and committee chairpersons. There is no doubt that board members who control this quasi committee on committees also wield power over the audit, compensation, nominating, and other committees in addition to acting as a checks and balances over management.

But there is something missing—who is to provide the vital entrepreneurship? Does the answer lie in an additional, still-to-be-designed committee on enterprise? This is essential because there can be no enterprise without an entrepreneur. There was a time when most American corporations were inextricably meshed and identified with the image of a Henry Ford, John D. Rockefeller, Harvey Firestone, and thousands of equally gifted leaders.

Although some contend that risk taking, innovativeness, superdedication, and the other attributes essential for entrepreneurship are atavistic and a thing of the past, the facts belie these contentions. Each year close to half-a-million new firms—each an entrepreneurial gestation—come into being. Even though 80 percent or more of these fledgling firms cease to exist within five years, there is nevertheless a steady flow of new entrepreneurship into corporate veins.

Admittedly, boards stressing the oversight role in audit, compensation, and nominating committees perform essential services. But what our corporations need most—and seem to be getting less—is entrepreneurial zest, a daring spirit. Enterprise, defined as a bold, arduous, and dangerous undertaking involving risk and a daring spirit, is the ultimate responsibility of the total board. It cannot be delegated. Consequently, there can never be a meaningful subcommittee of any board supposedly fulfilling the board's entrepreneurial responsibility. What we desperately need is not more peripheral committees, but rather the entire board acting as a "committee of the whole." Its role, in lieu of the dynamic and dedicated individual enterpriser, is to provide the corporation with a dynamic and dedicated *composite entrepreneur.*

CHAPTER 5

INTERNAL CONSTRAINTS

THE CHAIRMAN

From the outside, it would seem that serenity prevails at corporate headquarters; yet it is not always so. Often there is contention, a sort of governance tug-of-war between president and chairman, and the prize for the winner is the post of chief executive officer. This headquarter's tussle is a fairly recent contest; historically, it was the president who also served as CEO. Then, upon earning a respectable retirement, the president-CEO relinquished both designations and moved to the chairman's post, basically an honorific and ceremonial position. The chairman presided over board meetings, but since boards did little more than nod approval to the CEO's proposals, the chairman simply enjoyed a comfortable sinecure.

During the turmoil of the late 1960s, when the activists focused on the corporation as a culprit, they seemed to discover the board of directors and its chief executive, the chairman. In their subsequent zest for corporate governance reform, the activists lobbied for more shareholder input, through the board and, consequently, through its chairman. Despite contentions, it is highly unlikely that much of today's progress in improved corporate governance would have been effected without this activist shock treatment.   But in their headlong charge into the boardroom fray, the activists failed to notice that among their staunchest allies were their mortal foes—the Wall Street financiers, together with Capitol Hill politicians and bureaucrats. This highly unlikely coalition had a common link, namely, all believed that inside-type boards of directors must go, and the CEO's scepter must be taken away from the president and given to the chairman. Of course, each of the unlikely coalition partners had his own reasons. Politicians, obviously, favored outside boards since these would provide a haven for former politicians, lame ducks, retired or defeated. Bureaucrats had come to look upon production- and marketing-oriented CEOs as their congenital enemies. Wall Streeters, likewise, have an affinity for members of their own financial fraternity. Since most production- or marketing-oriented CEOs come up from the ranks, they generally lack elitism and exclusive business club credentials. Surprisingly, after these up-from-the-ranks CEOs win their spurs and invitations to the elite business clubs, some invariably act as zealous converts by stacking their boards with outsiders, and in so doing, earn their keys to the financial fraternity.

This incongruous and incompatible coalition, uncoordinated and even unacknowledged, has made tremendous strides. A facilitating factor was the lack of any united opposition; neither the pro-inside directors nor the pro-president-CEO forces had any organization. Only once did the opposition rise to be counted. When the chief of the SEC, Chairman Harold Williams, proposed that all boards consist entirely of outside directors—with one possible exception, the chairman-CEO—several thousand protestations were uttered. Their extent and vehemence forced Williams to back down.

Despite this single setback, the coalition seems to have succeeded, at least for now. The activists demanded more outside directors, audit committees, representative directors, proxy reform, more pertinent disclosures, and similar changes—all in the name of shareholder democracy and corporate responsibility. The bureaucrats, politicians, and financiers, likewise, opted for most of these reforms. Judging from the record, most of these changes have been effected and the net result has been a significant decrease in officer-directors and an increase in outside or independent directors. Equally noticeable has been the shift in power from the president to the chairman. Control becomes more centralized as an increasing number of chairmen appropriate all three designations—chairman, president, and chief executive officer. Although this trend is attracting some unfavorable attention, since it removes all pretense of checks and balances on the chief executive, it has established a different kind of corporate governance control center.

In being relieved of his chief executive officer's role, the president—if he is still a separate entity—now justifies his existence by becoming the chief operating officer (COO). Following this logic, the third and fourth ranking officers, with ranks of vice chairman or vice president (usually executive or senior), are designated in sequence—chief financial officer (CFO) and chief administrative officer (CAO). With twenty-six letters in our alphabet, the number of "chiefs" can be expanded into thousands, depending upon a given organization's size, needs, and preferences.

Considering preferences, we can expect a great assortment not only of chiefs, but also of chairmen-CEOs, cloaked in varying degrees of authority. Robert K. Mueller, chairman of Arthur D. Little, Incorporated, expresses the complexity. "Servant or master? Board agent or team leader? Guide or whip? Moderator or task advocate? The satyrlike biformity of corporate governance often makes for a fuzzy system at the top, as far as roles and structures are concerned."[1]

Another chairman, Ira G. Corn, Jr., views the presumed governance functions and compresses the prime considerations as follows:[2]

1 *Compatibility.* The chairman should have those characteristics which tend to satisfy, complement, and otherwise be compatible with major holders of capital stock and with the executive team.

2 *Visible leadership.* The chairman is a reflected image of the company to the rest of the world.

3 *Decision role.* The chairman should have a proven record of success as a decision maker.

4 *Building a team.* The chairman must be responsive to members of the board.

5 *Board organization.* The chairman should be the leader of the board in the judgmental role of appointing directors to committees where they can serve most effectively.

6 *Membership on the board.* The chairman has to assume the responsibility of arriving at a consensus in choosing members.

7 *Replacement of the chief executive officer.* The chairman must ensure survival of the corporation and the maximizing of success by replacing the CEO when necessary.

8 *Public image.* Because good relations are essential with government, customers, suppliers, employees, media, trade associations, and others, the chairman must spend an increasing portion of his time in building the corporate image.

9 *Social responsibility.* The chairman should monitor the company's compliance with laws and regulations while helping it become a good corporate citizen.

10 *Data dissemination.* A major test of the performance of the chairman as a monitor may be found in his ability to keep the members of the board of directors informed about the operations of the company.

[1]Robert Kirk Mueller, *New Directions for Directors* (Cambridge, Mass.: Lexington Books, 1978), p. 83.

[2]Adapted from Ira G. Corn, Jr., "The Role of the Chairman of the Board," *NACD Corporate Director's Special Report Series,* vol. VI, 1978, pp. 4–11.

Meanwhile, there might be some unforeseen shifts in the tug-of-war between the chairman and president over the CEO designation. At a meeting of his peers, C. William Verity, chairman and CEO of Armco, suggested a new title and role: the corporate governance officer (CGO). Verity pointed out that Armco and most major corporations have already isolated five specific areas of managerial responsibility which call for closer board overview[3]:

1 *Capital formation,* the prime responsibility of the chief financial officer

2 *Corporate strategy,* reviewed by the chief administrative officer or a strategic planning officer (SPO)

3 *Corporate human resources,* the purview of the principal personnel officer (PPO)

4 *Corporate operations,* headed by the chief operating officer

5 *Corporate leadership,* the obvious task of the chief executive officer

But in today's environment, corporations are ever more pressed to find ways and means to respond to outside demands and, in particular, to fulfill their obligations to society. Many a corporation has found that it is not enough to delegate all such problems or situations to vice presidents of public relations, of corporate affairs, of public policy, or of management issues.

Consequently, Armco has considered separating governance from management. It would identify governance at the very corporate pinnacle by designating the board chairman as the chief corporate governance officer. At Armco, this would mean that the chairman would no longer be the chief executive officer. While the CEO would continue to manage the company's routine operations, the CGO would oversee the board's expanded role. To avoid any semblance of demotion, the CEO would not report to the CGO, but rather to the entire board. Logically, this would depict the board as the corporate boss.

THE VICE CHAIRMAN

While the title "chairman" has been used since the beginning of the modern corporation, the use of the title "vice chairman" became widespread only during the present generation. It is a concomitant of the recent shift in the locus of corporate control, from the president to the chairman. With this shift in power, there almost had to be vice chairmen, if only to corroborate Parkinson's law of multiplication of subordinates. In most organizations, the measure of power is the number of subordinates one oversees, plus their

[3]Adapted from "Should There Be a Corporate Governance Officer?" *Boardroom News,* National Association of Corporate Directors, vol. 2, no. 10, 1978, p. 11.

titular stature. Consequently, even one or two vice chairmen can enhance the chairman-CEO's stature.

At the recent changing of Bethlehem Steel's corporate guard, four vice chairmen were designated; interestingly, the company's president was "promoted" to one of these spots. This order of succession is evident in the rank sequencing shown in the company's annual report, where the chairman-CEO is followed by his several vice chairmen, then the president, executive vice president, and finally the two senior vice presidents.

Vice chairmen serve in a variety of ways, depending upon individual company preferences. At Eastern Air Lines, where the chairman is also the president and CEO, the vice chairman also carries the title of executive vice president. In this dual capacity, he is actually, albeit unofficially, serving as president without the title. He oversees and coordinates eight senior vice presidents who are the heads of the several functional components.

At American Telephone and Telegraph Company, there is a vice chairman and chief financial officer. In addition, a second vice chairman— seemingly without portfolio—presumably serves as a "super" executive vice president, coordinating five ordinary executive vice presidents.

The genesis of the vice chairman is best illustrated at General Electric Company. As far back as 1955, General Electric set up an Office of the President, consisting of seven top executives, strictly limited to planning as distinct from operations. Note that even though the company's chairman was a member of the group, it was called the Office of the President. Following the death of its chairman, GE's president-CEO was elevated to the post of chairman-CEO, and the president's position was eliminated. This eventually led to the formation of an Office of the Chairman, with four vice chairmen now serving in roles formerly filled by vice presidents.

In spite of its lofty title, the Office of the Chairman also serves a utilitarian purpose—it is the proving ground for heirs apparent. And herein lies the problem. When the office was restaffed in 1979, three of GE's most promising vice presidents, having been passed over, simply quit. All three moved on to top jobs at other firms: one to president and CEO at General Telephone and Telegraph, another to vice chairman of American Express, and the third to vice chairman of Rubbermaid, Incorporated. While the loss of such talent is lamentable, the Office of the Chairman does work for succession purposes, at least at GE. Late in 1980 when Reginald Jones, GE's chairman-CEO, announced his retirement, he concurrently announced his successor, one of the office's vice chairmen.

Another reason for the widespread use of vice chairman is that presidential and vice presidential titles have suffered from overuse. As will be pointed out later, presidents have proliferated for a variety of reasons. Just as the title of vice president has been demeaned—particularly in banking—so, too, the presidential title has lost its luster, particularly in cases where a major firm has a dozen to a hundred presidents of divisions and subsidiaries.

It is interesting to note that the media, only a decade ago, referred to vice chairmen with headlines such as "Vice Chairman: What's My Line?"; "Job of Vice Chairman Means Most Anything Firms Happily Discover"; "To Be Vice Chairman Isn't So Bad After All." Note that the commentary was equally noncomplimentary: "For years, whenever an executive was elected vice-chairman of the board, his close associates offered condolences instead of congratulations. The move was synonymous with being kicked upstairs. The job has traditionally been a ceremonial one, with limited authority and little responsibility. It was a way to accommodate a veteran executive who had lost the race for a top slot. The vice-chairman was solicitously treated but not necessarily listened to in the executive suite."[4]

Another sympathetic commentary from the same period stated, "You've been named vice chairman of your company? Congratulations! But just what does a vice chairman of a corporation do, anyway?"[5]

THE CORPORATE SECRETARY

The effective functioning of every board of directors depends largely on its corporate secretary. The use of the title "secretary" is confusing since there are hundreds of thousands of secretaries in our corporations, performing stenographic, typing, duplication, filing, and, more recently, word and data processing functions. While the average person is not overly impressed with the secretary's role in the corporate hierarchy, the title is often respectfully used at the very top—our Secretary of State, for instance, and more important, the Secretary of the Communist Party in the U.S.S.R.

At one time, particularly in smaller, closely held firms, corporate secretaries were almost always seated on the board. However, with the accelerating trend toward independent and outside directors, relatively few corporate secretaries currently hold directorships. While this unseating might have lessened their importance, there have been some added compensations. In a survey of its members, the prestigious American Society of Corporate Secretaries found that 43 percent held the title of vice president, another 7 percent were senior vice presidents or executive vice presidents, and 47 percent held dual titles of corporate secretary and general counsel.

Even though secretaries seldom hold directorate seats and thus have no voting power, the corporate secretary is present at all board meetings and

---

[4]*Business Week,* April 29, 1972, p. 53.
[5]Lewis M. Phelps, "Job of Chairman," *The Wall Street Journal,* May 19, 1970, p. 1.

frequently at important sessions of committees of the board. The secretary not only takes and transcribes the minutes of the meetings, but often indirectly determines the agenda. In either of these functions, whether intentionally or inadvertently, secretaries can influence the board's course of action. Moreover, they can detail the agenda to the point of unreadability, or they can reduce it to a few meaningless phrases. By judiciously placing and spacing agenda items, they can focus more or less attention upon specific issues. Obviously, the sage and seasoned corporate secretary will not openly attempt subversion without the tacit approval of the chairman.

Similarly, the minutes of meetings can be elongated or crisply condensed, and their mailing to the directors can be delayed to the point where they become irrelevant. On the other hand, an effective corporate secretary can, through the agenda and minutes, provide a lucid compendium of supporting materials for helping directors get a meaningful comprehension of the important issues. This role of judicious and accurate scribe is a tremendously helpful service considering that directors—insiders and outsiders—tend to be extremely occupied individuals. In particular, as directors' liability becomes more plaguing, corporate secretaries can provide essential documentation and interpretation, helping to avoid pitfalls. Considering the avalanche of paper burying most corporate executives and directors, the secretary can provide a real service by arranging a priority reading list. Moreover, by underscoring and digesting pertinent materials and including interpretive comments, the secretary can be of even greater assistance to the outside directors.

The kind and number of reports provided to the directors, by the secretary, will vary from company to company and according to particular circumstances. Forecasts, for example, capital requirements, and schedules of financing are generally integral parts of the information flow. Operational and current business reports are highly likely inclusions; yet these are materials with which the outside directors can easily become swamped. With the one-process, line-product company a thing of the past, directors need to be informed on a multiplicity of products, new technologies, and frequently fluctuating prices. Competitive complexities can confound even the most apperceptive part-time outside director.

In addition, there are special reports whose scope, content, and frequency are unpredictable. In the recent past, the sudden emergence of problems related to the Occupational Safety and Health Act (OSHA) forced most of our major corporations into serious and extended introspection. Soon thereafter, the Foreign Corrupt Practices Act partially obscured OSHA, and then ERISA and ESOPS/ESOTS demanded inordinate attention. Even the ancient oracle at Delphi would not have foreseen what comes next.

If the current practice of filling more than half of all the boardroom seats with outsiders continues, the corporate secretary will have still another onus. While textbook theory grandiosely tends to assign the "breaking in" of new outside directors to the chairman of the board, this is generally not how it works. The chairman does fulfill the social introduction functions and then proceeds to delegate any onerous chores to the corporate secretary.

Some forward-thinking firms are attempting to save time by producing a "book of the board," giving copies to each director. "Other companies provide a series of letters, memoranda and other materials to the new director concerning various aspects of the company's affairs. The basic types of information given to new board members can be categorized under the general headings of Security Law Compliance, Basic Corporate Documents, Board Policies and Procedures, Major Corporation Policies, Other Corporation Information, and General Reference Material."[6]

Regarding securities law compliance, an increasingly sensitive area, directors must be advised particularly of their obligations under Section 16(a) and Section 16(b) of the Securities Exchange Act of 1934. These require the filing of Forms 3 and 4 and other reports regarding financial transactions relative to the company, in particular, insider trading situations.

The basic documents every new or reappointed director should get include the certificate of incorporation, bylaws, annual reports, prospectus, proxy statements, and Form 10-K, 10-Q, 8-K, and all interim reports. When available, copies of the company's code of ethics should be an integral part of the information package, as well as copies of all other corporate policies such as those dealing with conflict of interest, with antitrust law observance, and even with contributions for charitable, educational, or political purposes.

This is only a partial coverage of the corporate secretary's role. Generally the secretary oversees proxy structuring and solicitation, supervises the preparation of quarterly and annual reports, and has the increasingly sensitive stockholder relations to contend with. The corporate secretary's role is further compounded by having to give attention to annual meeting details and to an array of other functions. For example, there is a trend for big companies to do their own stock transfer work, and there is the contact work with stock exchanges, financial analysts, and assorted others—all adding to the corporate secretary's responsibilities. Yet, in spite of all these complexities, this modern-day Figaro, this corporate factotum, seems willing to undertake any and all tasks.

---

[6]John B. Megahan, "Keeping Directors Informed: The Role of the Corporate Secretary," National Association of Corporate Directors, Board Practices Monograph No. 8, May 1980, p. 6.

DIRECTOR AND OFFICER LIABILITY

"Our free enterprise system is a quid pro quo arrangement. These three little words can mean: 'You get what you pay for,' 'There is nothing for nothing,' and 'Good things do not come cheap.' These truisms apply not only to the common marketplace but are equally relevant at the highest level of decisionmaking, in this instance, the corporate boardroom. In the past, all directors, corporate or otherwise, were expected to perform in an eleemosynary capacity, or 'for free,' their services balanced 'quid-wise' by minimal duties and liabilities. Board meetings were infrequent and perfunctory. Little serious 'homework' preceded such meetings and directors were rarely liable for any boardroom action or inaction. But the increasing complexity of corporate governance has caused profound changes in director duties, responsibilities, and liabilities.

"The old boardroom honorific plums have gradually ripened into lush sugar plums, with retainers, fees, bonuses, options, and performance shares totaling more than $100,000 in the leading cases. In *Fortune*'s top 1300 firms, costs per director are now well above $25,000 annually with the median about twice that figure. The duties, responsibilities, and liabilities of directors have expanded in proportion to this better pay. Which came first, 'the quid' or the 'pro quo,' is a matter of speculation."[7]

The first sign of a profound change followed the "phases of the moon" electrical-equipment conspiracy. Although the twenty-nine corporate defendants were found guilty and fined a total of almost $20 million, subsequent stockholder suits resulted in Westinghouse Electric Corporation paying more than $52 million in settlements. Even more momentous were the indictments of thirty-seven officers-directors who were fined a total of $137,000—seven defendants were sent to jail with thirty-day sentences and twenty-five received thirty-day suspended jail sentences.

The reflex reaction in the corporate governance sector was one of immediate scurrying for cover, but only Lloyd's of London provided any kind of directors and officers (D&O) liability insurance. Probably the first American coverage available was with St. Paul Insurance Companies, and the rush of insurers soon turned into a stampede. The rush was dramatically accelerated by the Penn Central fiasco, where director apathy—and even ignorance—created a national revulsion toward do-nothing directors, and a concerted effort was made to identify and punish law-breaking board members. After 1974, when Penn Central shareholder suits were merged and settled out of court for about $10 million, claims against corporate directors more than quadrupled in the next seven years. Average individual

---

[7]Stanley C. Vance, in *Directors and Boards,* Summer 1979, p. 61.

claims now exceed $1 million annually. As an illustration, late in 1977, the Federal Deposit Insurance Corporation filed a $13.7 million suit against the twenty-one former directors of International City Bank and Trust Company of New Orleans after it failed. "If the directors had performed their duties even to a minimal degree, the FDIC suit charged, they would have adopted policies that would have prevented the losses. Instead, the suit alleged, the directors failed to scrutinize adequately insider transactions, neglected to supervise the loan portfolio, approved loans to borrowers known to be in financial difficulties, and didn't adhere to applicable laws resulting in extension of credit in investments in excess of legal limits of the bank."[8]

The record-setting suit, to date, was filed by Charles Rodman, trustee of the bankrupt W. T. Grant estate, against twenty-two former officers and directors. It seeks a total in excess of $10 billion from the defendants, ranging from $100 million to $800 million against each director. In a seventy-eight-page complaint filed in New York State, charges were made that the retail chain was grossly mismanaged and the officers and directors were negligent. The $10 billion in claims, if allowed, would very likely have a domino bankruptcy effect upon even the biggest of the insuring companies.

Without adequate company liability insurance coverage, the onus of court judgments, of course, is on the person. When William F. (Bill) Buckley, Jr., agreed to a consent decree in the Starr Broadcasting Group case—to pay an estimated $1.4 million—it was strictly a personal matter since his transgressions were of a kind that could not have been covered by liability insurance.

Lawsuits involving directors and officers continue to increase dramatically. For example, a generation ago, *Fortune*-listed companies had a near-zero of D&O claims; in 1979, however, an intensive survey[9] by the Wyatt Company showed that in the previous decade, on an annual basis, one out of twenty of the major publicly held U.S. corporations had a D&O claim. And the tempo is increasing, reaching one out of eleven *Fortune*-listed companies in 1978, one out of nine in 1979, and an estimated one out of six by the mid-1980s.

There are three types of suits that can threaten company directors: (1) derivative suits, (2) third-party actions, and (3) class-action suits. Briefly, *derivative suits* are actions brought by a stockholder, not for his own personal benefit, but for the benefit of the corporation. *Third-party actions*

---

[8]"FDIC Sues Directors of Collapsed Bank in New Orleans; $13.7 Million Is Sought," *The Wall Street Journal*, August 18, 1977, p. 14.

[9]The 1979 Wyatt Directors and Officers Liability Survey, quoted in *Director's Monthly*, National Association of Corporate Directors, June 1980, p. 4.

may involve legal action by a creditor or suits by competitors or by the government and its agencies such as the SEC. *Class actions* involve the pooling of several shareholders' claims, on their own behalf, into a single legal action.

The causes for legal action against directors are difficult to classify and enumerate because of varying state laws, the viewpoints of judges, and the pertinent facts that have surfaced. The Wyatt survey[10] found the following leading causes:

Misleading representation, 21.4 percent
Collusion or conspiracy to defraud, 13.6 percent
Civil rights denial, 7.9 percent
Antitrust violations, 7.6 percent
Failure to honor employment contract, 6.5 percent
Improper expenditures, 6.2 percent
Breach of duty to minority stockholders, 6.0 percent
Conflict of interest, 4.6 percent
Nine other specified causes, 23.5 percent
Not available, 24.7 percent

The sum of these figures exceeds 100 percent since some claims involved more than one set of allegations. Also, the causes for legal action can vary from year to year, depending upon a great many impelling forces. But one of the perturbing features for anyone seeking a factual base is the one-in-four figure of "not available." Another obstacle investigators must contend with is the reluctance of insurers to release any statistics about actual losses paid or about the losses which are claimed.

Then, too, there are the increasing number of exclusions. "Most D&O policies being sold today have nine basic but sweeping exclusions, meaning they won't cover any losses arising out of:

1 Libel or slander
2 Personal profit
3 Short swing profit
4 Excess remuneration
5 Dishonesty
6 Failure to effect and maintain insurance
7 Any risks already covered by any other insurance policy
8 Claims that should have been or were filed under a previously held D&O policy
9 Claims already indemnified by the corporation."[11]

---

[10]Ibid.
[11]Susan Alt, "D&O Liability Insurance: An Overview," *Directors and Boards,* Fall 1976, p. 37.

The list lengthens: nuclear energy-related liability; environmental protection-initiated claims; pension law controversies concerning fiduciary responsibilities; and claims arising from payments to foreign government officials or from political contributions, here or abroad, are almost always excluded. "It's difficult to find *anything* that's covered by the insurance because nearly every risk which could reasonably be foreseen to cause a loss is specifically excluded. Just three standard exclusions in the policies— for dishonesty, profit-taking and self-dealing, and conflict of interest— coupled with recent broad deletions of coverage 'may well take away just about everything,' according to a legal expert."[12]

Another caution is the extremely restrictive wording of policies. For example, some policies deny coverage for *all* directors and officers of a company, even if just one of those insured by the policy had any knowledge of a fact, circumstance, or situation which could lead to a claim under the policy. And all policies have a standard clause excluding losses arising from criminal actions or activities.

Regardless of the many inherent uncertainties, most users are convinced that they need more and better protections. Lloyd's of London has begun offering policies called tender offer defense expense insurance. This policy would pay 80 percent of certain costs associated with hostile takeover attempts, up to a maximum of $1 million. But as with most D&O policies, there is a proviso attached—the company must win to collect on the insurance. Other considerations cloud the issue. "There is a real question about the propriety of a company spending money for this kind of insurance . . . it makes fighting (tender) offers easier, but could look like the use of corporate funds to perpetuate management. The company might be sued by shareholders."[13]

As already stressed, despite the many legal and semantic limitations, the need for officer and director protection is obvious. The need extends even beyond the for-profit sector—hospital litigations involving millions of dollars are becoming commonplace. More and more boards of nonprofit organizations are being forced to see that their enterprises adhere to the same systematic, businesslike methods that are standard practice in industry.

As much as a decade ago, five directors of the Eugene (Oregon) Water and Electric Board were declared personally liable for $13,318 by the Oregon Court of Appeals. The five directors had authorized the sum to pay expenses for promoting nuclear power measures. The attorney for the accused summed up the sentiment of all directors—whether associated with

[12]Ibid., p. 38.
[13]G. Christian Hill, "Lloyd's Offers U.S. Concerns Insurance for Fighting Hostile Take-overs," *The Wall Street Journal,* May 12, 1980.

profit-making enterprises or serving in the nonprofit sector—when he stated that the court decision "puts chills down the spine of every public official serving without pay. If he cannot vote in good faith for what he thinks is right after obtaining advice of designated counsel, he will not want to vote, nor, in fact, serve."[14]

INTERLOCKS AND CONFLICT OF INTEREST

To put it simply, a boardroom interlock is a linkage or reciprocity arrangement: "You put me on your board, and I'll put you on mine." This mutual interchange constitutes direct interlocking and frequently stems from top-placed individuals striving for ego fulfillment. There is also an increasing number of "professional" directors who, in multiplying their outside directorships, seek to boost their retainer or fee income. While the "ego trip"- and "dollarmania"-induced interlocks can lead to ineffective boardroom performance, even more serious legal and ethical consequences result from another form, namely, collusive interlocks. These generally begin as friendly or buddy deals involving borrower and lender, buyer and seller, or adviser and advisee. Invariably, because gain is involved, these initially innocuous friendships lead to situations of preferential dealing, conflict of interest, insider trading, or other forms of monopoly and restraint of trade.

Far more prevalent are indirect interlocks, where directors from competing firms serve on the board of a third or neutral company. For example, a regular board meeting at American Telephone and Telegraph would almost seem to be a meeting of an auto-industry board, because in addition to three members of the General Motors board, members of the Ford and Chrysler boards also serve as AT&T directors. While this is presumed to be legal—not violating Section 8 of the Clayton Act—it raises questions of propriety.

Earlier interlock abuses led to passage of the Sherman Anti-Trust Act of 1890, and to the Pujo Committee (1913) which resulted in the Clayton Act of 1914. During the 1960s Congressman Emmanuel "Manny" Celler pursued the problem as chairman of the House of Representatives Committee on the Judiciary. Arguing for more restrictive legislation on interlocks, he stated: "Perhaps the most significant aspect of the common (interlocking) director problem is the concern that, by means of this device, inordinate control over the major part of USA commerce would be concentrated in the hands of so few individuals that the normal social and political forces relied upon to maintain a free economy would be ineffective to correct abuses. Ingrown relations, closely knit corporate identities, and the ability to wield economic power on a wide front were feared because they carry the seeds

---

[14]"Five Liable for Board Outlay," *The Oregonian,* December 21, 1972, p. 27.

of a 'business aristocracy' that would not be compatible with basic tenets of the political and economic democracy embodied in the antitrust laws."[15]

The 270-page report in support of Congressman Celler's bill, HR 11572, contained some disconcerting facts. For example, although insurance companies and banks are in direct competition, the staff study disclosed that the 10 largest life insurance companies had more than 195 interlocks and that the 10 largest fire and casualty companies had more than 160 direct interlocks with banks. It also pointed out that 6 leading interlockers, our 3 biggest automakers plus AT&T, B. F. Goodrich, and Phelps Dodge, had a total of nearly 400 direct interlocks, 26 of them with the 5 biggest New York banks. Note that all data dealt only with direct interlocks, that is, with the reciprocal seating of company A's director on company B's board and vice versa.

Unfortunately, boardroom interlocking and its related abuses are difficult to contain. As soon as therapy is applied to one sector, breakouts occur in other areas. For example, even after some progress was made following the Celler Committee disclosures, new rashes of abuse led to Congressman Wright Patman's renewing the fight. As chairman of the House Banking and Currency Committee, Patman introduced the Banking Reform Act of 1971 (HR 5700). This bill, in part, was sparked by the Penn Central collapse. Patman detailed the numerous interlocks among the railroad holding company's directors and many of our leading banks, insurance companies, buyers and vendors, and major corporations. There were charges that these self-serving interlocks involving Penn Central's directors ignored stockholder interests and unwittingly led the railroad into bankruptcy.

Even more recently (1978) a Senate Governmental Affairs Sub-committee emphasized that the continuing large number of interlocking directorates among the nation's largest corporations poses an overwhelming potential for antitrust abuse. In a 999-page study of 130 of the country's largest companies, the staff of the sub-committee found 530 direct and 12,193 indirect interlocking directorates. The 13 largest companies had 240 direct and 5547 indirect links.[16]

However, the study did not find any violations of current antitrust laws which bar competing companies from sharing directors. The staff also made no allegations that any of the specific direct or indirect links led to "predatory practices," and as such violated the antitrust laws. But the study did say that the close links among business leaders "may lead to a concentration of economic or fiscal control in a few hands" and may

---

[15]*Interlocks in Corporate Management,* U.S. House of Representatives Committee on the Judiciary Staff Report, Washington, D.C., March 12, 1965, p. 5.

[16]"Sharing of Directors Seen Posing Threat for Antitrust Abuse," *The Wall Street Journal,* April 24, 1978, p. 17.

"provide a linkage for communication and discussion which can result in elimination of competition."[17]

Obviously, the whole issue of interlocks gets clouded and complicated, particularly as our enterprise system expands and becomes more fine-tuned. For example, should a bank continue to carry a corporate CEO on its board if (1) the bank also manages that firm's pension funds; (2) its trust department deals heavily in that firm's equities; (3) the bank is a prime lender to that corporation? This lender-client, trustee-pension fund relationship is sometimes justified by variations of the "Chinese Wall" defense, namely, that what takes place on one side of the wall is of no concern and completely hidden from the view of those on the other side. This is counterpart to the well-known monkey trio, sitting together amiably in the classic no-see, no-hear, no-speak posture.

But directors do see, hear, and speak, and therefore they can collude. An increasing number of directors and corporations no longer take advantage of the "transactions-at-arm's-length" loopholes. To cite some instances described in *The Wall Street Journal:*

1 Even before any allegations were made, a university president resigned from a bank's board because the university had nine checking accounts, totaling over $3.2 million, with the bank (August 1, 1975).

2 The president of Equitable Life Assurance Society left Chase Manhattan's board because there was "the possible appearance of conflict of interest," even though there was no specific pressure from the Department of Justice or any other agency (March 3, 1978).

3 Earl G. Graves, the only black member on International Telephone and Telegraph's board, resigned because of the "increasing potential risks of conflict of interest," even though he served on no other boards. But because of the enormity of ITT's far-reaching businesses, Mr. Graves, who had a desire to take advantage of other board opportunities, felt he could incur conflict of interest (March 4, 1981).

Early in 1981 the Federal Trade Commission (FTC) and Gould, Inc., settled a charge that Gould violated federal antitrust laws by having two interlocking directorships with competitors, namely, at Midland-Ross Corporation and at Narco Scientific. Gould made and sold various electrical and electronic medical devices, as did the other firms. Gould's predicament was typical of that faced by an increasing number of multiproduct firms.

In addition are the numerous social, educational, political, religious, and other nonbusiness associations which can prompt preferential dealings. The domination by Ivy League graduates in some of our large publicly owned

[17]Ibid.

corporations, banks, and insurance companies has been amply document-ed. Also, membership in exclusive clubs such as the Links, Bohemian, or Laurel Valley have presented even more imponderables on the impact of interlocks.

The most serious legal objections to interlocks stem from the continued incidence of conflict of interest and insider trading. Basically, conflict of interest refers to a director's fiduciary duty to devote himself to corporate affairs with a view of promoting the common interests and not his own. Never should a director utilize his position to obtain any profit or advantage other than that enjoyed also by his fellow shareholders.

Within days after Walter Cronkite bowed out as anchorman and manag-ing editor of "CBS Evening News," he created a big stir in media circles by accepting a seat on the board of Pan American World Airways. While no interlocking was involved, the seating of this eminent newscaster on the board of a company about which he might, on occasion, relate news or other items caused consternation among his colleagues. Spokespersons for both ABC News and NBC News said that such a board position would constitute a conflict of interest within their own companies. While CBS News stressed that it would guarantee that Cronkite does not work on any assignments dealing with airlines, the TV community's decisive sentiment was that Cronkite should not have ventured into this conflict-of-interest potentiality. Apologists emphasized that Cronkite did not need the director-ship compensation, which initially was set at a $10,000 annual retainer, $300 and expenses per meeting, and unlimited free Pan Am travel for Cronkite and his wife. But in less than half a year, Cronkite left Pan Am.

Equally reprehensible is the insider trading evil. By law and precedent, a corporation has a proprietary right to information it obtains in the course of running its business. Directors and officers have a duty to protect this information, and they cannot use it for personal advantage; doing so constitutes insider trading. For example, the Securities and Exchange Commission charged a director of Riggs National Bank with profiting from information related to an imminent takeover of the bank.[18] The individual was accused of selling his stock to the acquiring firm, and meanwhile, purchasing additional shares from stockholders who were unaware of the takeover discussions. Because takeovers generally increase the value of the firm being acquired, the profit, in this instance, came to $20 per share, or a total of almost $1 million, which a federal court ordered be compensated to the original owners.

Directors, since they are privy to all major issues at their firms, are in a particularly vulnerable position in regard to insider trading allegations. In

[18]"Riggs National Director Charged on Insider Trades," *The Wall Street Journal*, March 10, 1981, p. 7.

the spring of 1981, a suit was filed against fourteen brokers and eleven investors, charging them with insider trading to the tune of $1.6 million in options on the stock of Amax, Inc., shortly before the announcement that Amax was the subject of a $4 billion takeover by Standard Oil Company of California (Socal). One of those charged was Thomas C. Reed, a prominent San Rafael businessman whose father, Gordon W. Reed, was a long-time Amax director (since the 1940s). Reed, who served as Secretary of the Air Force in 1976 and 1977, allegedly purchased at least 1000 Amax options just before the merger offer. Half of these options were purchased on the day before Socal made its offer for Amax. Thus, Thomas Reed and his children presumably made $446,850 in this shortest-of-short options deals.[19]

Periods of intensified merger activity are usually times of high insider-information leakage. A 1981 *Fortune* study[20] of twenty recent tender offers and acquisitions graphically demonstrated how, over a four-week period, there were sizable stock price rises before information of takeover intentions was released. Assuming there were no public pronouncements, the speculators either possessed excellent crystal balls or had unauthorized access to insider information since prices of the target companies spurted by an average of 20 percent. It should be mentioned that in an attempt to forestall leakage, many companies take elaborate precautions by using code names, hiring electronics specialists, shredding confidential papers, and limiting the number of those privy to merger dealing.

The New York Stock Exchange, likewise, is sensitive to insider abuses. It has a supersophisticated computer system, referred to as the Big Board's Stock Watch Department, which immediately recognizes abnormal stock movements for any of its listed securities. But, of course, unethical dealers in insider information often evidence an ingenuity that transcends even the best computer capabilities.

Each year a dozen or more directors get unfavorable mention in the press because of insider dealings. Virtually all the transgressors are affiliated with small and closely held companies. Relatively few major company directors are so indiscreet. Nevertheless, since directors are presumed to have full-information access, they will always be suspect. Consequently, eternal vigilance is recommended.

Evolution in the boardroom is creating new potentials for unethical access to insider and privy information. The slowly evolving concept of worker representation on boards poses such a threat. While several European nations have accepted this comanagement practice, American

---

[19]"Amax Director's Son Bought Call Options via Dean Witter," *The Wall Street Journal*, March 16, 1981, p. 5.

[20]Katherena Leanne Zanders, "The Unwinnable War on Insider Trading," *Fortune*, July 13, 1981, p. 72.

labor leaders, from Samuel Gompers through George Meany, have held that labor and management co-opting in the boardroom would be a serious conflict of interest.

In 1980 we witnessed the first big reversal of this separatist policy when the United Auto Workers bargained a seat on the ailing Chrysler Corporation board. This did not necessarily set a precedent. When American Motors Company tried to follow the Chrysler example, the Department of Justice initially refused the UAW bid. The federal regulatory authorities stressed that such action would give rise to serious conflict of interest and other antitrust questions.

The union argued that the AMC nominee would not be Mr. Fraser; thus there would be no direct interlock. The nominee, likewise, need not be an official or employee of the union, thus minimizing indirect interlock connotations. While the Department of Justice raised objections, it eventually backed away. What the ultimate will be in comparable conflicts and compromises cannot be predicted. Evidently, while interlocking is as old as the most rudimentary corporate governance, it is constantly adapting to changes in environment, and is far from becoming a paleontological curiosity.

REPRESENTATIVE BOARDS

The social and political activism of the late 1960s sparked a revolution of sorts in corporate governance. Before that tense period, directors had always been a relatively homogeneous group of WASPs, males with Ivy League encrustations, excellent family connections, and outstanding cash positions. Now, however, a new focus became visible, with less stress on gentility, more on representativeness; less stress on the candidate as a stockholder, more on the candidate as a stakeholder. The word "stakeholder," broadly defined, means anyone who holds anything of value which is being chanced or wagered on the uncertainties of a contest. In this instance, the contest is the corporation's attempt to utilize all its resources most effectively. The stakeholders include not only owners—who obviously take chances—but also customers, vendors, the community, workers, and virtually everyone within the immediate socioeconomic radius of the company's impact.

Not until 1980 could workers, as stakeholders, be considered for boardroom service—Douglas A. Fraser, president of the United Auto Workers, broke this barrier. Black Americans have become more welcome even though they did not make their first breakthrough until 1965 when Asa T. Spaulding became the first black to serve on a major company board (W. T. Grant). The following year, Jackie Robinson, of baseball fame, joined the board of Hamilton Life Insurance Company as cochairman. Although boardroom seats were available to women much earlier, usually they were limited to wives or daughters of male entrepreneurs. Mrs. Henry Ford held a seat in the Ford Motor Company as early as the 1930s; Mrs. Merriweather Post and Mrs. Claire Hoffman also occupied seats on family-run enterprises. Despite their association with ownership, their acceptance was cosmetic and exceptional.

One of the first efforts to diminish the "old boy" network and institute a mild form of representation occurred in 1954 during Robert Young's attempt to take over the New York Central Railroad. Young sought the votes of the railroad's 41,000 stockholders, promising dividends of $7 to $10 versus the $1 per share they were receiving. In addition, he announced that his slate of candidates would include a woman and also a Catholic. Either because of his enlightened approach to representativeness or because of his promise to increase dividends, Young won 60 percent of the vote. Then for unfathomable reasons, he sold most of his stock two years later (1956), and in 1958 he was a victim of a tragic suicide.

Robert Young's naming of a woman to his board did not start a rash of imitators. But today a number of the "Fortune 1300" do have a woman on their boards, and some—Armstrong World Industries, American Telephone and Telegraph, Dow Jones, Textron—even have two women directors. Gulf Oil Corporation, however, seemed to take Robert Young's innovative experiment most seriously; in 1976 it named (and subsequently reelected) Sister Jane C. Scully, president of Carlow College, and a nun, to its previously all-male board.

Certainly there are better reasons—other than representativeness and democracy—for opening boardroom doors to women. One good reason (if I dare quote myself on this sensitive issue) is that: "In not a single instance of serious corporate mismanagement has a woman been on the firm's culprit board of directors or even on its top executive staff. This also applies to any major corporation that has collapsed or become so ailing that it had to be absorbed by another firm. . . . The list of male-mismanaged enterprises could be expanded with another category—the sorry plight of railroads. Until recently, roundhouse history has never included a woman director or major executive. Perhaps with better balanced leadership, railroads today might not be begging for federal alms."[21]

But in spite of the number of women-held boardroom seats in major corporations (expanded from a handful of relatives before 1965 to more than 400 presently), there is still a dearth of women officers and directors. In the past, virtually all corporate career paths detoured capable women employees into lower-level, dead-end jobs. Fortunately, today at least a

---

[21]Stanley C. Vance, "Women Directors: From Bedroom to Boardroom," *University of Tennessee Survey of Business,* May/June 1975, p. 7.

dozen women key executives also serve as company directors, compared to not a single one in 1965.

The logic and pattern observed for women directors holds equally well for black Americans. Since Asa Spaulding's inauspicious entrance into W. T. Grant's boardroom in 1965, the number of black directorships has expanded to almost 200. Evidently, this is not as good a record as that shared by women. However, a large proportion of multiboard seats are filled by blacks, including those held by such stalwarts as:

Jerome H. Holland (AT&T, General Foods, Union Carbide, Manufacturers Hanover Corporation, Continental Corporation, Chrysler Corporation, Federated Department Stores, Culbro Corporation, Pan American Bancshares, and Zurn Industries)

Andrew F. Brimmer (UAL, Du Pont, International Harvester, Bank America Corporation, Bank of America National Trust and Savings Association, American Security Corporation, Ford Foundation, and Commodity Exchange)

There are times when all representative directors will act as partisans for their constituents. Black directors, in particular, are under special pressures —they must be sensitive to domestic problems pertinent to their constituents and to international issues as well. In this area, one of the greatest services rendered by a black director was provided by the Reverend Leon H. Sullivan, elected to General Motors' board in 1971. Reverend Sullivan put together the well-known "Sullivan Principles" or "Sullivan Code," an action plan for U.S. companies to help institute increasingly progressive labor policies in South Africa. Within a decade there were 138 signatory companies. While nonwhite strikes and riots in South Africa continued, wage patterns, job opportunities, and working conditions did improve markedly at the signatory firms. Even though extremists from both sides were displeased with the compromise, common sense indicated that the Sullivan Principles offered the best course of action available. And the Sullivan Principles worked.

There are, of course, dozens of other groups that could seek representation on boards. Ethnically speaking, despite their numbers, only a mere handful of Latin Americans sit on major American corporate boards. Among descendants of Asiatic Americans, Dr. Fujio Matsuda, president of the University of Hawaii, is one of the very few to hold boardroom seats; his directorships include UAL, Incorporated, C. Brewer and Company, and Hawaiian Electric Company.

Late in 1979 , a New Jersey-based automobile dealer organization sent a formal request to Chrysler's CEO, asking that a Chrysler dealer be added to its board. " 'We plan to get around to all the auto makers but we're going to Chrysler first because it opened the floodgates with the nomination of Mr.

Fraser,' said a dealer spokesman. 'We think it's a good idea to put Mr. Fraser on the board to get some balance, and we also think a dealer on the board could give Chrysler some fresh conceptual and practical approaches to its problem.' "[22] Chrysler shelved the proposal.

Another very significant form of representation on boards is touched upon in other chapters. This is functional representation, namely, the election of top-level executives to the board, where they serve as inside and functional directors and become spokespersons for their respective functions, product lines, or geographic divisions. While there has been a decline in the incidence of functional officer-directors, the probabilities for product-line and geographic representation have been enhanced because of conglomeration and multinationalism. Note the commentary on sector executives and proliferating presidents. Likewise, on the multinational score; for example, how can any major firm strive to be multinational if its board of directors is strictly regional or provincial, excluding all foreigners?

While representation on the basis of conglomeration and geography has good prospects, the more commonly alluded to constituency (demographic, social caste, or political forms of representative boards) seems to be plateauing.

Securities Exchange Commission chairman, Harold Williams, in delineating board functions and structure, aptly put it by first outlining what he did not advocate for the board: "First, I do not favor constituency (representative) directors. In my view, the board is not a political body and cannot function effectively when populated by individuals who have special interest to champion and little concern or sense of responsibility for the overall welfare of the company. Additionally, some of those who advocate constituency directors seem to have in mind persons unconcerned with—or actively hostile to—the basic economic purpose of private business. For these reasons I strongly oppose constituency directors."[23]

Equally convincing is the obvious pragmatic reason: there is no demonstrable proof that adding representatives of constitutencies improves sales, productivity, growth, morale, or even better relations with the constituents in question. Moreover, sustained effort for such representation is essential, and such continued dedication is rarely forthcoming from any group.

There are other objections. Although representative boards may be viewed as a vital part of industrial democracy, they can easily lead to collusive action, factionalism, favoritism, and endless bickering. Also, if each vested group demands an excessive piece of the production pie, this taken-for-granted industrial democracy will definitely lead to industrial chaos.

---

[22]*The Wall Street Journal,* October 29, 1979, p. 6.
[23]Harold M. Williams, "Corporate Accountability and Corporate Power," *Corporate Governance Review,* National Association of Corporate Directors, 1981, p. 17.

A less radical and more sensible view of industrial democracy and representativeness has been advocated for almost half a century by the Gilbert brothers, John and Lewis. Undaunted by a near-zero batting average at annual stockholder meetings, these 'gadflies" have persisted in their quest for reform through stockholder resolutions. Their Corporate Democracy, Inc., which has published the *Annual Report of Stockholder Activities at Corporation Meetings* for forty-one years, provides an incisive but sane corporate representative course of action. The Gilberts have consistently argued for restructuring boards with a new focus on representation, but what they sought, and continue to seek, is more representation of independent stockholder interests. Lewis Gilbert argues that directors should stop thinking in terms of boardroom harmony. "We must have boards on which directors are not afraid to cast dissenting votes. For after all, the boardroom is supposed to be the council chamber of the owners."[24] This view of representation is certainly different from the notion that minority and special groups should have vested seats in major boardrooms.

ILLUSTRATION: First Pennsylvania Bank

In 1971, John R. Bunting, president of First Pennsylvania Banking and Trust Company, attempted a dramatic restructuring of the bank's board, with the intent of increasing representativeness. A year earlier he had proposed making banks more responsive to present needs, thereby turning over up to one-third of his bank's twenty-four seats to the disenfranchised. He went so far as to suggest a "poor-man's seat" which could be held only so long as the director earned less than $10,000 a year. "The idea that only 100 people in Philadelphia are capable of holding all of the important corporate and civic boards in the city may have been sound years ago but it's certainly no longer justifiable."[25]

Bunting partially implemented his radical notion by adding to his bank board its first black, first woman, and first student. This dramatic experiment in boardroom structuring also made dramatic headlines, leading some critics to accuse Bunting of an inordinate penchant for publicity. The critics might have been more right than wrong.

Of interest is the fact that this same board, earlier, had included some of the most blatant direct interlocking—William L. Day, its chairman, sat on the Penn Central board, while Stuart Saunders, the railroad's chairman, sat on the bank's board. It is hard to prove what led First Pennsylvania into the doldrums and then into serious financial embarrassment; was it the earlier elitism and interlocking or the inexperience of the new representative board?

Nevertheless, by the fifth year of Bunting's tenure as chairman and chief executive, Federal Reserve Board examiners were on the premises, checking on

---

[24]"The More Representative Board," *The Conference Board,* February 1972, p. 43.
[25]Jack H. Morris, "A Banker's Startling Idea on Directors," *The Wall Street Journal,* August 5, 1970.

questionable practices. Federal officials were particularly not enthusiastic about Bunting's attention-getting schemes and some of his far-out banking policies. " 'Every time you'd pick up the paper, there would be another article about Bunting running off somewhere to give a speech,' says one Fed source. 'You had to wonder who was running the bank. I remember [one of the Fed's seven governors] saying, This guy Bunting is a wild man. We ought to put a harness on him.' "[26]

Whether it was due to banking irregularities, the high-level corporate interlocks, the representative board innovation, the overstress on long-term government bonds in the investment portfolio, or the flamboyance of its chief executive, bad times did befall First Pennsylvania. It slumped on the basis of all financial yardsticks, dropping from nineteenth by asset size among commercial banks to, in 1981, a less impressive forty-first position. Of all the larger banks, it produced about the worst operating record. In 1980, the company reported a loss of $164 million. Among the top commercial banks, it ranked fiftieth out of fifty on both net operating income and net income as a percent of equity norms. First Pennsylvania had to be rescued by a $1.5-billion aid package, including an FDIC loan.

Bunting lost his job, his successor cut the dividend rate drastically, and several stockholder suits were instituted. These suits alleged, in part, that the company had been mismanaged, and demanded that the company appoint enough new directors to assure that a majority of its board consist of members who were not on the board between 1977 and 1980. This was a unique action in that it more than implied culpability in the bank's directors. Alas, the nation's once nineteenth biggest bank holding company, with assets of almost $11 billion, saw its assets shrink to about $5 billion. It lost many of its customers, including former trust department stalwarts such as the state of Arizona, PPG Industries, and Kansas Power and Light Company. "Many officers have left. 'They're losing good people in middle management, and that's where work gets done,' observes the chairman of a competing bank holding company."[27]

Ironically, First Pennsylvania did not treat its departing chairman-CEO too harshly. It granted him nearly $100,000 severance pay, plus $4883 a month for the rest of his life. This aroused the fury of the stockholders. At the 1980 annual meeting, "exclaimed angry stockholder Herbert C. Hannemann: 'He's not bunting. He's a home-run hitter.' "[28]

ILLUSTRATION: College Boards

In the Charter Provisions of the University of Tennessee, Article VI, there is a real attempt at structuring a representative board. The Board of Trustees is to consist of five ex officio members and eighteen additional appointive members. The ex officio

[26]Thomas J. Bray, "Did the Bank Switch Rather Than Fight the Fed Examiners?" *The Wall Street Journal,* April 26, 1976, p. 1.

[27]John Helyar, "Big Philadelphia Bank Faces a Hard Struggle to Regain Its Health," *The Wall Street Journal,* August 24, 1981, p. 1.

[28]"A Tale of Two Troubled Banks," *Time,* May 12, 1980, p. 61.

members represent state departments closely concerned with the university: the governor, the commissioners of education and agriculture, the executive director of the Higher Education Commission, and the president of the university system. While they are representative in a sense, the real representation is in the other eighteen appointive trustees. These include one from each congressional district, two each from the two counties providing the most students, one each from the other principal counties, and one student on an annual rotating basis from one of the five campuses of the university.

Totally, there shall be at least one woman; at least one-third of the appointive members shall be of the principal minority political party in the state; and at least one-third shall be alumni of the university. This last proviso might seem superfluous since, in recent years, practically all the trustees have been UT graduates. This accent on alumni, as trustees, is not purely accidental. Years ago, less than a majority of the board were alumni. This annoyed the UT Alumni Association, which launched a protracted campaign for a legal right to place alumni on the board. Their sentiments were expressed in a prediction that if alumni met year after year with nothing to do but talk about old times, they soon would be trying to govern their alma maters. And this is precisely what happened, not only at Tennessee but in most major public universities.

Safeguarding the minority political party's position on the board is vital, not only in the South, with its century-old one-party bias, but in every state as well. The role of the student trustee, likewise, proved to be beneficial. Invariably, the student trustee is a superactive campus leader, with a strong student constituency. Having students serve on the board has stimulated interest and dedication to the university, not only among student trustees but particularly throughout the student body.

It is probably worth mentioning that even after the first alumni association was formed at Williams College in 1821, it took almost a century to accept a legal basis for designating a specified number of seats for the alumni of University of Tennessee. After this victory, one-third of the trustees were to be alumni of the university they governed. Historically, even though the board has always included at least one-third alumni, proponents of the legal mandate stressed they wanted a legal guarantee and not a mere probability of having representatives on the board.

There are increasing signs—certainly not a ground swell as yet—that a comparable move could take place among corporate shareowners. Although most alumni are stakeholders rather than shareholders, it should be pointed out that they have succeeded in being guaranteed at least some representation on the board.

CORPORATE SOCIAL RESPONSIBILITY

The last bastion of noblesse oblige has finally been breached; corporations are more and more expected to behave like ordinary responsible citizens. It had been universally assumed, since the beginning of the industrial era, that because all corporations were authorized to do business by the political sovereign (the crown or Congress), they were answerable only to the sovereign. Consequently, they were outside the general reaches of the law. As evidence, a tour of the coal mining areas of the anthracite region of

Pennsylvania shockingly reveals the atrocious strip-mining despoilation of past years. A run through Oregon's beautiful coastal and Cascade regions reveals hills of timberland horribly desecrated and left to grow into useless scrub thickets. Regretfully, the story has been the same in industry after industry.

The abuse of nature's beauties and bounties was more than matched by a callous disregard for company employees. As a result, we have black lung, brown lung, asbestiosis, and a host of other industry-induced ills, proving man's inhumanity to man. Yet apologists for exploitation of resources—human and inanimate—have quoted clichés such as assumption of risk, nolo contendere, caveat emptor, or innocent till proven guilty.

Some of the deferential treatment accorded industry might have followed from Chief Justice John Marshall's 1819 landmark definition. When Marshall stated that a corporation was an artificial being, invisible, intangible, and existing only in the contemplation of the law, his words, unfortunately, were taken literally. Even when a corporation was obviously guilty of bad conduct, it seemed impossible that anyone would punish an artificial, invisible, intangible being that existed only in the contemplation of the law. An ectoplasmic corporation can feel no pain. So for years, whenever our invisible corporations behaved as poltergeists or impish spirits, the heaviest punishment accorded was a cease and desist order; in other words, "Now don't let me catch you again." At worst, there were token fines.

The long-overdue transformation has finally come about. Without violating John Marshall's definition, modern corporations have become more real and less artificial, somewhat more visible and tangible. While still existing only in the contemplation of the law, today's corporations are also subject to the law. This new and radical view is a by-product of the anti-Vietnam war resentment of the late 1960s. Significantly, this sociological change was not due to congressional initiative; in fact, corrective actions such as the Occupational Safety and Health Act (1970) and the Foreign Corrupt Practices Act (1974) were the effects of this new attitude. Nor did federal regulatory bodies such as the SEC, FTC, or the Departments of Justice and Labor do much to gestate the new view. Actually, corporate and business associations and professional bodies, even the several stock exchanges, were invariably defensive and sometimes outright hostile to the new movement.

The new focus on corporate social responsibility was fundamentally a grassroots reaction to authoritarian abuses in business. Since much of the corporate social responsibility terrain is covered later in other sections—"Foreign Corrupt Practices Act," "Corporate Democracy Acts," "Campaign GM," "The Gadflies," and a half dozen other topics—it will not be repeated here. But there are some facets that could be burnished; in particular, what should society expect of executives outside corporate headquarters?

The section "Who's Watching the Store?" points out how difficult it is for even the most capable and willing corporate executives to wear a wide array of hats. Yet there is persistent pressure, particularly for chief executive officers, to volunteer their services for civic and professional duties. " 'Herbert E. Strawbridge, chairman of Higbee Company, a Cleveland-based operator of department stores, is one of the city's biggest boosters, and still spends roughly 30 hours of his 70-hour workweek on municipal affairs. He used to spend more—at a price. Higbee's suffered from a lack of guidance.' "[29]

Good citizenship, a fundamental thesis of corporate social responsibility, carries a big price tag. " 'We can't get a decision on anything around here,' grouses a vice president at one big Mid-western manufacturing company. 'The chairman is running around on Savings Bond drives or some other do-gooder activity so much that he's never here for us to talk to.' "[30]

It is an exceptional executive who has the courage to face up to his real responsibilities. "One recent weekend, Fletcher L. Byrom, chairman and chief executive officer of Koppers Company in Pittsburgh, dictated letters to five social-concern groups resigning his memberships. The outside activities, he had decided, were taking more time than he had to give them. 'Koppers comes first,' Mr. Byrom says."[31]

Much of the civic and social-responsibility duties that were foisted upon top executives in the past two decades were carried out only because executives delegated their prime corporate duties. This resulted in higher costs, confusion, dwindling productivity, and trouble—sometimes big trouble. Yet the impractical activists continued to make exaggerated claims. Milton Moskowitz, editor of *Business and Society Review,* argued that the socially aware corporation possesses the special sensitivity that will enable it to surpass competitors. He then tested this interesting hypothesis on a sample of fourteen companies, with remarkable positive results. Each of the fourteen firms had similarly good social responsibility credentials and was selected on the basis of its outstanding contributions to socially responsible actions. For example, the list was headed by Chase Manhattan Bank. "Chase has compiled a superlative record in many categories associated with corporate responsibility . . . the company was also one of the first to report a social budget expenditure for its various activities—$3.5 million a year. In a recent poll, Chase outranked forty-four other competitors that were being rated on social performance."[32]

[29]Margaret Yao, "Civic Duties Become a More Beastly Burden for Chief Executives," *The Wall Street Journal,* June 11, 1980, p. 1.

[30]Ibid.

[31]Ibid.

[32]Milton R. Moskowitz, "Choosing Socially Responsible Stocks," *Business and Society Review,* Spring 1972, p. 72.

Moskowitz did seem to prove his thesis, using only 1972 data. In the stock market for a twelve-month period, the socially responsible firms did do better than the Dow Jones averages. But in a subsequent replication (1975) by an outside analyst, there seemed to be a distinct reversal in results; most of the fourteen socially aware companies did considerably worse than the Dow Jones averages.[33] Perhaps their negative performance was exaggerated by exceptional problems plaguing some of the test group. For example, First Pennsylvania Bank and Trust, Chase Manhattan, and Xerox had to contend with unusual circumstances.

In several 1972 issues, *Business and Society Review (BSR)* had obtained rankings of companies on the basis of how they were perceived to behave as responsible citizens. The Spring 1972 issue published a "Survey of Businessmen," and the Summer 1972 issue presented "How Business School Students Rate Corporations." From these rankings, another independent test was made in the 1975 replication study. The top twenty socially responsible, or "good guy," companies were compared with the twenty lowest-ranked, or "bad guy," companies.

The overall results indicated that if an investor had just $1000 in each of the twenty socially aware firms in early January 1974 and then sold the portfolio a year later, he would have lost a whopping 44 percent. His pragmatic counterpart, who at the same time bought and sold similar shares in the twenty "bad guys," would have lost only 18 percent. Even though 1974 proved to be a poor market year for both portfolios, investing in firms that businesspeople and college students had rated as socially responsible corporations was the faster way to go broke.

A single failure, however, does not disprove a theory. A recent quick check was made to compare the top and bottom twelve industrial firms in the *BSR* 1972 surveys. "Fortune 500's" total return to investors, over a ten-year period, was the yardstick used. This final test corroborated the earlier negative relationship: the twelve good guys (between 1970 and 1980) had an average annual return to investors of 5.07 percent; the twelve bad guys averaged 9.59 percent.[34]

Comparisons of this sort, naturally, are tenuous. There are so many variables and subjective factors; there are uncontrollable forces and a lot of imponderables. The negative analyses are not intended to discredit corporate social responsiveness, but rather to temper the ardor of proponents and antagonists. The point to be made is that the supposed investment superiori-

---

[33]Stanley C. Vance, "Are Socially Responsible Corporations Good Investment Risks?" *Management Review*, August 1975, p. 18.
[34]"Fortune Directory of the Largest U.S. Industrial Corporations," *Fortune*, May 4, 1981, pp. 322 ff.

ty of companies deemed to be socially responsible needs to be proved—and also vice versa.

Perhaps intentionally, the demogogic activists of a decade ago missed one big point: enlightened self-interest can also be enlightened social interest. Take the example of G. F. Swift, founder of the once-dominant meat packer. Swift was exceedingly cost-conscious, perhaps even parsimonious. His son tells the story of G. F.'s daily visitations to Chicago's old Bubbly Creek, back of the stockyards. "Bubbly" was a malodorous open sewer into which the company emptied its waste. As Louis Swift put it, "But down to Bubbly Creek father would go and scrutinize the sewer for a few minutes every once in a while."[35] Then he pointed out that G. F.'s visits to this bloody, repulsive, reeking sewer were not in the best ecological interests. Neither was he contemplating the fate of the animals dispatched that day. "He was on the lookout for waste. If he saw any fat coming out, that evidenced waste in the packing house. Briskly he would head for the superintendent's office and before the episode was closed someone would smart."[36]

Gustavus F. Swift typified the breed of entrepreneur who got things done because he was on the scene. He was concerned because it was *his* enterprise and waste was *his* loss. (If macrocorporations could somehow resurrect this old-fashioned self-interest, and enlighten it to present-day standards, there probably would be fewer Love Canal incidents.) He was *the* inside director—on the scene, competent and concerned. Unfortunately, the experience of past generations shows that far too many directors either were removed from the scene or simply did not consider social responsibility as being their business. This has changed.

Within the past decade, an increasing number of corporations have set up boardroom committees to monitor environmental, consumer, and related issues. Currently, several hundred companies in sensitive industries have developed a new kind of executive—one concerned with the environment. " 'We're facing up to the fact that good environmental policy is as much a part of running the business as profits,' says Monte C. Throdal, a senior vice president of Monsanto Co. It wasn't always so. A decade ago most companies relegated environmental matters to the engineering department, where a small staff designed equipment to meet the few existing pollution-control requirements. Now faced with heightened public awareness of environmental problems and increased government regulation,

---

[35]Louis F. Swift, *The Yankee of the Yards, the Biography of Gustavus Franklin Swift* (Chicago: A. W. Shaw Company, 1927), p. 4.
[36]Ibid.

almost every major chemical company has an organized program for handling environmental issues."[37]

And there are unexpected bounties when even the most sophisticated of today's corporations go back to using G. F. Swift's century-old Bubbly Creek waste-watch program. As an illustration, Allied Chemical, well known environmentally because of its unfortunate Kepone experience, has been particularly alert to industry problems. At one of its Baton Rouge plants where fluorocarbons are processed, calcium chloride was a burdensome waste product; it was treated and then discharged into the Mississippi River. "Allied decided to look for a market for the calcium chloride and found one. 'We turned a liability into an asset,' says the plant manager."[38]

There are uncounted millions of profit dollars awaiting recovery from what is now dumped as slag, sludge, discards, and other waste. We might emulate the hog-processing industry where the whole animal, except its squeal, is utilized. If action is to come, it must be now, before we are preempted by the Japanese, as we were in total quality control and quality control circles. And if we are to embark on a universal total materials utilization program, the basic decision should not rest with the production executive, the engineering department, or the environmental manager—it should come from an enlightened and economically advanced board of directors.

ILLUSTRATION: Non-Linear Systems

The Andy Kay caper is probably the best documented management-experimentation case of its time. It proved that idealism simply cannot contend in the tough arena of realism even with full support of CEO and board. In the early 1960s, Non-Linear Systems owner and president, Andrew F. Kay, provided motivational theorists propounding the teachings of A. H. Maslow, Rensis Likert, Douglas McGregor, and Frederick Herzberg with a super laboratory—his company—to test their behavioral science notions.

Among his many innovations, Kay eliminated assembly lines and time cards. All production workers were put on salary—at 60 cents an hour more than the prevailing wage in the home city of San Diego. Members of independent production units of six or seven workers were free to organize and work as they wished. "They can decide to break the work down and specialize in different assembly operations, or they can decide that each man should take an entire product unit through every phase of operation."[39]

---

[37]Georgette Jansen, "New Breed Environmental Managers," *The Wall Street Journal*, July 30, 1981, p. 50.
[38]Ibid.
[39]"When Workers Manage Themselves," *Business Week*, March 20, 1965.

Not only was the production process modified, but so were staff functions. "The accounting department chalked up a success—by being eliminated. Accountants were dispersed to purchasing, shipping, personnel. . . . Now departments keep their own books, report balances to the Treasurer."[40]

The new approach, variously called "permissive management," "nonstructured management," "eupsychian" or "enlightened management," seemed to work for a decade. Several factors favored it—NLS was in electronic instrumentation and test systems and was largely protected by patents. Moreover, the company was privately held; Andy Kay owned all the stock, and he was a one-man board of directors. Moreover, there were government contracts.

In less than five years, *Business Week's* initial glowing commentary became a totally different story, a reversal—"Where Being Nice to Workers Didn't Work." When the aerospace industry fell apart, in 1970, so did NLS. "Kay says the behavioral experiments caused him to lose touch with what was happening to his company. Top and middle managers were preoccupied with trying out new participative techniques, sensitivity sessions, and long-range planning. 'I assumed that the day-to-day operations of the company would take care of themselves,' Kay says. 'I found out differently.' "[41]

Assembly lines were returned, salaries were brought into line with the area's prevailing scales, and NLS once again became a conventional manufacturer of electronic and testing equipment. One of the experiment's architects, Richard Farson, former president of the Western Behavioral Sciences Institute, earlier had commented on NLS's social responsibility adventure: "There was so much excitement it was almost seductive."[42] Now, however, consultant Farson reflected, "I think we now know that human relations don't have to do with profit and productivity. We should pay much closer attention to the style of the top guy of the company. That is a fact we must accept. We are working at considerable odds in democratizing management."[43]

POSTSCRIPT

It is evident from the discussion in Chapter 5 that every corporate governance mechanism has its own internal constraints. These constraints vary in proportion and emphasis from board to board—some stress structural aspects, others look at functional features, while others give greater importance to policy and philosophical considerations. These differences in focus were variously touched upon in the three previous chapters dealing with board purpose, characteristics, and structure.

Of the many internal constraints, the most significant is a board's value system—its outlook on corporate life plus a clear-cut differentiation of right

[40]Ibid.
[41]"Where Being Nice to Workers Didn't Work," *Business Week,* January 20, 1973, p. 100.
[42]Ibid., p. 98.
[43]Ibid., p. 100.

from wrong. This strong ethical posture might be translated into a list of attributes such as integrity, honesty, loyalty, faith, and dedication. While until recently, directors and boards were grandiosely described in these angelic and abstract terms, there were those who suspected that few possessed these virtues to any marked degree. These skeptics pointed the same accusing finger at directors as the presiding judge of the Michigan Supreme Court, in his 1926 pronouncement:

> It is the habit in these days for certain well-to-do men with influence in their respective communities to accept positions on boards of directors of corporations as honorary directors, and then never render any service except to sign on the dotted line, vote as requested by the one in charge and afterwards to cash their director's check for attending the meeting.
>
> They give no thought to the affairs of the company, exercise no judgment upon questions of business policy and make no investigation of the real financial conditions of the company.
>
> It is this kind of service by directors that helps to extract such a tremendous toll out of the public who happen to own industrial securities. The law requires a different kind of service of them.[44]

Fifty years later these classic words were repeated by A. A. Sommer, Jr., formerly of the Securities and Exchange Commission. In uttering these same words, SEC's Sommer was implying that when a board's value system is at a low level, virtually all other internal constraints are at a minimum. Such a board is a liability to our system.

[44]"Drawing a Tighter Line for Corporate Directors," *U.S. News & World Report,* October 6, 1975, p. 67.

CHAPTER 6

EXTERNAL CONSTRAINTS

SECURITIES AND EXCHANGE COMMISSION

Of all the external constraints affecting corporate governance, the Securities and Exchange Commission is the most formidable. Initially, its thrust was aimed directly at the financial community, and its concern was with corporate affairs associated with raising funds. In the past decade, however, the SEC has assumed a different role; namely, that of a referee in corporate governance matters.

Created by the Securities Exchange Act of 1934, the commission's prime function is to protect the interests of investors and the public in securities transactions. Basically, the SEC engages in two activities—regulation and enforcement. When the SEC investigators feel there is sufficient cause, they can institute civil injunctive actions and administrative proceedings, but only when authorized by the commission. Only then do SEC staff attorneys prosecute. If the situation involves matters of a criminal nature, then it must be referred to the Department of Justice for further investigation and possible prosecution. In some cases the matters might be passed on to other regulatory agencies if the issues are within their purview.

The five SEC commissioners, each appointed for five-year terms, meet three times weekly for approximately three hours. With a staff of 1550 (not much bigger than it was thirty years ago), they head one of the smallest federal agencies. Its organizational structure is made up of six divisions— Corporation Finance, Investment Management Regulations, Enforcement,

Market Regulation, Corporate Regulation, and Opinions and Reviews—and six offices—Chief Counsel, Chief Financial Analyst, International Corporate Finance, Economic Research, Public Information, and Chief Accountant. The architects of the SEC were fully cognizant of political realities, and so there are never more than three commissioners who are members of the same political party. Moreover, the commission reports annually to the Congress, providing a review of how the commission administered the pertinent laws and regulations.

In almost a half century of refereeing the toughest of all games, the corporate contest, the SEC, on the overall, has enjoyed a reputation as one of the government's most effective and admired agencies. Even critics consider it to be dynamic, vigilant, productive, and unbeholden to politicians, the financial community, or our nation's corporate governors.

But despite this quality and an outstanding record of accomplishments, the SEC has its share of setbacks. For example, a few years ago it announced that it was considering requiring major corporations to make public the names of their thirty largest stockholders. The intent was to respond to the charge—increasingly heard—that a relatively small number of financial institutions have effective control of our bigger enterprises. The vested interests immediately took action with a barrage of letters, vehemently objecting to such disclosure. Some objected because such a listing would expose their executives to salespersons, fund and charity solicitors, and even kidnappers and extortionists. No one thought this was a good idea.

Meanwhile, congressional pressures continue to increase for precisely such information. Congress wants to know who actually owns and who controls our corporations—perhaps because of the chauvinistic fear that foreigners are taking over too many of our industries. Another reason is the increasing use of "street names," under which securities firms and banks hold securities for the actual or "beneficial" owners. At present, SEC rules require a corporation to report only the names of owners holding 10 percent or more of the company's shares or 5 percent of a company being acquired. Only these big holders, together with the company's officers, must file when they buy or sell the company's securities.

Out of this Swiss-bank secrecy has come a movement to change the meaning of the term "beneficial." While it now refers to the one who bears the economic risks and the benefits of ownership, "beneficial" redefined would pertain to voting power and control rather than to ownership. This would further compound the regulatory agency's problems, making it more difficult to track down violators of laws and even of "insider" traders. The equitable enforcement of Internal Revenue Service rules would, likewise, be more readily circumvented.

The SEC's forward momentum is both slow and often resented. For example, for many years it was assumed, even by corporate governance authorities, that it was nobody's business what a corporation paid its top executives. In the mid-1950s, *Business Week* began publishing a list of those receiving the highest corporate salaries. Much of this reporting was voluntary. More recently, the SEC began requesting the names and salaries of the top three recipients. While this was a quantum leap forward, it was only partially satisfactory since indirect payments were not included. Seeking more meaningful salary information, the SEC broadened its requirements by asking for total payments made to the top five executives. Perhaps out of sheer pettiness, some companies, which before the ruling voluntarily listed a dozen or more of their high-paid executives, now cut back to the required five. Compounding the confusion even more was the lumping of salaries and bonuses. Previously, on a voluntary basis, about two-thirds of all reporting firms listed salary and bonus separately. Now the SEC began to require that all compensation be reported by type of payment—salary, bonus, and long-term income.

A few years ago, the proxy rules were modified by the SEC, requiring, among other things, disclosures of certain economic and personal relationships between directors and the company and its management. After an initial show of irritation, the corporate respondents adjusted to the new rulings. While the SEC definitely deserves credit for these disclosures, bear in mind that these and related proxy changes were proposed a decade earlier by Campaign GM-style activists.

Even when the SEC is seemingly successful, as in its campaigning for audit committees, it is not free from serious criticism. For instance, the SEC considered passing a law requiring audit committees for the more than 10,000 publicly held companies it oversees. The law failed to materialize because, while the SEC temporized, most of these firms installed such committees voluntarily. Referring to a law proposed by former Senator Frank Church in regard to audit committees and the SEC: "The law says the audit committee 'could' report directly to the Securities and Exchange Commission, which implies something voluntary and almost casual. But since the committee would itself be a creature of federal law with a responsibility to keep an eye on management's obedience to a federal law, that description seems too casual by far. Audit committee members would be charged with a clear duty to represent Washington while sitting in the innermost deliberations of corporate boards. In Stalinist Russia, having agents of the state record acts and utterances of operators in the field was known as the commissar system."[1] *The Wall Street Journal,* while expanding on these fears, made the point that once having established a beachhead within the boardroom, it would conceivably make further inroads. The audit committees "could be charged, for example, with reporting board

[1]"Commissars for Corporations," an editorial, *The Wall Street Journal,* May 12, 1976.

discussions of prospective price increases or anything else deemed anti-social by Congress at any given time."[2]

Coupled with the previous is the SEC's own secrecy, in light of the government's Sunshine Act of 1976. "It's ironic that the commission's meetings are so cryptic, not only because the SEC forces others to make full disclosure, but also because the commission is hardly bashful about formally closing its meetings when it wants to protect confidential information. In one recent 12-month period, it held more closed meetings than any other of the 48 agencies surveyed in a Congressional Research study for Sen. Chiles's subcommittee. In fairness it should be pointed out that the Commission also held more meetings than any other agency and many of the SEC meetings were closed for good reason."[3]

In rebuttal to an SEC spokesperson's contention that the votes are taken in public, and that is all the law requires, " 'It is not sufficient for the purposes of open government to merely have the public witness final agency votes. . . . The whole decision-making process, not merely its results, must be exposed to public scrutiny.' "[4]

In view of the SEC's intrusions, its equivocation, and, particularly, its mistakes, this federal watchdog definitely needs watching. Yet considering its successes in a generally hostile environment, the SEC deserves plaudits for helping corporate governance adapt to the twentieth century while preparing for the next.

THE FEDERAL TRADE COMMISSION

The FTC was established under the Federal Trade Commission Act of 1914, expressly to perform as an independent law enforcement agency. Its prime function is to protect the public against anticompetitive behavior and unfair and deceptive practices. Although the commission has no power to imprison or fine, recent legislation has empowered it to seek civil penalties in federal court, up to $10,000 per day, per violation, if a final cease and desist order or FTC rule is violated. This, plus the procedure of referring cases to the Department of Justice, seems to give this agency adequate muscle.

The FTC is administered by five commissioners, appointed by the President and approved by the Senate. The chairman, designated by the President, makes all the staff appointments and serves as chief executive officer. The members serve staggered seven-year terms.

---

[2]Ibid.
[3]Stan Crock, "Those 'Open' Meetings at the SEC," *The Wall Street Journal,* August 2, 1978, p. 14.
[4]Ibid.

Of the FTC's six offices and three bureaus, the component with the most significance to corporate governance is the Bureau of Competition. While the FTC has many corporate-related interests, including mergers, the interlock issue has been paramount. The Clayton Act specifically forbids direct interlocks, namely, those between competitors in the same industry. But as competition transcends narrow industry lines, the FTC's job becomes more complex. For example, it has ruled that a steel producer and an aluminum maker cannot share the same director; neither can companies producing copper and aluminum use the same director on their boards. There are many comparable examples.

To avoid FTC confrontations, major corporations are extremely cautious in checking prospective directors' backgrounds. Yet, with the trend toward continuing conglomeration, interlocking potentials are multiplied. Even more serious is the increasing threat of congressional action against indirect interlocks. These arise when directors from competing firms sit on a third, presumably neutral board. If interlock through a third party is ever declared illegal, the FTC will have a tremendously increased caseload.

GOVERNMENT-MANDATED DIRECTORS

One of Gilbert and Sullivan's operettas has a line "Let the punishment fit the crime." This makes good common sense. Yet when it comes to "crime in the suites," punishment continues to vary from too light to too heavy. Following the self-confessions and self-incrimination of more than 400 of our leading corporations, during the post-Watergate illegal political contributions and foreign bribery episodes, the Securities and Exchange Commission attempted something new in punishment. For the first time ever, a federal regulatory agency took serious steps to punish boards of directors for their so-called crimes in the suites.

While CEOs and other high-ranking executives occasionally have been indicted and punished for illegal actions, boards of directors, as boards, have escaped indictment. However, when the courts began a concerted program, not so much to punish but rather to reform and rehabilitate the corporate culprits, serious doubts began to rise. In particular, critics began to question the law-enforcing agency's authority to compel corporations to change their life-styles, even their very structures. Serious doubts arose when the SEC began to mandate that the offending corporations change their boards of directors by adding more outsiders. This was an extreme interference, particularly when many of those selected as outside directors for the restructured boards were actually inside directors in their own firms.

Although there had been previous instances of the courts taking a role in restructuring corporate boards, all these cases dealt with bankrupt or, at least, failing firms. Here, the federal agencies were presumably protecting the shareholders by naming new, more capable and trustworthy trustees. In the following illustrations, there is no question of impaired corporate performance; in fact, previous to the accusations, most of the companies had better-than-average profit patterns.

Phillips Petroleum Company, accused of making half-million-dollar domestic political contributions, plus over a million dollars in foreign payments, was forced to change its board composition. Before transgressing, it had been highly successful with its board of eight insiders and three outsiders. Nevertheless, after the accusation, to please the court, it had to change the balance to nine outsiders and eight insiders. Of the new outsiders, three were "activists," proposed by the Center for Law in the Public Interest.

Northrup Corporation, even earlier, was similarly punished by a precedent-setting court order. It had to agree that, henceforth, at least 60 percent of its directors must be genuine outsiders. The executive audit and compensation committees were each ordered to have majorities of outsiders. Ironically, and presumably ignored by the courts, was the uncontestable fact that even before the court order, Northrup's board consisted of six outsiders and three insiders. The charge in this case was that some of these outsiders had close ties to the company.

Lockheed Aircraft Corporation, after signing an SEC consent decree on foreign payments, promised to revamp its board of directors. Even at the time of its transgression, and later its trial, Lockheed—as shown in the 1975 Standard & Poor's Register of Corporations, Directors, and Executives—had only four officer-directors as opposed to thirteen outside directors. But the SEC insisted that Lockheed add still more outsiders. In particular, three "tainted" outsiders on Lockheed's special committee of outside directors investigating the company's foreign business practices had to be replaced. Lockheed agreed to, henceforth, have a two-thirds majority of outsiders on its board.

A special committee, investigating charges of McDonnell Douglas Corporation's involvement in $21 million of questionable payments, recommended more outsiders. "Having an independent outside board of directors probably would have resulted in a more timely disclosure of questionable payments and an earlier implementation of the preventive policies and procedures currently in effect."[5] Again, ironically, there was no reference to the fact that most of the companies punished for FCPA-related misdeeds were even, at the time of their transgressions, overwhelmingly dominated by outside directors.

The list of contrite culprits continues to lengthen. Rapid-American

---

[5]David P. Garino, "Panel Finds More McDonnell Payments, Urges Outside Control of Concern's Board," *The Wall Street Journal*, July 30, 1980, p. 4.

Corporation's Meshulam Riklis, charged with conflict of interest, agreed to add four new independent members to his board. Conglomerator Victor Posner agreed to appoint two new independent directors, satisfactory to the SEC, to six of his major companies. Zale Corporation signed a consent decree which required it to add three new outside directors; Rusco Industries did likewise. Continental Connector Corporation promised to add four independent directors; Kaiser Steel Corporation added one additional director to give outsiders a majority. At the beleaguered Playboy Enterprises (discussed in the section "The Audit Committee"), "a Playboy spokeswoman said that part of the settlement includes adding a new outside director to its board and maintaining its compensation and audit committees as part of its structure."[6]

The list of SEC-ordered board restructuring continues to expand: Invesco Industries, Ormond Industries, Potter Instrument Company, and more than a hundred other companies. A particularly perturbing SEC-mandated boardroom restructuring took place at Mattel, Incorporated, the Los Angeles toymaker turned conglomerate. In a case that dragged on for four years, Ms. Ruth Handler, cofounder of Mattel, and four other company officials were accused of adjusting the company books to maintain the appearance of corporate growth, even though real data did not support the increases. Eventually, Ms. Handler entered a plea of nolo contendere, meaning that while not admitting guilt, she offered no contest to the charges and waived all right to appeal. She explained: " 'I have decided to plead nolo contendere and conclude these many years of seemingly endless investigations and litigations. My life is now totally consumed by a thriving new business providing breast prostheses to mastectomy patients. I don't want to jeopardize it by a lengthy trial.' . . . Ms. Handler's husband, Elliot, with whom she cofounded the company, wasn't mentioned in the indictment."[7]

The really critical part of the Mattel incident was the SEC's demand that a majority of the boardroom seats be filled by individuals with no current ties to the company. On the surface, at least, this looks like a federal usurpation of the rights of stockholders in the guise of protecting them. Yet Mattel needed no protection.

Before its SEC problems, its family-dominated board had embarked on an ambitious diversification program, acquiring Ringling Bros.–Barnum & Bailey Combined Shows, Inc., a film company, a circus theme park in Florida, Ice Follies and Holiday on Ice, Incorporated, and Western Publishing Company. It made financial headlines in 1979 when it tried to acquire

---

[6]"Playboy and Hefner Draw SEC Charges Involving Expenses," *The Wall Street Journal*, August 14, 1980, p. 4.

[7]"Mattel Founder Pleads No Contest to Charges of Falsifying Reports," *The Wall Street Journal*, September 6, 1976, p. 21.

the book publisher Macmillan, Incorporated, for $329 million. More recently, it has embarked on a joint venture with General Instrument Corporation, to offer cable subscribers a twenty-four-hour channel of Intellevision games. Despite strong-arm government interference into its boardroom, Mattel is coping well. It is likely that the company that has provided a generation of young Americans with such pleasures as Barbie dolls and Hot Wheels will survive the bureaucrats.

PUBLIC CORPORATIONS

Federal bailment of prominent U.S. corporations—Chrysler, Penn Central, First Pennsylvania Bank and Trust—has brought up the specter of outright federal boardroom control. As was stressed in the historical introduction, all corporations are creatures of the state; this fact holds for free enterprise, socialist, and communist economies. In our society it is the sovereign, the state, which permits a group of enterprises to band together to seek specified business objectives.

Sometimes the state even joins forces with enterprisers to initiate a venture—our railroads are a good example. As our nation began its great westward-ho expansion in the early nineteenth century, it needed better transportation than that provided for early trailblazers who took off on foot, via packhorse, and by canoe. Since waterways provided the easiest mode of travel, state-owned or state-supervised canals became the rage, but only for a brief period. Inventions, from Nicholas Cugnot's steam-propelled automobile to Richard Trevithick's steam engine railroad prototype, have challenged transport by canal. It was at this critical time that our own states could have become public transport monopolists.

One of the earliest railroading ventures in the United States was later to become the Pennsylvania Railroad. It was chartered by the Pennsylvania Legislature, in 1823, as a state-owned, state-operated enterprise. Interestingly, even in those early years of the Republic, long before the bureaucratic heyday, this pioneering venture ran into typical bureaucratic confusion. Competitively, it was anemic. In its dealings with its employees, it was pliant and prone to featherbedding. (Note that this was more than a century before the era of unionism.) Faced with the inability to make on-the-spot vital decisions, the original venture tottered and eventually fell.

After several attempts, it finally got started again in 1846. Public agencies, particularly the counties of Philadelphia and Allegheny, held most of the stock and exercised their ownership prerogatives by placing directors on the board. Proponents of the all-outside board should note that the first Pennsylvania Railroad board of directors, in March 1847, consisted of thirteen members: nine local merchants, two manufacturers, one banker, and one financier-lawyer. There were no officer-directors; however, one of the original thirteen, though lacking expertise, served temporarily in the capacity of chief executive.

Interestingly, even today's government-controlled Amtrak and Conrail have organizational similarities to the Pennsy, when it was a government-owned and controlled enterprise. For one thing, these boards were, and still are, structured with corporate eyes glued to political ramifications. Presently, at Conrail, only two of the thirteen directors are officers of the railroad; among the others, three are former federal officials, two are there to represent minorities, and three are educators. Amtrak's board distribution is similar except that a United Transportation Union executive is included, as are three members who represent the railroads that own Amtrak stock. The President of the United States designates eight directors; the other two are Amtrak's president and the Secretary of Transportation. A comparable pattern was proposed for the U.S. Synthetic Fuels Corporation.

A decidedly different structure is evident at Tennessee Valley Authority (TVA), where a three-man board runs the multibillion-dollar federally owned energy corporation. The directors (present and past), few of whom have been career energy-industry experts, are nominated by the President and confirmed by the Senate. Presidents Roosevelt and Eisenhower each appointed four; Truman, Kennedy, and Carter, three each; the others, one each.

Although (theoretically) politics is not an issue, and directors' nine-year terms supposedly are a guarantee against the spoils system, several attempts to "pack the board" have been made. In 1975, at a time when the TVA board reflected Republicanism, Tennessee's Governor Blanton, a Democrat, sought to expand it by adding four directors, each appointed by the governors of Tennessee, Alabama, Kentucky, and Mississippi. This proposal fell flat. That same year, another proposal to expand the board to five members, all appointed by the President, also died in committee.

Even though expanding a board does not guarantee improved performance, there are some arguments in favor. For example, during half of 1978 the newly designated Democratic chairman could not function because he simply had no board—the other two members had quit, leaving him without a quorum. Subsequently, even when the board was fully staffed with Carter-appointed Democrats, there was little business as usual because of political in-house feuding.

Being a government agency, and having so small a board of directors, has led to accusations of TVA insensitivity to consumer interests. These charges intensified with rising power costs in the 1980s. In an appeasing gesture, the board set up a TVA citizens action line, providing customers and others with a toll-free number to call and lodge complaints. During the first six months, 7200 calls were recorded.

But hot lines are not substitutes for ineffective boards of directors, as was evidenced in a series of headlining episodes. There was the Sharlene Hirsch case. Ms. Hirsch headed TVA's Community Development Office for a few months in 1979. In that short time she had caused so much aggravation that she was "let go." In typical bureaucratic magnanimity (with TVA consumers' money), she was allowed annual leave time even though she had not worked the required full year. Moreover, she was retained as a consultant at her former $49,000 salary even though she had moved 3000 miles away, to California. This outrageous waste of TVA consumers' dollars aroused considerable criticism in the Tennessee Valley. This fiasco should have qualified TVA for Senator Proxmire's famous "Golden Fleece Award."

Even before the Hirsch reverberations had ceased, TVA's board manifested extremely poor judgment in recommending massive pay raises of $35,000 for a dozen or more key executives who had already reached the federal pay limit. The underlying logic was that comparable jobs in private industry paid considerably more than the low-ceiling federal posts. TVA's impolitic action antagonized politicians—even long-time TVA friends—and TVA's board retreated ignominiously. Top pay raises of $5000 were authorized.

TVA again displayed gross boardroom misdirection. Its economists issued a formal report recommending that TVA retreat from its ambitious nuclear facility building program. Presumably, the economists had suddenly concluded that coal would be a cheaper energy source and much of the current construction of nuclear facilities was a waste. The report recommended cessation of construction on three plants. Note that a conversion to coal would cost TVA's consumers billions of dollars more.

In this era of strategic long-range planning, it is difficult to believe that a multibillion-dollar federal agency could commit so many blunders. How much of this blame could be placed on TVA's "troika" is a matter of conjecture.

A real danger of having any corporation under federal aegis is that its board can too easily become a refuge for retired or defeated politicians and other party faithful. TVA's recent experience corroborates this. According to a high-ranking TVA executive: "Packing it up with a bunch of losing politicians is not going to help much. I hope TVA doesn't become the dumping ground for losers."[8]

A fate even worse than packing the board with phased-out politicians would be packing it with current bureaucrats. When Reagan replaced seven Carter appointees to the board of the National Consumer Cooperative Bank, all seven new members held assistant or deputy posts in federal agencies. The board, in addition, includes six representatives of cooperatives, one

---

[8]John Moulton, "Efforts to Expand TVA Board Gather Steam Despite History of Rejections," *Knoxville (Tenn.) News-Sentinel,* March 8, 1981, p. A-4.

from small business, and the head of the National Credit Union Administration. The government is entitled to majority representation because currently it holds the majority stock interest in the bank. However, when stock purchases will eventually be increased by cooperatives, the board will switch toward the private sector.

The travesty of having political appointees serve as directors of a major industrial enterprise was dramatically illustrated at General Aniline and Film Corporation. In 1942, with the United States at war with Germany, the Secretary of the Treasury (as authorized by Executive Order 8389) invoked the Trading with the Enemy Act. It was determined that 459,488 Common A and 2,050,000 Common B shares of General Aniline stock were the property of nationals of an enemy nation, and so were taken over by the U.S. government. It was not until March 1965 that the U.S. government divested itself of this stock. Having been converted into 11,166,438 new shares, it was sold on the open market for almost $330 million. During its confiscation, GAF's board became a political football—in a period of twenty-three years it had eight chief executives and more than sixty directors. Tenures averaged about five years, depending on a director's political clout and connections.

There is considerably more to this lamentable corporate governance episode. In a comparison with two chemical companies—Dow and Monsanto—neither much bigger than GAF in 1942, Table 6-1 shows the difference between free enterprise and federal control.

Perhaps we can accept *Fortune's* brief explanation for the first twenty years of General Aniline's poor performance, made as it was being returned by the government to public ownership: "The board members were often ill-acquainted with the chemical industry, and tended to feel that conserving the assets the Attorney General had temporarily entrusted to them was their main responsibility. Back in 1953, President Jack Frye confessed to a senatorial committee, 'One of the problems of this company is that, due to the ownership situation, the management, the board of directors, and all

TABLE 6-1
PERFORMANCE OF THREE CHEMICAL COMPANIES, 1942 and 1980

	1942			1980		
	Sales, $ millions	Net income, $ millions	No. of employees	Sales, $ millions	Net income, $ millions	No. of employees
GAF	43	4	8,200	1,230	−(234)	13,000
Dow	78	9	14,000	10,600	805	56,800
Monsanto	69	5	18,600	6,600	149	61,800

concerned are extremely cautious about making expenditures. In trying not to make mistakes, they actually move more slowly than do their competitors.' ''[9]

That was twenty years ago. Today's continuing lackadaisical performance, especially the $234 million loss recorded in 1980, cannot be so easily rationalized. Perhaps, as Prime Minister Margaret Thatcher experienced, when she tried to revivify a British economy seriously ailing from prolonged Labour Party nationalization, complete rehabilitation does not come easily.

Corporations, unlike nations, can take expedient measures when it comes to lopping off an ailing "province." One remedy, divestiture, is increasingly used by overexpanded or ailing corporate giants. It is precisely what GAF Corporation attempted almost twenty years after it regained its autonomy from government control. In a single swing of the corporate cleaver, GAF's long-tenured chairman chopped off eight different businesses, thus reducing the corporation to its two best performing endeavors— roofing products and specialty chemicals. By using the $233 million gained from selling these components, GAF not only reduced its debt to $125 million, but became a smaller and more financially stable firm.[10]

By 1982 GAF had effected most of its retrenchment. Its president, nevertheless, resigned because of a policy disagreement with the chairman-chief executive. This led to the formation of an Office of the Chairman, consisting of seven key operations executives. This was a switch since previously production and marketing technicians did not have a prominent part in running the company.

Much of GAF's previous ordeal was summed up in one financial analyst's observation that somewhere, somehow, GAF caught a bad case of the "blahs." Even its least apperceptive executives recognized that GAF had remained a static, moribund company in a rapidly changing field. Despite its massive modifications in product mix and asset deployment, GAF will suffer a relapse of the "blahs" if it fails to cure the cause, namely, an unimaginative, overcautious, inadequate board of directors.

FOREIGN CORRUPT PRACTICES ACT

Judeo-Christians have a readily identifiable norm for morality measurement —the Ten Commandments. Business, to the contrary, does not have a single identifiable composite code, either carved in stone or engraved on a headquarter's plaque. Instead, there are statutes, ordinances, laws, acts, rules, edicts, and a near-infinite sequence of "thou shalt nots." Some of this profusion follows from the multiplicity of rule makers. In addition to

---

[9]Irwin Ross, "General Aniline Goes Private," *Fortune,* September 1963, p. 125.
[10]*Business Week,* January 22, 1979, p. 68.

executive orders, judicial pronouncements, and congressional acts, we have fifty zealous—and jealous—state sovereignties, plus counties, municipalities, and special bodies legislating business controls. This is confusing, to say the least. Not only do the majority of businesspeople know how not to break the law; it is next to impossible to know how to obey it.

One of the most confusing of recent federal mandates was Public Law 95-213, bearing the titles Foreign Corrupt Practices Act of 1977 (FCPA) and Domestic and Foreign Investment Improved Disclosure Act of 1977, signed by President Carter December 19, 1977. As so many corporations discovered subsequently, this was no Christmas package.

The FCPA had a five-year period of gestation: it was conceived when the Watergate Special Prosecutor's Office discovered that a large number of U.S. corporations had made illegal campaign contributions during the 1972 presidential campaign. During the initial investigation, it was also discovered that some corporations had made questionable payments to foreign officials, including political candidates.

Several federal agencies joined in the witch hunt, but the lead was taken by the Securities and Exchange Commission. The Securities Act of 1933 and the Securities Exchange Act of 1934 gave the SEC broad authority to determine what matters must be disclosed to investors. This gave rise to the classic concept of "materiality." Basically, what mattered to the investor was profits, assets, and similar quantifiable items. The SEC now stretched materiality to encompass the qualitative, so that, for example, the character and consequence of a payment, not its size, differentiated its materiality from the immaterial.

To expedite identification of culprits, the SEC issued a sort of amnesty appeal: it would go easy on self-incriminators. "By the end of 1976 approximately 250 corporations had disclosed illegal or questionable payments, and the commission had brought enforcement actions against 19 corporations which had allegedly misstated or omitted material information."[11] With such a manifest need, Congress passed Public Law 95-213.

The FCPA specifically prohibits U.S. companies from making payments to foreign government officials or political parties in order to win contracts. A second feature of the Act mandates strict records and accounting standards. The internal accounting system must provide reasonable assurances that management is in control of a corporation's operations and assets.

The stringent penalties imposable under the FCPA—fines up to $1 million and jail sentences up to five years—understandably slowed to a halt all forms of under-the-table, "grease," baksheesh, and similar international tipping. Most analysts concluded this was detrimental to our foreign trading

---

[11]"A Backdrop to the Act," *Directors and Boards,* Fall 1979, p. 47.

since many countries not only allow but require facilitating payments. " 'The public servants here are not paid enough to live on,' says an American businessman in Manila. 'Everyone denies making bribes or greasing palms, but it is a way of life here.' In Zaire, telephone operators must be paid privately to secure overseas lines. In Nigeria advance bookings must be 'reconfirmed' with the receptionist, and in much of Southeast Asia traffic cops must be tipped on the spot to allow a left turn."[12]

Even though certain kinds of payments for expediting business actually are permissible under American law, the FCPA made most American companies baksheesh-shy. Few were as outspoken and detailed in their facilitation-payment attitude as the Honolulu-based Castle & Cooke, Incorporated: " 'You've got a banana boat that comes in at 2 or 3 in the morning with its perishable cargo,' says a spokesperson. 'Every hour means something, so you must get a customs official out of bed. You are not going to be very successful unless you make it worth his while to come down.' C&C's budget for facilitating payments typically exceeds $200,000 a year."[13]

The presumed hardship and loss of business led to a General Accounting Office (GAO) study, published in March 1981. The survey studied 250 *Fortune*-listed industrial companies and found that 98 percent of the respondents had, in the light of the Act, reviewed their corporate policies, while 60 percent had made changes in their policies. Furthermore, 70 percent believed the Act effectively reduced questionable foreign payments by U.S. companies, and more than 60 percent perceived that, all other conditions being equal, American firms could not successfully compete against foreign companies that were paying bribes.

A redeeming feature in our system is that even when a bad or questionable law is enacted, aggrieved citizens can work for its repeal. The Eighteenth Amendment (Prohibition) and its enforcement authorization—the Volstead Act—were the law of the land for fourteen years; yet it was repealed when a majority of citizens felt otherwise. On March 12, 1981, shortly after the GAO study was made public, Senator John Chafee and thirteen cosponsors introduced a bill in the Senate (S708) to amend the FCPA. Senator Chafee's bill sought to temper the "materiality" complexities by using the same definition of the term "material" as is given in generally accepted accounting principles (GAAP). This linkage with GAAP provides meaningful norms and makes compliance less difficult. The bill also restates the term "in reasonable detail" by equating costs and benefits as viewed by prudent individuals.

A major improvement is the Chafee bill's scienter requirement which imposes liability only for knowing violations. In the accounting sector, this

---

[12]"Misinterpreting the Antibribery Law," *Business Week*, September 3, 1979, p. 150.
[13]Ibid.

means knowingly falsifying records, knowingly attempting to circumvent the accounting system, and knowingly maintaining an inadequate system. Neither the corporation nor its officers are to be held liable for inadvertent violations.

On the more prominent side of the FCPA, namely, payments to foreign officials, the Chafee bill, likewise, makes such payments illegal only if they are in violation of the recipient's duty as a public official. "The Chafee bill makes it clear that if the country in which the official operates does not consider this payment illegal, then it is not a violation of the Act to make the payment."[14] The bill specifically sanctions payments customarily made to facilitate or expedite performance of official duties, those considered normal marketing expenses, and small sums as tokens of esteem or appreciation. In essence, we are now removing ourselves as missionaries of the world, no longer seeking to evangelize according to our own gospel. When in Rome, we will do as the Romans do.

In December 1980, *Fortune* conducted a survey on crime in the executive suites during the 1970s. It canvassed 1043 companies which, at some point, have appeared on its listing of the largest corporations, and found that 117, or 11 percent, of the companies were either convicted on federal criminal charges or in consent decrees. Many of the defendants pleaded nolo contendere, which is tantamount to pleading guilty. The degree of corporate corruption was based on five categories of crime, and some companies were multiple offenders; consequently, 117 firms had "163 separate offenses: 98 antitrust violations; 28 cases of kickbacks, bribery, or illegal rebates; 21 instances of illegal political contributions; 11 cases of fraud; 5 cases of tax evasion."[15]

Fortune listed the 117 companies, ranking them from Allied Chemical to Zale, the year and nature of the crime, and the court verdict. "Fifty executives from 15 companies went to jail in various of these cases. Fines were levied on most of the convicted companies but aren't listed unless they come to $500,000 or more. Minor cases of corruption far down the chain of command have been excluded."[16] There were actually thirteen fines in excess of $500,000, ranging up to a $4 million fine for illegal payments to customers by R. J. Reynolds Industries.

While the 11 percent crime rate among our giant corporations indicates something, our interpretation is limited because, over the ten-year-period, this averages out to only a bit more than 1 percent. Also, we have no way of knowing if the rate is rising. The 117-company sample, with 188 citations,

[14]Elliot M. Schnitzer, "Foreign Corrupt Practices Act," National Association of Corporate Directors, Board Practices Monograph No. 14, April 1981.
[15]Irwin Ross, "How Lawless Are Big Companies?" *Fortune*, December 1, 1980, p. 57.
[16]Ibid., p. 58.

might just be the tip of the iceberg—a lot of crime is never detected or brought to justice. Not to justify corporate crime, but is its rate any higher than the crime rate in any of our metropolitan areas? And how do corporate transgressions compare with the ordinary individual's record on breaking the Ten Commandments?

ILLUSTRATION: Lockheed's Peanuts

Without doubt, the most flagellated corporation during the post-Watergate industrial inquisition was Lockheed Aircraft, the nation's largest defense contractor. It was prominent among several hundred major firms accused of foreign payoffs and other assorted illegal deeds. In August 1975, after months of denials, Lockheed finally conceded publicly that, over the previous five years, it had paid at least $22 million to individuals and political organizations overseas. In turn, these payoffs had helped win lucrative contracts—in Japan, the Netherlands, West Germany, and a half dozen other countries.

One of the "punishments" for the transgressions was the requirement that four more outside directors be added to Lockheed's board, thus giving the outsiders a ten to seven majority. Ironically, even during the payoff years, Lockheed had a six-member outsider contingent, which did nothing to detect and denounce the wrongdoing. It was naive to assume that adding four or even a dozen more outsiders would geometrically compound the board's integrity and apperception. It was neither a company officer nor an outside director, but rather Lockheed's auditors, Arthur Young and Company, who first discovered something was wrong. They had detected excessively large foreign payments to individuals. The outside directors composing Lockheed's Audit Committee were not perturbed at the extraordinary large commissions being paid abroad. " 'We didn't realize the severity of the problem until the Arthur Young people started stumbling across these things,' says one outside director. 'We were all taken by surprise.' "[17]

Seven months after Lockheed's misconduct was publicly revealed, a special investigatory committee of four directors, unaffiliated with the company, was set up. Of course, there was criticism of the board of directors concerning the lag in setting up this special review committee. One rather weak rationalization came from an outside director: " 'We've been talking about such a committee for several months, but we've held off forming one because we felt that as one component of a consent decree with the SEC, we'd probably have to form such a group under SEC guidelines.' "[18]

Whether Lockheed's special review committee of outside directors added anything of value to the investigation is debatable. Yet the directors spent fourteen months and $4 million investigating their own company. "Their report issued in May

[17]Stephen J. Sansweet, "Embattled Executives of Aerospace Concern to Face the Directors," *The Wall Street Journal,* February 13, 1976, p. 12.
[18]Ibid.

protected the corporation by concentrating on the causes of improprieties rather than revealing what Its chairman J. Wilson Newman calls 'the raisins in the pudding'— who got paid off. As the report states, 'the most conclusive reason for not naming payoff recipients abroad is the grave damage this might do to Lockheed.' ''[19]

Some looked upon the special review committee's findings as a not-so-subtle whitewash. The $4 million spent to have this committee come up with such an inconsequential finding was probably more than the total payoffs in some of the countries involved. In addition, both prime culprits, Chairman Daniel J. Haughton and Vice Chairman A. Carl Kotchian, were terminated but then rehired, and given ten-year contracts as senior advisers. Each will receive—over the ten years—pay totaling $750,000. To compound the travesty, the new CEO, Robert Haack, an investment banker and a former president of the New York Stock Exchange, was designated chairman. Haack had been a longtime outside director on Lockheed's board. Naturally, this raises serious questions as to propriety—while his credentials were commendable, his intimate participation on Lockheed's board tainted him with at least guilt by association.

But the really big uproar over Lockheed's misdeeds did not come from here at home, but from Japan. Marubeni Corporation, the highly successful and aggressive Japanese trading company, was named as a party to Lockheed's scandal. The early Lockheed disclosures indicated that "Marubeni was instrumental in distributing up to $2.1 million in bribes to Japanese government officials to influence plane purchases. 'We deny almost everything,' insists Hideyuki Kobayashi, assistant public relations chief at Marubeni's Tokyo headquarters. 'People want us to name the government officials who got the money but we don't know. We are in a most awkward position because we cannot prove we are innocent.' ''[20] But Marubeni paid a steeper price than did Lockheed: it "lost its chairman and two executive directors who admitted carelessness in signing receipts for 'peanuts,' 'units,' and 'pieces'— words that apparently were codes for bribery payments in blocks of 1 million yen."[21]

Lamentably, Marubeni lost face. It was boycotted by more than forty local jurisdictions then under socialist party control, including Tokyo, Yokohama, and Kobe. These jurdisdictions refused to do business with Marubeni on ethical grounds. "The children of Marubeni's 8000 employees have been jeered by schoolmates because their fathers work for 'the bad, bad company'. . . . The demoralizing form of social ostracism suffered by Marubeni employees and their families is part of what one Tokyo newspaper calls the 'peanuts' elegy. Marubeni was the company accused of handing out the 'peanuts'—local slang for bribery packets—in Japan's Lockheed scandal. Anybody connected with the disgraced corporation is subject to a kind of shame by association."[22]

The Japanese reaction was more than a show of morality, as we understand it. The melding of Japanese workers and their employers is so close that an insult to the corporation is an equally deep hurt to its employees. "As the furor over Marubeni's

[19]Louis Kraar, "How Lockheed Got Back Its Wings," *Fortune,* October 1977, p. 210.
[20]"An Aftershock of the Lockheed Affair," *Business Week,* April 12, 1976, p. 43.
[21]Ibid.
[22]"Shame by Association," *Time,* March 22, 1976, p. 26.

role in the Lockheed scandal has intensified, the social status of its employees has plummeted. Many employees complain that their families are being shunned or ridiculed because they work for Marubeni. One employee said that his child was nicknamed 'Lockheed' by his schoolmates. . . . Some wives of Marubeni workers have taken to shopping at night to avoid the cold stares of neighbors. Perhaps most insulting of all, Tokyo's Crown Record Company is trying to profit from Marubeni's misfortune. Next month it will release a pop-rock single that parodies the Lockheed payoff. Title: *Peanut Song.*"[23]

ILLUSTRATION: Exxon and Esso Italiana

Although Exxon is remembered as Standard Oil Company of New Jersey, it was once popularly known as Esso—actually, for much of its first hundred years. As John D. Rockefeller's creation, it became one of our biggest turn-of-the-century trusts, withstanding vehement and persistent populist-muckraker attacks and the Sherman Antitrust Act of 1890. Then in 1911—more than twenty years after monopolistic trusts were officially declared illegal—the Supreme Court, in the first big test of the Sherman Act, ordered Standard Oil to be dismembered. The huge oil trust of $400 million in assets was then fragmented into thirty-three separate companies. Interestingly, what was too big and monopolistic in 1911 would be classified today as just another moderate-size firm. Note that within seventy years after the Court ordered Standard Oil's dismemberment, there are now almost 500 industrial firms with assets exceeding $400 million. Of the cloned and cleaved Standard Oil offspring, the six most successful—Exxon, Mobil, Standard Oil (California), Standard Oil (Indiana), Atlantic Richfield, and Standard Oil (Ohio)—had 1980 sales approaching $300 billion and assets totaling $160 billion. This means that their combined assets are more than 400 times the size of their dismembered forefather. Exxon is the most colossal of the six petroleum colossi; its assets (in 1980), exceeding $60 billion, continue to rise rapidly.

For almost seventy years after the Sherman Antitrust action, Exxon hewed to the straight and narrow, like a converted sinner, firmly resolved never to relapse into oligopoly, restraint of trade, or any other corporate transgression. Then, in 1975, in the swell of the post-Watergate corporate confessions of bribery and illegal political contributions, Exxon admitted an indiscretion. With a public mea culpa, the corporation provided the charges and testimony against itself. Over a ten-year period, Exxon made nearly $30 million in authorized secret political contributions in Italy. In addition, the company states that its subsidiary, Esso Italiana, disbursed another $30 million in unauthorized payments. Even though corporate political contributions were legal under Italian law, there were allegations that some of the unauthorized payments were actually bribes, given for specific government favors. Even some of the authorized payments were questionable.

Howard Kauffmann, former president of Esso Europe and subsequently president of the parent, Exxon, was confronted with the issue of whether to approve a $700,000 "contribution" in Italy—some alleged it was an outright bribe to help

[23]Ibid.

settle a $30 million Italian tax claim against Esso Italiana. Exxon felt there was no basis for this tax claim. However, Esso Italiana's managing director, presumably, had already agreed to make the "contribution." Failing to go through with the deal probably would have led to political recrimination. "One familiar with the case says that 'there was a commitment to the highest levels of the Italian government, and unless he approved the payment, that company (Esso Italiana) would have been in deep yogurt. You know you can really foul up a company if a host government decides to be unfriendly—they can tie up your shipping, crippling operations.'"[24] While Esso Europe's president, Kauffmann, was outraged at such blackmail and disagreed vehemently, he nevertheless approved the sum.

Note that no one connected with the case actually called it bribery. While U.S. legislation specifically outlaws bribery, it does not consider payments made to settle tax disputes as being illegal. Nevertheless, the Securities and Exchange Commission sued Exxon, alleging bribery and violations of security laws. Exxon settled without admitting or denying the charges.

Earlier, Exxon had set up a three-member committee on litigation to investigate the charges. The committee of outside directors rejected the notion of bribery. It also exonerated Kauffmann on a related charge that he had been negligent in failing to block the questionable $700,000. Nevertheless, Kauffmann's judgment was questioned, and several stockholder suits were filed, charging that his negligence had cost the company $700,000. The courts, however, accepted the report of the committee on litigation and dismissed the stockholders' suits. The disappointed parties charged the outside-director committee with being far too charitable with Kauffmann and called their report a whitewash. It was pointed out that the report had omitted many relevant facts; for example, nowhere in the report are the sums in question stated. The only way interested parties can get an index to these amounts is through SEC documents.

Because of Exxon's seven-decade, relatively clean slate, and because there were no flagrant violations, "Even certain government investigators who tend to be tough on corporate executives, believe that Mr. Kauffmann made his decision in good faith. 'First of all you have to remember that this was 1971, before Watergate and before overseas payments had become a big issue,' one investigator says. 'It was before people had become sensitive to these kinds of issues.'

"As to Mr. Kauffmann, this investigator adds, 'His instincts were good. He was caught in a difficult position. His response was, 'Okay, make this one last payment, but damn it, don't make any more.'"[25]

ILLUSTRATION: Textron

A number of interesting cases illustrate the uncertainties, confusions, and even the contradictions associated with FCPA objectives. The Textron episode is one of the more intriguing, particularly since it involved Textron's chairman, president, and

[24]William Carley, "To Pay or Not to Pay. How Exxon Official Decided on a Donation," *The Wall Street Journal,* July 14, 1978, p. 27.
[25]Ibid.

CEO, William Miller, subsequently named chairman of the Federal Reserve Board and then U.S. Secretary of the Treasury. In the hearings before the U.S. Senate Committee on Banking, Housing, and Urban Affairs, in connection with Miller's nomination to the top Treasury post, a series of "push money" charges were made, including an alleged $2.9 million payment to an Iranian general—in effect, a bribe. There were other equally serious charges emanating from the Securities and Exchange Commission's private investigation of Textron, to determine whether Textron had violated certain sections of the Securities Exchange Act of 1934. The SEC subpoenaed certain Textron documents and took testimony from past and present employees. It charged Textron with concealing $5.4 million of questionable foreign payments and implied that the transactions were known at the highest levels of the company's management. Textron, in its defense, set up a Special Committee of outside directors to conduct an independent study. The committee members were paid sums comparable to consultant fees for these special services.

Two years after the charges, the SEC made a settlement: Textron agreed to the civil complaint without admitting or denying the allegations of the complaint. Textron also consented to the entry of a permanent injunction, which enjoins violation of federal securities laws by failing to disclose material information concerning payments—directly or indirectly—to or for the benefit of any foreign government official or employee in connection with obtaining or retaining business. At this point, Textron terminated its Special Committee, but the SEC still continued its investigation. Now, however, the SEC wanted to know if there was any evidence of perjury or obstruction of justice in connection with the investigations and earlier congressional hearings.

Subsequently, in lengthy testimony before the Senate Banking Committee, William Miller, later to become Secretary of the Treasury, admitted he was not properly vigilant as head of Textron. " 'I could have and should have done much more to be sure that Textron's policy on standards of conduct and ethics was widely understood and that more compliance checks were made.' Furthermore, he said, he should have recommended a 'special Textron investigation' at the time that improper payments began to surface at other U.S. corporations."[26]

When several senators talked about naming a special prosecutor to continue the investigation, "Mr. Miller wondered aloud whether two years of government investigation of Textron's affairs weren't enough. 'Am I ever to be free?' he asked. . . . 'My statements were made in good faith.' . . . He said it was correct and reasonable for him to say that he didn't know of any improper payments. 'But of course the investigations have disclosed that there were improper payments. It turned out that I was incorrect.' "[27]

FEDERAL CHARTERING

Although the Civil War ended the controversy over federal or states' rights, it did not settle all the issues. Business incorporation is one of them. For

[26]"Miller Says He Wasn't Vigilant Enough Regarding Textron's Improper Payments," *The Wall Street Journal*, February 11, 1980, p. 7.
[27]Ibid.

example, there is the "Delaware syndrome," the inordinate competition among a number of our states to attract incorporating enterprises. Delaware's hard sell (discussed in "Board Incorporation") basically consists of setting minimal requirements along with a highly conducive speed factor— incorporation can be completed in less than a day, in fact, in about fifteen minutes if the participants are in a hurry. Delaware is also unique in that its corporation law states that a board of directors shall consist of *one* or more members.

But it is not Delaware's accommodation alone that raises the hackles of good corporate governance proponents. Some contend that in our society the corporation plays too vital a role to be manipulated for individual state benefits. Consequently, they and proponents of the Corporate Democracy Acts argue for federal chartering. Since 1976, Ralph Nader, through his Corporate Accountability Research Group (CARG), has periodically pushed for this reform. If or when the federal government does take over the corporate chartering function, it will be because the fifty states could not agree on reasonable standardization in fees, format, function, and policing. It is claimed that federal chartering would have a greater impact on the conduct of enterprises and businesspeople than the New Deal's reforms of the 1930s.

The proposed need for chartering reforms was tempered, in the early 1980s, by the attitude of the Supreme Court. According to Harvey L. Pitts, former general counsel for the Securities and Exchange Commission, "The Supreme Court is shifting the question of directors' responsibilities to the state courts. He attributes this shift to the Supreme Court's belief that federal law should be applied cautiously in overriding the good faith business judgment guideline set for outside directors."[28] This change of attitude in our highest tribunal makes it more difficult for private individual plaintiffs to maintain lawsuits under the antifraud provisions of the federal securities laws. Some interpret this changing sentiment as a resurgence of states' rights. Others believe the Supreme Court is telling us it presently lacks authorization to interfere. If the public really wants responsible court-enforced overviewing of corporations, then Congress must enact more stringent federal securities laws—this sets up the case for federal chartering.

However, opponents point out that the move for federal "leveling" of chartering requirements could discourage incorporating in the lowest-cost-combination location. This has been demonstrated in studies by the Managerial Economics Research Center, University of Rochester, which show that in the past half century most reincorporations have resulted in higher prices for the stock of the firm that moves. Critics also claim that neither the financial community nor the shareholders have evidenced any

[28]*The Corporate Director Newsletter*, National Association of Corporate Directors, June 1981, p. 1.

real need for a broad federal chartering law. They argue that the corporate system works despite Delaware, Nevada, New Jersey, and other states providing "pirate sanctuaries."

But occasionally even Delaware is to be complimented. For example, in the past several years, Delaware's Supreme Court has handed down a number of decisions that protect minority stockholders from "squeeze-outs." The squeeze-out tactic consists in a public company going private by buying out minority shareholders at grossly unfair prices. The Delaware Court, in just a few decisions, is credited with having done more in this area than the Securities and Exchange Commission, after many years of talk, threat, and backing away.

Other states have moved with speed and decisiveness on other problems. In a ten-year period, virtually all the states enacted laws extending the time that must elapse before a takeover is consummated. These individual state actions were prompted by the so-called Saturday night special, a blitzkrieg takeover. On this and many other issues, federal agencies simply take their time—a lot of time.

There is also a growing compromise group, willing to accept some form of federal minimum standards law. This would establish criteria for internal corporate conduct. Such an approach would provide the area of corporate governance with a "Taft-Hartley Act" for corporations. Although narrower in scope than the chartering concept, a federal minimum standards law would go beyond it in one key way—it would embrace far more companies. Nader suggests concentrating the proposed reforms on the top 700 macro-corporations. But even corporate critics must agree that, in spite of the bribery and illegal contributions accusations of the late 1970s, our biggest corporations have remained overwhelmingly law-abiding and most highly respected. They have to be—they have tremendous investments in public acceptance and goodwill. Conversely, it is among the smaller, less-known, unobtrusive companies that we find the highest percentage of questionable practices.

Minimum standards, favored by a number of key legislators and the chairman of the Federal Trade Commission, would place the burden of affirmative actions on corporate directors to protect the interests of the shareholders and the public. It would strengthen the principle of division of power, in particular, giving greater shareholder participation in corporate decision making. Shareholders would have the right to vote on all company transactions involving an amount over a certain percentage of the corporation's assets. Among the other and more radical changes, shareholders would be given the right to attend board meetings to ask questions or present grievances. Any investor who discovered corporate violations would be empowered to bring derivative lawsuits against the directors without risk of financial loss.

While neither federal minimum standards nor federal chartering is about to become a certainty, it is very likely that within this generation, one of these reforms will be enacted. Meanwhile, the corporate citizen has received ample warning.

MODEL BUSINESS CORPORATION ACT

The American Bar Association's Model Business Corporation Act has been either adopted or adapted by a majority of states to serve as a legal corporate governance framework. As its title indicates, it is a model and in itself has no legal force. Even though its real impact comes from the specific legislation of the adopting states, and there is considerable variance, the Model Act does serve to anchor standards. Moreover, the Act is periodically modified to fit current needs.

In its 1974 Model Act revision, the ABA's Committee on Corporate Laws set forth the basic requirement that "A director shall perform his duties as a director, including duties as a member of any committee of the board upon which he may serve, in good faith, in a manner he reasonably believes to be in the best interests of the corporation, and with such care as an ordinarily prudent person in a like position would use under similar circumstances."[29]

This statement and other expressions in the Model Act emphasize the concept of good faith reflected in both the "business judgment rule" and the "personal affairs rule." In particular, the Act considers the duty of care and the duty of loyalty. The former stresses the requirements of diligence and prudence. For example, while directors may rely upon officers, employees, counsel, accountants, and board committees, most statutes embodying the Model Act stress that every director must make reasonable inquiries when the need arises.

The duty of loyalty implies that "in essence, a corporate director declares his allegiance to a corporate enterprise and acknowledges that the best interest of the corporation and its shareholders must prevail over any individual interests. A director must not use a corporate position to make a personal profit or gain other personal advantage."[30] This is a clear caution against conflicts of interest, real or potential, and the use of inside information.

Of the Model Act's several sections, the following serve most directly as constraints upon corporate governance:

Section 5: Indemnification of Officers and Directors
Section 35: Boards of Directors

---

[29]William E. Knepper, *Liability of Corporate Officers and Directors*, 3d ed. (Indianapolis: Allen Smith Company, 1978), p. 16.
[30]"Legal Briefs for Directors," *Director's Monthly*, National Association of Corporate Directors, September 1980, vol. 4, no. 8, p. 6.

Section 40: Quorum of Directors
Section 41: Director Conflict of Interest
Section 42: Executive and Other Committees
Section 48: Liabilities of Directors

The most frequently quoted part of the Model Act is Section 35, which stresses the purpose and powers of the board. It begins with the statement that "all corporate powers shall be exercised by or under authority of, and the business and affairs of a corporation shall be managed under the direction of a board of directors except as may be otherwise provided in this Act or the articles of incorporation."[31]

Some states still use the earlier form of Section 35, which more forcefully states that the business and affairs of the corporation shall be managed and controlled by the board of directors. As stated in Chapter 2, the rephrasing of the board mandate, now meaning *to be managed under the direction of the board,* implies a great deal more than semantics.

Other sections of the Model Act are addressed to specific issues. For example, Section 42, which covers committees of the board, warns that a director, presently not serving on a given board committee, should not assume he or she is exonerated from actions of that committee. *All* directors are presumed to be fully informed of *all* committee doings and are equally liable. While this caution will most likely be tested in the courts, it does seem clear that directors simply cannot slough off ultimate responsibility by delegating authority to committees.

The Model Act is the fruition of the American Bar Association's Committee on Corporate Laws, which continues to make studies and recommendations on refinements. Its Subcommittee on Functions and Responsibilities of Directors is unusually productive—its pamphlet "The Overview Committees of the Board of Directors" (1980) set the tone for the overview committee and independent directors.

A year earlier, *The Corporate Directors' Guidebook* suggested a model for the governance of a publicly owned business corporation. The ABA's paramount recommendation, in addition to the establishing of audit, compensation, and nominating committees, was the exhortation that committee members be free from personal involvement or self-interest in all matters that might come under consideration.

The American Bar Association's endeavors are commendable. Even if motivated by self-interest it is precisely this kind of *enlightened* self-interest that reduces the need for bureaucratic interference in a corporate self-governance mechanism.

---

[31]Knepper, op. cit., p. 703.

CORPORATE DEMOCRACY ACT

The Corporate Democracy Act of 1980 was the most recent in a series of proposed wholesale legislative actions to curb alleged corporate governance abuses. The Senate Subcommittee on Citizens' and Shareholders' Rights and Remedies, chaired by Senator Howard Metzenbaum, held extensive hearings and then drafted the Act. In that period, Senator Metzenbaum became the articulate voice for liberalizing shareholders' rights and participation, insisting forcefully on much more disclosure by corporations. In a sense, the senator was emulating the populist leadership exercised by two late congressmen, Wright Patman (Texas) and Emanuel Celler (New York).

The proposed act consisted of seven titles:

Title I: Directors and Shareholders
Title II: Corporate Disclosure
Title III: Community Impact Analysis
Title IV: Constitutional Rights of Employees
Title V: Interlocking Directorates
Title VI: Criminal and Civil Sanctions
Title VII: Jurisdiction and Penalties

"At the heart of the proposed legislation is a precedent-setting provision for citizens who have been injured by the non-performance of a standard to go to court. This provision would open federal courts directly to shareholders and other so-called stakeholders, among them consumers and employees."[32]

While all seven titles have pertinence, since they would reshape corporate governance, Title I, "Directors and Shareholders," sets the scenario for the entire Act. For example, Title I, Section 101, provided that a majority of the board of directors must be "independent"—basically the same as proposed by the SEC. Section 102 recommends that at least nine board members shall have special responsibilities to oversee. The stress on responsibilities, which are spelled out, simply means this would be a constituency board. Section 103 forbids persons serving on more than two boards of directors. Section 104 mandates independent audit and compensation committees.

The remaining titles provide for public policy and law compliance committees, for cumulative voting, and for certifying that the lawyers and auditors—both internal and external—have been instructed to report illegal or probable illegal actions to the board. Specifically, each of the six titles

---

[32]*Director's Monthly,* National Association of Corporate Directors, January/February 1980, vol. 4, nos. 1 and 2, p. 6.

spells out, in reasonable detail, additional corporate governance constraints. In Title II, for example, it is emphasized that the disclosures are not meant to be a "fishing for data expedition." The objective is a corporate social self-audit. Title V is also quite significant because its Section 501 would amend Section 8 of the Clayton Act. It would forbid any person, who is a director or officer of any corporation under the jurisdiction of the Corporate Democracy Act, to be concurrently a director or officer of more than two corporations under the Act.

Passage of any legislation comparable to Senator Metzenbaum's proposal is probably a few years away. It is discussed here because it, or subsequent legislation modeled after it, would be a distinct conditioning force on corporate governance. Its proponents, particularly the Americans Concerned about Corporate Power, a coalition of distinguished citizens in various walks of life, do not seem intimidated by corporate management's resolute resistance.

Even if by some remote quirk of fate a similar act were to be legislated, the vast majority of American enterprises would not be affected. Title VII, in establishing jurisdiction, is very selective. It pinpoints by making the Act apply only to establishments with sales or assets in excess of $250 million *or* with more than 5000 employees. Also, dollar and personnel ceilings would be increased annually by 10 percent. This would exempt all but the top 750 corporations. The approximately 9,999,250 remaining business enterprises would be outside the jurisdiction of the Corporate Democracy Act of 1980.

CAMPAIGN GM

President Eisenhower would have been astounded if, in his lifetime, some social activist would have addressed him as the Father of Campaign GM. Yet in his classic references to a powerful military-industrial complex, Eisenhower was evidencing the same concerns as those that prompted Campaign GM. "The dual engines of industrialization and war have created a tightly planned corporate complex that dominates the economy. . . . The great corporations should somehow be made responsible to workers and consumers."[33]

Campaign GM, or the Campaign to Make General Motors Responsible, was not the first to charge corporations with acting irresponsibly—thousands of laws and dozens of governmental agencies, acting as watchdogs over business, prove that others have been concerned with corporate lack of social awareness. Neither was Campaign GM the first attempt at getting shareowners to exercise their ownership rights—for almost a half

---

[33]Todd Gitlin, "Power and the Myth of Progress," quoted in *The Radical Attack on Business* (New York: Harcourt Brace Jovanovich, 1972), p. 9.

century, the Gilberts and other corporate gadflies have been doggedly trying to get stockholders to take a keener interest in corporate governance. Campaign GM was different in its choice of first target, its stress on legalities, its timing, and its recourse to a coalition effort.

Back in the 1960s, when the high cost and disillusionment of our no-win entrapment in the Vietnamese war gave the "new left" a stronger position than it had ever had before, those seeking causes and "whipping boys" found their best prospects in our macrocorporations. Our business enterprises, following twenty years of scarcely interrupted prosperity, were fat and contented and not in the best battling form. Nor were they prepared for the Campaign GM kind of fight.

Early in 1970, a small group of young, unestablished, lawyers pooled their resources and purchased twelve shares of General Motors common stock. They formed the Project for Corporate Responsibility (PCR), and then called a news conference to announce they were going to tackle the giant automaker head on. Their strategy was entirely new. As owners of GM stock, they planned to submit nine resolutions to the corporation's 1.3 million shareholders at the 1970 annual meeting. They indicated that they chose GM because of its size and status and not because of its particular guilt. The PCR founders were tactically emulating Ralph Nader's clever "David and Goliath" scenario, a real sympathy-arouser among little-guy-oriented Americans. Campaign GM was characterized by a seemingly sincere desire to "work within the system," particularly, the corporation. Change would come about through the gradual and legal introduction of public-interest laws.

A natural concomitant was PCR's premise that as economic power became more concentrated, so did authority become more centralized in corporate headquarters. A corollary followed; namely, that as practiced then, shareholder democracy was a sham. They recognized the value of the Securities and Exchanges Act of 1934, with its focus on the concept of "fair corporate suffrage," and they also recognized its limitations. "The paucity of proxy challenges proposed during the Act's first thirty-five years suggests that the floor of the stock exchange rather than that of the annual meeting is the arena most frequently employed to define the relationship between management and shareholders. The proxy system has proven to be peripheral in protecting the financial interests of shareholders: when displeased with management for whatever reasons, they sell their shares."[34]

In reaction, General Motors cited legal precedent on its side and notified the SEC and PCR that it would exclude all the project's shareholder proposals. Their attitude was bolstered by Rule 14a-8 of the SEC, which details three principal grounds for excluding proxy proposals: those which

[34]David Vogel, *Lobbying the Corporation* (New York: Basic Books, Inc., 1978), p. 76.

by state law are not proper subject for action by security holders; those relating to the conduct of the ordinary business operations of the user; and promotions of political, social, and similar causes. The SEC rejected seven of PCR's proposals but ruled favorably on the remaining two. This was a momentous decision—it opened up an entirely new domain for shareholder democracy activists. For the first time, the SEC required management to include a resolution whose implications were clearly social rather than financial. Campaign GM, phase one, was really under way.

As can be expected, considerable public debate followed. General Motors was clearly on the defensive; it ran full-page advertisements in about 150 newspapers and mailed a twenty-one-page booklet, detailing its position to its 1.3 million shareholders. PCR, on the other hand, sent a fifteen-page statement to 200 institutional investors, explaining its stand. As a result, at least thirty-five institutional investors—largely universities, foundations, and religious groups—wrote to General Motors expressing their concern.

GM's 1970 annual meeting, held May 12, attracted a record-setting 3000 shareholders plus 130 reporters. The proceedings, which subjected management to a siege of acerbating, precise questioning during 6½ hours, were marked by only one tense confrontation. "Staring dispassionately at the podium, a pretty, young, black law student from the University of California at Los Angeles, Barbara Williams, said sharply: 'Mr. Roche, you have not answered my question. Why are there no blacks on the GM board of directors? Why no women?' The chairman's answer that 'none were elected' served only to encourage the interrogation."[35]

Although civility prevailed during most of the meeting, this single outburst emphasized the fact that here were two mutually antagonistic and unyielding forces. Some commentators felt that, aside from the common courtesies, this was more like a confrontation of adversaries, with Campaign GM's representatives behaving as prosecuting attorneys. " 'This is a new departure,' says John T. Connor, chairman of Allied Chemical Corporation, and a GM board member. 'Up until this time, stockholders have always appreciated and observed the sanctity of the board room. I think it is essential for a board to have free and frank discussions. . . . I was quite upset by the nature of the questions and the tone of the questions—as if the board was a public body whose deliberations were a matter of public record.' "[36]

As expected, the two PCR proposals went down in defeat, each getting less than 3 percent of the shares voted. The PCR spokesperson complimented GM's chairman for his courtesy and his stamina in holding up under the

---

[35]"GM's Ordeal May Set the Fashion," *Business Week,* May 30, 1970, p. 84.
[36]Ibid.

long ordeal, and stated he looked forward to next year's encounter. Mr. Roche thanked all the shareholders for a most gratifying expression of confidence and stressed that GM was more determined than ever to fulfill its responsibilities.

As both sides removed themselves from the annual meeting arena, it might have seemed that the corporation's mighty clout had flattened the challengers. Not so. Within three months, General Motors had acted on PCR's proposal that GM set up a committee for corporate responsibility. Once established, this group was called the Public Policy Committee. In responding to Barbara Williams's direct challenge, GM invited its first black—the Reverend Leon Sullivan—to its board. Soon after, GM named its first woman to its board—Catherine B. Cleary, president of First Wisconsin Trust Company, who later was asked to serve on the boards of American Telephone and Telegraph, Kraftco, Kohler, and other firms.

Because of its success, Campaign GM I (1970) automatically led to Campaign GM II (1971). The tactics now were modified because of the previous year's experience, and only three new proposals were introduced. There was no overt sociopolitical slanting, with focus strictly on legal aspects. For example, the "Proposal for Shareholder Democracy would have required GM to list on its proxy statement, directors nominated by shareholders as well as those nominated by management. A proposal for Constituent Democracy provided that three of GM's constituencies—employees, dealers, and vehicle owners—could each nominate a candidate for director. The final proposal required GM annually to disclose its progress in the areas of minority hiring, air pollution, and auto safety to shareholders."[37] In the voting, Campaign II did no better than Campaign I—all three proposals were resoundingly defeated. While management won a smashing victory, it came close to losing the whole war. "In what became probably the worst gaffe uttered by a chief executive at a modern stockholder meeting, Roche replied to a question about GM's accountability by affirming that 'yes, we are a public corporation owned by free white. . . .' Following the crowd's gasp, Roche hastily added, 'black and yellow people all over the world.' "[38]

To date, there has been no Campaign GM III even though periodic outbreaks, reminiscent of 1970, occasionally surface. For example, the Council to Advocate Public Utility Responsibility (CAPUR) waged a battle to force Northern States Power Company (NSP) to elect a public-interest representative to its board. Although initially CAPUR lost its fight, NSP's management later elected two public-interest representatives, one a woman.

[37]Vogel, op. cit., p. 87.
[38]Ibid., p. 89.

Soon thereafter, the Investor Responsibility Research Center (IRRC) was established jointly by twenty major institutional investors, largely universities. Its objective was to provide accurate and balanced studies of issues raised in public-interest proxy proposals.

Related but independent is the Interfaith Center on Corporate Responsibility (ICCR). It has held firm despite few victories. Ten years after its founding, in 1970, it included 170 Roman Catholic orders and dioceses and 17 Protestant denominations with investment portfolios of over $6 billion. In the ten-year period, it has been instrumental in filing about 500 shareholder resolutions with nearly 100 corporations. One very intriguing and important area of concern to ICCR is the question of who owns and who votes stock in our corporations. This group's studies confirm the obvious— that concentration of voting power is held by a few banks. ICCR, presumably, will seek to reduce this massive power concentration because the banks are now exercising the voting rights that technically belong to others, namely, the owners. Banks will be pressed to pass these voting rights on to the beneficial owners of stock. And unions, with significant pension stakes, will be encouraged to demand that the power of the proxy and investment decisions be turned over to them.

While Campaign GM might now be a matter of history, its spirit lingers on. An interesting revival by a Ralph Nader coalition, Americans Concerned about Corporate Power, illustrates this persistence. The coalition set April 17, 1980, as Big Business Day. The organizers included Ralph Nader and others—representatives of the United Auto Workers Union, International Machinist Workers Union, Consumer Federation of America, Americans for Democratic Action, and other groups.

Big Business Day had an ambitious program: it planned teach-ins and mock trials of companies, spotlighting on corporate abuses and crime in the suites. Union representatives and members of citizens' groups served as judge, jury, prosecutor, and defense attorney. There was even a corporate Hall of Shame. Moreover, "shadow" boards of activists were appointed to monitor specific companies, among them, American Electric, Castle and Cooke, Citicorp, Du Pont, Eli Lilly, Exxon, Fluor, Grumman, Occidental Petroleum, U.S. Steel, and Winn-Dixie Stores. There was considerable confusion over why these particular corporations were selected out of the 10,000 SEC-supervised companies. Du Pont's chairman philosophized: "It is an honor we didn't seek but we accept with equanimity."

Interestingly, the "shadow" boards were modeled after Great Britain's shadow cabinets. The boards, monitoring these "socially bankrupt" firms, were to issue annual reports. "Naturally, directors will be able to serve on only one shadow board—interlocking directors aren't allowed."[39]

---

[39]Stan Crock, "Every Dog Has His Day, but Big Firms Gladly Would Skip Them," *The Wall Street Journal,* April 9, 1980, p. 1.

THE CONGLOMERATE CONSTRAINT

In substance, conglomeration is growth by acquisition. As such, it is just one form of merger: a fusion of two or more companies by the transfer of all property and authority to a single corporation. What makes conglomeration a special kind of merger is its strategic emphasis on keeping the corporate "eggs" in several baskets, through diversification. Consequently, whereas conventional mergers are between similar components, conglomeration combines unlikes.

Until recently, most mergers were severely constrained because the articles of incorporation, the bylaws, custom, or the enterpriser's competency confined merging to a given product line, to a specific process, or to selected market areas. Our experience with trusts in the latter half of the nineteenth century was typical. These trusts were amalgamations in a single line of endeavor: petroleum, wool, sugar, tobacco, and so forth.

In the second half of the present century, mergers took a totally unexpected turn. While there were still many vertical backward, vertical forward, and horizontal mergers, there was now an increasing preference for conglomerate merger, namely, for acquiring firms not related to the company's current endeavors. There were a number of reasons for prompting such unorthodox action: the need to diversify, the implied synergy, innovation, changing technology, and a dozen other reasons. Initially, at least, it was the prospect for making a fast buck.

The very first to organize conglomerates were a breed of fast-acting, high-risk takers, derogatorily called the "raiders." To them, certain target companies could be worth more dead than alive, and so, consequently, they would acquire, unobtrusively, sufficient voting shares to gain control. Generally, in publicly owned companies, this could be as little as 10 percent of the outstanding stock. Once in control, the raider would begin to sell off the more salable parts of the victim. Having disposed of the best components, the raider might then sell the marginal units at their scrap value, or even abandon the unwanted parts. No wonder the raiders had few friends; communities and workers put out of jobs had no love for such heartless enterprisers. But the greatest animosity came from members of the business establishment, who feared they might be the next to be dismembered.

Yet the raiders did perform a necessary function—they were corporate surgeons, lopping off injured or defective limbs from an ailing corporate body. More caustically, the raiders were likened to morticians, who, in preparing the corporate corpse for burial, removed everything of value, even the gold teeth.

Although seldom alluded to as being one, the earliest of raiders was Royal Little, who parlayed a classic raid into one of our most respected conglomerates: Textron, Incorporated. In so doing, he contributed much, not only to the theory and practice of merging, but equally to corporate governance. Royal Little's target was American Woolen Company, itself the result of a turn-of-the-century horizontal merger. At its birth, American Woolen, an amalgam of twenty-seven woolen manufacturers, with a total of seventy mills, was called the Woolen Trust, and flourished under the founding enterprisers. When ownership and control became the prerogatives of second- and third-generation family scions, the Trust lapsed into inertia. It lost money regularly, even during the prosperous post-World War II period.

Royal Little viewed this stumbling giant as a perfect raiding target. It had a net worth of $77 million, with more than two-thirds of that value in cash and other very liquid assets. Moreover, the million-dollar-per-month operating losses had generated a $30 million tax carry-forward opportunity. So Little decided to raid. It was a long and complicated process, but in the end, brashness and ingenuity defeated the unimaginative hired-hand outside directors, who ran the firm for the absentee third-generation owners.

In his autobiography, Royal Little marvels at what audacity, plus knowing where you want to go, can accomplish. He stressed that tiny Textron had a net worth of only $35 million compared with American Woolen's $77 million. Moreover, American Woolen's very liquid position meant that an imaginative leadership could actually have bought up the brash aggressor, Textron, whose entire common stock then had a market value of less than $15 million. "This is an interesting concept since our 470,000 shares of American Woolen would have been extinguished, 100 percent of Textron would have been owned by American Woolen, and there would thereafter have been only 530,000 American Woolen shares in public hands. If you are planning to make a tender offer for some company three times as big as you are, be sure to pick a company whose board of directors isn't smart enough to take advantage of a reverse acquisition of this sort."[40] This is the significant point: rarely does the public blame the real culprits when disaster strikes a corporation. Even when the leadership is singled out, only the chief executive officer and a few of his henchmen usually "get the axe." The corporate helmsmen, the policy makers, the board of directors, are almost never tarnished with blame. Yet as Royal Little stresses, an imaginative and forthright American Woolen board of directors could easily have subverted Textron's machinations.

The sequel to this episode is conglomerate history. Royal Little immediately disposed of most of American Woolen's assets. The more promising textile facilities were regrouped in a new firm, Ameritron, which was sold off in 1963. Having liquidated most of the sluggish former Woolen Trust,

[40]Royal Little, *How to Lose $100,000,000 and Other Valuable Advice* (Boston: Little, Brown and Company, 1979), p. 146.

Royal Little embarked on his classic course of unrelated diversification, which translates into conglomeration. He accentuated the concept of asset redeployment, subsequently glamorized by "Jimmy" Ling of Ling-Temco-Vought (LTV) and by others. Yet, as Little admits, "Without the American Woolen merger, Textron would never have amounted to anything. It would have been a very small company with three or four diversified operations still primarily in textiles."[41] For the past twenty years, however, Textron, with twenty-six major divisions, has been completely out of the textile industry.

In developing and popularizing conglomeration, Textron also faced up to essential changes in corporate governance for the conglomerate. Textron was among the very first, for example, to change its annual report structure so as to show how the different company activities contributed to operations. Textron, likewise, was one of the first to designate heads of divisions as presidents. This concept, now widely practiced, is more fully developed in the section on proliferating presidents. Governance of conglomerates, as envisaged by Royal Little, necessitated an alternative control mechanism.

Giving some gratuitous advice on board structuring, Little emphasizes that "in a diversified company such as Textron, never have a division president on the board—don't put the chief executive officer in a position where someone reporting to him is, as a director, his boss. If possible never have commercial bankers or investment bankers on the board—it restricts your options when you need capital. Never have suppliers or customers on the board. Don't invite your lawyer to join."[42]

Royal Little gives a considerable amount of other boardroom advice, but the critical point here is that preemptory exclusion of division presidents does create a void of knowledge and technology in the boardroom. As a consequence, some successful conglomerators today choose to ignore Little's sage advice. At the extreme end are corporate confederations such as Alco Standard, a Valley Forge, Pennsylvania, conglomerate which proudly proclaims: "Alco Standard has 135 men who call each other 'partner.' Once these men owned and managed their own successful companies. But they were frustrated by increasing complex administrative details and the difficulty in obtaining investment capital. So they merged their companies into Alco Standard's 'Corporate Partnership' to gain the financial leverage of a (multi-) million dollar corporation."[43]

There are a number of comparable illustrations, but with less emphasis on the partnership concept. For instance, Nate Cummings, founder of Consolidated Foods Corporation, used owner-officer-directors very effec-

[41]Ibid., p. 145.
[42]Ibid., p. 271.
[43]*The Wall Street Journal*, March 11, 1970.

tively. Up to recently, there generally were fourteen insiders on the seventeen-director board. These insiders, known as the barons, were men who had owned their own companies which they sold to Con Foods. As major shareholders, they were interested owners, and directors with a real stake in the company. Under their leadership, Con Foods had a phenomenal prosperity. When, however, the current CEO reformed the board so that only four barons remained, the giant food processor–merchant faltered. Its stock today is selling at less than half the price it commanded ten years ago.

These examples corroborate another extreme in headquarter's decentralization, such as described by Northwest Industries, Incorporated, in a full-page ad of *The Wall Street Journal:* "You Can't Run 10 Successful Companies with Just One Man." It "requires 10 strong chief executives with 10 good management teams."[44] Photographs of ten key Northwest Industries' divisional presidents are featured. What is not stressed in this glamorizing of conglomerate divisional autonomy is the fact that there is but one management member on the corporation's board of directors. The dominant CEO, Ben Heineman, while handing out divisional presidencies, tolerates no peer power on the board, which is entirely outside director in composition.

Some companies try to provide their boards with technical competency by elevating a number of heads of the leading divisions to director status. Fuqua Industries rotates a directorship among a number of its key divisions. Other firms, concerned that a hundred or more autonomous divisions can lead to disintegration, try to combine their multiplicity into a few related units, calling the heads group vice presidents or sector executives.

This area is still in an early evolutionary phase. It will be interesting, ten or twenty years from now, to review how corporate governance theory has adapted to conglomerate reality. But whatever the course, proper credit should be given to Royal Little, the imaginative founder of Textron, Incorporated. Although he operated as a raider, he is never alluded to as such. Instead, he goes into business history as the entrepreneur who gave respectability to the concept and technique of conglomeration.

THE GADFLIES

By definition the word "gadfly" means a pest, a fly that bites and torments large animals. Its use in corporate governance signifies an irritating, bothersome shareholder who asks embarrassing questions of the chairman and his colleagues at annual stockholders' meetings. Among the most prominent gadflies are Lewis D. Gilbert, the father of the shareholder revolution; his brother, John Gilbert; Wilma Soss; and Evelyn Y. Davis. At

[44]*The Wall Street Journal,* July 28, 1977.

least a dozen other imitators have cropped up, including Ralph Nader, but so far they have not earned the sobriquet.

Lewis Gilbert pioneered the corporate democracy and gadflying movement, beginning his campaign back in 1932. As a young newspaper reporter, he attended the annual meeting of Consolidated Gas Company, chaired by George Courtelyou, a former politician. "He was given the job as chairman of the gas company as a plum," says Gilbert, now seventy-three. "In those days one way of rewarding long-time politicians was to give them chairmanships of businesses."[45]

Arriving at the meeting, Gilbert found a small group of bored people whose boredom was accentuated by the hour-long monotone verbatim reading of the company's annual report. Toward the end of the meeting most of the shareholders in attendance were asleep. "Finally, Courtelyou finished the reading. Then in a flash there was a motion to adjourn and it ended. Courtelyou happily announced that a delicious lunch was waiting in the lobby for those attending."[46]

Little did Courtelyou realize the reaction he was creating—then and there Lewis Gilbert vowed to fight for corporate democracy. In the half century following his crusader's decision, Gilbert has attended close to 6000 corporate annual meetings, averaging about 130 each year. His brother and others in his crusade have attended about another 6000 annual meetings. The Gilberts were loners until the late 1940s when Wilma Soss joined the fray. Although they fought for the same cause, Lewis Gilbert and Wilma Soss never became admiring allies. For one thing, Mrs. Soss staged theatricals, frequently donning outlandish costumes to dramatize a point. For example, after one chairman had remarked that she was making a circus of his meeting, Wilma Soss took him literally, rented a clown suit and an elephant, and proposed to ride it down Wall Street.

Another gadfly, Mrs. Evelyn Y. Davis, came on the scene in the early 1960s. As if to catch up because of her late entrance, she set the ultimate in theatrics, sporting various outlandish costumes: a Batman mask, a red miniskirt, an orange pith helmet, a gas mask, a black sweater emblazoned with "I was born to raise hell." Moreover, her behavior at times seemed to be rude, even boisterous.

In seeking to make their contributions more coordinated and permanent, the Gilberts organized Corporate Democracy, Inc., whose sole function is the publication of the *Annual Report of Stockholder Activities at Corporation Meetings*. Forty annual publications of the *Report* have provided the best detailing of Lewis Gilbert's aspirations and very slow crawl toward idealistic goals.

[45]Geoffrey Thompson, "Gilberts' 48-Year Battle for Corporate Democracy," *Business,* Gannett Westchester Newspapers, June 22, 1980, p. 2.
[46]Ibid.

How successful are the gadflies? The answer depends on one's angle of vision. As viewed from the corporate dais, and particularly from the chairman's podium, their efforts are irritating but insignificant; from a gadfly perspective, the view is one of marked accomplishment. Consider some of the Gilberts's and Corporate Democracy's objectives[47]:

1 To ask questions of management at the annual meeting and to encourage other owners to do the same at this forum provided by law for shareholders

2 To urge constantly the holding of annual meetings in convenient locations

3 To urge better and more informative annual reports and better and more postmeeting reports in order to keep owners well-informed voters

4 To urge that all directors be stockholders with 100 shares as the average minimum holding

5 To campaign for increased recognition of preemptive rights for owners

6 To keep reasonable watch over executive compensation, options, and pensions for executives in order to ensure that both sides are treated fairly

7 To encourage cumulative voting in order to ensure independent directors

8 To introduce, from the floor, resolutions in order to register shareholder expression of opinion

A reading of the list should indicate that the Gilbert objective is not so much to win on a specific issue, but rather to shake shareholders out of their bottom-line trance. Making shareholders aware of corporate governance, its meaning, its potential—that is the objective.

Of course, winning a battle—even a skirmish—is always a pleasure. At the 1974 annual meeting of J.P. Morgan and Company, a Gilbert-Soss proposal was finally approved by convened shareholders. Not only was it approved, but it was actually endorsed by management. Under the proposal, proxy cards sent to shareholders before a meeting would inform them of their right to cross out the names suggested by management and enter any names they wish. Actually, this right was already guaranteed by law, but few shareholders were aware of it. "In an unusual example of corporate support of a minority shareholder proposal, the Morgan management recommended the resolution be approved." It passed overwhelmingly. "Asked after the meeting how often he scored a win, Mr. Gilbert conceded, 'It's rare, very rare.' "[48]

To emphasize the difficulty of the uphill fight to democratize corporate governance, the next recorded victory occurred years later at Western

---

[47]Adapted from Proxy Statement, Corporate Democracy, Inc., 1980.
[48]Charles N. Stabler, "Gilberts, Wilma Soss Score Rare Victory at Annual Meeting," *The Wall Street Journal*, March 21, 1974, p. 4.

Union's annual meeting. This was a proposal that would require proxy statements to include a disclosure of the amount of fees paid to the company's auditors. According to Lewis Gilbert, a big jump in fees would be a "red flag," warning stockholders that something is amiss with the company. The two-to-one victory even surprised its sponsors. " 'I've been working for Mr. Gilbert for seven years and this is the first time I've been on the winning side,' said William Frisher, who introduced the resolution on Mr. Gilbert's behalf."[49]

But the really big winning is in the educating of our public. Thirty years ago, the Gilberts's goals were viewed as far left of center; today, they epitomize pure capitalism where shareholders have meaningful input and control. In the learning process, many an authoritarian chairman—and there have been an abundance—has been forced to introspect. "Of the oft heard comment that the Gilbert brothers have 'mellowed' as the years have gone by, the two proudly agree: 'We haven't mellowed, the corporate chairmen have.' There are a lot of corporate chairmen who would agree with that."[50]

POSTSCRIPT

Of the many external constraints, let us consider one more—religious zest. Even though the days of the Inquisition have long been gone, and church and corporation have been effectively separated, a modicum of morality still remains in the boardroom. For the most part, this morality is exercised by governmental regulatory agencies, Congress, and the courts. Nevertheless, a growing number of Americans believe there would be less need for morality custodians—OSHA, FCPA, NLRB, SEC, or FTC—if God were not so effectively shut out of the boardroom.

However, it was different at National Student Marketing (NSM), where board meetings began and ended with a prayer. NSM was a high-flier favorite of financial analysts during the late 1960s. It went public in 1968, at a price of $1.50 per share, and within a year hit a high of $36 per share. Founded by Cortes W. Randell, the company uniquely used a cadre of business school graduates to sell a great variety of products and services on campuses. After a fantastic short-run success, it was charged by government officials with fraud and a variety of improper activities. As a result, National Student Marketing collapsed in 1970, and after ten years of litigation and salvaging of assets, the shareholders approved a liquidation plan with an initial distribution of about $6.50 per share.

The Wall Street Journal commented on NSM's final meeting: "In keeping

[49]Victor F. Zonana, "Gadfly Gilbert Bites Western Union Corp. and Gives It Message," *The Wall Street Journal*, April 25, 1980, p. 41.
[50]Thompson, op. cit., p. 3.

with company tradition, Mr. Cottrell (chairman) opened the meeting yesterday with a prayer followed by a moment of silence. He offered a prayer lamenting the company's failure to provide shareholders with a better investment adding that he hoped the liquidation plan would turn out all right."[51] Actually, Cottrell's prayer of lamentation should have been a prayer of thanksgiving for some shareholders; namely, the true "believers," the original investors. Even assuming that the first liquidation disbursement of $6.50 is the only cash they receive, based on a $1.50 initial offering price, this is a 333 percent profit over an eleven-year period, not including dividends. For those of lesser faith who purchased shares subsequently at the $36 high, neither lamentation nor expletives would suffice.

[51]*The Wall Street Journal,* September 11, 1980.

CHAPTER 7

EVOLUTION THROUGH PRECEDENT

BARCHRIS CONSTRUCTION CORPORATION: DIRECTOR LIABILITY

The *Escott v. BarChris Construction Corporation* (S.D.N.Y. 1968) decision is important in that it probed into the meaning of Section 11 of the Securities Act. This section "imposes civil liability upon the issuer of securities and designated persons when an effective registration statement contains an untrue statement of a material fact or an omission to state a material fact required to be set forth."[1]

"Materiality" is defined in SEC Rule 405 as the matters about which an average prudent investor ought reasonably be informed before purchasing the security registered. In defining "material" under Rule 14a-9 of the Securities Exchange Act, the Supreme Court has stated that an omitted fact is material if there is substantial likelihood that a reasonable shareholder would consider it important in deciding how to vote.

Knepper points out that the BarChris decision to probe Section 11 "defined a material fact as that which if it had been correctly stated or disclosed would have deterred or tended to deter the average prudent investor from purchasing the securities in question."[2]

BarChris was a small Long Island company engaged in building bowling alleys, a booming business in the late 1950s. BarChris publicly sold $3.5 million of convertible debentures early in 1961, and in the fall of 1962, it went bankrupt—a casualty of overbuilding in the bowling industry. In the

---

[1]William E. Knepper, *Liability of Corporate Officers and Directors,* 3d ed., Indianapolis: Allen Smith Company, 1978, p. 249.
[2]Ibid.

legal action that followed, the company, together with a consortium of eight underwriters, and nine members of the board of whom five were officers, was sued for issuing a registration statement that contained false statements and material omissions. As required by law, the officers and directors had signed the registration, in effect vouching for its accuracy and completeness.

When a federal district court found the defendants guilty, four of the five officer-directors were judged to have been aware of all or part of the inaccuracies and so were automatically guilty. There was doubt about the guilt of the fifth officer-director. Yet to be innocent, he had to prove that he had exercised "due diligence"—since he could not, he joined his guilty colleagues.

The significant contribution in this precedent-setting legal decision concerned the four outside directors and their exercise of due diligence. Apparently, none knew they were signing a flawed document; yet none had made a reasonable investigation. Two of the outsiders who had legal or financial relationships with the company, and who had helped prepare the registration form, were undeniably guilty.

It was the other two outside directors who created a problem. Both had joined the board with an implied understanding that their own firms were to get business from BarChris. In the process, they investigated the company's performance record and found it very good. They even went so far as to check its Dun & Bradstreet rating and received favorable reports. They did not, however, diligently investigate the accuracy of the registration statement—yet they signed it. Despite the fact that both had joined the BarChris board less than a month before the bankruptcy, and even though all they signed were papers to which the registration statements were not attached, the judge held that neither had done sufficient investigating and so they were guilty.

The lesson to be learned from this incident is that every director should at least go through the motions of investigating—in this case it would have meant at least reading the prospectus (which they did not do). Before signing, the directors should have asked specific questions relating to the substance of the prospectus, and a record of their questioning should have been kept. To date, the legal interpretation seems to be that directors do not have to ask the right questions provided they ask pertinent ones.

PHASES OF THE MOON: CONSPIRACY AND COLLUSION

If corporate governance scandals could be rated on a scale of 1 to 10, the electrical equipment conspiracy of 1959 would definitely be a 10. General

Electric, Westinghouse Electric, and twenty-seven other manufacturers of electrical equipment had been rigging bids and prices over a twenty-five-year period. The "phases of the moon" was their ingenious technique whereby each conspirator had a position in the "lunar system" and knew when it was supposed to be high or low. Each took turns in this rotational bidding, hence, the reference to phases of the moon. The executives and their henchmen worked like true conspirators, meeting at odd times in out-of-the-way places, using passwords and codes. The conspiring covered almost all electrical equipment product lines, from tiny $2 insulators to multimillion-dollar turbines. The annual volume involved was estimated at just under $2 billion.

It was only by chance that the smoothly functioning "lunar system" was discovered. Officials at Tennessee Valley Authority became suspicious when they noted that there was a succession of nearly identical bids. They alerted the Department of Justice, and soon there were indictments. Then another chance factor helped explode what might have been only a conventional criminal case into a national scandal. Just at that time "four Ohio businessmen were sentenced to jail for antitrust violations, the first in history to go to jail after pleading nolo contendere in an antitrust case. (One of them committed suicide on the way to jail.) This news sent a chill through the electrical-equipment executives under investigation and some agreed to testify about their colleagues under the security of immunity."[3]

Round one climaxed with Federal Judge J. Cullen Ganey referring to the cases of the twenty-nine companies and their forty-four executives as a "shocking indictment of a vast section of our economy." Imposing sentences, he implicitly blamed the chief executives and their boards of directors. "This court . . . is not at all unmindful that the real blame is to be laid at the doorstep of the corporate defendants and those who guide and direct their policy . . . for one would be most naive indeed to believe that these violations of the law . . . involving so many millions upon millions of dollars, were facts unknown to those responsible for the corporation and its conduct."[4]

Pressed by the Senate Antitrust and Monopoly Subcommittee, some former GE employees, fired for their alleged part in the conspiracy, also "blew whistles." The witnesses swore that "former GE President Robert Paxton encouraged the conspiracy and that Chairman Ralph Cordiner at least knew about it. From Paxton and Cordiner came outraged denials. As the testimony unfolded, Michigan's Democratic Senator Phil Hart, a sub-

---

[3]"The Great Conspiracy," *Time,* February 17, 1961, p. 85.
[4]Richard Austin Smith, "The Incredible Electrical Conspiracy," part I, *Fortune,* April 1961, p. 132.

committeeman, said: 'Either somebody is lying, or somebody is crazy.' "[5] There was considerable similar testimony, seriously hurtful to corporate governance and our business system. For example, one smaller firm president, justifying his conspiratorial actions, stated: "It is the only way a business can be run. It is free enterprise."

Regretfully, some of the companies had long-standing codes of ethics, expressly forbidding such scandalous action. Under Charles E. Wilson's presidency, General Electric promulgated General Instruction 2.35, which states: "It has been and is the policy of this company to conform strictly to the antitrust laws . . . special care should be taken that any proposed action is in conformity with the law as presently interpreted. If there is any doubt as to the legality of any proposed action, the advice of the Law Department must be obtained."[6] In 1954, the new CEO, Ralph Cordiner, replaced this mandate with the even more explicit Directive Policy 20.5.

Among the penalties handed down by Judge Ganey were thirty-day jail sentences for seven of the defendants and thirty-day suspended jail sentences for twenty-five other defendants. All told, thirty seven executives were fined a total of $137,000, and twenty-nine corporations were fined $1,787,000. Yet rarely do cases of this magnitude end with the judge's verdict; soon a series of civil antitrust suits followed, reaching a total of more than 1800 private antitrust suits. Most were incidental and quickly settled. The last big case was settled, late in 1965, when a federal court found General Electric and Westinghouse Electric guilty and, with triple damages, fined them a total of $16,873,203.

The "phases of the moon" reflected upon managerial mores, showing the low-ethical level to which some corporations, and particularly their governors and directors, had sunk. Note that the judiciary put the blame squarely upon those who guide and direct policy. Referring to GE's Directive 20.5, Judge Ganey noted that it was observed in the breach rather than in its enforcement. Out of a grand total of about 400 directors in the 29 companies, only a handful were indicted, namely, a few presidents of some of the smaller firms. Even GE's and Westinghouse's directors, with the exception of their chief executives, who were only incidentally implicated, escaped censure. Moreover, not a single outside director was even mentioned by name.

Several months after the trial, Henry Ford II, chairman of Ford Motor Company and a member of General Electric's board of directors, commented upon this governance failure. In a talk before the Minneapolis Junior Chamber of Commerce, Ford decried the tendency of business, caught in

---

[5]"Confidence in Cordiner," *Time*, May 5, 1961, p. 77.
[6]Smith, op. cit., p. 135.

dishonest acts, "to blame a few bad apples," or to complain about persecution by the government. He emphasized that the only course of action for top executives, implicated in phases of the moon embarrassments, is to drop the alibis and explanations and to "have the fortitude—the plain guts—to stand up and say, 'This is our failure. We are chagrined and sorry. It will not happen again.' "[7]

Ford was the first, and probably the only one, to implicate the corporations' outside directors. "With a mea culpa, as a General Electric director, he also suggested that outside directors should make it their business 'to be aware of the pertinent codes and policies of the companies on whose boards they sit. If the companies themselves fail to keep their own houses in order, this house-cleaning job certainly will be put in less friendly hands.' "[8]

In a seemingly high-moral gesture, Henry Ford relinquished his General Electric outside directorship. To some this indicated rectitude, Ford practicing what he preached; to others, it meant just another outside director abandoning a sinking ship. As a member of both Ford and GE boards, Henry Ford was in a highly suspect position. General Electric was one of Ford's big suppliers of various components, and legal entanglements could have arisen out of this potential for conflict of interest. The issue of why Ford left GE's board—to avoid litigation or out of principle—was never resolved.

Almost a quarter of a century has elapsed since the phases of the moon scandal. Although no single corporate connivance has matched the intrigue of the electrical equipment conspiracy, there have been a series of embarrassments, namely, Texas Gulf, Penn Central, and others. In order to halt questionable practices, Congress enacted the Foreign Corrupt Practices Act of 1977. To date, more than 450 American firms have been implicated under the FCPA. Yet in spite of all the questioning and investigating, no one seems to place the blame on incompetent and lackadaisical outside directors; instead, corporations continue to use increasing numbers of outsiders.

Of all the headlines and commentary of that time, it was a generally unnoticed letter to *Business Week*'s "Readers Report" which best summarized the awkward corporate governance situation, then and even to the present. The author argued that drafting outside and professional directors presents serious problems. Among these is the question of business principles, which, he suggested, ought to be checked before the outsider is elected to the board. But, he concluded, "Further, I would like to withdraw

---

[7]"Management: This Is Our Failure," *Time*, April 28, 1961, p. 89.
[8]Ibid.

my last suggestion and say instead: if men in business require a checking out of their ethics, then it may be best to do without directors."[9]

TEXAS GULF SULPHUR: INSIDER INFORMATION

When, in December 1971, the Supreme Court declined to review an earlier Securities and Exchange Commission's victory over Texas Gulf Sulphur Company (TGS), the seven-year litigation in the lower courts seemed to have come to an end. By refusing to hear the case, the Supreme Court apparently supported the SEC's attempt to establish new corporate disclosure and insider trading standards. Two years earlier, the High Court had declined to review a companion case, growing out of the same 1964 Texas Gulf press release incident. This earlier ruling was also in favor of the SEC.

The incidents leading to the litigation started in early November 1963, when Texas Gulf began exploratory drilling on a tract of land it owned near Timmins, Ontario. Four days of drilling " 'yielded one of the most impressive drill holes completed in modern times,' showing the presence of high-grade copper and zinc ore to a depth of 400 feet."[10] Elaborate precautions were taken so that spies or snoopers could not learn the significance of the find. After removing the drilling rig, planting trees to camouflage the drilling site, and even leaving a false clue—a worthless core at the site—the entire drilling team was sworn to secrecy.

According to SEC charges, a number of high-placed Texas Gulf officials began to buy the company stock in quantity after November 12, 1963, and the purchasing process continued at prices around the $18-per-share level. In early April 1964, *The New York Times* reported that Texas Gulf had discovered a great deposit of copper 10 miles north of Timmins, and the next day Texas Gulf issued a counterstatement intending to downplay *The New York Times* release. This denial eventually became the key issue in the litigation. Not until April 16th was Texas Gulf's board of directors informed about the major discovery. Meanwhile, two months earlier, the directors, unaware of the Ontario project's potential, had granted the president options for 12,800 shares at slightly under $24 per share. The executive vice president and three other key executives were granted a total of 18,400 additional shares—allegedly, these executives were aware of the major discovery from its inception.

A series of other involvements ensued. One concerned an outside director, Francis G. Coates, who was accused of buying TGS stock immediately after the April 16th board meeting which authorized a news

---

[9]Robert T. Erlichman, "Readers Report—Director Ethics," *Business Week,* May 19, 1962, p. 6.

[10]"Texas Gulf Suit Opens New Door for SEC," *Business Week,* April 24, 1965, p. 25.

release to the press. The records show that Coates made his telephone order for 2000 shares at 10:51 A.M., before the Dow Jones News Service began disseminating the story at 10:54 A.M. In subsequent legal entanglements, the court said Coates should have waited a reasonable time for the news to appear over the Dow Jones ticker tape. Coates contended that he had decided on the previous day, while on board a plane en route to the board meeting, to buy more stock for four family firms. His decision was made after he was told a major discovery was going to be announced. He had delayed because he felt the price would decline.

Even more newsworthy was the episode involving another outside director, Thomas S. Lamont, scion of a leading Wall Street family and a recently retired officer of Morgan Guaranty Trust Company. Lamont was similarly accused of "jumping the gun" by leaking the news. While he did not buy stock in his own account, Lamont did call an executive vice president of Morgan Guaranty after the Texas Gulf board meeting, and advised the banker to watch the Dow Jones ticker for good news about the company. Between 10:45 and 10:59 A.M., Morgan Guaranty bought 8000 shares for its accounts. Even though Lamont did not buy any shares in his own account, the SEC sought restitution to the shareholders from whom Morgan Guaranty bought its stock.

Among the many legal questions, the most perplexing was: Just when is inside information considered to be public knowledge? Lamont argued that the information he had, when he phoned the bank, was generally available to many other investors. Purportedly, the night before the Texas Gulf meeting, a Canadian weekly, *The Northern Miner,* carried a front-page headline: "Texas Gulf Comes Up with a Major." Lamont's lawyer argued that a director is not required to await publication of information in one particular medium—in this case the Dow Jones ticker—before he joins in disseminating it.

Several corporate governance clarifications evolved from this long and involved legal battle. For example, "SEC's Rule 10b-5 prohibits anyone who has access directly or indirectly, to information intended to be available only for a corporate purpose and not for the personal benefit of anyone, from taking advantage of such information, knowing it is unavailable to those with whom he is dealing when trading for his own account in the securities of the corporation."[11]

Further clarifying the SEC's sequential Rule 10b-5(2), the court broadened the interpretation of the use of untrue statements or omissions of fact through any instrument of interstate commerce. It now included corporate press releases and other statements regardless of any ulterior motive by

---

[11]"Court Draws the Line on Insiders," *Business Week,* August 24, 1968, p. 34.

management whether or not they were buying or selling securities. "Insider trading benefits . . . in essence, are forms of secret corporate compensation derived at the expense of the uninformed investing public and not at the expense of the corporation which receives the sole benefit from insider incentives."[12]

In the wake of the Supreme Court's resolution of the case, some stockholder suit action followed. The ultimate was *The Wall Street Journal* 's advertisement on January 17, 1973, requesting all persons who sold common stock of Texas Gulf Sulphur Company between April 12, 1964, and 10:55 A.M., April 16, 1964, at a price of $33 per share or less, to present proof of claim. The restitution settlement followed a class action entitled *Victor M. Cannon, Jr., et al. v. Texas Gulf Sulphur Company et al.,* settled in the United States District Court, Southern District of New York.

While Texas Gulf's experience cast a number of doubts, not only on the integrity, but also upon the competency, of its 1964 board of directors, there was a more favorable sequel. On October 30, 1974, Charles F. Fogarty, one of the directors involved, and now chairman of Texas Gulf, announced that the company would give away $1 million in stock to its employees. Thus, it was the first large publicly owned corporation to make such an outright gift of shares to all its employees. Except for senior officers, all full-time employees—depending upon the length of their service—received from one to fifty shares of Texasgulf (the new name) stock. Evidently, this magnanimous and commendable gesture by the company's directors proved them to be more progressive than they were a decade ago. In their allocation of company stock to the workers, the directors were advancing the concept of *people's capitalism,* discussed in a subsequent section. Chairman Fogarty, the product of a Catholic home for underprivileged children, views the corporation as akin to an extended family: "We are a unit, we are a team."[13] As for the board of directors—of which some earlier members were guilty of sins of commission by breaking the law, and some were guilty of sins of omission in not knowing what was going on—it now set a positive and laudable precedent: converting workers through ownership into people's capitalists.

But less propitious sequels were soon to follow. In February 1981, four of the company's top executives, including chief executive Charles F. Fogarty, were killed in a plane crash. A few months later a second catastrophe threatened when the French government-controlled Societe Nationale Elf Aquitaine, together with the Canada Development Corporation, offered almost $2.5 billion for 63 percent of Texasgulf's stock. The remaining 37

---

[12]Ibid.
[13]"Spreading It Around the Family," *Fortune,* December 1974, p. 40.

percent was already owned by Canada Development (90 percent Canadian government-owned).

Ironically, Texasgulf's board survived an SEC inquisition only to suffer consequences of today's technology—a plane crash that decimated its management and an unexpected takeover by a foreign-based conglomerate. How one should contend with such eventualities is not detailed in any director's primer.

THE PENN CENTRAL COMPANY: APATHETIC DIRECTORS

The venerable Pennsylvania Railroad, only a few recessions ago, could properly have been called a widow's best friend—for decades more than half of its stockholders were women. Their investment in the Pennsy sprang from a fervent faith in the organization's solidity, stability, dependability, as evidenced in its long and generous dividend record. Incorporated in 1846, the Pennsylvania Railroad had continuously paid dividends since 1848.

After World War II, when many railroads teetered and tottered, the Pennsy barely swayed. And when it ventured into a mammoth horizontal merger with the New York Central (its longtime arch rival), stockholder faith in the merged giant reached its zenith—its common stock climbed to an all-time high of 86.5.

Faith in this cornerstone of our railroad system received another boost when the newly merged Penn Central ventured into the fascinating free-for-all game of conglomeration. To the new Penn Central board of directors diversification seemed in line with the paraphrased financial saw as applied to railroads: Don't put all your eggs in one caboose. Consequently, a "one-railroad" holding company, Penn Central Company, was set up. Penn Central Transportation Company fulfilled the traditional role of railroading, while a second subsidiary, Pennsylvania Company, was allowed to function like any other conglomerate.

When the "boxcar bubble" burst, following the June 21, 1970, petition for bankruptcy under Section 77 of the Federal Bankruptcy Laws, Penn Central's stock slumped to a barely visible 5⅝ per share and investors dropped a total of nearly $2 billion. Not only did many grieving widows ask why, but so did bankers, congressmen, and millions of other Americans. What brought about the financial embarrassment of the twelfth largest (in assets) corporate entity (outside banking and insurance) in the world?[14]

Of course, no single reason would suffice. "Most of the blame, however,

[14]See Stanley C. Vance, "Penn Central—A Lesson for Bank Boards and One-Bank Holding Companies," *The Bankers Magazine*, Winter 1971.

falls on the directors of Penn Central and its railroad subsidiary. The average shareholder could ask no questions; he could make no policy. Yet the directors charged with that task raised virtually no questions and blandly endorsed the practices of management. Although they had the power to demand that the books be restated in more realistic fashion, the directors did nothing. Even in the complex and often conflicting tables that Bevan [financial vice chairman] and Saunders [CEO] set before them, the directors had ample material for gaining an inkling of Penn Central's true health. But they accepted the financial statements at face value and, until this spring, made no demands for more information. Ten directors resigned within a month after Saunders was fired. Their performance was half-hearted, but their failure was absolute."[15]

Keep in mind that of Penn Central's twenty-three directors all but four were outsiders, most of whom were foremost business leaders. Some maintained they had been hoodwinked by management; others claimed that the first information they had about the sad state of affairs was what they read in the May 1970 prospectus offering $100 million in P-C debentures. The prospectus listed losses of $193 million in 1969 plus 1970 first-quarter losses of $106 million. The debenture offer failed, and as is so well known, Penn Central toppled.

Even before the fall, some outside directors had come under stockholder inquisitioning. One irate owner filed charges against Howard Butcher III, senior partner of Butcher and Sherrerd (now Butcher and Singer), charging him with using secret information acquired as a P-C director. Butcher had been exceptionally bullish when he stated publicly that P-C stock selling at 29 would easily go to five times that figure. Yet four months later, just before P-C announced its 1968 loss, Butcher sold his large holdings and those of his customers. He was charged with conflict of interest, which he denied, commenting that " 'theoretically anyone who has any business at all is going to have conflicts of interest. The question is: How do you avoid liability?' Butcher's answer: he quit all of his directorships in close to 70 outside firms. His five partners, who held twelve directorships among them, did the same. 'The potential liability of being a director,' says Butcher, 'has become too great for the active, experienced businessman to suffer.' "[16]

Butcher maintained that none of the directors even had an inkling that the railroad was losing so much money. " 'Even when I was on the board of directors, I never saw the raw railroad results.' Mr. Butcher was asked why he had not seen those results. 'Why not? Because they didn't show them to me—that's why.' "[17]

---

[15]"The Penn Central Bankruptcy Express," *Fortune*, August 1970, p. 171.
[16]*Time*, October 18, 1968, p. 100.
[17]Robert Metz, *The New York Times*, June 24, 1970.

In a *New York Times* book review of *The Wreck of the Penn Central,* Robert Townsend, former head of Avis-Rent a Car, pointed an accusing finger not only at Penn Central's nineteen outside directors but at the very concept. "Part of the corporate scenery is a group of important people who don't know the first thing about the business: the outside directors. The typical outside director is a businessman, a banker, aristocrat, socialite or retired Government or military official.

"They all have one thing in common: they share a firm belief in the efficacy of the non-function known as the board meeting."[18] Townsend goes further in terming most board meetings as periodic get-togethers of friends and sycophants of the chief executive. The real objective of such meetings is to provide a forum for the mutual admiration group where they "cluck over their problems to the extent they can understand them, listen to a superficial review of the state of the economy, bitch about labor costs, rubber stamp the recommendations and ratify the actions of the chief executive, grab their fees and go back to their various businesses until next month. Do you suppose it ever occurred to the directors of the Penn Central to wonder how in the name of reason any outsider could spend 40 hours *a year* in this kind of scene and have any idea what the hell was going on?"[19]

The Penn Central debacle raised a host of corporate governance issues too numerous and complex to detail. One particularly important issue was Penn Central's attempt to get bailed out by the federal government. By 1976 the government did take over the railroad properties for $2.11 billion. These assets were combined with those of six other bankrupt railroads to form Consolidated Rail Corporation (Conrail). Here was a multibillion-dollar precedent for subsequent bailouts such as Chrysler Corporation.

Another big issue dealt with the cost of a $10 million director liability insurance policy, purchased in June 1968 from Lloyds of London at an initial annual charge of $305,360. Lloyds later threatened to rescind the policy and to return the premium because it claimed it received false and misleading information. The ethics of providing blanket protection for directors when questions are raised about their competency or behavior is very touchy. If Penn Central's directors were inattentive or incompetent, should company funds—which could go to stockholders as dividends—be diverted into director liability insurance premiums?

Ex post facto, some evidence did indicate there were halfhearted attempts to avert P-C's abuses before the bankruptcy. For instance, six months before the collapse, Robert S. Odell, a director from San Francisco, invited the other directors to dinner one night before a regular board

---

[18]Joseph R. Daughen and Peter Binzen, *The Wreck of the Penn Central* (Boston: Little, Brown and Company), reviewed in *The New York Times Book Review.*
[19]Ibid.

meeting. Presumably, the idea was to get support to shake up management. Because only three of seventeen board members were willing to attend, the dinner was canceled.

Not surprisingly, one of management's first cleanup moves was to demote twenty-four of thirty-five vice presidents, who then were given lesser titles. But a spokesperson declined to say if their salaries were reduced. This was an obvious "whipping-boy" tactic—far short of punishing the real culprits.

As the situation worsened, a wholesale resignation of directors became evident. One, Daniel E. Taylor of West Palm Beach, Florida, had been provided with special transportation to board meetings because of his aversion to flying. He generally came to Philadelphia on a private Penn Central railroad car at company expense.

Meanwhile, numerous class-action and derivative lawsuits were filed. Eventually these were consolidated in the Federal District Court in Philadelphia and were resolved after five years of litigation. The settlement totaled $12.6 million and was assessed against seventy defendants, none of whom admitted any wrongdoing. The court's judgments reflected the various culprits' degree of presumed guilt, and provided an index of a shifting legal onus. Recall that in the phases-of-the-moon example, operating executives were most severely penalized while the directors went unscathed. In this instance, a group of seventeen vice presidents and other officers were fined a total of $25,000, while in sharp contrast, another group of forty-eight transgressors, including twenty-four *former* directors, were collectively assessed $6.4 million. Note that among the several directors whose tenures antedated Penn Central's collapse, Walter H. Annenberg, former ambassador to Great Britain, was among the guilty.

In addition, the brokerage firm of Butcher and Sherrerd, together with Howard Butcher III, had to pay $250,000. The auditors for Penn Central and Penphil (an investment club), Peat, Marwick, Mitchell and Company, were also heavily fined. The SEC contended that Peat, Marwick failed to give due professional consideration to the economic substance of several Penn Central transactions, schemes, and devices. Comparably, Goldman, Sachs was charged with violations of antifraud provisions of federal securities laws in connection with marketing $83 million of Penn Central commercial paper just before the bankruptcy.

The Penphil case brought other irritations to light. Penphil was a private investment club through which at least twenty-six Penn Central officers, directors, friends, and relatives made investments in companies that Penn Central later invested in or acquired—Kaneb Pipe Line Company, Tropical Gas Company, Great Southwest Corporation, Continental Mortgage Investors, and National Homes Corporation. Participants were accused of making huge profits through insider trading.

The remarkable recuperative force latent within this giant of our railroad system manifested itself a decade later. By 1981 Penn Central set tentative dates for settling all its creditors' claims. The settlements would be made out of the $2.11 billion paid by the federal government for Penn Central railroad properties, transferred in 1976 to Consolidated Rail Corporation (Conrail).

Even more remarkable was the conglomerate's regeneration. In 1980 Penn Central acquired GK Technologies and then, the following year, tried to acquire Colt Industries, Inc., for cash and stock valued at about $1.4 billion. Combined revenues would have been in excess of $5 billion, with net income optimistically approaching $300 million. A significant advantage in the merger would have been the use of $600 million of Penn Central tax-loss carry-forwards.

However, an active and effective Stockholders Committee, using full-page ads in *The Wall Street Journal,* was able to defeat the proposal. Among its convincing arguments, the committee had disclosed that P-C's lead investment banking firm would receive $4 million and another bank would get $625,000 for managing the merger. Moreover, the committee pointed out, Penn Central would be paying almost twice the preproposal price for Colt stock; when it was announced there would be no merger, Colt stock dropped a precipitous $23 in one day.

Although this merger failed to take place, Penn Central continues its rejuvenation. Its market quotations on the New York Stock Exchange (NYSE) are up considerably from a low of $1.625 six years ago. While Penn Central is not ever likely to regain the esteem it once had as "a widow's best friend," it has dramatically changed the course of corporate governance.

GULF OIL CORPORATION: ILLEGAL CONTRIBUTIONS

The Mellons have always run their financial-industrial empire like a limited monarchy. Even today Mellon "viceroys" continue to run Gulf Oil Corporation, Mellon National Corporation (Pittsburgh's biggest bank), Aluminum Company of America, Koppers Company, and assorted other interests. Meanwhile, the Mellon "monarchs," an increasingly large number of descendants of Judge Thomas Mellon, perform like British royalty, serving as ceremonial figureheads. This pattern endures as the philosophy handed down by two of the judge's sons, Andrew W. and Richard B., continues in practice. "As the Mellons explained it, it went like this: Find a man who can run a business and needs capital to start or expand. Furnish the capital and take shares in the business, leaving the other man to run it except when it is in trouble. When the business has grown sufficiently to pay back the money, take the money and find another man running a business and in need of money and give it to him, on the same basis."[20]

[20]Charles J. V. Murphy, "The Mellons of Pittsburgh," *Fortune,* October 1967, p. 249.

This philosophy-strategy worked exceedingly well for the Mellons. Note that they grubstaked Henry B. Rust, the founder of Koppers Company; Edward G. Acheson, developer of Carborundum Company; and the small group that started Aluminum Company of America, just three years after the electrolytic process was developed by Charles Hall. Equally eventful was their staking of Colonel James Guffey and John H. Galey, who made the great oil strike at Spindletop in 1901. But while the Spindletop discoverers had good noses for oil, they had little ability for processing and selling the petroleum. The Mellons soon bought out their "roughneck" partners and went on to form the Gulf Oil Corporation, presently our seventh largest industrial company.

The sequence of Gulf Oil's responses to the illegal campaign contribution scandals of the mid-1970s typifies the Mellon philosophy. Unlike the Du Ponts, who even now continue to have family members actively engaged in the business and on the board of directors, only one member of the Mellon family, at the time of Gulf's public ordeal, had any direct association with the company. Hired hands ran the operations—until the big trouble.

In July 1973, Common Cause, the citizens' lobby, won the right to gain access to "Rose Mary's Baby"—the undisclosed list of campaign contributors which was maintained by President Nixon's secretary, Rose Mary Woods. One of the surreptitious contributors was Claude Wild, Jr., a vice president heading Gulf's Washington office, who gave $100,000 to the Nixon campaign. At the August board meeting, Bob Rawls Dorsey, who had become Gulf's chief executive officer just a few months earlier, revealed the $100,000 contribution. Some time later it was mentioned that illegal giving had been standard practice, and initiated with a $50,000 contribution to Lyndon Johnson shortly after his election to the vice presidency in 1960. Other alleged recipients, during the next dozen years, included members of the Senate Watergate Committee; Senators Hubert Humphrey, Henry Jackson, and Fred Harris; Congressman Wilbur Mills; and other notables.

Since Bob Dorsey had so recently become Gulf's CEO, there was, initially, a feeling that he might not have been personally involved. But subsequent testimony proved otherwise; moreover, he had personally authorized the largest payments—totaling $4 million—to South Korea's President, Park Chung Hee.

Slowly, as the scenario unfolded, investigators discovered the existence of Bahamas Exploration Company, a Gulf subsidiary that laundered slush-fund money. Eventually, the total of the illegal political gifts came to over $10 million. It was here that the Mellon four-generation-old strategy—find and trust competent hired hands—failed miserably.

Gulf Oil's board of directors, at that time, consisted of two officers, a former officer, and seven outside directors. Among the outsiders, five were identified as Mellon directors, but only one of them was a Mellon family member. As new evidence was found and as the Securities and Exchange Commission began to take a keener interest, the Mellon board members awoke to their responsibilities. Heard at first were the typical outside-director protestations, that they were innocent because of ignorance. "Charles M. Beeghly, retired chairman of Jones & Laughlin Steel Company, indicated in a sworn statement last November [1975] that 'Bahamas Exploration' was 'a new name to me' when it was cited in a Dec. 11, 1973, report to the Gulf board by the Pittsburgh law firm. Yet, Mr. Wild had identified Bahamas Exploration as the location of the slush fund in nationally televised testimony before the Senate Watergate Committee a month prior to the report."[21]

A number of similar conflicting explanations only served to emphasize how nearly impossible it is for outside directors—removed from, perhaps even disinterested in, the scene—to do an effective job. As in the case of the Penn Central fiasco, the evidence points overwhelmingly to the inattentiveness of outside directors. Note that nowhere in Gulf's earlier board minutes was there any evidence that the directors were seeking more information. "But Gulf's outside directors grew noticeably more concerned about the details of the slush fund after the Securities and Exchange Commission started an investigation in October, 1974, according to minutes of various board meetings. The worries mounted when the SEC filed a lawsuit in March 1975 attacking the slush fund, and the agency demanded that the board name a special review committee led by a complete outsider to investigate the entire affair."[22] John J. McCloy, an eighty-one-year-old New York lawyer and former public servant, was the outsider choice.

The situation intensified as shareholders, emboldened by the SEC action, filed lawsuits naming most of the directors as defendants. The lawsuits claimed the directors should have been more alert, and sought to have them reimburse Gulf for the $10.3 million channeled through the slush fund. Belatedly, and seemingly to protect their own individual interests, Gulf's board decided to fire its CEO, Bob Dorsey. The mutiny was spearheaded by the five Mellon-connected directors. " 'The atmosphere in the board room was sort of like a jury room,' reports an insider. There was argument but 'they didn't take any written ballots and there was little parliamentary maneuvering.' "[23] Several of the outside directors suggested a more conventional ouster. For example, there was a proposal to set up an office of the president where Dorsey would serve as one of the troika, but in a superficial

[21]Byron E. Calame, "Cleaning Up the Slush," *The Wall Street Journal*, January 13, 1976, p. 41.
[22]Ibid.
[23]Byron E. Calame, "Gulf Officers' Ouster Was Boldly Engineered by Mellon Interests," *The Wall Street Journal*, January 15, 1976.

way, perhaps as honorary chairman. Meanwhile, the Mellon majority warned Dorsey that they were not bargaining for a resignation and that they had the votes to oust him if he refused to resign. After an emotional six-hour ordeal, the board announced that it had accepted Dorsey's resignation.

Interestingly, two recently appointed directors—one a nun, the other an educator—voted differently. George Kozmetsky, dean of the College of Business Administration at the University of Texas, sought to establish the troika and gently ease Dorsey out of the CEO post. Sister Jane Scully, president of Carlow College, voted with the Mellon interests. Even though Sister Scully had been selected as a director by Dorsey, she voted for outright ouster. Her reasoning was that Gulf Oil, as a corporate citizen, had an obligation to society and she simply could not absolve the guilty. She opted for significant management changes in order to restore a sense of rectitude in the company. Sister Scully's corporate-citizen posture was beyond questioning, but the Mellon directors' motivation was viewed with cynicism. Critics reasoned that with the increasing threat of shareholder suits and with SEC inquisition, the Mellon directors feared there was real danger of court action, and they dreaded the embarrassment.

Chairman Dorsey was stunned by the turn of events. No doubt he thought the board would typically let the entire episode evaporate; after all, almost three years went by before the board took any action. Its punishment of the chief culprit, Vice President Wild, consisted of firing him from his post, but immediately putting him back on its payroll as a consultant, at approximately the same salary. Wild's rehiring probably would have gone unnoticed except that, at the 1975 annual meeting, one stockholder asked if Wild was still on the payroll. Dorsey then mentioned the consultant arrangement. Some directors seemed startled, even shocked, claiming they did not recall ever being told about Wild's being retained as a consultant. This, in itself, was a negative reflection on Gulf's uninformed directors. Considering the magnitude of the problem, and the legal responsibility of all directors to keep informed, it is hard to believe that some directors would feign ignorance. By releasing the principal culprit, Claude Wild, from all liability, and rewarding him with a retainer, Gulf's board was equally and, perhaps, even more guilty than its chief executive officer.

Other ramifications followed. As a direct consequence of the scandal, Gulf Oil broke up a forty-six-year mutually rewarding relationship with Price Waterhouse & Company. This outstanding accounting firm was fired because it refused to share, with certain Gulf directors, the stigma and costs of an out-of-court settlement of shareholder litigation. Despite persistent pressures to contribute as much as $2 million as its share for settling out of court, Price Waterhouse maintained its posture of rectitude. It refused, even when Gulf's Mellon directors, in an eleventh-hour appeal, dropped the asked-for figure to $50,000. Late in 1976, a judge dismissed Price Waterhouse as a defendant and approved a settlement. The major cash reimbursement ordered by the court against Gulf's directors, and in favor of the corporation, was set at $2 million. Payment was to be made by the insurance company that provided the directors' and officers' liability insurance coverage. Herein might be the answer to why the outside directors insisted on getting Price Waterhouse to share the onus: It would have improved their chances that the insuring company could not default, claiming the directors had prior knowledge. (All D&O liability coverage is conditioned by the proviso that none of the directors has had prior knowledge.) Price Waterhouse did pay a price for its firm stand—it was replaced as an outside auditor of the $2 million account by Coopers and Lybrand.

The Gulf Oil case has an important bearing on corporate governance, particularly where there is a fairly high concentration of ownership. Even though their sizable stock sell-offs (during the early 1970s) reduced the Mellon family and bank holdings in Gulf from about 30 percent to about 18 percent, the Mellons still remained dominant, but lacked an efficient family-member overseer. "The events at Gulf reflect a distinct loosening of the family's control since the 1970 death of Richard King Mellon, known as 'the king,' who was a dominant overseer of the family's corporate interests. 'If R. K. had still been around, there wouldn't have been a special review committee report' one Gulf insider says. 'There would have been a new management in 1973. He was a power.' "[24]

At the time of their transgression, Gulf's outside directors were being paid retainers of $20,000, plus meeting fees and all expenses. They were derelict in assuming they had sinecures rather than jobs with very real, nondelegating responsibilities. "In discussing the problem of illegal campaign contributions, the McCloy committee said: 'It is hard to escape the conclusion that a sort of 'shut-eye sentry' attitude prevailed upon the part of both the responsible corporate officials and the recipients as well as on the part of those charged with enforcement responsibilities.' The key phrase is from a Kipling poem, 'The Shut-Eye Sentry,' which contains the lines:

But I'd shut my eyes in the sentry-box,
So I didn't see nothin wrong.

"If there is a lesson for directors in the Gulf episode, it is that as surrogate sentries for the shareholders, they must be alert at the watch. And, if they doze, they are apt to be rudely awakened by unfriendly lawyers rapping loudly at the box."[25]

---

[24]Calame, "Cleaning Up the Slush," op. cit., p. 40.
[25]Wyndham Robertson, "The Directors Woke Up Too Late at Gulf," *Fortune*, June 1976, p. 210.

GENESCO: OFFICERS BLOW THE WHISTLE

Patricide is known to have been a favorite pastime of impatient heirs apparent. In the corporate sovereignty game, however, patricide is bloodless and generally takes place in the boardroom. The heir, usually in the boardroom only by the sufferance of the intended victim, organizes his cabal, which invariably consists of outside directors with strong financial stakes in the firm. This type of usurpation was perfectly executed, in 1973, at Genesco, Incorporated, the billion-dollar retailing and apparel conglomerate, and Tennessee's biggest industrial firm.

W. Maxey Jarman, in a tremendously successful thirty-year career as chief executive, built a small family shoe company into one of our nation's top corporations, comprising a variety of companies—Bonwit Teller, Jarman Shoes, I. Miller, Flagg Bros., Roos Atkins, S. H. Kress. Jarman then dutifully retired at age sixty-five; earlier he had initiated mandatory retirement requirements for all Genesco employees, and he now followed his own mandate. Almost immediately, Franklin M. Jarman, his son, was catapulted into the chief executive's office when the person selected to succeed Maxey suddenly took sick and left the company. Some felt Franklin was too young, at age thirty-seven, and minus executive seasoning. Within the first year of his tenure, even Maxey, who endorsed him at first, now "declared that Frank couldn't handle the job." Three years later, as Genesco's earnings' slide accelerated, Maxey came out of retirement and replaced his son.

Within six months Franklin engineered a coup, and when the twenty-three-member board convened, giving Franklin a narrow preference, Maxey, the entrepreneur, was promptly ousted. When he capitulated and resigned from the board, there was no testimonial of any sort to mark the end of fifty years of service to his company. Similarly, Franklin "rewarded" the board which gave him victory by cutting its size to ten members.

Back in power, Franklin initiated a stringent financial control system. "Controls were an obsession with Jarman. According to insiders he centralized management to the point of frustrating the company's executives and causing red tape and delay. Operations were virtually paralyzed by paper work."[26] "By the first Friday of every month, Jarman gets 'a jillion numbers—beautiful accurate numbers' on operations for the previous month. Ask him a question about Genesco and he inevitably turns to a thick black book that holds every conceivable statistic."[27]

The financial constraints were obviously onerous, as was the organizational complexity. There were seventy-eight operating company presidents who reported to eleven group presidents, who in turn reported to five chief

---

[26]"What Undid Jarman: Paperwork Analysis," *Business Week,* January 24, 1977, p. 67.
[27]"Genesco Comes to Judgement," *Fortune,* July 1975, p. 178.

operating officers. In the presidential pyramid there were, thus, ninety-five presidents, headed by the chief operations officer, Ralph Bowles. Bowles was also a member of a troika, an "office of the chairman," which Jarman set up. The office also included Jarman and the chief administrative officer, Larry Shelton.

Despite the installation of sound financial controls and innovative organizational management methods, a director observed that a lot of people left Genesco. Among the managers, 230 either quit or were fired that first year. The board began to have qualms about Franklin's ability to attract and keep top-notch managers.

Conditions continued to deteriorate, and by the end of 1974, a board-room coup was engineered by the two inside directors on the board. Surprisingly, both these "regicides" were much indebted to their CEO—he had named them vice chairmen, to serve in the office of the chairman. It was this triumvirate which ran Genesco. Presumably, as conditions worsened, the two insiders became alarmed and made a surreptitious visit to a prominent Genesco outside director in Washington. They convinced him that immediate action was necessary but that they felt powerless because the problem was their boss. The telling argument against Franklin was the demoralization of the managers—it was a revolt of the troops.

A special meeting of the board was quickly convened, and "from the start the sentiment against Mr. Jarman was so strong that when votes were taken they were all unanimous. When he saw the handwriting on the wall, even Mr. Jarman voted for his own demotion."[28]

Observers close to the board discounted any personality clashes between Franklin and the other directors, since it was he who had handpicked all of them. As for the two "whistle-blowing" officer-directors, they were more than beholden to their chairman. "Mr. Jarman for his part says, 'The board's action wasn't the best solution: obviously the best solution would have been to keep me. But what happened was the second best answer.' "[29]

Four years after the "palace revolt," Genesco was partially successful in that it still survived. But annual sales had slumped to half their former level, and profits were minuscule. More than fifty of the eighty-plus companies that once constituted Genesco, the conglomerate, were sold off or merged. If something positive could be said, it would be that Genesco did avoid bankruptcy, the unfortunate destiny of another retailer, W. T. Grant. It also avoided falling into foreign clutches, as was Greater Atlantic and Pacific's fate.

[28]Bill Paul and Douglas R. Sease, "Demotion of Genesco's Chief Was Set in Motion by a Trip by Two Inside Directors to See an Outside Director," *The Wall Street Journal,* January 5, 1977, p. 1.
[29]Ibid.

In this grand finale of the Jarmans at Genesco, it might be said with humor that now Franklin realized a youthful aspiration. As a youngster, he did not want to work for his father. Maxey threatened his reluctant son that unless he joined the family firm, his inheritance would be cut off. Now Franklin's reluctance had ended with his reluctant departure from the family firm.

As for the whistle-blowers, when, in 1980, the company went outside to select a president-chief operating officer who would be the presumed heir to the chairman, the two "Brutuses," Ralph H. Bowles and George A. Langstall, resigned their executive vice presidencies.

If there is anything to be gleaned from this narrative, it is that no one is actually beyond suspicion and temptation when corporate control is at stake. Even a father cannot be sure of his scions. Nor is there any guarantee that, as a CEO, your own hand-picked board will always do your bidding, unless you own a controlling stock interest. Finally, do not accept the dictum that all inside directors or officer-directors are forever spineless and will always subordinate themselves to the CEO. As Franklin Jarman learned too late, officer-directors can "blow whistles," and when they do, they are usually heard.

MCGRAW-HILL/AMEX: TENDER OFFER

Are directors obliged to allow shareholders to make the final decision in regard to tender offers? This is one of the issues that erupted from an "unfriendly" tender offer made by American Express Company (AmEx). Early in 1979, AmEx tried to acquire all 24.4 million common shares of McGraw-Hill, Incorporated, plus the preferred shares, at a total purchase price of about $880 million. The opening offer was $34 per share at a time when the stock was selling for about $26 on the New York Stock Exchange—a 30 percent markup. At the time of the offer, AmEx already was the owner of 7.1 million shares, or 29 percent of McGraw-Hill (MH) stock.

Harold W. McGraw, Jr., chairman of McGraw-Hill, immediately coun-teracted by mobilizing family, friends, investors, and even McGraw-Hill authors to protect the company's autonomy and integrity. This unexpected stiff opposition quickly prompted AmEx to raise its price to $40 per share, thus resulting in a 54 percent premium. Immediately the media referred to this as a "friendly" offer. But McGraw-Hill's chairman was neither tempted nor placated. His irritation stemmed, in part, from what he perceived to be a gross violation of near-sacred corporate governance precepts, by AmEx and its sponsoring financial institutions. In fact he felt betrayed, and for justifiable reasons.

AmEx's president, Roger H. Morley, was a member of the MH board. Morley "sat quietly as an outside director on McGraw-Hill's board while his own company's investment firm (Lazard Freres and Company), for at least three months, was developing plans for a McGraw-Hill takeover. Indeed, Mr. Morley and Jonathan O'Herron, the Lazard partner in charge of the McGraw-Hill project, were Harvard Business School classmates and long-time friends."[30] *Business Week* stated that it was believed by insiders that Morley was scouting MH during the two years he was on its board. Obviously, if this charge were true, then Morley was guilty of unethical boardroom behavior and very likely could be charged with conflict of interest. In a sense, he was a double agent.

A second charge was equally serious, namely, that Morgan Guaranty Trust Company, McGraw-Hill's principal banker for more than fifty years, was financing the AmEx deal as the lead bank in a six-bank consortium. Because of this, McGraw-Hill's chairman accused Morley in a two-page newspaper advertisement: "Any company that would use its financial power to cause a bank to violate its relationship with a client lacks the integrity and morality essential to the business of McGraw-Hill."[31] However-er, Morgan Guaranty, whose trust department held 1.1 million McGraw-Hill shares, was not the only bank implicated; involved also was Chase Manhattan, with 318,000 shares. Together, they stood to gain approximate-ly $20 million. Meanwhile, Morgan Guaranty held 2 million AmEx shares, Chase Manhattan held 1.8 million, and Manufacturers Hanover held 1.4 million shares. These three banks were party to the six-bank consortium engaged in financing AmEx's attempt to take over McGraw-Hill.

In this merger attempt, involving such enormous bank investments in both companies, only the naive could accept the Chinese Wall reasoning. As defined in an earlier illustration, the "Wall" establishes internal proce-dures to ensure that a bank's lending officers and its trust investment officers do not communicate information to one another. Evidently, the banks and Morley assumed this was a rational defense. It was said that Morley had done a conscientious job in keeping all papers pertinent to his McGraw-Hill directorship segregated and properly safeguarded under lock and key.

Now there are serious questions as to what precautions would be considered adequate by the New York courts under that state's fiduciary and corporate governance laws. Commenting on Morley's Chinese Wall ambiv-alence, *The Wall Street Journal* stated, "But initially at least it puzzled State Court Judge Martin B. Stecher. 'He (Morley) may not have disclosed it to his associates, but he certainly disclosed it to himself.'"[32] A Pennsylvania orphans court judge concurs: "Chinese walls are total fiction."

The outstanding feature of this episode was the vigorous counterattack

[30]Priscilla Meyer and Bill Abrams, "McGraw-Hill Girds for Its Board Meeting," *The Wall Street Journal*, January 15, 1979, p. 5.

[31]*The Wall Street Journal*, January 18, 1979, pp. 14–15.

[32]Priscilla Meyer, "McGraw-Hill Puts Outside Directors in Legal Slumber," *The Wall Street Journal*, February 2, 1979, p. 12.

staged by Harold McGraw, Jr. Financial odds proved to be against him—during the past ten years 85 percent of all target companies had been acquired sooner or later, sometimes by a "white knight," a supposedly friendly firm with even greater financial clout than the original unfriendly aggressor. There were *fifteen* assorted white knights waiting to rescue McGraw-Hill. Yet, considering the magnitude of the deal, it is questionable whether a suitable champion could really have come to the rescue.

In its counterattack, McGraw-Hill (as previously mentioned) purchased two-page advertisements addressed to American Express directors. It stressed, for example, that in the spring of 1978, AmEx's chairman had approached MH, soliciting interest in a merger. Upon being told a merger would not be in the interests of MH, AmEx's chairman, Morley, gave his absolute word and assurance that if MH was not interested in pursuing the matter, nothing further would be done.

A list of potential conflict-of-interest situations for AmEx's directors was published, in the event merger with McGraw-Hill materialized. These conflicts would arise from American Express directors' membership on boards of MH competitors, and would result in multiple violations of United States antitrust laws and the Federal Communications Act (1934). Conflicts would also arise out of MH's many ventures such as *Business Week* and Standard & Poor's credit rating service. Moreover, the independence and credibility of McGraw-Hill would be diminished, with serious loss to the academic, educational, and scientific communities.

Consequently, McGraw-Hill's board of directors, prompted into taking appropriate legal action, authorized a lawsuit against American Express, Morley, the AmEx directors, and every other person or entity participating in the conspiratorial breach of fiduciary duty to McGraw-Hill's stockholders. The suit intended to recover hundreds of millions of dollars in damages resulting from this wrongful conduct. According to legal convention, American Express retaliated by suing McGraw-Hill for libel—an action believed to be the first of its kind in a takeover battle.

In view of the fact that the McGraw family had only a 20 percent interest, compared with the enormous size of the banks' financial entanglements, McGraw showed tremendous courage. His strong offensive play, his use of checkmating via the public advertisement, plus the threatened lawsuit, unnerved the opposition, and AmEx allowed its last offer, $40 per share, to expire.

Harold McGraw's strategy was confirmed at the annual stockholders' meeting when 67 percent of the votes favored management's actions and only 11 percent voted against. Probably the most bitter attacks on MH management's steadfast refusal to sell out came from a few investors, who felt they had lost potential profit. Arbitragers, in particular, who were reputed to have speculated on as many as 5 million shares, were vehement.

No doubt Guy P. Wyser-Pratte was the most bitter because he had the most to lose—he had purchased 46,900 shares at between $30 and $31. When the merger deal fell flat, so did MH stock—dropping back to its premerger level of $26 per share. Meanwhile, Wyser-Pratte, who was paid on a formula, and had earned $864,855 from arbitraging in the previous year, in his pique philosophized: "Everyone in these things always claims they're doing what's in the best interests of the shareholders—the boards, the investment bankers, even the class action lawyers. But everyone's really out for themselves. No one represents the interests of the shareholders."[33]

But back to the introductory question—are directors obliged to allow shareholders to make the final decision in regard to tender offers? The answer and the real test is still a few years away, and will come from judicial pronouncements. Harold McGraw, Jr., risked much. He realized that McGraw-Hill was a temptation, with $64 million in cash and very little debt. It had a 20 percent growth in earnings in each of the three prior years. Yet its book value only came to about $13 per share. His stance was very risky. "If a lawsuit went against MH directors, they would be liable for about $290 million—the difference between the stock's post-offer price and the $40 offered by AmEx. The willingness to take such a risk is evidence of their commitment to their position. MH holds only $10 million in directors' and officers' liability insurance."[34]

This observation is very important, particularly since the general public feels that directors are so afraid of being sued that they are breaking their fiduciary duties by not putting up an adequate and honorable resistance. Their refusal to fight inadequate or harmful offers with resoluteness is a betrayal of trust. Fortunately, there have been cases where an aroused board, determined to survive, defends its sovereignty and autonomy. McGraw-Hill's directors had some splendid precedents, such as B. F. Goodrich's ingenious defense against Ben Heineman's Northwest Industries' unfriendly merger attempt. Giant Chemical Bank, likewise, resisted unflinchingly the audacious takeover by raider Saul Steinberg and his pygmy Leasco Corporation. And both American Motors and Montgomery Ward staved off the advances of raider Louis E. Wolfson. In turn, McGraw-Hill's heroics might subsequently have inspired others to resist.

In less than two years after the American Express–McGraw-Hill fracas, a similar situation involved Standard Oil Company of California's attempt to take over Amax Incorporated (formerly American Metals Climax Corporation). Rejection led to a $2.5 billion lawsuit against Amax. At the time of the tender, California Standard's offer was $2.5 billion above the market price

[33]Priscilla S. Meyer, "Cancelled Poll of McGraw-Hill Holders Signals End to American Express Bid," *The Wall Street Journal*, February 26, 1979, p. 11.
[34]*Business Week*, February 12, 1979, p. 41.

of Amax stock—Amax was trading at $38 per share when California Standard offered $78.50 per share. Yet Amax directors rejected the offer. " 'I frankly don't understand it (the Amax rejection),' Mr. Rosenblatt, a private investor said in an interview. 'I've never seen a more generous offer in my life. I can't understand when you have an offer that's more than twice the market value, why it is rejected summarily. . . . If Amax directors were holding out for a higher offer, I think the stockholders would be delighted.' "[35]

As previously mentioned, many stockholders were irate when Harold McGraw and his MH directors rejected the American Express initial offer of $40 per share—a 54 percent premium over the NYSE quote. As if to justify the board's action, in less than two years, the stock market had revalued MH stock, setting a 1981 high of $56 per share. Even the most rabid of yesterday's critics would have to admit that tendering their shares would have been a mistake. McGraw-Hill, Incorporated, is now worth considerably more as an independent entity than as a publications subsidiary of a big conglomerate.

Typical of so many jilted suitors, the rebuffed American Express soon found other new infatuations. Within a year it had purchased a 50 percent interest in Warner Communications' cable TV subsidiary for $175 million. With that purchase, American Express had to give up two of its directors who had other board seats on companies with TV connections. The next year, American Express, ever the ardent wooer, in a tax-free stock swap valued at $915 million, acquired Shearson Loeb Rhoades, the nation's number-two brokerage house.

Earlier, just months after AmEx lost its bid for McGraw-Hill, it also lost its president—Roger H. Morley resigned. As for Harold W. McGraw, Jr., when "asked if he used an American Express card, 'yes,' he replied, 'but two weeks ago in preparation for a trip to Japan I obtained a Master Charge and a Visa card. I'll leave it to you to speculate which I will make primary use of.' "[36]

WILLIAM F. BUCKLEY: CULPABLE IGNORANCE

Not all precedent-setting corporate governance cases have involved major corporations. In what was termed "the first case ever brought against all of a corporation's outside directors,"[37] the SEC charged nine officers of Starr Broadcasting Group, Incorporated, with violating securities laws. Among

---

[35]Richard D. James, "Amax Holder Urges Board to Reconsider Acquisitions Offer," *The Wall Street Journal*, March 18, 1981, p. 26.

[36]"McGraw-Hill's Directors Takeover Move," *The Wall Street Journal*, January 19, 1979.

[37]"Outsiders on the Board Face an SEC Squeeze," *Business Week*, July 17, 1979, p. 35.

these were four inside directors who, the SEC said, knew of, but failed to apprise stockholders of, the true motive for their illegal action. This action was the purchase—by Starr Broadcasting—of drive-in theater properties in Texas, from a partnership whose most visible member was William F. Buckley, Jr., the famous talk show Torquemada. Buckley also was chairman of Starr Broadcasting.

In the testimony, it appeared that Buckley engineered the deal by setting up a separate venture called Sitco. This new firm bought the seventeen Texas theaters—the investment, however, was bad to begin with and soon went from bad to worse. Fearing that Sitco would go bankrupt, Buckley had Starr Broadcasting buy the theaters from Sitco for $8 million. Although Buckley claimed this was an "arm's length" transaction, the SEC charged it was improper use of Starr's assets since, in Starr's 10-K report, there had been no mention of Sitco losing money. There were many legal convolutions, most of which were devised by Buckley. For example, he claimed he was never active in managing Starr but was preoccupied with his "hectic and itinerant professional life." Yet documents and witnesses' testimony showed that Buckley was definitely not a passive bystander.

"Mr. Buckley now says that although he was chairman, he didn't read the 10-K reports. 'Nixon didn't read the SALT I Treaty,' he says, adding that he wouldn't have spotted any errors or omissions in the 10-Ks anyway."[38] On the same theme: "I did not even know what a 10-K was (at the time). I live in a world in which people are simply unaware of the uses of boiler plate."[39]

There were a number of interesting ramifications; for instance, some questions arose as to Starr's paying $70,000 in operating expenses for the schooner *Cyrano,* leased from Buckley; the respected *National Review* was almost dragged into the affair; and then there were the outside directors. One of these, Glenn R. Burrus, had made an $850,000 loan to Buckley and his partners. When Starr got the theaters, it guaranteed the loan, which would have been defaulted if Buckley had gone bankrupt. It is interesting to note that three of the outside directors were Buckley's old Yale classmates— in fact, Buckley and two of the directors had been members in Skull and Bones, a Yale secret society.

An important lesson for outside directors is pointed up in the resolution of charges against one of Starr Broadcasting Group's outside directors, Maurice L. McGill, a Phoenix, Arizona, accountant. The SEC did not accuse McGill of personally benefiting from the transactions, or of preparing reports that failed to indicate the disclosures, but the commission did contend that he was responsible for making sure the reports complied with the securities law. "Mr. McGill said, 'The question wasn't whether I had

---

[38]June Kronholz, "On the Firing Line," *The Wall Street Journal,* September 24, 1976, p. 23.
[39]"Firing Line: W.F.B. vs the SEC," *Time,* February 19, 1979, p. 51.

personally benefited from the transactions but rather what the responsibilities of an outside director are. It would be interesting to take it to trial but my decision to settle was purely economic. The cost of fighting the SEC to completion would be enormous.' ''⁴⁰

Starr's chairman, Bill Buckley, likewise, signed a tough consent decree, saying that he wanted to avoid costly litigation. According to the decree, Buckley would surrender about $600,000 worth of Starr stock to a court-administered fund, to be distributed to Starr shareholders. Total cost to Buckley was estimated to be about $1.4 million.

There were further SEC pressures. In 1980 dissident stockholders of United Canso Oil and Gas, Ltd., the crown jewel of the Buckley financial empire, ousted John W. Buckley—a brother—from the company presidency. The holders were irate because excessive royalties—the latest a whopping $3.2 million—were being funneled from United Canso to the 98 percent Buckley-owned Catawba Corporation. The SEC also probed Catawba's entanglements with six publicly owned oil companies. In November 1981, Catawba in a consent agreement paid $175,000 to four of the energy companies.

In a swan-song parting with corporate directorships, "Buckley says he will never again sit on a public company's board. 'The evolution of a director's responsibility is running ahead of inflation,' he complains. 'The contemporary director is supposed to know more about accounting than the company accountant and more about the law than the company lawyer.' ''⁴¹

J. P. STEVENS AND COMPANY: CORPORATE CAMPAIGN

Despite the many vaunted advantages of outside boards, and oversight boards in particular, they have been known to possess an Achilles' heel. The seventeen-year tussle with the Amalgamated Clothing and Textile Workers Union (ACTWU) at J. P. Stevens brought this vulnerability to public attention. Back in 1963, as remnants of the textile industry continued their exodus from New England to the South, the labor unions intensified their membership recruiting.

In a representation election at J. P. Stevens's Roanoke, Virginia, plant, the ACTWU—in 1974—squeaked through with an initial victory over the nation's second largest textile firm. This victory precipitated a lengthy feud, with each side engaging in questionable tactics. The courts issued three

---

⁴⁰SEC's Charges Settled by a Former Director of Starr Broadcasting,'' *The Wall Street Journal,* June 25, 1979, p. 5.
⁴¹''Firing Line: W.F.B. vs the SEC,'' op. cit., p. 51.

contempt citations against the company for violating earlier court orders, and the union, supported by the AFL-CIO, called for a consumer boycott against J. P. Stevens products. Interestingly, the union forces were led by Murray Finley, and the J. P. Stevens cause was championed by James Finley, chairman and chief executive officer. Although unrelated, their identical surnames gave a label to the struggle—Finley versus Finley.

The strike earned a place in labor union history—for its duration and for its final breakthrough despite a most resolute employer's resistance. The intriguing thing, from a corporate governance viewpoint, was the union's "corporate campaign." The idea was to put pressure on other corporations having dealings with J. P. Stevens, and thus isolate Stevens on the business scene. This strategy was devised by Raymond F. Rogers, ACTWU's corporate campaign director. Rogers cleverly decided to attack the company via the company's boardroom interlock route.

Although the company bears the family name, J. P. Stevens is not a family-owned firm; actually the Stevens family owns less than 4 percent. The current CEO, Whitney Stevens—a family scion—owns only $\frac{3}{10}$ of 1 percent of the equity. This diminished family ownership is reflected by the use of several very influential business leaders who serve on the board.

The first test of corporate campaign strength came in Rogers's foray against the giant Manufacturers Hanover Bank, when the existence of two direct interlocks between J. P. Stevens and Manufacturers Hanover was made known. Stevens's CEO, James Finley, and another Stevens director, David Mitchell, chairman of Avon Products, Incorporated, were on the bank's board. Rogers got the cooperation of eight unions which threatened to sever their financial dealings with the bank. One union actually removed $6.4 million of investments handled by the bank, and another union closed a $400,000 account. William Winpisinger, president of the International Association of Machinists, was the first union official to openly suggest removal of pension funds from Manufacturers Hanover because of its tie with Stevens. The union debated whether it should drop the bank as the money manager of its $160 million fund, covering 150,000 machinists. Earlier, the United Auto Workers Local 259 ended a thirty-six-year relationship with Manufacturers Hanover when it closed its $50,000 checking account because of the tensions at Stevens. (It was estimated that as much as $1 billion in total union deposits, individual members' deposits, and pension funds was handled by Manufacturers Hanover.) Within months, the Stevens CEO was forced off the bank's board, saying he decided "not to go where you're not wanted." The other Stevens director, David Mitchell, also declined to seek renomination, attributing his decision not to union pressure but to business-time conflicts.

The corporate campaign, instigated by Rogers, produced other notable results when Mitchell also resigned from the Stevens board. This time

Mitchell was more forthright in stating, "I cannot permit Avon to be drawn into the conflict and to be subjected to the pressures which the union is exerting as a result of my Stevens board membership."[42]

Meanwhile, pressure mounted on R. Manning Brown, Jr., a member of both the Stevens and Avon boards, and also chairman and CEO of New York Life Insurance Company. Here, again, boardroom resistance to the union crumbled. In less than six months, with deep regret, Brown resigned from the Stevens board, and James D. Finley, Stevens's interlocking director, resigned from the New York Life board.

The union maneuver at New York Life was particularly intriguing. A key factor in the union's campaign was the announcement that it would run two independent candidates, in an attempt to unseat Brown and Finley. Neither of the union's candidates was a New York Life policyholder, nor a member of the textile workers union. Thus they were far more independent than Stevens's or New York Life's outside directors.

The union strategists were faced with some intricate issues. Realizing that New York Life does not have stockholders—only policyholders-owners—it meant there would be no conventional stockholders' meetings. The only resemblance to such meetings was the annual voting ritual, where a room at headquarters was kept open for six hours. Interested policyholders could come and deposit their votes, thus electing one-third of the total board to three-year terms. Ballots were mailed only upon request. If the union were to nominate its own candidates, it had to present a petition signed by $\frac{1}{10}$ of 1 percent (about 6500) of the policyholders. If this process were followed and were then approved by the proper state authorities, New York Life would have to send election ballots to all its policyholders, listing both slates of candidates. Considering the intricacies of such an election, a company spokesperson said that if such an opposition slate were successful in gaining enough signatures, it would create a nightmare for the insurance company.

As stated earlier, Rogers's corporate campaign succeeded when the J. P. Stevens–New York Life directorate interlocks were severed. The union strategists now had to reevaluate their battle plans. Finley, J. P. Stevens's chairman, was still on the Sperry Rand and Borden boards, and E. Virgil Conway, chairman and president of Seamen's Bank for Savings, continued on the Stevens board. Rogers warned Sidney J. Weinberg, Jr., a partner in the investment firm of Goldman, Sachs and Company, and also a Stevens director, that he might be the next union target. Rogers also stressed that Morgan Guaranty Trust Company was an important Stevens stockholder and was very vulnerable to outside pressure.

---

[42]Deborah Sue Yaeger, "Union Scores Second Victory at Stevens as Avon Chairman Resigns from Board," *The Wall Street Journal,* March 3, 1978, p. 2.

Meanwhile, J. P. Stevens was striving to shore up its shaken battlements. With a grand total of eighteen National Labor Board citations for labor law violations, it had earned itself the title as the nation's number-one labor law violator. Likewise, it had attracted unfavorable attention because it had neither a woman nor a black on its board, even though its labor force was distinctly female and black. In a conciliatory gesture at its 1979 meeting, J. P. Stevens elected its first black and also its first woman. The charges of tokenism were denied by the chairman and by the black director, Henry Ponder, president of Benedict College, Columbia, South Carolina. However, Winifred T. Wells, an attorney, conceded that tokenism " 'might have been the case in her election' adding that 'if I can't contribute something and I won't be listened to, I won't stay on the board. So far we've been listened to.' "[43]

Actively resuming its corporate campaign in the first half of 1980, the union tried to oust Finley from the board of Sperry Rand, but Finley remained firm and Sperry would not budge. Then, by a masterstroke, the union switched its strategy and attacked Metropolitan Life Insurance Company, J. P. Stevens's biggest lender. Meanwhile, J. C. Penney, the textile company's biggest seller, was another likely target. In these two instances, interlocking was not focused on those occupying boardroom seats because neither Metropolitan Life nor J. C. Penney had any direct interlock with J. P. Stevens. However, there was indirect interlocking: The chief executives of the new targets, Metropolitan and Penney, were members of the committee that, in mid-1980, nominated Stevens's CEO to another term on the Sperry Rand board.

Zeroing in on Metropolitan Life, the ACTWU proposed to contest two of the insurance company's twenty-two board seats. As its nominees, the union proposed a black woman minister and a Metropolitan insurance salesman. It followed the same procedure used at New York Life—signatures obtained from twenty-five policyholders were used to solicit permission from the New York State Insurance Department to get access to Metropolitan Life's policyholders' records. Reflecting that it had never had a contested election, Metropolitan's chairman felt that such an election would create acute embarrassment. Mailing ballots to more than 23 million policyholders, plus legal and other costs, would have totaled close to $7 million.

Metropolitan Life's CEO was not accused of applying pressure, but he was credited with some very effective behind-the-scenes actions: " 'Without my ever having to say anything,' stated Mr. Shinn [Metropolitan Life's CEO], 'J. P. Stevens realized that if in the course of good business

[43]Jeffrey H. Birnbaum, "J. P. Stevens Posts Record 1st Quarter Net at a Meeting Enlivened by Union Dispute," *The Wall Street Journal,* April 21, 1979, p. 2.

dealings they could settle with the union, it would minimize our election problems with the textile workers.' "[44]

This was the coup de grace, the blow that unseated the errant knight, J. P. Stevens. After almost two decades of chronic defeat and humiliation, the union won the joust. J. P. Stevens signed a contract covering ten plants, and the troublesome seven Roanoke plants signed shortly afterward; but more than sixty plants remained outside the union domain. Pay raises and checkoff of union dues were granted. For its part, the union agreed to halt its boycott against Stevens's products and to end its corporate campaign. Most significantly, one clause in the agreement "prohibits the union from working to remove directors from the Stevens board and 'from restricting the availability of financial or credit accommodations to Stevens.' "[45]

Considerable debate followed in the aftermath—Ray Rogers's corporate campaign strategy was denounced as an illegal secondary boycott. While some businesspeople deplored becoming pawns in games in which they were not directly involved, the textile union's response was that corporations act out of self-interest and, therefore, in defense of its interests, the union had the right to wage corporate campaigns.

Emulation invariably follows success. Because the corporate campaign at J. P. Stevens was successful, the United Food and Commercial Workers, in mid-1979, similarly tried to marshal their financial clout against Seattle-First National Bank, the largest bank in the Pacific Northwest. The union, seeking to organize clerical workers at the bank, tried to persuade other unions to withdraw their funds from Seattle-First. However, after several months, only about $2 million was withdrawn from the bank's $7 billion assets.

Again, another test of the concept occurred in mid-1981, when the Air Line Pilots Association threatened a corporate campaign against Texas Air Corporation (TAC) and its subsidiary, New York Airways. Basically, the intent of the pilots' campaign was to prevent the acquisition of Continental Airlines by Texas Air. Fueling this conflagration was the fact that Texas Air's subsidiary, New York Airways, was nonunion. Ray Rogers, the supersuccessful corporate campaigner in the J. P. Stevens fight, agreed to organize and direct the pilots' campaign. Union members bombarded the companies with which Texas Air's outside directors were associated, using public criticism and personal letters and threatening boycotts as a means of persuasion. In trying to emulate the corporate campaign effort at J. P. Stevens, this latter attempt at TAC raised many new issues, even imponderables. For instance, the first endeavor involved low-paid, "exploited" textile

---

[44]Jeffrey H. Birnbaum, "How the Textile Union Finally Wins Contracts at J. P. Stevens Plants," *The Wall Street Journal*, October 20, 1980, p. 1.
[45]Ibid., p. 24.

workers—would the public be as sympathetic to the aggrieved airline pilots, who are among the nation's highest-paid workers? Then, too, J. P. Stevens had a hard-line antiunion record whereas Texas Air had no such record. More significantly, what happens if the target company has no vulnerable outside directors?

Whether good or bad, a new weapon has been added to organized labor's arsenal. It needs more testing to gauge its impact and continued effectiveness. Even with one victory, labor has shown it can win major concessions by exerting pressure on interlocking directors. Outside directors, in the future, will be reluctant to expose themselves and their firms to potential loss not only of boycotted business but also of hard-earned image. Neither will liability consequences be ignored. Several stockholder suits were filed against J. P. Stevens, but no pattern has evolved as yet. For better or for worse, the successful use of the corporate campaign has created just one more constraint on corporate governance.

BENDIX CORPORATION: THE CUNNINGHAM-AGEE SOAP OPERA

Harvard's Graduate School of Business has produced some fast-track master of business administration graduates, but the fastest record to date simply has to be Mary Cunningham's. As a Wellesley magna cum laude graduate, Cunningham had no business administration education before attending Harvard. Yet within a year after earning an MBA, Cunningham was promoted to vice president for corporate and public affairs at Bendix Corporation. Three months later, she was elevated to a higher post as vice president for strategic planning.

The grumblings that followed Cunningham's first vice presidential promotion were nothing compared with the uproar created over her second promotion. The controversy was amplified by William M. Agee, the forty-three-year-old chairman and chief executive, and also a Harvard MBA. Indignant over the rumors buzzing around—linking Agee and Cunningham romantically—Agee hired a hall near headquarters and convened a meeting "to explain to" 600 Bendix staff members. Agee believed that a face-to-face confrontation was necessary; "When talk gets above the noise level it is time to address it. I know it has been buzzing around that Mary Cunningham's rise in this company is very unusual and that it has something to do with a personal relationship that we have. Sure it's unusual. Her rise in this company is unusual because she's a very unusual and very talented individual. . . . Her rapid promotions have been totally justified."[46]

[46]"Miss Cunningham's Very Rapid Ascent," *The Wall Street Journal*, September 26, 1980, p. 35.

In her own justification, Mary Cunningham considered Mr. Agee as her mentor and served as his sounding board—"She's his key advisor," a company spokesperson says. "She counsels him on the most important things in the company."[47] At other times she considered herself as his alter ego and most trusted confidante—Agee referred to her as his best friend. In his public disclaimer, he "hardly dispelled the notion that Cunningham's rise might have been due to cronyism. 'It is true,' Agee told the employees, 'that we are very, very close friends, and she's a very close friend of my family.' . . . Then in August, Agee and his wife of 23 years got a divorce so quickly it surprised even top officials at Bendix.

"What was one to think? Here were two young, attractive unattached people working together, even staying in the same two-bedroom suite at the Waldorf-Towers. They *had* to be having an affair—and that would explain Cunningham's sprint up the ranks."[48] It should be pointed out that Cunningham's "unattachment" was actually her separation and pending marriage annulment. During her senior year at Wellesley, she met "Howard R. Gray, a black man 11 years her senior who was then attending Harvard Business School. Within a year they were married. 'It was not a typical relationship,' Cunningham said recently. 'We were much more focused on the message we were sending to society from our marriage.' "[49]

The public airing of Bendix headquarters' "hanky-panky" created an opposite effect, not what Agee had intended. A Detroit newspaper reported his remarks and immediately the news media picked up the choice morsels. Within a week Cunningham requested a temporary leave of absence from her post as vice president of strategic planning. However, the board's organization committee unanimously declined her request and urged her to stay on despite the allegations. The committee emphasized that it had complete confidence in her and that it would be unjust for the corporation to respond to speculation by granting her request.

But shortly thereafter, the full board of directors met and indicated they had come to a consensus—Cunningham had to go. The adverse publicity and the internal bickering impaired her effectiveness. Cunningham then resigned.

There are a number of significant corporate governance implications in this case. Corporate boards have had to consider all sorts of accusations against their chief executives—there was even a scandal involving the chief executive of Olympia Brewing Company, charged in a homosexual act—but the Cunningham caper was the first time two top executives of a major corporation were implicitly accused of being romantically involved.

Of course, some would agree with Agee that "In the future I do not

[47]Ibid.
[48]Peter W. Bernstein, "Upheaval at Bendix," *Fortune,* November 3, 1980, p. 54.
[49]Ibid.

believe that I owe the management committee, the board, or external audiences a discussion or explanation of any aspects of my personal life unless I am accused of breaking the law. Henry Ford II, and before him Benjamin Disraeli, had already said it more succinctly: 'Never complain, never explain.' "[50]

On the other hand, those who differed with Agee were quick to stress that a public corporation's key executives are public figures, and must conform to prevailing moral standards. While a single impetuous sexual aberration might incur some public displeasure, a prolonged affair, particularly on company time and expense, is still anathema. It is the board's unpleasant duty to ferret out such deviations. If directors expect the public to look with deference upon the boardroom, then it is up to the directors to keep this sanctuary undefiled. Unfortunately, the directors at Bendix initially tried to whitewash the affair—fortunately, they failed.

But more serious are the repercussions from this episode—they seem to support Mary Cunningham's feelings that business is still macho-managed and she unjustly paid the penalty for straying from conventional morality. Ironically, the other main character in this scenario escaped unscathed. Some of Agee's fellow executives felt that during the four years he had been chairman and chief executive, the company's goals "have swerved across industries and veered from concept to concept. . . . Discontent over this erratic course of planning showed up last year when two top executives quit."[51] What most of Agee's executives resented was not so much the sexual implications, but rather the feeling that the Agee-Cunningham coziness was effectively isolating them from the executive group. "You always feel, as a senior executive, that you know what is going on, but it didn't work that way."[52]

But Agee's aberrations were evidenced even earlier when, consulting no one, he ordered the corporate boardroom table removed. In getting rid of Bendix's table, Agee said, "I didn't tell the board because I knew the answer would have been no."[53] Agee referred to the boardroom table as being brown and drab and looking "like a surfboard. He termed it just a security blanket. Some directors mildly disagreed. Mrs. Jewel S. Lafontant admits to being more self conscious about her posture and worrying whether her shoes are polished. She also says she'll have to avoid 'slipping off my shoes' in the meetings as she has done in the past."[54] Another critic states, " 'the table may be a crutch, but a big open space is a problem; eye-to-eye,

---

[50]Ibid.

[51]"Bendix: The Ongoing Mystery of Bill Agee's One-Man Show," *Business Week,* April 27, 1981.

[52]Ibid.

[53]"Board Room Table Banished at Bendix for Being a Barrier," *The Wall Street Journal,* March 6, 1978, p. 34.

[54]Ibid.

feet-to-feet contact is somewhat graceless.' He adds: 'your arms become a helluva nuisance.' "[55]

The shape, size, or even absence of a boardroom table is trivial in comparison with Agee's other atypical actions. Just before the Cunningham affair, he ousted Bendix's president and chief operating officer, William P. Panny; and Jerome Jacobson, executive vice president for strategic planning, resigned. Agee also terminated or transferred 250 of the 800 employees at company headquarters. The issue here revolved over divestitures and acquisitions, with close to a billion dollars—at Agee's discretion—for future endeavor.

One version of events leading to the Cunningham climax is that a number of disgruntled executives brought their complaints about the affair to President Panny, who then planned to take the matter to the board. "The next day, so the story goes, Agee fired him before he had a chance. Panny is mum on the subject, but Agee vehemently denies any link between the Cunningham issue and Panny's departure. 'He never raised the topic of Mary with me,' says Agee."[56]

There are a number of pertinent sequels: A year later, Bendix was doing very well. Its sales for 1981 amounted to $4.4 billion; net earnings, $453 million. Mr. Agee received a $300,000 raise, boosting his salary plus long-term income to $1,650,000. Earlier in 1982, Bendix, with a cash trove of $572 million, took aggressive action by purchasing a 7.3 percent interest in troubled RCA, presumably as an investment, but with acquisition possibilities.

Some contend that Agee engineered the resignations of three outside directors by seemingly seeking to acquire a high-technology company. Since the three outsiders had close ties to Burroughs Corporation, the intended acquisition would have raised questions of potential conflict of interest.

Only one director, Robert W. Purcell, who had served on the Bendix board since 1965, found the courage to speak up. Almost a year after the incident, Purcell made this statement: "Having lost confidence in top Bendix management and having tried without success to remedy the situation, I have resigned as a member of the Bendix board."[57] Purcell, senior member of the board, was then only two months away from the mandatory retirement age of seventy. Incidentally, his was the only action to rock the Bendix boardroom boat in the wake of the Cunningham-Agee caper.

---

[55]Ibid.

[56]Bernstein, op. cit., p. 53.

[57]John Koten, "Robert Purcell Quits as Bendix Director," *The Wall Street Journal,* August 28, 1981, p. 4.

Meanwhile, Cunningham accepted a six-figure salary position as vice president for strategic planning and project development at Joseph E. Seagram and Sons. She continues her protestations of sexual innocence, claiming "that she and Agee were never anything more than good friends. But she has resumed seeing Agee on a regular basis, though he lives in Michigan and she has taken an apartment in Manhattan."[58] Highlight of this sequel was the late spring 1982 announcement of Mary Cunningham's and William Agee's marriage.

Earlier in the episode, Cunningham had observed: "There are certainly no Harvard Business School cases on how to deal with this. Maybe there should be."[59] As if in response, Stanford University made her adventures the subject of a case study in its course—Power and Politics in Organizations.

POSTSCRIPT

In the Latin hymn "Magnificat," there is a very pertinent line: "He [God] puts down the mighty from their thrones and elevates those of low degree." What is true for political kingdoms is also true for industrial empires. Even a casual reflection will bring to mind numerous American enterprises that flourished, became dominant, and then passed into oblivion—their boards of directors and managements toppling with them.

Some of these examples: American Woolen Company, once *the* Woolen Trust, was subsequently acquired and cannibalized by Textron, an insignificant competitor. American Tobacco Company (now American Brands), foremost in the tobacco industry, is not even considered a runner-up today. Kennecott and Anaconda, once the world's copper kingdoms, are now mere duchies in the empires of other conglomerates. (Kennecott was acquired by Standard Oil of Ohio; Anaconda by Atlantic Richfield.) Great Atlantic and Pacific Tea Company, the greatest of grocers, has seen its dominion shrivel from a peak of almost 16,000 "economy stores" two generations ago to a lesser 4500 supermarkets one generation ago. More recently, A&P slumped from 3200 stores in 1975 to less than 800 in 1982. It also suffered the ignominy of being taken over by a foreign invader, Germany's Tengelmann Group, a family-owned firm.

Fifty years after World War I, the automobile industry continued to generate some mighty empires—General Motors, Ford, Chrysler, American Motors, and a dozen others with shorter life spans—until the invasion, first from the east (Europe) and then from the west (Japan), caused our mighty auto moguls to give ground. In a single year (1980), the combined losses of

---

[58]"Mary Cunningham Redux," *Time*, March 9, 1981, p. 61.
[59]Bernstein, op. cit., p. 56.

the four leaders approached $5 billion, presaging the mightiest monarchical humbling of all time.

There is a common strain in this litany of corporate lamentations: namely, all these industrial monarchs once had secure thrones, they were impervious to change, and they failed to adapt. Chapter 7 has presented some recent episodes having high potential for corporate humiliation. An apperceptive director will study and index not only these highlighted examples, but also all similar cases. When directors and boards recognize their own corporate failings, they will be in less immediate danger of being toppled.

CHAPTER 8

NEW/INNOVATIVE DESIGNS FOR BOARDS

PROLIFERATING PRESIDENTS

Thousands of ambitious American executives, in the 1970s, were fortunate that they were striving here and not in Zambia. Kenneth Kaunda, mercurial head of state, decreed, in 1973, that as head chief of his African nation, only he could use the title of "president." All other leaders of organizations would have to find other titles. There were even to be no presidents of school boards or of rotary clubs, much less of business enterprises.

Unwittingly, Kaunda, in his "purge of presidents" campaign, was echoing the convictions of another African, this one an invader. In the third century A.D., Servaeus Africanus, the district governor of Middle Egypt, wrote: "It is apparent from the accounts alone that a number of persons wishing to batten on the estates of the Treasury, have invented titles for themselves, such as comptroller, secretary or superintendent whereby they procure no advantage to the treasury but swallow up the profits."[1]

Whatever the reasons that motivate title iconoclasts, whether to cut costs or to cut political opposition, executive egalitarianism is an idle dream. There never has been an organization—not even the family—without a hierarchy, and titles are an inherent part of the hierarchical system. Congress has its Speaker of the House and President of the Senate, and Soviet commissars have their designations.

[1]British Museum Papyrus 752.

The eminent Italian philosopher-economist Vilifredo Pareto is credited for his succinct inference on the *inevitability of inequality*. So, if inequality is inevitable, then some are more equal than others, and the more equal invariably will invent appropriate titles for themselves. A glance at the organization chart of any American macrocorporation will, undoubtedly, show a maze of neat squares, rectangles, or circles, beautifully layered and neatly intertwined with lines of authority. Each entity on this hierarchical chart has a specific title, sounding more superlative with each upward rung on the corporate ladder.

Yet Henry Ford, one of the best-known proponents of centralized control, cautioned against a too great reliance upon organization charts, or any other formalized hierarchical structuring. To him, titles were an abomination, and for many years only two titles existed in his organization: a president-treasurer and a secretary-assistant treasurer. Ford's much-quoted observation on the genius for organization states: "This usually results in the birth of a great big chart showing after the fashion of a family tree, how authority ramifies. The tree is heavy with nice round berries, each of which bears the name of a man or of an office. Every man has a title and certain duties which are strictly limited by the circumference of his berry."[2]

Even after he relinquished his presidency to his son, Edsel, in 1918, Ford did not relinquish control. Although he used no title, there was absolutely no question about who was the boss. The company's business boomed, and it was inevitable that success would bring on increased size and organizational titles. Whereas Ford Motor Company had only two presidents in its first fifty years [excluding the short two-year tenure of its first president, John Gray (1903–1906)], it has had seven presidents in the past twenty-five years. Along with increased presidential succession have come organizational and performance problems, culminating in multimillion-dollar losses in the early 1980s. Organizationally, Henry Ford, Sr., would not recognize his corporate offspring which now compares with the average hierarchy in its use of rank and titles. There are, in fact, presidents of subsidiaries—Ford Motor Credit, Ford Motor Canada, Ford Europe, Ford Asia-Pacific. Even more of a departure from the past, the parent company has a tripartite office of the chief executive. In other words, Ford Motor Company has joined in the presidential proliferation game.

Some of the proliferation was due to the merger-conglomeration boom of the 1960s, which injected a span-of-control variable—how could one president encompass the expanded conglomerate domain? Also, how could the newly absorbed components be made to feel represented and "at home" in their new headquarters? The first and logical step in adapting

[2]Henry Ford, *My Life and Work* (Garden City, New York: Doubleday & Company, Inc., 1922), p. 91.

newly acquired companies to their conglomerate environment is to invite the chief executive of the merged company to sit on the parent board. However, because some conglomerates have exceeded more than a hundred acquisitions, and because of the limited number of boardroom seats, there have been some serious physical and political consequences. For example, International Telephone and Telegraph Corporation, at its acquisition peak, encompassed over 270 separate companies and divisions under Harold Geneen. In 1965, ITT had a lean, centralized headquarters structure, with basically just one president-chairman-CEO, Harold Geneen. This lean organization consisted of fifteen vice presidents, superintended by five senior vice presidents and overviewed by one executive vice president. Geneen's lean and swift corporate headquarters philosophy was epitomized in a graphic quote: A former ITT vice president remembered Geneen starting a meeting by saying, "Gentlemen, I've been thinking. Bull times zero is zero bull. Bull divided by bull is infinity bull. And I'm sick and tired of the bull you've been feeding me."[3]

A decade later, ITT's expansionism resulted in a flurry of divisional presidents. There were, for instance, presidents heading ITT General Controls, ITT Lamp Division, ITT Sheraton, Avis, and dozens of other divisions. In addition, more than a score of these president-headed divisions had their own boards, with chairmen.

Textron, the highly successful conglomerate, founded by one of our nation's great entrepreneurs, Royal Little, has twenty-five divisional presidents plus two managing directors. For administrative reasons, the major divisions are combined into groups such as aerospace, consumer, industrial, metal products, creative capital, and international. It is interesting to note that here we have twenty-seven presidents and managing directors reporting to group vice presidents. If this appears to be a reverse chain of command, that is, presidents reporting to vice presidents, it is because of the presidential proliferation problem.

Similarly, at Arthur D. Little, Incorporated, one of the most dynamic management consulting firms, there is, besides the corporate chairman and president, a team of nine senior vice presidents, sixty vice presidents, fourteen presidents, two chairmen, and six managing directors of divisions and subsidiaries. Again there seems to be an inconsistency regarding divisional presidents who serve as vice presidents of the parent.

Efficiency through organization seems to be the prime reason for this plethora of presidents. Our biggest corporate entity, American Telephone and Telegraph Company, for example, could scarcely coordinate its huge assets (approaching the $200 billion level before its 1982 breakup) and its million-plus employees without a judicious regionalizing. Considering that

[3]*The Oregonian* (Portland, Oregon), March 14, 1972, p. 15.

it then had twenty-three associated and near-autonomous companies, each headed by its own president, chairman, and board of directors, it is obvious that AT&T resembled a holding company.

Even Exxon Corporation, the number-one industrial enterprise, has fourteen peripheral presidents, six in charge of Exxon divisions and eight (including one chairman) heading affiliated companies. Similarly, at Union Carbide Corporation, there are twenty divisional presidents, most reporting to headquarter's officers of senior vice presidential rank.

This focusing on the multiplicity of presidential titles in our most eminent macrocorporations is intentional. It strengthens the contention that if the giants grow bigger and if the increased use of outside directors continues, new "mountains" will have to be created for overzealous executives to climb. Outstanding executives, therefore, must be sufficiently challenged to ascend the mountain. But in corporations with only one or two officer-directors, virtually all key employees come to dead ends at the executive level. In reality, only one or two key executives will, at any one time, reach the mountaintop, otherwise known as the board of directors. Invariably, they will be joined by outsiders who possess only a superficial acquaintance with the technological and business affairs of the company they are directing. At Exxon, for example, twenty years ago there was tangible evidence that fifteen hard-working, competent and loyal officers had reached the summit—they had earned seats in the boardroom Olympus. Today, despite Exxon's tremendous growth, only nine outstanding executives can attain the corporate Olympus, and these nine must share their boardroom with ten outsiders. Although these outsiders are eminently qualified in their respective fields, one wonders how many would know the difference between catalytic cracking and wildcatting, or if they would be able to differentiate between sweet and sour crude. By generating fourteen new presidential titles, Exxon hopefully multiplies its key executive motivators and gets performance results. It has charted fourteen new routes, but few lead to the ultimate boardroom Olympus.

But caution should be exercised. In the example of Genesco, Incorporated, detailed in a separate case illustration, Franklin Jarman, upon wresting the corporation away from his father, instituted a variety of modern management methods. He even set up a chief-executive troika, an office of the chairman. Among other innovations, he designated the seventy-eight heads of the operating companies as presidents. These seventy-eight presidents reported to eleven group presidents, who reported to five chief operating officers, who reported to one chief operations officer. Here, too, the titular sequencing of presidents responding to operating officers seems to be out of kilter and could raise doubts in the divisional presidents' minds. That titles alone are not enough to generate profits is obvious in the subsequent travails of Genesco.

If improperly used, multiplying of presidents or of vice presidents can even downgrade the titles. This was the case with the overabundance of vice presidents in our banking industry a generation ago. At that time our ten biggest banks had a total of 1268 vice presidents, an average of 127 vice presidents per bank. During that same era, our ten biggest outside-director-dominated firms averaged thirty-four vice presidents each. In marked contrast, the ten biggest officer-director-run companies averaged only nine vice presidents each. There were, at that time, relatively few cases of presidential proliferation. It was virtually standard practice that there should be but one president per corporation.

The present proliferation of vice presidencies in banks, and both vice presidencies and presidencies in the corporate sector, has come about for a variety of reasons. There was a time when banks had abominably low pay scales, and so titles were the natural recourse. While salaries today are considerably better, promotional opportunities to the boardroom are virtually zero in most of our outside-director-run banks. Similarly, in the industrial sector it is becoming progressively more difficult for an able and ambitious executive to cross the boardroom threshold. To compensate for the scarcity of directorship titles, a plethora of presidential titles is being bestowed—executive, senior, group, staff, and an expanding assortment of others. President Kaunda of Zambia would indeed have good hunting, bagging big titles in our management jungle.

But far better hunting for big-game titles can be had abroad. "Italians, who rarely agree on anything, generally concede—indeed sometimes boast—that their country is just about as inefficient as any in Europe. No one can say precisely why."[4] But a survey compiled by Mediobanca, Italy's biggest investment bank, may have found a reason—too many government chiefs and not enough Indians. The survey found that "there are 59,340 presidents running government agencies, or one president for every 900 men, women and children in the country."[5]

The survey goes even further, showing that most agency presidents are entitled to a board of directors. Conservatively figured, this means about 1 million Italians sit on government boards. In a nation of 54 million, such boardroom multiplicity and staffing are an absurdity.

Mediobanca's survey goes further in this presidential dilemma—how can they be put to good use or be eliminated? "They can scarcely be sent to private industry: there are already 41,336 corporate presidents holding sway there. They certainly cannot join the armed forces. Italy presently has 541 generals to command an army of 267,570 men. As for the Italian navy, it has 123 admirals for every vessel in the fleet."[6]

---

[4]"A Plethora of Presidents," *Time*, January 29, 1973, p. 36.
[5]Ibid.
[6]Ibid.

SHARED AUTHORITY: THE OFFICE OF THE PRESIDENT[7]

The "office of the president" has a spatial sound and connotes visions of a suite where the firm's chief executive holds forth. It also carries hierarchical, functional, or process implications associated with the members of that "office." Early in the 1950s it assumed another meaning: the office of the president (or chairman or chief executive) was a sharing of chief executive authority and responsibilities by two or more key executives. In theory, the members of the office of the president (OP) are coequal; what one member enunciates in the absence of his coequals holds legally and effectively for the entire office. Ideally, there is also an allocation of the prime functions, so that in a four-member office, for example, there is a chief executive officer (CEO), a chief operating officer (COO), a chief financial officer (CFO), and a chief administrative officer (CAO). This functional allocation follows the classic division-of-labor precept. The increasing complexity of modern large-scale corporate endeavor virtually precludes that any one person can perform optimally in every one of the chief executive roles. Having two, three, or more coequal "chiefs," sharing duties where needed, maximizes their expertise and allows the CEO more precious time.

Critics, however, claim that the OP is simply another committee with all the frailties inherent in governance by committee. Some say that the OP innovation is nothing more than the relabeling of a long-established mechanism—the executive committee—which has been used since the turn of the century. As was pointed out earlier, a majority of our larger corporations have executive committees of the board of directors, which act for the entire board in interim periods between board meetings. But an executive committee is not an office of the chief executive, or of the chairman, or of the president. A typical executive committee shares no authority, nor does it pretend that the committee members are all coequals.

While there is some disagreement about the purpose and effectiveness of an office of the president, there is one area of near-agreement; namely, it can be useful for testing or training chief executive successors. For example, back in 1974 Ingersoll-Rand Company established a three-person office of the chief executive, with CEO succession in mind. In addition to the chairman-CEO, the troika included the vice chairman and chief financial officer and the president, who also served as chief operating officer—eventually one would succeed the CEO. Together, and with presumed equality, these two "junior" members of the troika oversaw a team of four executive vice presidents and twenty-one vice presidents. The chairman-CEO remained preeminent—he set company policy, which was then

---

[7]Stanley C. Vance, adapted from "Shared Chief Executive Authority: Chaos or Collegiality?" *Directors and Boards,* Fall 1980, pp. 5–10.

executed by the two "equal" members of the troika. But late in 1980, as the mandatory retirement of the chairman-CEO approached and a successor had to be selected, *The Wall Street Journal* mused: "Which of the two equals is more equal?"[8]

In addition to the chairman-CEO's unquestioned supreme authority at Ingersoll-Rand, a significant pay differential was also very evident—the chairman-CEO received almost $800,000, while the two "equal" members each were paid about $450,000. As we have come to recognize, in a money-exchange economy, relative pay is the best measure of a person's worth, of power, and of equality or inequality. On this basis alone it might be said that no major U.S. firm has as yet applied the OP concept in a theoretically pure form since there are no instances where all OP members get equal pay. Armstrong World Industries, for example, has used the OP concept informally since 1950 but, even to the present, adheres to conventional compensation and authority allocation among its key executives.

General Electric Company, which seems to have been the first major corporation to institute a formal OP, initially proclaimed a measure of equality in function but not in power or pay. General Electric established its innovative seven-member office of the president as an integral part of its major 1951 reorganization. In this prototype, several theoretical shared-executive-authority ideals were clearly enunciated. When the office of the president was not in session as a group, each of its seven members had the authority of the president. When speaking on company policy before any group, each of the seven supposedly assumed the "posture of the president." Since each of the office members spent up to 40 percent of the time on the road, the group approach made presidential authority more available to all concerned. Among other features, the members of the office were charged with spending three-fourths of their time on problems of the future—they were free to think.[9]

The innovation, however, was premature and soon went into disuse until the late 1960s when, with some fanfare, it was revived as a five-member president's office. Shortly thereafter, upon the death of its chairman, Gerald L. Phillippe, GE abolished the presidency and reconstituted the top control group as the Corporate Executive Office. In addition to the chairman, the office included three vice chairmen who were also designated "executive officers." They were also elevated to membership on GE's board. This was a major change since, historically, GE had predominantly outside-director boards. Previously, except for the chairman and the president, the remaining eighteen board members were all outside directors.

[8]*The Wall Street Journal,* November 5, 1980, p. 23.
[9]"The Overhaul of General Electric," *Fortune,* December 1955, pp. 110ff.

Yet even at such a progressive and successful enterprise, the Corporate Executive Office has not functioned without flaw. Admittedly, it has been an excellent proving ground for developing chief executive officers. But there have been great losses, particularly when bypassed key executives quit the firm. One heavy loss occurred in late 1979 when three "comers," elevated two years earlier to GE's second management layer as sector executives, resigned their key posts because they had been bypassed during the restaffing of GE's Corporate Executive Office. Significantly, the three "quitters" were almost immediately hired in presidential or vice chairman positions by other major firms.

But neither GE, Armstrong Cork, Caterpillar Tractor, nor any other firm can claim full credit for initiating shared chief executive authority. Variations of shared chief executive authority existed in the business sector even before the first balance sheet. Partnerships, formal and informal, limited and less limited, with silent and not-so-silent partners, were (and remain) very instrumental in shaping our business structure and philosophy. In 1891 when Edouard Michelin invented the demountable pneumatic bicycle tire, his inventive and production genius needed the complementary marketing talent of his brother, André. Together they formed their working partnership, an effective but informal Office of the Entrepreneur, which Edouard once described in a classic statement: "If I am the champagne, he is the bubbles."[10]

Another example of similar coequality was the promotion of two close friends and coentrepreneurs at Genstar, Ltd.[11] Genstar, a housing and land development firm with sales of about $1.5 billion, faced the dilemma of picking a new CEO from two potential successors—each judged equally capable—by selecting both to serve simultaneously as chief executive, swapping chairman and presidential titles annually.

A similar job-swapping experiment was innovated several years earlier at Saga Corporation, a $700 million food and restaurant chain. For almost thirty years after its founding by three college friends, Saga was successfully run by the three founders who shared the duties of the CEO. During the last several years of their triumvirate, they even practiced a month-by-month rotation of duties.

Even more revolutionary is the extended partnership concept as practiced at Alco Standard, a highly successful miniconglomerate. Here each of the more than 100 small, mostly privately held companies comprising Alco Standard still retains considerable autonomy. The chiefs, generally the company founders, are coequals, partners, and Alco Standard brags about

---

[10]Vance, "Shared Chief Executive Authority," op. cit., p. 5.

[11]"Elusive Genstar, Ltd., with Two Bosses . . .," *The Wall Street Journal*, December 28, 1980, p. 11.

this partnership. Among other examples, Northwest Industries proclaimed in full-page ads, "You Can't Run 10 Successful Companies with Just One Man,"[12] implying that each of the firm's eleven major components has considerable autonomy and even coequality. But for almost two decades, there was no challenging of Northwest Industries' dynamic CEO, Ben Heineman, or his singular executive role.

Despite the claim of critics that "it won't work," the OP concept has continued to gain acceptance, though slowly. By 1970, at least thirty-seven corporations, including leaders such as Boise Cascade, Borden, Ford, General Foods, W. R. Grace, IBM, ITT, Singer, and Union Carbide, were experimenting with this new corporate governance technique. A decade later the users and experimenters numbered 113 firms, several of which had tried, abandoned, then revived the office. Newcomers in 1981 included Du Pont, Alcoa, Alcan, United Airlines, J. C. Penney, North American General, GAF, Avon Products, and others.

Greyhound Corporation instituted a five-person executive office in 1975, its paramount reason being that succession to the top spot would come from one of the four "junior" members. However, Greyhound's first venture in shared authority never really worked since the chairman-CEO retained total control. By late 1980, as the retirement of the "strong" chairman-CEO approached, the board resuscitated the executive office, which now included the chairman, president, and two vice chairmen. Presumably the earlier office failed to work because the chairman-CEO ran Greyhound as a one-man show. As *The Wall Street Journal* quoted: " 'You never know where you stand in that company. . . . There is very little discussion and give and take before he [Gerry Trautman] announces a decision.' "[13] Not only was Greyhound's executive office ineffective; its board, also, evoked negative comment. The board, made up of three officers and ten outsiders, had been described as a "rubber stamp." One board member stated: " 'The board was excellent and fully aware of what's going on'; however, he can't ever recall one negative vote cast on any issue. 'We do things by consensus.' "[14]

At Greyhound, as at General Electric and other firms with preponderantly outside-director boards, including OP members as the only officer-directors might portend a trend. It could be the inception of a two-tiered board such as that initiated in West Germany in 1951. In the German *Mitbestimmung,* the supervisory board, or *Aufsichtsrat,* composed equally of employees and stockholder representatives, forms the policy-setting tier. The second level,

---

[12]*The Wall Street Journal,* July 28, 1977, p. 15.
[13]"At the Wheel: Chairman Trautman Finds Greyhound Post Remains a Hot Seat," *The Wall Street Journal,* November 20, 1980, p. 24.
[14]Ibid.

the *Vorstand,* is the executive management board. It consists of three or more top managers appointed by and answerable to the *Aufsichtsrat.* While the second-tier members have an implied directorial status—the key executive even being called the managing director—these "directors" are not members of the supervisory board. In the United States, by contrast, most OP members are also members of the board of directors.

In instances where the OP members are excluded from the firm's board of directors, the shared authority tends to be more show than substance. At Bendix Corporation, just before the classic Agee-Cunningham caper (see "Evolution through Precedent"), the strong-willed chairman and CEO, William H. Agee, deposed the firm's president and set up a ten-member "chairman's council." Ms. Lillian Panny, wife of the evicted president, made an observation on the power struggle with Mr. Agee. "She said the company announced her husband's departure without even warning him about it, and she commented: 'It's too bad so much power has to be in the hands of one man.' "[15]

This concentration of excessive authority in the CEO's hands was evidenced a few months later when the alluded-to Agee-Cunningham caper surfaced. Mr. Agee was obviously annoyed when rumors persisted that he had preferentially promoted Mary Cunningham, his twenty-nine-year-old friend, a fresh Harvard MBA graduate, to the level of vice president for corporate and public affairs—after only one year at Bendix. Three months later Cunningham was elevated to the position of vice president for strategic planning—a top spot—and also to the ten-member chairman's council. *Fortune,*[16] in addition to a detailed and not-so-flattering story, even dedicated a cover photo to the two principals. Significantly, the Bendix "chairman's council" was not even mentioned in the article. Neither was there any mention of the boardroom's ambivalence in its initial committee support for Cunningham, and the subsequent boardroom consensus for firing.

Probably OP's most serious limitation is that many of its users are uncertain about whether or not they want to use the concept. In July 1973, *Business Week* headlined the lead article in its Management Section: "Making Aetna's 'Corporate Office' Work." But, then, in a February 1976 issue, *Business Week* proclaimed: "Aetna: Where Group Management Didn't Work."

It is remarkable that the vision of corporate collegiality should have been so fleeting at Aetna Life and Casualty, the $20-billion-plus number-one diversified financial services company in the country. At his impending retirement in 1972, Chairman Olcott D. Smith set up a four-executive

---

[15]*The Wall Street Journal,* September 15, 1980, p. 5.
[16]Peter W. Bernstein, "Upheaval at Bendix," *Fortune,* November 3, 1980, pp. 48ff.

corporate office. Designated as chairman and chief executive officer, John H. Filer optimistically stated that the purpose of the new corporate office was to focus the attention of the quadrumvirate on the company's major problems and expectations. This was not supposed to be a decision-making body, nor was it a committee. "It's more a process by which all of us can bring our backgrounds, intelligence and judgment to company problems."[17]

Yet even before promulgation, there was considerable skepticism that shared authority would work at Aetna. One of the quadrumvirate members stated at the outset: " 'I like to reach a decision quickly and get on with it. When the idea of the corporate office came along, I had two concerns: Would it be management by committee? And would it slow up the process of decision-making?' The new head of the foursome, John H. Filer, commenting on these apprehensions stated: 'Within the Office we operate as peers, we really do. If someone thinks something is stupid, he says so.' "[18] Unfortunately, Chairman Filer, who a short time ago had so optimistically described Aetna's corporate office as "A process by which all of us can bring our own backgrounds, intelligence and judgment to company problems," now condemned the mechanism saying, " 'it has tended to lead to delays or impede the decision-making process on occasion.' "[19]

Aetna's well-organized and well-publicized, but short-lived, experiment does not hold the record for brevity. Late in June 1979, ITEL, the computer equipment manufacturer with a high-flying record, set up a four-man office when performance nosedived. Then, "after experimenting only two months with a new office of the president consisting of four equal executives, the board relieved the chairman and vice chairman, the company's co-founders, of all operating duties. . . . At the same time, it scrapped the newly created presidential office . . . nor were they slow to conclude that major operating decisions were too difficult to make under the office-of-the-president format."[20] The yes-no impetuosity at ITEL, Aetna, and a dozen other seemingly uncertain firms should raise red caution flags for any analyst seeking definitive answers to top executive shared-authority questions.

On the more positive side (mentioned earlier) is the increase of OPs, from 37 to 113 between 1970 and 1980, most of the gain occurring in the period between 1977 and 1980. Equally interesting is the proliferation in titles; in 1980 there were twenty-one, the most frequently used being[21]:

---

[17]"Making Aetna's Corporate Office Work," *Business Week,* July 1973.
[18]Ibid.
[19]"Aetna: Where Group Management Didn't Work," *Business Week,* February 1976.
[20]"End of the Directors' Rubber Stamp," *Business Week,* September 10, 1979, p. 75.
[21]Vance, "Shared Chief Executive Authority," op. cit., p. 9.

	Percentage	
Title	1980	1970
Office of the President	18.6	32.4
Office of the Chief Executive	18.6	5.4
Office of the Chairman	16.8	10.8
Executive Office	15.9	8.1
President's Office	6.2	16.2
Other titles	23.9	27.1
	100.0	100.0

Note that there has been a noticeable shift toward increased frequency in the use of titles that stress the preeminence of the chairman and of the chief executive; offices identified by the presidential title declined from more than half to less than a quarter of the total. Much of this follows from the growing number of firms that have chairmen, rather than presidents, serving as chief executives. Also, a significant number of larger corporations are increasingly bestowing the rank of president to heads of major divisions. For example, there are at least seventeen presidents of divisions at Singer, twenty-one divisional presidents at ITT, and five divisional chairmen plus sixteen divisional presidents at Gulf & Western, Incorporated. Since many head multibillion-dollar components, there is logic in their elevation to presidential rank, dignity, and compensation. However, this proliferation of presidents is more a delegation, not an abdication or any real sharing of CEO authority.

In summary, offices of the president, chairman, or chief executive are:

1 Innovative attempts at shared chief executive authority, initiated in the mid-1950s

2 Strictly an American business phenomenon, not to be confused with two-tiered *Mitbestimmung*

3 Not widely used, and yet users include a score or more of our largest and best-managed firms

4 Different in function and title

5 Not one size, varying from two to ten members, with three and four being the preferred size

6 Too often hierarchical rather than coequal

7 Invariably flawed by compensation differentials

8 Not substitutes for executive committees

9 Effective for training and development at the top level, with chief executive succession as an objective

ILLUSTRATION: Delta Air Lines

Most shared-authority experiments come into being through chance and, therefore, have relatively short tenures. A major exception is Delta Air Lines's not too widely publicized office of the chairman. After Delta's imaginative and strong-willed seventy-year-old founder, C. E. Woolman, suffered a serious heart attack, he encouraged his key executives to work as a group. The teamwork was most effective, and after Woolman died suddenly in 1966, the group went full-flight ahead in the endeavor.

Presently, nine key executives constitute the governing board. Heading the group is the president and CEO, David C. Garrett, Jr., who is assisted by Richard S. Maurer, vice chairman and secretary. Seven senior vice presidents complement these two. The nine team members are all longtime Delta employees, averaging twenty-six years of on-the-job experience.

" 'We have taken the interchangeability-of-parts concept we have in our standardized fleet of airplanes and applied it to management,' says Garrett. 'We have a group of senior officers who are almost interchangeable because lines of communications are so short you never have to worry about someone not knowing what is going on. It's not a committee structure. People have very clearly defined responsibilities to make decisions in their areas. But the way the interchangeability of it works is that at our meetings every Monday morning everybody is constantly being updated.' "[22]

Not only does Delta brief its office members regularly and completely, but the same communications policy extends all the way down the line. Top managers meet frequently with groups of employees. Generally, one of the nine key policy makers, together with a specific group's supervisor, relays current information to that group. The supervisor then excuses himself, and the top executive is available for questions, complaints, and suggestions.

Moreover, there is an effective open-door policy for anyone with a need for privacy. While the company basically adheres to the chain-of-command principle, it does provide for easy access and an understanding reception of employee suggestions and grievances. The company's open-door policy continues to be used, but not abused.

There are several other practices which might help explain the airline's success; for instance, Delta promotes entirely from within, which means that most competent and dedicated employees can project their careers all the way to the ruling council. This democratic process, promotion from within, is a powerful motivator. It should be stressed that this policy simply would not work unless it were coupled with another equally important policy, that is, no layoffs. Delta, in twenty-five years, has not laid off or furloughed a single full-time employee for economic reasons. This practice prevailed not only in more normal periods, but also in the hectic days of the 1973 fuel crisis and during the 1981 air traffic controllers' wildcat strike. Delta's no-layoff policy closely approaches the equally successful lifetime employment practice of the Japanese. Delta pays its workers well and provides a most generous

[22]"Delta: The World's Most Profitable Airline," *Business Week,* August 31, 1981, p. 72.

retirement plan so that employees have not been pushed to unionize. Only pilots and flight dispatchers are union members.

The net result: Delta has a loyal, competent, and cohesive work force with a fantastic decision-making speed factor. " 'We do respond very quickly to fires that develop,' says Finance Senior Vice President Oppenlander. 'We've all been working here together for a long time so we can work together very quickly. We're also not cluttered with a great deal of committee-type or staff-type operations around this company. People can get to us and get to us very quickly. If half the senior management is not here, including the president, and if a difficult decision comes up, whoever is here will make it and make it very quickly. He'll make a 10¢ decision or a multi-million-dollar decision right on the spot. He can do this because we try to keep each of us well enough informed every Monday morning about each other's division that we have the knowledge to make the right decision.' "[23]

MULTIPLE MANAGEMENT

McCormick and Company, the half-billion-dollar spice and extract maker (currently diversifying into fast foods), made headlines late in 1979 when it rejected an unfriendly tender offer. Sandoz, Limited, a Swiss conglomerate five times McCormick's size, had quietly purchased 4.8 percent of its nonvoting stock and offered to buy the rest, plus all the voting stock. Sandoz's offering price of $37 a share was a premium of 67 percent over McCormick's market price.

Anticipating hostile takeovers as early as 1947, McCormick had differentiated its stock, designating 1.8 million shares as voting and 9.6 million shares as nonvoting. The voting shares were closely held by 730 individuals, while the nonvoting common was more widely disbursed among 6500 owners. The employees, together with the company's profit-sharing plan, hold about one-third of the voting shares, and members of the McCormick family hold other significant blocks.

While the Sandoz interests pledged to retain McCormick management, the takeover target had seen and heard enough about such vapid pledges. Consequently, McCormick rejected the Sandoz offer and indicated it would put up a stiff resistance. Chairman Harry K. Wells stated: "McCormick is more than a mere commodity to be traded like a contract for pork bellies. It is a group of dedicated people . . . and a name that has earned the respect of consumers, suppliers, and the communities where we operate."[24]

Arbitragers and other fast-buck types were furious. McCormick's fixation on independence was attacked particularly by stockholders who had recently purchased large blocks in anticipation of arbitraging fast profits.

[23]Ibid.
[24]"McCormick: Independence in a Storm over a Takeover Bid," *Business Week*, April 21, 1980, p. 121.

What these gambler types overlooked was the philosophy that had made McCormick one of the most profitable of food processors. In an industry where operating margins of 2 or 3 percent are considered good, McCormick has consistently been above 10 percent.

What could account for this phenomenal success which obviously attracted Sandoz? In the first place, McCormick's board comprises seventeen officer-directors, all insiders; most are natives of Baltimore, the headquarters city. The officers and directors are all owners of McCormick stock, with a combined ownership of almost one-third of the voting shares—these are interested owners and participating directors.

In addition to its complete reliance on officer-directors, McCormick's success is facilitated by a corollary device. In the depths of the depression year 1932, Charles McCormick, who had just succeeded to the presidency of the family-owned firm, set up a novel junior board of directors. This experimental group, also consisting of seventeen members selected from the salaried personnel, "functions after the fashion of a full-fledged board of directors. It has its own bylaws, board room and officers. The members receive a fee for serving on the board. . . . Nearly all the suggestions approved by this body have in turn been accepted by the senior board. Since the introduction of multiple management, practically every addition to the senior board of directors has been a former member of the junior board. In this respect, multiple management is a device for grooming qualified functional, or inside directors. The morale-boosting stimulus of such opportunity for advancement to the highest level in the organization is obvious."[25]

This twenty-five-year-old quotation, about an experiment which has celebrated its golden anniversary, is as effective today as it was two generations ago. Its success is also evident in McCormick's expansion of this concept to production and sales boards. Over the past fifty years, the experiment has been duplicated in several hundred small companies with varied success. Yet no major corporation has even considered giving it a try. The reason seems to be that dominant financial interests, far removed from a particular corporate scene, will never willingly relinquish control to any local group of operating executives. Even as McCormick's ambitious diversification program expands—and particularly if it succeeds—the need for progressively more outside financing will sharpen the Damocles sword. By reducing its reliance on spices—which presumably will grow at only about 3 percent each year—McCormick has been prompted to move from a spice house to a specialty foods company. Shifting some of its emphasis to fast foods could give McCormick more flexibility, but it could also reduce

[25]Stanley C. Vance, *Industrial Administration* (New York: McGraw-Hill Book Company, 1959), p. 228.

its operating margin significantly. It would require considerable external financing with a real danger to local ownership and multiple management control. Not only could this lead to a medley of financial voices in the beholden-firm's boardroom, but it could also attract shareholders with a propensity for stockholder suits.

OFFICERS OF THE BOARD

A novel experiment at getting competent and available directors was attempted at Texas Instruments, Incorporated, and at Westinghouse Electric Corporation at least a decade ago. In mid-1967, Texas Instruments (TI) inaugurated its "officer of the board" program when it retired a senior vice president for long-range planning and elected him to the board of directors. Although serving now as an officer of the board, the former vice president, who remained on full time and full salary, was free to ponder Texas Instruments' role in a changing world. This arrangement would correct the fundamental weakness of inside directors, namely, that they are too close to the action and that they are preoccupied with daily routine. As expressed by TI's chairman, this key executive, as an officer of the board, would be freed of mundane duties and would have time to study, to reflect, and to comprehend the impact of rapidly changing internal and external environments. Removed from all operating responsibilities, this officer of the board would serve as a high-level advisor.

The second officer of the board appointee at TI was John B. Connally, former governor of Texas and former Secretary of the Navy and of the Treasury. It was assumed that Connally, a seasoned politician, would bring another dimension to the board. If he had been appointed as a conventional outsider, Connally would have had all the limitations of outsiders, that is, a minimal presence and minimal concern with the firm. But by creating this new kind of director, TI would correct this basic fault—Connally would be available, and he would be concerned. In substance, whether an officer of the board comes from within the company or from outside, he or she is expected to be available when needed. The officer must actually perform at least 25 to 30 days a year but no more than 110 to 125 days. The upper time limitation is to assure that he has sufficient time to develop meaningful activities, other than those at Texas Instruments.

A decade after its inception, TI's novel officer-of-the-board concept was modified and the company's board was radically restructured. Only two of the directors now were actively engaged in operations, another was a conventional outside director available for scheduled board meetings, and the remaining ten were "general" directors, namely, officers of the board. While these could be either former employees or outsiders, they had to be more available for special board and committee duties than conventional nonemployee directors. General directors, of course, receive additional compensation for their greater responsibilities and time commitments. For instance, they are expected to participate in the three- or four-day strategic planning conference held every spring. The general directors might also be expected to serve as directors of one or more TI subsidiary corporations. Furthermore, committee service is mandatory, with each general director devoting approximately ten to eighteen days each year to committee work.[26]

Westinghouse Electric's "step-down-at-sixty" policy, initiated in 1972, bears some resemblance. At age sixty, the top seven executives must either retire or become officer-directors, working two-thirds of their time for two-thirds pay. At sixty-five they can retire with full pension rights. For instance, Donald C. Burnham, architect of the step-down-at-sixty plan, became an officer-director at age sixty. In so doing, he sacrificed nearly a million dollars in compensation by not staying on as the company's full-time, full-pay chief executive. But even though he received reduced compensation, as an officer-director, Burnham was able to devote his maximum efforts to socially important issues and long-range considerations.

At about the same time, International Business Machines Corporation also initiated a retirement-at-sixty program for its key executives. IBM's program, however, was more early-retirement-oriented than it was concerned with utilizing retired executives as members of its board.

There are some comparable instances where key executives and directors, relieved of their regular duties before retirement, are given advisory-employment contracts. It is hoped that these sweeteners will somehow reduce the trauma of being fired. Recall the situation at Lockheed Aircraft Corporation, where after forced resignations, both the company's chairman and vice chairman were given ten-year advisory-employment contracts, at a combined total of $1.5 million.

Sometimes elaborate precautions are taken to ensure the freedom of the consultant executive or director. When Westinghouse Electric's Burnham reached the mandatory retirement age of sixty, he commented on his own retirement and that of two predecessors: " 'We've gone to some lengths to avoid horning in,' he says. 'First of all, all three of us immediately took two-month vacations when we stepped down, to get us off day-to-day things entirely. Our offices are in a different part of the building from the officers' and we even take different elevators.' "[27]

But in spite of the good pay and elaborate precautions safeguarding

---

[26]Bryan F. Smith, general director, Texas Instruments, Inc. From an address at the University of Texas, Austin, December 7, 1979.

[27]Frederick Klein and David Elsner, "Sweet Deal: Few Duties Involved for Many Ex-Officers Named as Consultants," *The Wall Street Journal,* June 30, 1976, p. 1.

independence, there is some criticism of using retired executive-director talent. The "consulting" agreements are too often concluded with no real intention that any significant work will be done. This is especially the case where, as at Lockheed, the executives were forced to resign. Presumably, the lesser of the two evils is to retain key executives and directors as high-paid consultants rather than cope with them in the boardroom. Says consultant Graef S. Crystal, " 'In the big majority of cases, calling a former executive a consultant is just a euphemism—window dressing for shareholders. Its real function is to make a top man's retirement easier or help save face for a guy who has been pushed out. I haven't heard of many cases where useful work was actually performed. It gives real consultants a bad name.' "[28]

So the dilemma in the boardroom persists. We cannot afford to push high-quality executives into costly quasiretirement by forcing them out of their jobs and off their boards, at any arbitrary age limit. Nor under prevailing circumstances can we expect to find outside directors, with fitting competencies, ample time, and super zest, to fill this need. Yet as Texas Instruments and Westinghouse Electric have demonstrated, we do have options: we can retire top talent when it plateaus—at its prime—and put it to exclusive policy-contemplation use in officer of the board or officer-director capacities. The advantage here is to be relieved of mundane operational chores so that talented executives can become more available for serving as officer-directors on their own boards and also on boards of other companies. With time and a respectable income, their extended high-level contributions to corporate governance can continue while zeal and zest endure.

SECTOR EXECUTIVES

General Electric Company has been the leader in pioneering ingenious and effective corporate governance innovations. One of these was corporate decentralization, introduced more than a quarter of a century ago and emulated by hundreds of companies. Shortly thereafter, GE also experimented with an office of the president, a concept it continues using to the present, in the guise of its office of the chairman. More recently, GE made headlines by focusing on strategic planning, contributing, in the process, SBUs to our management vocabulary. These SBUs—strategic business units—are still the subject of business application and professional-meeting discussion. Even more recently, GE has given us the concept of sector executives.

The notion of sector executives is not really new. It is simply an attempt

[28]Ibid.

to keep a complex and expanding organization's span of control manageable by adding still another layer to senior management. Theorists will probably continue to argue for generations over the merits of lengthening the chain of command as versus widening the span of control. As inaugurated at GE, the sector executives are hierarchically placed just below the chief control center, the office of the chairman, which consists of the chairman plus two or three vice chairmen. Initially, there were five sector executives; however, the president of GE's huge subsidiary, Utah International, Incorporated, might be considered a sixth. This layer of sector executives was interspersed between the group heads or group executives who formerly reported to the office of the chairman. Currently, these group executives report to one of the sector executives, who, in turn, report to one of the vice chairmen in the executive office. The strategic business units, of which there are approximately fifty, also are under the sector executives' supervision.

As in its decentralization move, in the early 1950s, this recent institution of sector executives is actually GE's way of rekindling the entrepreneurial spirit. The new system attempts to develop institutional leadership. It sets up the sector executives, making each synonymous with "Mr. GE" in the specific industry in which that sector operates. In a sense, the sector executive is a quasi CEO.

The five basic sectors (excluding Utah International) are international operations; consumer products, including GE credit; power systems, including turbines and nuclear energy; industrial products and components; and technical systems and materials, including aeronautic and aerospace operations. Integrating such widely different components into an effectively functioning single organism is a complex task. The purpose of sector executive structure is concisely put forth by Robert R. Frederick, senior vice president for corporate planning and development, who headed the team that redesigned GE's management system after three years of structuring and testing. Frederick says: "It involves an objective, total assessment of key resources, financial, human and technical. In this way resource planning provides a matrix look at GE and identifies issues for the next year's plan. . . .

"At GE, the new emphases are on value-added management, a variety of new, supportive, integrated planning systems, and an organization structure that accommodates growth for the foreseeable future. The intent is to balance business strategies and corporate resources."[29]

In making the dramatic change, GE's chairman and CEO, Reginald Jones, assigned four of the sector executives to totally new areas "to broaden their knowledge of the company, a strategy that is also part of Jones's effort to

---

[29]Robert R. Frederick, "Sector Executives: Management Evolution," *AMA Forum*, vol. 67, no. 10, October 1978, p. 30.

develop institutional leadership. 'If you are going to understand the many markets we serve, you shouldn't have experience in just one,' Jones declares. 'So don't be surprised if, in a couple of years, we shuffle again to give some of these operating people staff experience and vice versa.' "[30] In less than two years, three of these peripatetic sector executives were deemed reasonably well groomed and were elevated to the penultimate level. They were designated vice chairmen, executive officers, and members of the corporate executive office.

Within half a year, W. R. Grace and Company followed GE's pattern. The company designated four of its executive vice presidents as sector executives. These new sector executives joined W. R. Grace's three top executives to form a new seven-member corporate executive office. As at GE, the sector executives at W. R. Grace constitute an additional layer of authority, superimposed upon a group of ten executive vice presidents.

At American Can Company, five of the ten senior vice presidents, similarly, were given additional posts as sector executives. Each heads one of the five major areas—packaging, consumer products, international, distribution, and resource recovery and chemicals. The architect of this plan, William S. Woodside, says: " 'All I'm doing is attempting to give broader development to some key people to relieve myself of a lot of day-to-day responsibility. . . . I've been like the proverbial paperhanger. . . . We will meet once every 10 days to deal with trade-offs in capital, technology, and human resources among the five sectors. . . . I want everybody to be a little bit involved in what's going on in the corporation as a whole.' "[31]

Even though they do not use the "sector executive" designation, many large corporations employ some comparable technique for grouping of executives. For example, in its most recent reorganization, H. J. Heinz and Company established four "area directors." Together they allocate the senior operating responsibilities for each of Heinz's thirty worldwide subsidiaries. Invariably, the area directors are also senior vice presidents and directors of the company.

There are dozens of other grouping arrangements, structured and titled to fit specific needs and preferences. As mentioned in "Proliferating Presidents," some corporations—such as Union Carbide, with five area allocations—even have presidents and chairmen of divisions reporting to corporate senior vice presidents.

Citicorp, one of the biggest financial institutions, tried an intermediate differentiation. It combined the two highest-ranking vice presidential titles—senior and executive—and designated three "senior executive vice presi-

---

[30]"GE's New Billion-Dollar Small Businesses," *Business Week,* December 19, 1977, p. 79.
[31]"Canco Adds a Rung to Its Executive Ladder," *Business Week,* August 30, 1979, p. 25.

dents." While they are not called sector or area executives, Citibank's senior executive vice presidents seem to supervise sector equivalents. Here again, this penultimate level in the hierarchy provides a proving area for testing chief executive officer talent.

Another approach is being used at Ashland Oil, Incorporated, where top management was realigned along the lines of a holding company. An eight-member "core group" was set up to function as a management team. The divisions report to this core group, which concentrates on long-range strategy and resource allocation. Presumably this arrangement enhances divisional autonomy yet facilitates deliberate planning. The core group's three top operating executives also act as a chief operating officer.

These are just a few of the more prominent examples of the great variety of titles and functions in the corporate governance ball game. It should be emphasized that even though many of the contending teams give different names to their several basic positions, and although they do not play by standard rules, the corporate governance game fans seem not to mind too much.

ADVISORY BOARDS

The difference between advisory and statutory boards is that statutory boards must provide advice in their fiduciary role, whereas advisory boards merely offer evaluative advice or provide specific services as requested. For example, Hiram Walker, Incorporated, organized a distributor advisory board, a rotating panel of eight distributors, drawn from a cross section of its markets. The panel members meet periodically with the president and other executives to discuss marketing-related problems and strategies. Theirs is a narrow, intensified focus on part of a single function of the organization. They do not replace the board of directors—they assist it.

The president of Hercules, Incorporated, following a decision to improve the review process before he brought new projects to the board of directors, established a four-person advisory council of prestigious outsiders. The president felt he needed evaluations more objective than those he might receive from his own staff or board of directors. He, likewise, felt he needed a continuing review board and not the ad hoc type of advising provided by most consultants.[32]

The rapidity and intensity of change on the international business scene has prompted an increasing number of multinational firms to set up advisory boards. Many of these operate as special committees, sometimes based abroad and using the services of outstanding citizens of the host country.

[32]"An Advisory Council to Back Up the Board," *Business Week,* November 12, 1979, p. 131.

This, in itself, is a splendid show of desire to cooperate and to appreciate other cultures and problems, in other words, to "listen to the natives" and to get an inside view.

General Motors Corporation instituted a seven-member European Advisory Council in 1974. On this council—which generally meets in London— are some of Europe's leading industrialists and most prominent politicians such as the chairman of Saint-Gobain-Pont-a-Mousson, the chairman of Bayer A.G., deputy chairman of Lloyds Bank, Ltd., and the former managing director of the International Monetary Fund. General Motors reciprocates by having its very top executives participate with the council. Among the reasons advanced for using this mechanism are "the benefit of the experience and insights of men with broad and varied knowledge of European economic, political and social developments. They can give, for example, early warning of a new type of union demand encountered in their own country, evaluate planned changes in the monetary system, spotlight a new demographic trend, assess the prospects of political realignments."[33]

Council members feel they get much in return; they not only hear the views of their own members but are privileged to consort with GM's top policy makers. " 'The world is not so small nor so simple any more,' declares Kurt Hansen, chairman of the supervisory board of Bayer A.G. 'It is very good for each of us to learn what other people of this caliber are thinking and doing to handle the problems we ourselves are facing or soon will face.' "[34] Such sentiments from council members, and the continued satisfaction among our multinational firms, are evident in the growth in advisory councils, from a handful a few years ago to approximately fifty.

One seeming advantage of advisory boards is their minimal legal or statutory entanglements; there are no comparable SEC or FTC harassments. Since the advisory group is much smaller, it does not need to meet as frequently as the parent board. Meetings are informal, and much of the actual work is accomplished on an individual basis, whenever the adviser happens to be in the vicinity of headquarters. Unless the courts or congress dramatically redefine duties and procedures, advisory board members have little, if any, legal liability as compared with statutory board members.[35]

But advisory boards are not limited to international operations. Their popularity and use are almost excessive in the federal government. In 1977, when President Carter tried to squeeze the federal bureaucracy into more manageable proportions, studies then showed that there were 1189 federal advisory committees with, perhaps, a grand total of 20,000 members.

---

[33]Alan Otten, "Advisory Councils," *The Wall Street Journal,* June 16, 1980, p. 22.
[34]Ibid.
[35]Robert Kirk Mueller, *Board Compass* (Lexington, Mass.: D. C. Heath and Company, 1979).

Employees of twenty-eight large corporations held more than a thousand seats on these committees. American Telephone and Telegraph led the list with 120; next in order, RCA with 94 members and General Electric with 74. Representatives from fourteen leading universities held over 1800 seats. The University of California ranked first with 394; University of Texas ranked second with 160, and was followed by Harvard's 140. Four labor unions held almost 200 posts. There were 173 multiseated individuals, holding simultaneously between four and twelve seats each.

With federal agencies setting the pace and pattern for advisory councils, the nonprofit sector comes in as a close second. Some nonprofit organizations, particularly those closely associated with the corporate sector, could even provide a proving ground for wider use of advisory boards and councils in industry. As an example, the National Association of Corporate Directors (NACD), an affiliate of the American Management Associations (AMA), has such an effective advisory board. This is a voluntary, unpaid group of eighteen, including industrialists, lawyers, consultants, and educators, who meet quarterly to review NACD's progress and problems. Fundamentally, the advisory board keeps an eye on the staff to see that NACD is adhering to its objectives, namely, to communicate with and educate directors and to study the area of corporate governance. The advisors also contribute their time and talent by writing articles for NACD's extensive publications and by acting as group leaders and speakers at conferences and seminars hosted by NACD.

Following the spirit of recent SEC-suggested boardroom reformations, NACD's advisory board adopted the currently popular committees-of-the-board structuring. It has three active committees: Nominations and Organization; Programs and Publications; and Membership and Marketing. The titles of these committees are self-descriptive. The committees, averaging about six members each, meet separately the same day as the regular board meets, and present their reports to the assembled advisory board.

Although the NACD's advisory board goes through the same motions as a corporate board, its differences are that NACD is a nonprofit organization, has no owners or shareholders, and is less affected by director-liability dangers. Despite the good intentions of the eighteen advisors, the advisory group's actions and resolutions can be nullified by the officers of the parent AMA. In a sense, then, NACD's advisory board has all the limitations associated with subsidiary boards and nonstatutory boards. But there is no denying its effectiveness—unassisted by these highly competent outsiders, NACD's staff would have a very limited terrain to explore and develop.

There is an increasing number of other kinds of advisory boards. The Commercial National Bank, Little Rock, Arkansas, has an interesting National Advisory Board. It consists of twenty-one Arkansas native sons who have achieved national and international prominence as leaders in their fields. Once a year, in October, they meet in Little Rock to study a carefully selected topic of current interest in Arkansas. They begin with a position paper, and after expressing their views in the meeting, a synthesis is ventured in a written report. Some recent topics considered by this National Advisory Board are Frost Belt vs. Sun Belt: Ways to Get More Corporate Headquarters to Little Rock; and Energy for Arkansas: A Question of Survival.

General Motors recently started yet another innovative advisory council. It is composed of GM's retired chief executive officers and other retired top officers and board members. This "Council of Elders"[36] gets much the same briefing reports that go to GM board members. They meet irregularly, as often as the CEO feels he can use their adult advice. The four former chief executive officers—Frederic G. Donner (1958–1967), Richard C. Gerstenberg (1972–1974), Thomas Murphy (1974–1980), and James M. Roche (1967–1971)—together with the other members, make this the most prestigious advisory board in the country. Not only is GM's advisory board prestigious; it is also utilitarian. A seasoned board of this type, exerting competency and past experience, gives GM a tremendous advantage over its rivals, as company performance seems to corroborate.

Retirees, however, are only one source of talent for advisory boards. Customers, distributors, local residents, educators, and many others might be used as particular needs arise. Unfortunately, one group is only infrequently recruited to serve in an advisory capacity—the shareholders. It is gratuitously assumed that owners of stock have very narrow perspectives, ever focusing intently on the bottom line. Even if this were the case, a little more focus on profits would surely not hurt most of our enterprises.

ILLUSTRATION: Du Pont–Conoco Merger

While GM's Council of Elders is praiseworthy, it is not the first such advisory board. E. I. Du Pont, for at least a half century, has effectively used the services of retired key executives in a comparable but less structured fashion. At one time Du Pont's board had a tripartite structure which consisted of one-third family representatives, one-third top executives, and one-third retired executives. Occasionally there was an outsider or two, generally a local resident with a longtime company association. Throughout the board there was a common bond—these were interested owners. Moreover, their interests were coordinated through Christiana Securities Company, a closed-end nondiversified management investment company, 80 percent owned by Du Pont scions. From its founding in 1917 until its merger into Du Pont in 1973, Christiana Securities held 29 percent of Du Pont common stock and dominated the directorate.

---

[36]Charles G. Burck, "How GM Stays Ahead," *Fortune*, March 9, 1981, p. 54.

A second and equally important boardroom bond was technical competence. Most of the top executives had backgrounds in chemistry and chemical engineering. At one time all nine of the working directors had advanced technical degrees.

The third binding force was the reliance on a strong representation of retirees— executives or family members—who provided a measure of continuity, maturity, and a fund of experience. The older family retirees served to coalesce and temper family factions; the retired executives contributed seasoned technical and managerial expertise.

Although the classic tripartite balance was continued even after the 1981 macromerger with Conoco, Incorporated, there were two major modifications: three Conoco and two Seagram Company representatives were added. The Conoco group, all working executives, reflects a pragmatic tactic—becoming increasingly more evident—whereby conglomerates give the acquired firm recognition and a voice at the top. In fact, Du Pont went so far as to set up a three-member office of the chairman, which includes the Conoco CEO, who is now also designated as vice chairman and chief operating officer for Conoco activities. The third member has served as vice chairman and chief operating officer for Du Pont divisions.

Du Pont's modified board, still tripartite in structure, now consists of:

Eleven active officer-directors (two family members)
Nine retired officers (three family members)
Eleven outside directors (three family members and two Bronfmans)

The addition of two Seagram Company representatives, Edgar M. Bronfman and his younger brother, Charles, reflects financial realities. In their unsuccessful bid to acquire Conoco, the Bronfmans had invested $2.6 billion in Conoco common stock, which subsequently was converted into a 20 percent ownership of Du Pont. As the single largest owners, it would be ludicrous to classify the Bronfmans as outside directors—they definitely are interested owners on a par with the Du Ponts.

It might take years to unravel the sequel to this merger triangle. In the aftermath, news stories featured captions such as "Seagram Tightens Its Grip on Du Pont" (*Fortune*, November 16, 1981); "Du Pont Could End Up in Seagram's Pocket" (*Business Week*, August 24, 1981); "Du Pont's Costly Bet on Conoco" (*Business Week*, July 20, 1981). Many considered this a Pyrrhic victory since Du Pont was now saddled with $3.8 billion of new debt.

Initially, it seemed, analysts berated Du Pont's board of directors for falling into a Seagram trap. With a better than 20 percent stake plus an option to buy another 5 percent, there was an imminent threat of another takeover—this one by the Bronfmans. But as Du Pont's stock price stabilized, dropping from the arbitragers' $56 to a more realistic $35 per share, the analysts recognized that the Bronfmans were overleveraged. They had invested $2.6 billion and saw their investment shrink—by an $800 million paper loss—as the stock market reappraised Du Pont's victory. Moreover, their investment would earn only about $100 million in annual Du Pont dividends, representing a 4 percent return compared with the 20 percent or more they would pay on further borrowings.

Amusingly, this episode illustrates that profitable mergers, unlike happy marriages, are made on Wall Street and not in heaven. Twenty-four leading institutional investors had a combined 20-million-share interest in Du Pont, 21 million in Conoco, and 38 million in Mobil. At the time, total investment of these twenty-four institutions in these three merger-prone firms had a market value approaching $5 billion. Representative Berkley Bedell of Iowa, chairman of the House Small Business Subcommittee on Energy, "says the Conoco bidding 'illustrates how incestuous the relationships have become. Thirty-six of the top 65 holders of Conoco stock also are listed among the biggest investors in Mobil or Du Pont.' "[37]

But a more significant point is that in the Conoco bidding, it was the Du Pont directors, a board with considerable "gray panther" caginess, that pulled a coup not only on a super aggressive Mobil, but also on the dynamic entrepreneurial Bronfmans. Even though rumors hinted of a Du Pont buy-out of the Seagram/Bronfman interest, Du Pont's board moved imperceptibly. Commenting on Seagram's longer-run prospects: "Argues one Du Pont board member, 'They are boxed in. Tying up that kind of money can't be their game plan. I think before long they will come to us to ask whether we'll buy back the shares.' "[38]

Even if the Bronfmans succeeded, they would have considerable technical and boardroom problems. "Du Pont is a company of engineers and experts. That culture makes it difficult for outsiders to influence things."[39]

Significantly, Irving Shapiro, Du Pont's former chief executive, with Edgar Bronfman, had once effected a compromise between the World Jewish Congress and the prestigious Business Roundtable in regard to the Arab boycott. Again they had structured another compromise. The two adversaries agreed not to invade any further into each other's domains for a period of fifteen years. The exchange of directors—two from Du Pont on Seagram's board and eventually three from Seagram on Du Pont's board—was a precautionary move. The adversaries could keep an eye on each other.

Asked what he would do when the fifteen-year truce expired, Edgar Bronfman replied "by telling the tale of a Jew sentenced to death by a sheikh, who promises to free the condemned man if he can teach the ruler's horse to talk within a year. The prisoner happily takes the deal, explaining later: In that time, the sheikh could die, I could die, the horse could die. Concludes Bronfman: In 15 years a lot could happen."[40]

TWO-TIER GOVERNANCE

Mitbestimmung, literally meaning "having a voice in," is a corporate governance technique which originated in Germany, spread throughout northern Europe, and just recently made the slightest of inroads into the United States. Familiarly known as codetermination or comanagement, the concept basically implies union or worker representation on the board of directors. A decade ago the universal rejoinder to *Mitbestimmung,* in the

[37]Charles J. Elia, "Overlapping Shareholdings Pervade Competition for Control of Conoco," *The Wall Street Journal,* July 24, 1981, p. 23.

[38]"Seagram: Its Cash Hoard Is Spent, and Its Future Is Up in the Air," *Business Week,* December 21, 1981, p. 100.

[39]Ibid.

[40]Louis Kraar, "Seagram Tightens Its Grip on DuPont," *Fortune,* November 16, 1981.

United States, would have been "it can't happen here." Not only did American management present a united front against this alien notion, but even our trade unions were equally opposed. George Meany, longtime head of the AFL-CIO, forcefully rejected the concept. "Who are you if you are a labor man on a board of directors? Whom do you represent? Labor doesn't want to run the shop. In the United States participation is absolutely and completely out. It will not work."[41] Another AFL-CIO official, Thomas Donahue, expressed the same view. "We do not seek to be a partner in management, to be most likely the junior partner in success and the senior partner in failure."[42]

Despite its Germanic flavor and its socialistic overtones, *Mitbestimmung,* the "German disease," by the mid-1970s had become endemic in northern Europe. It was here that governing boards of American subsidiaries first became acquainted with this new view of workers' rights. For years General Motors has run its biggest overseas subsidiary, Adam Opel AG, through a board of directors including members elected by the employees. Presently, more than 650 firms, including at least 40 subsidiaries of American companies with facilities in Germany, must abide by the provisions of the 1976 law: The Act on Co-Determination by Jobholders. Keep in mind the word "jobholder" is synonymous with "worker."

As is universally known, the United States's first bruising contact with codetermination was at the Chrysler Corporation early in 1980. Earlier Chrysler's United Kingdom subsidiary, severely ailing even before the travails of its American parent, went so far as to offer two seats on its board of governors to union representatives. Presumably this whetted the codetermination appetites of Chrysler's union leaders at American headquarters. For instance, in May 1976, while addressing his union's 225 delegates considering a new contract, Douglas Fraser stated that the contract should include worker representation on the company's board of directors. "I'm not saying this would resolve all our problems but it would be refreshing to get the point of view of workers in the atmosphere where all the decisions are made which affect every Chrysler worker. Maybe we could save them [the boards] from some of their own mistakes."[43] Fraser's proposal for codetermination in the United States, however, was a few years premature.

Subsequently Chrysler's chronic poor performance in the late 1970s and early 1980s led to financial embarrassment which only government funds and union wage concessions could alleviate. In a trade-off that amazed both American industry and trade unions, the chairman of Chrysler, Lee Iacocca, offered to nominate Fraser to the board as one of the management slate. This

---

[41]"Workers on Boards of Directors," *Nation's Business,* February 1976, p. 52.
[42]Bruce Stokes, "Answered Prayers," *MBA,* 1979, p. 20.
[43]"UAW Goal—Workers in the Boardroom," *San Francisco Chronicle,* May 7, 1976, p. 56.

endorsement was tantamount to election. Soon after his election to Chrysler's board (May 1980), Fraser commented "that his union's membership is overwhelmingly in favor of representation on corporate boards and that 'we think we are entitled to more representation than a single seat on any company's board'."[44] Soon after he stated: "Almost inevitably, workers are going to realize it's not enough for a labor movement to react to decisions made by management. We've got to be where the decisions are made."[45]

Contrary to all the misgivings, ten months after his election, Fraser was given the greatest of praise by his fellow Chrysler board members: "He's been a surprisingly strong addition. We are lucky to have him," said Lee Iacocca. "He has handled his dual interests very well," stated one outside director. "Doug could speak with credibility to the workers because, as a director, he had seen the detailed financial data."[46]

The pattern set by Chrysler soon had an emulator, American Motors Corporation, which agreed to add a UAW member to its board if it could get government assurances that there would be no legal problems. The AMC-UAW maneuver, however, elicited considerable negative comment to the effect that this would be conflict of interest since the UAW president already served on one automaker's board. The union countered that, to avoid possible conflict of interest, it would nominate Raymond E. Majerus, its secretary-treasurer and director of its AMC department. Although some obstructionists contended that having two unionists serve on competing automakers' boards would be tantamount to handing the union all the industry's trade secrets, these same objectors raised no questions on the ethics of having two or more members of the same bank or law firm serve on the boards of competing firms.

As for industry-company trade secrets, an increasing number of corporate boards are providing union leadership with data once viewed as solely management's prerogative. For example, in the 1982 negotiations between the United Rubber Workers (URW) and Uniroyal, Incorporated, the union requested that its president have the right to appear before Uniroyal's board at least once a year, and that the union have the continued right to audit the company's books. In this context URW President Milan Stone reflects: "Maybe we'll be looking for seats on boards."

At Pan American World Airways, another troubled enterprise, the Teamster's bargaining committee proposed seating three new directors to represent the interests of the union's new employee stock ownership plan. Also, a union spokesperson accused Pan Am's management of ineptness,

---

[44]*The Wall Street Journal,* May 14, 1980, p. 6.
[45]"The Risk in Putting a Union Chief on the Board," *Business Week,* May 19, 1980, p. 149.
[46]"Chrysler Lauds Strong Performance of UAW's Fraser as Board Member," *The Wall Street Journal,* March 2, 1981, p. 33.

bungling, and waste, and asked that an employee-nominated director be added immediately to act as an overseer reporting back the facts to the union.

A more tangible but indirect action took place at Western Airlines where, early in 1982, three new directors were added—one a Western pilot. Even though the pilot had been a longtime acquaintance of Western's new chairman-CEO—and this could have influenced the choice—it, nevertheless, corroborates the sentiment that pilots can perform as members of airline boards—and might even do better than outsiders.

Acceptance of unionists on boards will undoubtedly face severe opposition, comparable to what women and minority persons had to contend with in the early 1970s. Yet today the majority of our 500 largest publicly owned corporations include at least one woman as a board member, and about one in five such boards also have admitted a black American. It is evident that worker representation will subsequently follow this pattern. Stockholder Proposal 5, voted upon at American Telephone and Telegraph's 1977 annual meeting in Kansas City, urged the inclusion of representatives of labor organizations on the board of directors. As expected, the proposal was overwhelmingly defeated by 97 percent of the vote. Similarly, Eastern Air Lines had to deal with an independent shareholder proxy solicitation for its April 28, 1981, annual meeting. Charles E. Bryan, a former Eastern Air Lines mechanic and then president and general chairman of District Lodge 100 of the International Association of Machinists and Aerospace Workers, nominated himself as a director candidate. Bryan's union represents 13,000 Eastern Air employees as well as employees of 22 other airlines and agencies.

Bryan's solicitation arguments stressed that employee participation on the board should accompany ownership. He stressed that in 1980 all employees received ten shares of Eastern Air Lines stock and so were co-owners of the firm. He also pointed out that the employees came to the rescue of the ailing airline by accepting the variable earnings plan. This was an agreement by which at least 3.5 percent of employees' wages are held back by the company in bad years, to be repaid only when the company achieves certain profit objectives.

Bryan's implied reasoning seems to follow the line that workers on the board provide members who are more technically qualified and more dedicated and have a bigger stake in the firm's future than what is provided by most investors and their outside directors. The board of Eastern Air Lines, for example, has only three officer-directors; the remaining thirteen are outsiders, with a preponderance of financiers and lawyers. Under this leadership the company has had below-average performance. To support the argument that type of board composition relates to performance, consider that the previously mentioned Chrysler Corporation and AMC both have equally disproportionate outsider representation: Chrysler's board, before its ordeal, had five officers and fourteen nonemployees, while AMC's board included two officers and thirteen nonemployees. In support of Bryan, one wonders how much worse a firm could perform if its board included one or two worker representatives?

But back to basics: What is this German disease, *Mitbestimmung,* that arouses so much animosity and seems about to spread its contagion in the United States? While recent articles on codetermination convey the impression that this is a new concept, its roots actually go back to the German revolutionary movements of the 1830s and 1840s. In 1848 the Frankfurt Constitutional Assembly debated a measure that would have established factory committees with powers to participate in owners' decision-making processes. The idea limped along until World War I when Germany decreed that working councils be formed in all war-related plants employing fifty or more workers. In true authoritarian fashion, the Nazis dissolved all work councils in 1933, and the idea lay dormant until 1948 when the British, in their military occupation of the Ruhr area, revived the concept for the steel industry.[47]

In April 1951, the *"Montanmitbestimmung"* bill was passed by the Bundestag. From the union point of view, this was a tremendous achievement. The law covered all steel and coal companies employing more than 1000. Supervisory boards *(Aufsichtsrat)* of eleven, fifteen, or twenty-one members, depending upon the nominal amount of share capital, were set up with five, seven, or ten labor representatives. In the *"Montan"* industries, shareholders had an equal representation, and the final member was a neutral party acceptable to both sides. Outside the steel and coal industries, covered enterprises had one-third of the supervisory board members representing labor.

The Act on Co-Determination by Jobholders (Co-Determination Act), effective July 1, 1976, widened the scope and coverage, giving an equal number of seats to labor and capital representatives. It should be noted that while this is a big step toward industrial democracy, voting power is tilted toward the owners. The board chairman is always a shareholder. In the event of a tie vote, there is a carefully prescribed ritual whereby the chairman casts the tie-breaking vote. Consequently unionists contend that on a twenty-member supervisory board, capital has eleven votes, labor ten.

Between 625 and 650 companies are covered by the Act. The *Aufsichtsrat,* or supervisory board, the top control tier, is now geared in size to the number of company employees:

---

[47]James Furlong, *Labor in the Boardroom* (Princeton, New Jersey: Dow Jones Books, 1977), p. 33.

1 Firms with less than 10,000 workers have 6 shareholder and 6 jobholder members.

2 Firms with 10,000 to 20,000 employees have 8 shareholder and 8 jobholder members.

3 Firms with more than 20,000 employees have 10 shareholder and 10 jobholder members.

There are rigid rules in prescribing how shareholder and jobholder supervisory board members shall be selected. For example, on a supervisory board with six jobholder members, four shall be employees of the company and two shall represent the trade union. On a ten-jobholder board, seven shall be company employees and three shall be trade union representatives.

The Act is quite comprehensive with each of its forty-one articles spelling out some aspect of the mechanism. For example, Article 10 prescribes that white-collar and blue-collar workers shall elect their representatives in separate and secret elections. The unions have the ultimate right to object to any jobholder selected, while the Labor Minister has the final authority to approve or disapprove. The unions, in nominating their representatives, are required to consult with the works council.

While the *Aufsichtsrat,* or supervisory board, selection and operations rituals are minutely detailed, the supervisory boards meet only about four times a year. And so some critics contend that the entire process of codetermination is largely cosmetic. Effective control, they contend, lies in the second governance tier, the *Vorstand,* or management board. It is the *Vorstand* which has the legal duty to run the day-to-day affairs of the company and to represent the company in dealings with third parties. The *Aufsichtsrat* is not allowed to interfere in the policy-making of the *Vorstand.* Should the supervisory board veto any of its plans, the *Vorstand* can appeal to a special meeting of the shareholders where a three-fourths majority will overrule the veto. In the counterpart of the American corporation, the *Aktiengesellschaft* (AG), the law mandates that some business activities, notably strategic decisions on investment and financing, be approved by the supervisory board. However, since the members of the *Vorstand* are hired and reappointed by the supervisory board, the incidence of serious friction is minimal. As a rule, *Vorstand* members are highly paid professionals, each excelling in certain areas where his competency is rarely questioned.[48]

While there are some similarities between codetermination's managing board and the executive committee of many American boards, the differences are greater. Some *Vorstands,* seeking an aura of mutuality, refer to the chairman as the speaker, and yet he, while a first among equals, does not

---

[48]Jeremy Bacon and James K. Brown, *The Board of Directors: Perspectives and Practices in Nine Countries,* The Conference Board, 1977, p. 28.

have the power to overrule the majority. In this respect the *Vorstand* resembles the ideal office of the president or chairman, described earlier, where in theory the CEO shares all rights and responsibilities with a team of coequals or peers. The two-tier similarities between German codetermination and American co-optation are more evident in actuality than in theory. In both systems the top tiers, the supervisory board in Germany and the directors in the United States, tend to let effective control slip out of their hands. The second tiers, eager U.S. chief executives and the equally eager German *Vorstand,* then assume control by default of the first tiers. Yet even when the first tier retains control, it too often gets into ineffective hands.

A precedent-setting situation occurred at Opel, General Motor's huge West German subsidiary. Under the 1976 *Mitbestimmung* law, Opel's board had expanded from six to twenty members—ten labor representatives and ten GM appointees—with the tie-casting vote in the hands of GM's general director.

Opel's worker-directors initiated demands quite alien to earlier *Mitbestimmung* practices. They insisted that "shop floor" issues be injected into Opel's boardroom: questions regarding retirement, plant ventilation, and even the workers' right to select the management board's personnel director. "As Opel President, James Waters, put it: 'These are issues to be settled by labor negotiations, not by the board.' Richard Heller, the head of the works council at Opel's Russelsheim works disagrees. 'We do not like to bring such issues before the board but we believe at Opel they are serious enough that the board should concern itself with them.' "[49]

Worker-directors want more information and more input into investment policy making. They argue that working conditions are just as important as product development and capacity improvement and should get equal consideration. Opel's president conceded that, in the past, management "presented worker representatives with investment decisions, after the fact. 'Now,' he says, they want to review them 'one at a time.' . . . As one Opel board member ruefully concedes: 'Common ground is still a long way off.' "[50]

Contrary to critics such as Alfred L. Thimm, a Union College management professor who vehemently condemns the system in *The False Promise of Codetermination,* there is considerable support.[51] In passing the expanded 1976 version of the law, the Bundestag voted overwhelmingly in favor, 391 to 22. Evidently the lawmakers who have to live with codetermination

---

[49]"West Germany: The Worker Dissidents in Opel's Boardroom," *Business Week,* July 23, 1979, p. 79.
[50]Ibid.
[51]Alfred L. Thimm, *The False Promise of Codetermination* (Lexington, Mass.: D. C. Heath and Company, 1981).

see much more of the positive than the negative. The courts, likewise, have validated the 1976 law. The West German highest court reiterated that the near-equal labor voice on supervisory boards of large companies does not infringe on the property rights of shareholders because they still have a slight voting edge. "While giving the unions a big victory, West Germany's highest court also left the door open for further action if the supervisory boards don't function as hoped. 'If, however, the existing legislation isn't adequate to safeguard effectively the independence of the boards, it will be up to the lawmakers to provide a remedy.' "[52]

The question of independence seems to be parallel with effectiveness in performance. For example, not long after the new law, Volkswagen and I. G. Metal, the biggest German union, "signed a contract that permits labor standards to be applied, extended or changed only with the full consent of the workers. This new contract covers 55,000 production workers at Volkswagen plants throughout West Germany."[53] The new system is based on methods-time measurement, a predetermined time technique used in some U.S. plants for at least thirty years. In addition, the agreement requires that workers be fully informed about why a particular operation is being measured. Significantly, "the company also agreed that the 'standard performance' levels imposed will meet the criterion of 'biological and social responsibility' based on a joint decision by union and management."[54]

Admittedly, the *Mitbestimmung* road to effective corporate governance is not a smooth one, and roadblocks such as hindered AMC in its bid to emulate Chrysler's breakthrough will continue to occur. James C. Furlong, an authority on codetermination, comments in an interview with Herman Rebhan, vice chairman of Ford-Werke, Ford Motor Company's 57,000-employee West German subsidiary: "The millennium hasn't arrived [even] in Germany as a result of the co-determination law, and he feels that boardroom representation of employees will spread to the U.S. He predicts that within five years it will be a prestige matter for American unions to have one of their officers on a company board. Rebhan, himself a former member of Ford-Werke's supervisory board, stresses that 'workers are more intelligent; they demand recognition; they want more to say about their jobs and their lives.' "[55]

Furlong concludes his interesting interview with Herman Rebhan, quoting the unionist that "worker representation on company boards is a reform rather than a revolution. What appears revolutionary in one decade is

[52]"West German Firms Lose in Their Test of Codetermination," *The Wall Street Journal,* March 2, 1979, p. 36.

[53]*World and Work Report,* May 1979, p. 34.

[54]Ibid.

[55]James C. Furlong, "Co-Determination," *The Wall Street Journal,* March 31, 1980, p. 20.

routine the next. 'The 10-hour day was once a revolutionary demand,' he points out. 'People died in Chicago for this.' He adds, 'The system is quite elastic. It can take many changes. I think that is why capitalism has survived. Today's capitalism isn't the one that Marx talked about.' "[56]

ILLUSTRATION: Germany: Deutsche Bank

German banks have a unique role in the country's economy because German law encourages their large-scale direct investment in manufacturing enterprise. For example, taxes on dividends reach 51 percent when a specific holding is less than 25 percent of a firm's outstanding shares. However, taxes drop to only 15 percent when the investment is over 25 percent.

Historically, this practice was reinforced because of the several major financial-industrial crises Germany had endured. It was accentuated during the depression when thousands of businessmen were forced to issue stock to the banks in order to obtain credit. After World War II, the scarcity of individual investors willing to risk their meager savings in Germany's chaotic economy forced the banks to continue their investment role. As a consequence of this investment opportunity, the larger banks have very diversified and substantial portfolios. Investment in bank shares is comparable to investing in our mutual fund shares. Many German citizens like this portfolio investment opportunity.

Because they are the nation's prime investors, German banks are prominently represented on corporate boards. Herman Josef Abs, postwar Germany's leading banker, at the peak of his activity served on twenty-four corporate boards. Until recently, there was no concerted effort to reduce this financial institution control over industry. Supervision by German regulatory agencies in no way matched the vigilance of the Securities and Exchange Commission or the Federal Trade Commission: conflict of interest, insider information, collusion, and similar American boardroom taboos lost their meaning in the German translation. In some respects German boards of directors resemble those that prevailed in the United States two generations ago.

A more contemporary similarity is the German "share depot" practice, much like the voting of customer and client shares held in trust by United States banks. Because the value of securities' portfolios fluctuates with stock market valuations, it is impossible to give precise figures. But a conservative estimate of the value of common stock held by the 13,681 U.S. commercial banks and trust companies would exceed $300 billion. Over 70 percent of these assets held in trust—according to the Federal Depository Insurance Corporation—are administered by our leading fifty bank trust departments. In this respect, both United States and German investment practices are parallel.

Specifically, the German share depot is considered to be a service provided by the bank, which offers to vote its customers' shares at annual meetings. Deutsche Bank (Germany's biggest), for example, regularly gets between half and two-thirds of

[56]Ibid.

its customers' voting rights. Carefully spelled-out instructions must be followed if the bank is to be denied these voting privileges. Typically, most of the bank's customers simply do not want to go through the bother of canceling the bank's privilege.

This practice, however, is not sacrosanct. "Exercising these depot voting rights has brought so much criticism down on the banks that Deutsche Bank says it is ready to drop the device."[57] Yet, a dozen years after that statement and even after a public stock market reform commission study and recommendations, the practice remains unchanged. Perhaps this is why the German public continues to support codetermination—where the bankers sit on one side of the boardroom and the workers and general public sit on the other.

Deutsche Bank, the country's leading commercial bank, provides some interesting examples in the application of codetermination and of shared chief executive authority. When Herman Josef Abs, the bank's venerable *Sprecher* (spokesperson-CEO), retired in 1967 after a long and colorful career, a two-person *Sprecher* was set up. In effect, this was an office of the *Sprecher,* comparable to the office of the president, where chief executive authority is vested in several coequal chiefs. When the experimental dual control came to an end because the principals had retired, a second joint *Sprecher* was set up in 1976.

Initially, this second shared-authority venture seemed destined to fail, particularly since both of the new *Sprechers,* F. Wilhelm Christians and Wilfried Guth, were headstrong and neither was willing to serve as the other's subordinate. Yet, fortunately, both recognized that unless they took drastic measures and compromised, there would be civil war in the boardroom. Recognizing their frailties, both vowed never to go into the boardroom unless they were in full agreement on every issue.

Not only are these dual chief executives quite different in temperament, but they operate from offices that are 100 miles apart. Each takes turns serving as chairman of the powerful *Vorstand,* which consists of twelve members. Collectively, it is this committee which runs the bank, chooses its own members, and elects the *Sprecher.* While this executive committee informs the supervisory committee, it does not necessarily seek its approval.

The twelve-member executive committee meets every Tuesday, and each member has an equal voice and vote. In sharp contrast to most American outside directors, each *Vorstand* member is supposed to have a considered view on all items of business. "Says Guth, 'It's not a situation in which specialists talk and others listen.' "[58]

The decision-making process in *Vorstand* meetings must tax even the combined patience of the dual *Sprecher*—all executive board decisions must be unanimous. Unanimity is also required in issuing the bank's annual report which must be signed by all the *Vorstand's* members. By contrast, a recent U.S. Securities and Exchange Commission requirement—that a majority of the directors must sign the annual report—has evoked considerable criticism.

[57]"Germany's Banks Flex Muscles," *Business Week,* May 24, 1969, p. 98.
[58]Robert Ball, "A Two-Headed Bank Nibbles at the U.S.," *Fortune,* August 24, 1981, p. 105.

Fortune made one other interesting observation: "Most of Deutsche Bank's senior managers come from rather modest backgrounds. There are few of the 'vons' that often grace German banks—none at all on the executive board and only two among 58 other senior executives."[59] *Fortune* emphasizes that Deutsche Bank's *Vorstand* members are all products of an intensive-training and promotion-from-within program. In the process, the successful candidates acquire a unique competency and polish. Yet the grooming process never ends: even after several years of serving on the executive committee, the new member learns his chores by doing; that is, taking the minutes of the meeting. Secrecy in German *Vorstand* meetings is rigidly observed; nonmember secretaries are not allowed.

For their full-time service on the *Vorstand*, each board member gets the same salary—the equivalent of over $400,000 a year. This approximates the salaries paid the "Fortune 500" chief executives but is far in excess of even the highest pay of any outside director in the United States.

This capsule comparison should suffice to show that significant differences exist between German banks and their boards and their United States counterparts. "German banks also function as investment bankers, underwriting issues of securities and as stockbrokers. Only the banks can be stock exchange members; nearly all the people who work in stock exchanges work for the banks."[60] Parenthetically, so do nearly all CEOs and directors in large-scale German industry.

ILLUSTRATION: Sweden: Codetermination College

Since 1973, Sweden has had a law requiring all companies with more than 100 employees to have worker representation on the board. The pragmatic Swedes immediately recognized that elevating "a hand" from the production line to the boardroom does not necessarily give the new director infused knowledge. Consequently, the giant Swedish Trade Union Confederation sponsored crash courses for blue-collar worker-directors at its training school outside Stockholm. Some white-collar unions, likewise, started cram courses for their director-designees, and even the Swedish Management Institute started briefing workers on their duties as directors.

The Swedish Trade Union Confederation's program, which costs several million dollars annually, is underwritten by the union and the government. Industry associations, while claiming to support the concept, fought hard to keep it voluntary. As the former head of the Swedish Federation of Industry and chairman of the largest chemical company put it: "This is starting at the wrong end. Workers certainly should be given greater responsibility but in those areas where they are working. Industrial democracy should be built up starting at the shop floor."[61]

Just as it would be unfair to judge a college on the basis of only three or four

---

[59]Ibid.
[60]"Germany's Banks Flex Muscles," op. cit., p. 96.
[61]"When Workers Become Directors," *Business Week*, September 15, 1973, p. 19.

graduated classes, the Swedish worker-director education experiment will have to be tested over a period of time. At one time even Volvo, the nation's largest company, had reservations about the concept's success—even though it put workers on its board before being mandated to do so. This overall uncertainty is reflected in two dichotomous views. Marcus Wallenberg, Sweden's leading industrialist-banker, questions the worker-director's dual loyalty: " 'You must remember you are sitting on the board and must take into consideration the total interests of the company, not just one side.' Britt Sweno, who conducts the blue-collar training school, disagrees. 'If the worker representatives forget their fellow workers' interests, this reform will be a failure,' she says. 'After all, men sitting on boards always represent special interests—banks, finance groups, stockholders. Why should it be different with the workers?' "[62]

The initial success of the experiment was acknowledged when, on January 1, 1977, an expanded law on codetermination made it mandatory for workers, both blue- and white-collar, to be consulted by management on operating decisions. "The gist of the law, which now applies to all companies with at least 25 workers, is that management must negotiate with labor before it makes an important change of activity or before it decides on any important change of the working or employment conditions. The final right of decision, however, is not taken away from management."[63]

ILLUSTRATION: France: *Liberté, Egalité, Fraternité*

Although the codetermination experiment has spread from West Germany to most of northwest Europe, it is the French who have put the supreme imprimatur on the technique. Keeping in mind the centuries-old rivalry and animosity between both banks of the Rhine, when one side imitates the other, you can be sure the imitation is worthwhile. In France, at the start of the 1980s, there was a shift of French corporate governance from the *societe anonyme*'s (or corporation's) conventional *conseil d'administration* (or board of directors) to the German-styled two-tier system. The upper tier, the *conseil de surveillance,* composed of elected stockholders, selects the two- to five-member *directoire,* comparable to the German *Vorstand*. This is management in charge of day-to-day operations.[64]

It will be interesting to see what level of success codetermination will achieve in France. So far it has at least two strikes against it: (1) it is considered a German disease, and (2) it has been superimposed upon a nation of small shopkeepers, small vintners, and various small enterprisers. In the wine-cellar sector, for example, there are more than 5000 chateaux and caves in the St. Emilion area; the Dordogne sector

[62]Ibid.

[63]"Swedes Ponder Long-Range Effect of Law Giving Workers More Say in Management," *The Wall Street Journal,* March 25, 1977.

[64]Maître Paul Le Cannu, "The Two-Tier Corporate Board in France," *Directors and Boards,* Spring 1980, p. 11.

has at least 2000. These are only two of a dozen equally important wine-producing areas. Add another hundred lines of endeavor, and shopkeepers and small enterprisers become very important in the nation's economics and politics.

The French have a history of being in the forefront fighting for *liberté, fraternité, egalité*. Since codetermination is definitely a battle of "little guys" against the establishment, it could appeal to this equalitarian mentality. There is, however, a major obstacle. All French governance—industrial, political, and even education— is dominated by closely knit graduates of the *grandes ecoles* (great schools). For instance, there is the Ecole National d'Administration (ENA). "No fewer than eight members of Mitterand's Socialist Cabinet, for example, are alumni of the vaunted ENA which also produced seven members of the outgoing Giscard government."[65] The *enarque*, or products, of this venerable institution run the French government. Similarly in the business world, graduates of Ecole Polytechnique, the science and engineering school molded by Napoleon, and the pedigreed products of the Ecole des hautes Etudes Commerciales tend to dominate. These three institutions, together with the Ecole Normale Supérieure (founded in 1794), constitute the French Ivy or "Fleurs-de-lis" League. They are extremely selective: annually the four *grandes ecoles* combined admit less than a thousand applicants. But "once they are accepted as full members, the other members will do everything possible to guarantee their success. . . . Once he graduates, the high-level functionary enters a separate social world. He will have his own preferred clubs (Polo de Bagatelle, Racing Club of France, Cercle Interallié) and discussion groups."[66]

This has a very familiar ring, especially when one recalls the U.S. Ivy League, Britain's "old boy" clubs, and University of Tokyo and University of Moscow patterns. This powerful built-in exclusivity makes it next to impossible for Jacques Doe ever to be admitted to the alma mater fraternities and secret societies. Yet the 1981 national elections that saw the advent of a socialist regime could portend another equally important French Revolution in the boardrooms—a Gallic codetermination.

ILLUSTRATION: Peru: The Industrial Community

Workers in the German, French, Swedish, and other European codetermination ventures get their stake through government decree and not through ownership. However, a few countries (including Denmark) have taken preliminary measures to legitimize this governance prerogative by giving the workers shares in the company. One of the more ambitious of these ownership-sharing schemes took place in Peru in the mid-1970s. A military junta, in 1975, seeking a middle course between South American-style capitalism and totalitarian Marxism, decreed the creation of "industrial communities." All enterprises with five or more employees had to gradually give ownership interests to the workers until ultimately the workers owned more

---

[65]"The Ties That Bind," *Time*, June 29, 1981, p. 30.
[66]Ibid.

than half the capital. This ownership distribution was to come about in the approximately 3300 firms affected, by an annual distribution of profits. Each year 15 percent of the profits must be recapitalized as shares that are distributed to the workers in the "industrial community."

The Pan-American version of codetermination has had a rough experience because very few of the Peruvian workforce have surplus funds for investment. As a consequence, most "industrial communities" have sought to disinvest and get more money immediately, rather than to wait for longer-term fruition. Instead of stressing productivity, quality, and innovation, most of the groups were interested in immediate gain.

In addition, there were some serious impediments from management and regular investors. "Firms are reported to have transferred much of their policymaking and executive authority from boards where workers are represented to shareholder committees where the employee voice is still faint. And some firms have frustrated employee-directors simply by holding unannounced meetings or by conducting business in English or German, which few workers understand."[67] Unfortunately for codetermination, its success continues to hinge too much on the fortunes of espousing parties, usually those of centrist-socialist persuasion. Consequently, as the fortunes of politics shift, so do those of codetermination.

But the long-run feasibility of workers as corporate directors just could become a reality. In the more developed industrial nations, increasing education levels and greater social awareness have definitely outmoded the old boss versus "hands" mentality. An American business executive in Peru commented: " 'The old days when the boss said, 'Jump,' and everyone jumped, are over. This [co-determination] is not an impossible concept to work with but it requires some mind-wrenching. It's a new business experience for me, and you know, I find it an interesting challenge.' "[68]

PEOPLE'S CAPITALISM

Even *Mitbestimmung's* most ardent proponents admit that the concept has some serious limitations. Despite all the ballyhoo about its democracy and its stress on the worker as a stakeholder, *Mitbestimmung* seems to be at variance with free enterprise. In only a few incipient cases are these workers also shareholders, and yet they hold up to one-half of the governance power. Their governance role does not come from ownership but rather from a political mandate.

As was emphasized in the historical introduction, corporations are legal entities. What the state creates, it can shape and reshape and even "uncreate." The creation process itself is conditioned by the character of the creator, and this character is a synthesis of culture, experience, and a

[67]Everett G. Martin, "Peruvian Regime Seeks Labor Harmony by Giving Employees Say in Management," *The Wall Street Journal,* February 4, 1975, p. 42.
[68]Ibid.

host of other variables. *Mitbestimmung,* as was described, is the consequence of centuries of struggle and striving by the Germanic people in a
tumultuous central Europe. What little possessions the common folk could
accumulate, they regularly lost to feuding barons and rapacious landlords.
Centuries of fear and deprivation condition the socialistic premise that the
means of production—factories, machinery, and all capital—belong to the
people, that is, the state. Consequently, while the people are the owners, it
is only in a generic or global sense. The bold concept of *Mitbestimmung*
naturally has appeal to disenfranchised individuals, who through an inter-
minable and infernally unhappy experience with owners, can only relate as
"them and us."

But as Adam Smith's free enterprise philosophy embarks on its third
century, greater numbers of workers, in an expanding circle of industrial-
ized nations, are getting opportunities to behave as capitalists. To them,
ownership of industry means individual possession and not a commonweal
treasure; they need to have tangible evidence of ownership—stock certificates, proxies, annual reports, and, above all, dividends. They also must be
able to dispose of their shares by sale or bequest, increasing or decreasing
their individual stakes.

In a sense, then, workers as citizens are evolving into their new role as
owners of industry. While the number of U.S. citizens individually owning
shares in our enterprise system fluctuates cyclically, there is a long-run
upward progression. Fifty years ago, at the depth of the depression, there
were probably only a million owners of stock in the United States; today the
figure is above 33 million. Expanding the count to include indirect
ownership (through mutual funds, savings accounts, insurance, and corporate stock investment plans) raises the figure to include virtually every
American. This widespread ownership can provide the basis for an American version of *Mitbestimmung* or codetermination—one based not on
government fiat but on meaningful stockholder ownership.

At least thirty years ago the retiring chairman of United States Steel
Corporation, Benjamin Fairless, made a most interesting speculation on
people's capitalism, which, incidentally, is only now beginning to make
headway. Fairless (after whom the giant Fairless Works in southeastern
Pennsylvania is named), in an address to the Pennsylvania State Chamber of
Commerce, focused on the Marxian premise that the means of production
must belong to the people. Fairless agreed with Marx on this score but
sharply disagreed on how such ownership should be effected. Marx,
obviously, proposed revolution, bloodshed, and expropriation as an instant
solution to all society's problems. Fairless recommended a gradual and
peaceful takeover through common stock purchase.

Fairless had a very logical proposition. At that time U.S. Steel had about
300,000 employees and an ownership represented by 26,100,000 shares of

common stock. Dividing these shares pro rata would have come to 87 shares per employee. At the prevailing market price of $40, if each U.S. Steel employee invested just $3500, the giant corporation would then be completely owned by its workers. But as is obvious, not even a figure as high as a 51 percent arithmetic majority is needed for effective control.

Fairless suggested that with an investment of as little as $5 per week the employees would have effective control in less than ten years. They could then elect their own directors, hire and fire management, put the president of the United Steel Workers Union in the company's chief executive office, and run the business to suit themselves. In a facetious fashion, Fairless concluded his talk to the chamber of commerce with: "Clearly Marx did not know all the Engles."

Bringing the Fairless proposal up to date, consider that before its Marathon Oil merger bid, U.S. Steel had 89 million common shares outstanding with a 1981 market price ranging between $23 and $35 per share (but with a book value of $70 per share). At the low point, therefore, the New York Stock Exchange had put a valuation on U.S. Steel's worth as low as $2 billion. Consequently, the employees, now down to 149,000, could have purchased "Big Steel" by investing an average $13,000. While this would have been four times the investment required in the original Fairless calculation, each worker now would get 600 shares as compared with 87 shares.

But Ben Fairless's suggestion was not accepted seriously, and almost a third of a century passed before a major corporation welcomed a union leader into the boardroom. Although the Chrysler-Fraser episode is precedent-setting, it did not result from union-member stock purchases—it was Chrysler's dire financial straits and its need for federal funding, plus union concessions, that swayed Chrysler's leaders toward heresy.

If Fairless were making suggestions today on how to improve the rank and file's ownership and control position, he might recommend a different approach. His present strategy would revolve not so much around individual workers as stockowners, but rather on their collective clout as future pensioners. There are, today, more than half a million private pension plans with combined assets approaching $650 billion. It is estimated that these funds, about two-thirds involving union members, will rise to a staggering $3 trillion by 1995. Keep in mind that the aggregate stockholders' equity in the 1980 "Fortune 1000" industrials totaled $584 billion. Even today's $650 billion in pension fund assets is sufficient to buy a 100 percent control in every major manufacturing firm in the country.

Another related pension-power factor—although unheralded but very significant for the future of corporate governance—is the unfunded prior service costs obligation. Unfunded prior service costs refer to the money a corporation must ultimately pay out in vested benefits and other promised benefits. To stretch a legal point, these might be viewed as "mechanics' liens"—a contractual obligation whereby pensioners would have first claim on an employer's assets. To date, the mechanic's lien concept has not been invoked for the simple reason that the federal government has increasingly provided pension guarantees. However, this puts the government in the position of figuratively taking a peripheral position in a near-bankrupt firm's assets and liabilities.

In Chrysler's case, the unfunded prior service costs came to almost $2 billion, more than eight times the market value of all Chrysler common stock at its 1981 low of 3⅛ per share. Hypothetically, if Chrysler's workers had pressed claims, they could have foreclosed on the company, ousted the board, and replaced the directors with bona fide unionists—this would be a giant leap beyond *Mitbestimmung,* where control is shared with outside owners.

Incidentally, Chrysler was not alone in its high unfunded prior service costs obligation. A *Business Week* survey (August 25, 1980) showed that 100 major reporting U.S. companies had a combined obligation of $46 billion. The magnitude of these very real yet overlooked obligations led to a shift in 1981 pension disclosure requirements by the Financial Accounting Standards Board.[69]

This accounting figment actually appeared to result in an overfunding by many firms. Consequently, a few hard-pressed companies, notably Atlantic and Pacific Tea Company, proposed taking a $200 million "surplus" out of its pension plan and using it for company revitalization purposes. A recent survey of 571 major pension funds, by Jeremy Bulow, Stanford University economist, "indicates that in the aggregate their assets exceed their liabilities by about $55 billion. Thus, if the economic conditions worsen and pension plan terminations accelerate, the use of 'surplus' pension funds could become an explosive political and economic issue."[70]

In some instances, especially in large multiemployer plans—as in the construction industry and trucking—pension funds are jointly administered. But since most unions adhere rigidly to the Samuel Gompers tradition of separation of union hall and corporate boardroom, most pension funds are managed by company-selected trustees, generally from trust departments of major commercial banks and insurance companies. For example, before its 1980 pension fund consolidation plan, American Telephone and Telegraph parceled out $28 billion of pension money to 115 managers, mostly banks. Naturally there is cause for ample suspicion when an elite financial

[69]"Pension Liabilities: Improvement Is Illusory," *Business Week,* September 14, 1981, p. 114.
[70]"Will Ailing Companies Tap Their Pension Funds?" *Business Week,* November 23, 1981, p. 44.

fraternity becomes the prime benefactor. *Note:* An investigation by the AFL-CIO Industrial Union Department showed that of the ten largest industrial companies, seven had interlocking directorships with J. P. Morgan and Company whose Morgan Guaranty Trust is a leading pension investment manager.

It is hoped that this summary of the pension fund potential for worker participation in the boardroom will stimulate more meaningful analysis. There is no argument against every American becoming an owner of American industry, but there is considerable confusion about how almost 250 million Americans can collectively become a really democratic and participative corporate governance mechanism. Among the several routes in this direction are:

1 Voluntary stock purchase
2 Income tax incentive plans
3 Stock saving plans
4 Saving and profit-sharing plans
5 Stock bonuses based on length of service
6 Purchase of company by employees
7 Employee stock ownership plan (ESOP)
8 Employee Retirement Income Security Act (ERISA) passed in 1974

However, as stressed earlier, by 1995 the $3 trillion from more than half a million private pension funds will certainly be sufficient to establish a right-of-way from the factory to the boardroom.

"Says Thomas H. Chase, a corporate planner for American Telephone and Telegraph: 'Pension funds have become the market maker in the stock exchanges of America. If one or two funds hiccup, prices move.' Control over these funds, says Chase, would provide union leaders an 'economic lever of greater importance than the greatest general strike.' "[71]

ILLUSTRATION: Vermont Asbestos Group: Success Kills VAG

Invariably employees get an opportunity to become majority stockholders only when management gets itself into inextricable situations. Such was the case with GAF's northern Vermont asbestos mine. Because of a poor market and because the Environmental Protection Agency was insisting on pollution control expenditures of over $1 million, the company decided to close the mine. Faced with losing their jobs, 174 workers organized and bought the mine. " 'The miners put up $80,000

---

[71]"Unions Bid for Bigger Voice in Pension Funds," *U.S. News & World Report,* June 8, 1981, p. 85.

toward the purchase price of a property worth at least $5 million,' said the president of Sterling Trust Co., the lead bank in a consortium of big Boston and small Vermont banks that lent $1.5 million to the miners now incorporated as Vermont Asbestos Group, Inc."[72] GAF facilitated the sale by putting a very low price tag on the property, by extending the payment period, and by giving the miners a very generous severance pay which some invested in the new firm.

Every miner owned at least one share, priced at $50; the miners as a group held 80 percent of the 2000 shares outstanding. At first, and on the negative side, it was assumed that only a six- to seven-year reserve of asbestos remained. World prices of asbestos had hit a new low. But the economic environment soon changed when subsequent testing revealed the reserve estimate to be doubled and asbestos prices rose more than 50 percent within the year.

Given the opportunity to run their enterprise as owners, the employees set up a board of governors consisting of seven hourly workers, seven salaried employees, and one outsider.

Within three years profits exceeded the million-dollar-per-year level, and a common share issued at $50 now had a book value of $2185. An independent appraisal by a member of a major brokerage house set a valuation of $3500 per share. The VAG directors opted for a diversification program, using the unexpected lush profits to guarantee work when the asbestos reserves ran out. But most of the stockholder-miners preferred cash in hand rather than reinvestment. (Dividends during the first three years totaled $144 a share on an investment of $50.)

The employee feuding built up to a point where the miners threatened to strike their own mine. The company's president was fired, and the chairman resigned. A local construction firm operator, Howard Manosh, then made a tender offer of $1834 per share. Aggravating the bickering even more, a local banker made a tentative offer of $2300 per share.

Shareholder disenchantment intensified because of seemingly arbitrary decisions made by the directors. Despite the shareholders' refusal to diversify into making wallboard, the wallboard plant was authorized by the directors.

Nevertheless, not all the miners soured on their capitalistic venture. One employee, a laborer who owns just one share of Vermont Asbestos, expressed the view many management theorists expect to hear from people's capitalism proponents. The miner-owner stated that, despite all the difficulties, he still likes the idea of having a stake in the company. "It's a good feeling to be able to say we own this company. One share doesn't make much difference, but I feel a part of things."[73] Of course, this was a minority view as compared with the many who wanted to "cash in their chips" and abandon employee ownership.

The issue came to a head at the 1978 annual meeting. After weeks of intensive vote solicitation, two opposing slates of candidates (management's and Manosh's) had a showdown. In a secret ballot election, the names of the candidates were printed on blackboards as they were nominated. Then shareholders voted by lining

---

[72]"Asbestos Workers Buy Out GAF's Mine," *Business Week,* March 31, 1975, p. 21.

[73]David Gumpert, "Discord in Eden: Miners Who Struck It Rich in Vermont Now Bicker over Loot," *The Wall Street Journal,* March 31, 1978, p. 1.

up to deposit secret ballots in two small cardboard boxes. The results: fourteen Manosh men, mostly outsiders plus one incumbent, were elected. "Richard Hamilton, an industrial representative of Vermont's Economic Development Department and the outsider member of the old board termed the results, 'a disaster. It's the end of employee ownership. They had it and they gave it away.' "[74]

ILLUSTRATION: C&NW: Will Success Wreck C&NW?

An equally interesting and longer-lasting success story is the employee ownership of C&NW, the former Chicago and Northwest Railroad component, spun off in 1972 from Ben Heineman's conglomerate, Northwest Industries. About 3500 of the railroad's 11,000 employees now own half of the 4.4 million outstanding shares. When stock was selling at an issuance price of $50 per share, the railroaders invested $3.6 million for 72,905 shares. Almost half of the initial purchasers were union members, including the president of the Brotherhood of Railway and Airline Clerks.

The new employee-run venture flourished from the start. Within a year the stock soared from $50 to $660 per share and later was split sixty for one. In mid-1981, the stock commanded a $58 bid; thus a $1000 original investment was now worth about $70,000. Several of the original purchasers, including the Brotherhood of Railway and Airline Clerks' president (who invested the $10,000 allowable maximum), were now millionaires. The stock soared because investors saw C&NW as a survivor in the midwest, where several competitors had been liquidated or drastically cut in trackage. Also, C&NW's strategic location in the grain belt, together with its proximity to the recently opened Powder River coal fields, gave it a competitive advantage. Moreover, it grabbed desired trackage and business from its bankrupt neighbors, the Milwaukee Road and the Rock Island Line. Much of its success is attributed to the management brought in by the employee owners.

But will success kill C&NW as it did Vermont Asbestos Group? Under the flush of success, some uncertainties exist, for instance, the threat of being gobbled up by a giant such as Union Pacific. More serious is the leverage problem; C&NW's huge debt of $428 million, as compared with $116 million in stockholder equity, is one of the worst ratios in the industry. Also, the railroad needs to abandon at least 1500 miles of unproductive track serving backwater communities. Equally disconcerting is its heavy dependence on federal subsidies; for instance, it sold the government $112.7 million in preference shares at a rate average of 2.3 percent to upgrade track and equipment. However, with the federal government becoming increasingly hard-pressed and cutting subsidies, this could be a fleeting advantage.[75]

Employee ownership and railroad governance, likewise, are not without irrita-

---

[74]David Gumpert, "Employee-Owners of Asbestos Mine Oust Directors Who Opposed Sale of Concern," *The Wall Street Journal*, April 4, 1978, p. 17.

[75]John Curley, "Route to Power Full of Risks for the C&NW," *The Wall Street Journal*, April 3, 1981, p. 23.

tions. On the overall, 1980 earnings were only $8.79 per share on sales of almost $1 billion. There are also many gripes such as the employee who paid $24,000 in taxes on the sale of 3000 shares. And there are jealousies. An engineer with about a quarter of a million in stock "says envious fellow workers tried to sabotage his car by putting screws and bolts in the tires. 'Some guys call me money-hungry,' he says. 'I tell them, yeah, but it sure tastes good.' "[76]

ILLUSTRATION: ESOP/ESOT: The Kelso Plan

An ESOP is an employee stock ownership plan, while the related ESOT is an employee stock ownership trust. Somewhere on the periphery are the TRASOPs, tax reduction act stock ownership plans. Fundamentally, ESOPs (of which there are more than 4000 in the United States) are tax-qualified employee benefit plans, designed to give employees an opportunity at easy acquisition of stock in the company. At the same time they provide the employer with an innovative method for raising considerable additional funding. TRASOPs provide for employers to purchase stock for the employees out of tax credit on corporate capital expenditures. Companies can claim an additional ½ percent credit when employees contribute an equal amount. Where an ESOP ends and a TRASOP begins, or vice versa, is a matter of conjecture.

Louis O. Kelso, an imaginative tax lawyer and economic theoretician, developed the employee stock ownership idea in the mid-1950s, and therefore, until recently, it was more familiarly known as the Kelso plan. Despite the Kelso plan's seeming attractions, it had very few adopters during its first two decades. Some of its much advertised positive features are:

The workers get a share of the action.
Productivity is stimulated.
The firm has a dependable and accessible source of funding.
There are significant tax advantages.
Most states and communities give special concession to ESOP firms.
A worker-ownership base provides friendly votes to thwart unwanted tender offers.

In general, economic theorists agree that ESOPs are great motivators and are needed to revive faltering productivity. Social theorists get a big uplift in assuming that ESOPs are a great stride toward a workers' utopia. Only die-hard unionists are adamant about the concept, just as they are with *Mitbestimmung* or any other corporate ownership or governance scheme.

In substance, the technique works as follows: An ESOT is set up and is managed by an employee committee. If the company wants to borrow $5 million, it approaches a bank with a request that the loan be made, not to the company

[76]John Curley, "Some Workers at the C&NW Find Positions Astoundingly Rewarding," *The Wall Street Journal*, March 27, 1981, p. 31.

directly, but rather to the ESOT. The employee committee then orders that the sum be invested in the company. Authorized stock is issued, at current market price, for the sum invested and placed in the trust, to be supervised by the trustees. Guaranteeing the transaction, the company commits itself to repay the bank loan indirectly through the trust.

The big attraction to the employer, in addition to ease in getting funds, is the repayment to the bank in pretax dollars. In effect, the company repays the entire loan as if it were making contributions to a pension plan. Legally the trust is an employee deferred compensation trust, and consequently, such payments are tax-deductible. This concept should be particularly attractive in periods of high and gyrating prime rates, as characterized the early 1980s.

After laying dormant for twenty years, ESOPs were given a powerful boost by the friendly and powerful support of Senator Russell B. Long, chairman of the Senate Finance Committee. Largely through the senator's efforts, Congress enacted the Employee Retirement Income Security Act of 1974 and the Tax Reduction Act of 1975. This legislation countervails ESOPs to a degree since it mandates pension fund diversification of assets.

As for immediate worker takeover of boardrooms, presently few of the 250 or more plans provide for voting rights passing through to vested employees. Most employee-owners do not actually receive the shares until they retire. Some ESOPs get only nonvoting stock, and even in cases where the stock is in ordinary voting shares, the vote is exercised by a voting trust of high-level executives. This is of vital significance in situations where, as mentioned earlier, unfriendly tender offers are a possibility. When the loan is repaid, usually after five years, the stock remains the property of the trust, that is, in friendly hands. But this is increasingly seen as an abuse, particularly in closely held corporations. A Senate Committee on Finance expressed concern in three areas: (1) the method by which privately held companies value the stock held by employees, (2) the voting rights of employee stock owners, and (3) the market for the stock.

Initially ESOP participants consisted of smaller, closely held, mismanaged, and financially embarrassed firms, but during the 1981 recession some well-known larger companies joined the roster. General Motors, for instance, faced with the possibility of closing a plant, offered it to the employees, who accepted and agreed on a $53 million purchase price. In addition to funds provided by three financial institutions, General Motors purchased $10 million of nonvoting preferred stock and bought another $13 million in notes. Significantly, the employees' purchase was conditioned on their acceptance of a 25 percent cut in pay and fringe benefits.

At Kaiser Steel Corporation, the employees bought the West Coast's only full-scale steel mill, and then made an attempt to buy the company. They hired Louis O. Kelso, originator of the ESOP idea, to help them set up a nonprofit corporation, Kaiser ESOP, Inc.

Rath Packing Company launched its program with an agreement that each employee purchase ten shares weekly through a $20 payroll deduction. The union also made governance progress when ten new directors were added; six were union members.

Immediately, productivity rose and absenteeism dropped. However, in a little more than a year *The Wall Street Journal* headlined: "Gripes of Wrath: Workers Who Bought Iowa Slaughterhouse Regret That They Did" (December 2, 1981).

As we know, there are always two sides to an issue, and so a few days later, *The Wall Street Journal* printed a reader's letter, "Rath Wrath," submitted by Lyle D. Taylor, president of Rath's union. Supported by a petition signed by 1200 Rath workers, Taylor disputed their supposed disenchantment and questioned the accuracy of the *Journal's* reporting.

ILLUSTRATION: South Bend ESOP: Workers Strike against Themselves

In 1975 South Bend Lathe, a failing division of Amsted Industries, Incorporated, was given new life through an ESOP, and 500 workers became owners of their company. South Bend Lathe's president had approached several local banks and the Economic Development Administration (EDA) for assistance. The EDA, seeking a meaningful test, approved a $5 million grant at 3 percent interest. The city of South Bend was the actual applicant for the grant, and it then lent the grant money to the ESOP. The banks provided another $5 million at a floating rate. The long-term loans were covered by 10,000 shares of stock serving as collateral. A portion of the company's profits was to be deposited in the employee stock ownership trust each year in order to pay back the loans. But the workers would not really become the owners until the loans were paid off. Then the stock was to be allocated to the workers on the basis of length of employment and salary level. The latter factor would mean proportionately more shares for managers. Nevertheless, by 1987, production workers should control about two-thirds of South Bend Lathe stock.

Initially, as expected, there was a significant boost (25 percent) in productivity; quality improved, and ESOP theorists were justified. But within two years the honeymoon had ended, and shortly thereafter, management-worker rifts developed. The chairman, president, CEO, and architect of the ESOP, J. Richard Boulis, stated: "Labor problems have destroyed the kind of spirit we really should have in an employee-owned firm."[77] On the eventual takeover by the employees, Boulis commented: "I feel that it was a mistake to agree to voting rights. Perhaps we tried to be too democratic when we put this whole thing together. Certainly there was no requirement to include voting rights."[78]

The big flare-up, and a discredit to the entire concept of the ESOP, came late in 1980 when 290 members of Local 1722, United Steelworkers, struck their own plant for nine weeks. In the contract negotiations that year, there was conflict over wages and, particularly, over an unrestricted cost of living adjustment. But as some ESOP watchers observed, the conflict over wages really concealed some deep animosities resulting from rank-and-file disillusionment with the basic structure of the South Bend Lathe ESOP, the first 100 percent employee-owned company. "We were

[77]*World and Work Report,* September 1979, p. 85.
[78]Ibid.

promised a piece of the action," said John Deak, Sr., president of the local. "What we got was misunderstanding."[79]

Boulis reflected that the dispute was the result of workers' unwillingness to think and act like owners. The strikers responded that they wanted to act like owners but that they had been allowed to select only one of eight board members. They wanted representation based on numbers employed. Yet since salary was a factor in the ultimate stock distribution, management would continue to have proportionately a greater share, about one-third of the total. The rank and file resented this privilege for a handful of managerial elite. In regard to the workers' gripe that their views had been consistently ignored, management's spokesman countered that "you can't consult with all the workers every time you make a decision."[80]

This episode, together with the Vermont Asbestos Group and C&NW cases, raises questions about the effectiveness of worker-owners running their own enterprises. In each of these instances the workers took over ownership of a failing firm. But in all instances they received either hefty governmental grants with unconscionably low interest rates plus more than reasonable prices on the acquired facilities or assorted other big breaks.

Again on the negative side, the workers were sold a bill of goods in that they were going to be their own bosses. In effect, there has not as yet been a real test of the effectiveness of workers as owners running their firm along ESOP ideals. *Time* aptly summarized the South Bend Lathe strike situation by quoting "bewildered Strike Leader Steve Kwiatkowski: 'I'm still confused why I'm here. If I'm an owner, then how can I be on strike?' "[81] *Time* then facetiously syncopated the situation: "The problems of South Bend Lathe are symptomatic of those that threaten to turn employee-owned companies into ESOP fables."[82]

WA: THE JAPANESE WAY

Kenji Takitani, a spokesman for Hitachi Metals, commented: " 'When I was in charge of a company in the US [board chairman of Hitachi Magnetic Corp. of Edmore, Michigan], I emphasized the *wa* spirit. You know the meaning of *wa?* Harmony. Harmony leads to strength, and this was very difficult to explain to the American executives and employees of that company. But gradually—and I was happy about this—they did understand. The *wa* spirit makes a great deal of difference in the attitude of businessmen or employees in Japan, compared with Americans. The lifetime employment system comes from the *wa* spirit. We try to keep good relations with the union; again this comes from the *wa* spirit. *Wa* means a kind of love. We

[79]"When Workers Strike the Company They Own," *Business Week,* September 22, 1980, p. 39.
[80]Ibid.
[81]"Trouble in Workers' Paradise," *Time,* September 22, 1980, p. 78.
[82]Ibid.

have to have patience, sacrifice, affection in every segment of the enterprise or the operation.' ''[83]

The *wa* philosophy applies to all company employees, from apprentice to chief executive officer. Observers stress that while the president of a big American company can be fired by the stockholders and the board of directors, there is no such custom in Japan. '' 'We have yearly or twice-a-year shareholder meetings but just for formality. In a sense the president of a Japanese corporation is a king. No one can remove him under normal circumstances. This may have some connection with the decision-making process,' says Toshihiro Tomabechi, Managing Director of Mitsubishi Corporation.''[84]

A Japanese CEO is ''king'' because Japanese industry is in the hands of doers, whereas U.S. industrialists are overwhelmed with reviewers. Our reviewing process is mandated by federal regulatory bodies, stock exchanges, internal and external auditors, and a host of other data seekers and self-appointed public watchdogs. Even the unions are demanding more information and a voice in decision making. Also, some legal and financial processes have become almost ludicrous. For instance, E. I. du Pont Company, contemplating merger with Conoco, sent its shareholders a 185-page 10-ounce prospectus. In addition, it had to file statements on Schedules 14D-1, 13D, and 14D-9 with the SEC, together with a registration statement. Less than a month later, Du Pont sent its shareholders an eight-page supplement to its prospectus. This is just a tiny segment of the bureaucratic and legal requirements which give us, on a per-capita basis, almost twenty times as many lawyers (approximately 600,000 today) and ten times as many accountants as there are in Japan.

Although they are described as ''doers,'' the Japanese do not neglect reviewing. They universally use a strictly internal procedure, the *ringi,* whereby a document proposing a decision or course of action is passed along for approval by persons concerned. There are two other interesting and pertinent terms: *ringisho,* the memorandum or document; and *hanko,* the initialing or signing of the *ringisho* or the seal affixed to it. Obviously, the *ringi* process is very time-consuming, but it has an advantage in a shorter chain of command—Toyoto has seven management layers compared with Ford Motor's twelve. So the *ringisho* has a shorter route, and once it has the requisite *hanko,* complete adherence is guaranteed.

In his innovative book, *Theory Z,* William Ouchi, professor at UCLA, states: ''Traditional American corporations encourage executives to be decisive, to act forcefully and to accept the consequences. Japanese

---

[83]''Japanese Managers Tell How Their System Works,'' *Fortune,* November 1977, p. 127.
[84]Ibid., p. 132.

corporate decisions are reached by a tedious process of collective compromising that can sometimes involve as many as 60 to 80 individuals, each of whom holds a potential veto. The process of consensus building is slow, but once agreement is reached, no one attempts to sabotage the project."[85]

It is evident, then, that both Japanese and Americans do a lot of reviewing; the difference is in reviewers. We answer to hosts of individuals outside the production and distribution processes; the Japanese almost exclusively seek reviews from those directly concerned with manufacturing and selling. There is a reason. "Japanese companies are run by professional managers. Since the 1950's stockholders have had little say in setting policy at most firms. Board members are usually people with corporate operating responsibilities and the general policy direction is invariably set by the company president. Emphasis, therefore, is on what is good for the company, not what will make the stockholders happy. Philosophically, there is a strong preference for long-term growth over short-term gains, which naturally benefits innovation."[86]

This system works in Japan because of the difference in separation of ownership and control from that premised, half a century ago, by Berle and Means.[87] They concluded, in their classic thesis, that the family firm had run its course and was being replaced by professional manager control. Berle and Means were only partly correct. Most family firms do, by the third generation, relinquish control to hired hands, to professional managers. But they also tend to lose their ownership positions as second- and third-generation scions fragmentize family holdings. There are, for example, an estimated 2000 to 3000 Du Ponts, with only minuscule shareholdings in their family firm.

As successful firms expanded, their need for huge aggregates of funds led them to borrowing. Consequently, financial institutions, which provided funding, have become the new owners. Until recently, the funding institutions had direct representation on corporate boards. Currently, since even this institutional ownership is quite fragmented, there is less direct representation and control. Instead, indirect control is maintained through the medium of independent or oversight boards.

In distinct contrast with yesterday's outside-director-type board, where financiers and lawyers were found in profusion, today's oversight board is more subtle in its financial institution tie-ins. But if one were to scratch deep enough, invariably one would find direct and especially indirect interlocks.

---

[85]Christopher Byron, "Review of William Ouchi, Theory Z," *Time*, March 2, 1981.
[86]"Japan: Quality Control and Innovation," *Fortune*, August 10, 1981, p. 36 (Special Section).
[87]Adolf A. Berle, Jr., and Gardiner C. Means, *The Modern Corporation and Private Property* (New York: The Macmillan Company, 1933).

Conversely, in Japan the *sogo shosha* ("all-out" or general trading firms), descendants of the pre-World War II *zaibatsu* (financial and trading "cliques"), tend to have their own internal sources of large-scale financing. Whereas in the United States major corporations generally have about half of their corporate financing in the form of bonds and bank debt, it would be distinctly rare for a *sogo shosha* to have as little as 50 percent long-term debt. Most of this borrowing is internal. Each of the six biggest *sogo shosha*—Mitsubishi, Mitsui, C. Itoh, Marubeni, Sumitomo, and Nissho-Iwai —have their own investment banks, insurance companies, and other financial components. Group members and allied companies do not have to go outside to borrow yen or any kind of foreign exchange. These six biggest groups each have over a hundred foreign branch offices, many of them bank representatives. Although the *sogo shosha* perform a variety of services for their clients, these associates are basically independent firms. Generally the associates concentrate on a limited line of endeavor; hence they become specialists and remain close to the operations scene. Yet these clients are tied to the parent in a unique multifaceted long-term relationship. "This enables the *sogo shosha* to influence its clients to coordinate their behavior so as to maximize long-term, total system welfare."[88]

Commenting on the Mitsubishi Group—the biggest of the *sogo shosha* with sales approaching $60 billion—the *Mainichi Daily News* states: "It is no exaggeration to say that the strength of the [Mitsubishi] group depends almost exclusively upon the capability of its bank to succeed in financing operations. Worth attention in this connection is the case of Mitsui Group whose members are considered generally to be less group-oriented. The Mitsui Bank occupies a less central position than does the Mitsubishi Bank."[89]

Perhaps, because of the bank's closer ties, Mitsubishi is able to manifest slightly more rigid corporate governance than its peer groups. The collective custodians of the group—its oversight board—include the chairmen and presidents of its twenty-eight major companies. They have a central meeting place and control center, the Mitsubishi Building (Tokyo), where at least twenty of the top companies have offices. Here are held the monthly meetings of the *Kinyo-kai* (Friday Conference), the supreme policy-making organ of the Mitsubishi Group. "At the monthly meeting, specific business dealings of the group are not discussed; the trading company's spokesman calls it a personal friendship affair. But the gathering exerts a pervasive influence over members' operations through the establishment of working

[88]Thomas B. Lifson, "A Theoretical Model of Japan's Sogo Shosha," *The Academy of Management Proceedings,* 1981, p. 71.
[89]"Mitsubishi Group," *Mainichi Daily News,* September 1971, p. 24.

committees on issues ranging from trademarks and quality control to public affairs."[90]

As in the United States, there is no rigid pattern among the *sogo shosha*. At Sumitomo, Japan's fourth largest group, ownership tends to be somewhat fragmented by a rather complex system in which group companies own one another's shares. In most cases there is a cross-ownership by Sumitomo Group members of about 40 percent. In some of the companies this cross-ownership is as high as 80 percent. "The maze of interconnections linking Sumitomo's diverse enterprises follows no pattern. Some of the companies go their own way, others are virtual captives.

"Nippon Electric has comparatively distant relations with the group. 'We do all our own domestic marketing, and we don't rely on Sumitomo Shoji too much for overseas sales, either,' says Sumitomo's Kobayashi. 'Our closest relations these days are probably with such companies as Brown Boveri, with whom we are working on a project in Nigeria, and with Siemens, General Telephone, and Page Engineering.' "[91]

Sumitomo's governance system has a central management council called *Hakusuikai* (White Water Club). It meets monthly and includes the sixteen core company presidents. These "directors" have considerably more independence in running their own companies than does the typical American subsidiary president. The chairmanship of the White Water Club rotates every month; yet as might be expected, there are some equals who are "more equal" than others. One of the more "unequal of equals" at Sumitomo, Bank Chairman Shozo Hotta, feels that while the *Hakusuikai* has considerable stature, 'it is not a central headquarters. It is a discussion group,' he says. The idea of going back to the intense control of the *zaibatsu* days seems plainly out of the question."[92]

To illustrate further the variability in Japanese corporate governance structure, consider Mitsui, Japan's second largest group, encompassing 178 companies. Mitsui's control center is its *Nimoku-kai* (Second Thursday Conference), an assembly of presidents of the group's nineteen major companies. No substitute persons are admitted. Here, too, the monthly meetings provide an opportunity for members to discuss common problems. In addition, there is the *Getsuyo-kai* (Monday Conference), whose members include the nineteen *Nimoku-kai* presidents, plus executives above the rank of managing director of sixteen other member companies. This is a sort of operations committee.

[90]"Mitsubishi, A Japanese Giant's Plans for Growth in the US," *Business Week,* July 20, 1981, p. 130.
[91]"Sumitomo: How the 'Keiretsu' Pulls Together to Keep Japan Strong," *Business Week,* March 31, 1975, p. 46.
[92]Ibid.

Perhaps it is the group dependence on the "brotherhood," coupled with management's independence, that gives Japanese corporate governance its unique strength. It resembles General Motors' classic control concept of a half century ago—decentralized responsibility for operations (profit centers) with centralization of staff. In Japan, the dependence follows from the heavy indebtedness and easy access to funding from the group's financial units, plus the considerable stock ownership within the several brotherhoods. The six largest trading companies, sometimes also referred to as the *keiretsu*, hold stock in 5400 companies in Japan, and the group banks own even more. In the United States, however, comparable interlocking would bring down the wrath of the FTC, SEC, and every reformist or populist politician.

Superficial analysts are quick to refer to the *sogo shosha* and their lesser counterparts as adjuncts of Japan, Inc. Generally, this is said derogatorily, the inference being that Japan's corporate governance system is basically more political than economic. There is some truth in this allegation insofar as the Ministry of International Trade and Industry (MITI) does take a very active role in assisting and refereeing. But when compared with U.S. practice, our composite interference of federal, state, local, industry, trade, and professional agencies more than surpasses MITI's role.

As we contemplate this dramatic *sogo shosha* success, there are moves in the United States to emulate the Japanese. A few years ago, Senators Adlai Stevenson, Jr., and John Heinz each sponsored bills to promote American-style *sogo shosha* to encourage U.S. world trade. Other nations, Taiwan, Brazil, and particularly South Korea, have gone even further in imitating the Japanese. Before we go all out in emulation, we should contemplate the "Three-Point Mitsubishi Principle:

1 To make contributions to promotion of social welfare through the company's business activities

2 To respect the spirit of fair play in all dealings

3 To contribute to the development of the Japanese economy through trade promotions

"This three-point principle was clearly spelled out in 1918 by Koyata Iwasaki, first board chairman of the newly independent Mitsubishi Shoji Kaisha as the watch for all Mitsubishi employees."[93]

Since these corporate ideals seem to be working well for Mitsubishi and most other components of Japan, Inc., perhaps it is time in the United States to set aside some of our mutual suspicions and distrust, our ingrained adversarial attitudes, and look upon Exxon, GM, AT&T, IBM, and ten thousand equally dedicated and enlightened public corporations, not as "them," but as "us." We, too, might benefit from a U.S., Inc. But before

---

[93]"Mitsubishi Group," op. cit., p. 1.

venturing in that corporate governance direction, we must first realize that what we need most is *wa*.

ILLUSTRATION: Phibro Corporation: U.S. *Zaibatsu?*

From what we have learned of "*Wa*: The Japanese Way," it is obvious that Japan has adapted the *zaibatsu*, or group companies, concept to fit the future. Its current corporate version, the *sogo shosha*, has several dimensions that are lacking in other highly advanced transnationals and conglomerates. One very obvious factor lacking in the United States, for example, is *wa*, the spirit of communality; another is the intensive integration and self-sufficiency in financing. Invariably when U.S. firms need huge sums, they borrow from the banks. There is hardly a major corporation that does not have frequently used lines of credit.

During the epic 1981 battle for Conoco, five major oil companies lined up a total of $24.7 billion in available new credit. Of course, not all of this potential borrowing was intended for a takeover of Conoco alone; yet it does illustrate the magnitude of big-bank willingness to get involved in major lending. Presumably, these macro-transactions would never be ventured if the lenders did not have complete confidence in the borrowers' boards of directors. Such confidence is engendered by having friendly and acceptable outside directors on the borrower's board. In Japan, this mutuality is attained by keeping the borrowing-lending transaction within the group. This is impossible in the United States because of the 1933 Glass-Steagall Act which separates banking activities from the securities business.

However, some recent financial maneuvers seem to indicate an end-run tactic around the Glass-Steagall prohibition. In mid-1981, Salomon Brothers, Wall Street's largest partnership and private investment bank, was taken over by Phibro Corporation, the world's largest publicly held commodity trader. With revenues of about $25 billion, Phibro was ranked as the fifteenth largest American company. Its executives prided themselves because, unlike other brokerage firms buying and selling on commissions, Phibro traded for itself. This has significant entrepreneurial advantages. Whereas an outside financier, particularly a staid bank, would hesitate assuming the exceptional risks inherent in commodity trading, Phibro, actively engaged in 150 commodities, might even welcome foreclosing on a loan backed by raw materials collateral. Disposing of bargain-basement collateral can be extremely profitable.

Dealing in huge quantities of many diverse commodities requires huge capital sums. Just before the merger, Phibro had $434 million of short-term bank loans and $707 million of commercial paper outstanding. Whenever banks advance such huge sums, they conventionally insist that the borrower's board have a majority of persona-grata directors. These acceptable directors, it is hoped, would impose a cautious philosophy upon the host board.

One of the peripheral bounties of this recent merger was the election of Salomon's managing partner as cochairman of the merged firm, and the election of the six members of Salomon's executive committee to the parent's board, expanding it from fifteen to twenty-one members. This is in the *sogo shosha* pattern, where corporate control is always in the hands of the "brotherhood," corporate insiders.

Keep in mind that Japanese enterprises are heavily leveraged; debt-to-equity ratios frequently run as high as 80 to 20. But in a sense, borrowers and lenders are one and the same. Not only do the sibling companies borrow from their own group's financial institutions, but they also buy large blocks of each other's common stock. Although these tactics do not guarantee autonomy, they do guarantee a better financial feeling, that is, to be beholden to one's own group rather than to outsiders.

A result of this urge to self-finance is the group's entry into every facet of financial life. Table 8-1 provides just a glimpse of the multiplicity of endeavors of the two leading *sogo shosha*—Mitsubishi Group and Mitsui Group. The table provides a cross section of activity showing how these two groups have either directly or indirectly related companies in virtually every financial, marketing, and manufacturing line, plus many other business-related activities such as economic research and publication, warehousing, construction, and even travel agencies and charge cards.

The Phibro-Salomon connection portends a comparable "American *zaibatsu*,"

TABLE 8-1 PARALLEL ACTIVITIES: MITSUBISHI AND MITSUI GROUPS

	Group Companies Ltd.	
Activity	**Mitsubishi**	**Mitsui**
Service		
General banking and foreign exchange	Mitsubishi Bank	Mitsui Bank
Banking and trust	Mitsubishi Trust and Banking Company	Mitsui Trust and Banking Company
Insurance: life, accident annuities	Meji Mutual Life Insurance	Mitsui Life Insurance
Insurance: marine, fire	Taisho Marine and Fire Insurance	Tokio Marine and Life Insurance
Ocean and regional development	Mitsubishi Shipbuilding and Engineering	Mitsui Ocean Development and Engineering
Leasing: offices, land, houses	Mitsubishi Estate	Mitsui Real Estate and Development
Manufacturing		
Beer	Kirin Brewery	Asahi Breweries Sapporo Breweries
Glass	Asahi Glass	Central Glass
Aluminum	Mitsubishi Aluminum	Mitsui Aluminum
At least 60 other lines		

with an increased level of self-financing and self-servicing. Inevitably, a major portion of Phibro's billion-dollar premerger external financing will be processed through the Salomon subsidiary. David Tendler, chairman of Phibro, noted "that in the past, Phibro has always been dependent on outside banks to help foreign producers secure financing. Declares Tendler, 'It is much cheaper and faster to do the whole process in one company.' "[94] The acquisition of Salomon was only an extension of this policy. Phibro had earlier acquired a Swiss bank and was actively engaged in financial dealings in forty-five countries, being recognized "in trading circles as having credit expertise in some regions that surpasses that of the multinational banks."[95]

But self-financing is not the only hallmark of the new American *zaibatsu;* there is also a close approximation to *wa* communality. In the first instance, the seventy-one-year-old Salomon Brothers was an eminently successful endeavor of sixty-two general partners plus twenty-nine limited partners. The latter were either major investors or retired partners who, combined, owned about one-third of the firm's net worth. The vested interests and communality in these groups were obvious.

Among the sixty-two general partners, zest for the new venture was engendered by the bounty of the merger's terms—they received shares in the firm's nearly $250 million in equity plus an additional $250 million in debentures, convertible into 9 million Phibro shares. Salomon's managing partner received $32 million, and several members of the executive committee each netted $16 million. The other general partners each averaged $2.7 million as their share of equity distribution plus another $3.2 million in convertible bonds as a premium. With such a generous windfall, it seems reasonable to expect a significant spurt in the merged Phibro communality.

Meanwhile, Phibro's stimulation of its old team has been outstanding. A year before the merger, five key executives each received over $1.6 million. Philbro's chairman/CEO received total compensation of $2.669 million in 1981 and its deputy chairman/COO was paid $2.221 million. Even its top nonexecutive traders were said to have earned in excess of $1 million.

Another *wa* communality characteristic was evident in both merging members— their major asset was not in expensive manufacturing facilities but rather in people. Typical of any successful partnership, Salomon Brothers prided itself on the rapport and reputation which annually attracted some of the best neophyte talent. Now, however, questions arise as to whether Salomon Brothers—the subsidiary—will continue to attract such promising talent. Even more worrisome is the fact that much of the aggressive entrepreneurial spirit of partnership will be lost as the partners are transformed into organizational executives.

Salomon's partnership base has been very much in line with the *zaibatsu* concept of lifetime employment. Not only did the firm tacitly guarantee effective performers a lifetime job, but it made the partnership rewards cumulatively so attractive that few partners were ever tempted to seek greener pastures. Similarly, Phibro had an equivalent lifetime employment policy inherited from its founders. Basic to this

[94]"A Trading Superpower Is Born," *Business Week,* August 17, 1981, p. 24.
[95]Ibid.

policy was the hiring of apprentices, internally called *lehrlings,* who, in typical apprenticeship fashion, were trained in all facets of the business. This, in the past, provided Phibro with a familial affinity; it also produced executives who were close to the scene. " 'You can't rely on agents,' sneers Ludwig Jesselson, a former chief executive officer of the company. 'Agents are only interested in commissions.' "[96]

The neo-*zaibatsu* pattern for large-scale, self-financed transnational firms, typified in the Phibro-Salomon union, seems to have prompted a new kind of merger: the Bache Group was purchased by Prudential Insurance Company of America, Bechtel Corporation bought a majority interest in Dillon Read and Company, and American Express Company acquired the second largest brokerage house in the United States, Shearson Loeb Rhoades (1980 sales were $653 million).

It is interesting to note that American Express (Amex), like Phibro, has important foreign activities, and even more in the neo-*zaibatsu* manner, it is expanding its many services. It has a 50 percent interest in a cable television subsidiary of Warner Communications and owns outright the $4-billion-sales Fireman's Fund Insurance. Amex's entrance into the insurance field, so typical of Japan's *zaibatsu,* is paralleled by dozens of other ambitious American neo-*zaibatsu* conglomerates (e.g., International Telephone and Telegraph's acquisition, more than a decade ago, of the huge Hartford Fire Insurance Company).

However, there are obstacles. As recently as September 1981, a U.S. Court of Appeals reaffirmed the Clayton Anti-Trust Act which prohibits individuals from serving, at the same time, as a director of a bank and of an insurance company with which the bank competes. The American Express experience, and more specifically the Phibro-Salomon juncture, could become forerunners of new and more effective corporate governance mechanisms, which in practice would bypass the Clayton Act. " 'We don't know what kind of financial services will be required in the future,' says David Tendler, Phibro's chairman and chief executive, 'but we want to be able to compete in a banking world that is obviously changing.' "[97]

POSTSCRIPT

Technological progress is sometimes measured by the number and quality of innovations registered by the U.S. Patent Office. A high incidence of patents and patents pending indicates dynamism, optimism, and accelerated productivity, whereas a sharp decline in new patents indicates a sluggish and, perhaps, a retrenching business system.

Similarly, the incidence of innovations in corporate governance mirrors the state of the art and reflects the system's enterprising zest. Chapter 8 provides specific illustrations of progression and zest in the boardroom. Had this chapter been written twenty years ago, it would have been considera-

[96]Roger Lowenstein, "Phibro Corp. Became a Commodity Giant by Taking Big Risks," *The Wall Street Journal,* August 18, 1981, p. 12.
[97]Ibid.

bly condensed simply because little experimentation occurred in this once-presumed sacrosanct domain.

Of the several experimental models described in this chapter, probably the most intriguing are those concerned with participative or shared authority ranging from the office of the chairman to the Kelso plan ESOPs. Works councils and codetermination, still distinctly European phenomena, also seem to be making strides. And, of course, people's capitalism through pension plan stock ownership is a factor for consideration. Equally important, though scarcely visible as yet in the United States, is Japanese *wa*, or societal harmony.

What will be the dimensions of tomorrow's directorate, and how will it serve society? From this chapter we have seen that an increasing number of today's corporate leaders are willing to experiment with new boardroom designs—some would even be considered as avant garde.

From such willingness to try new things, it is possible that one day a boardroom experimenter will make an Archimedes "bathtub" discovery—and react in the same way. It is said that when Archimedes was asked by his king to determine if a certain crown was pure gold or alloyed with silver, Archimedes was baffled. Then one day while taking a bath he noted that the overflow of water correlated with the density of an immersed substance; gold and silver with different densities would displace different weights of water. In his exultation, Archimedes jumped from his tub and, minus toga, ran into the street shouting "Eureka—I have found it!"

It is hoped that one day a lucky boardroom architect will make a comparable discovery of the ideal twenty-first century board and similarly dash out into the street, over to the SEC, and exult: "I have found it!"

CHAPTER 9

BOARD EVALUATION

DIRECTOR DIMENSIONS

Robert Kirk Mueller, chairman of Arthur D. Little and prolific author of ten corporate governance books, aptly refers to many management leaders, and particularly directors, as random-walk practitioners. The term "random walk" is a statistical expression referring "to the path traversed by a particle which moves in steps, each step being determined by chance either in regard to direction and/or in regard to magnitude. The theory of random walks has many applications in biology, business, industry and the military in such matters as determining the migration of insects, sequential sampling, and in diffusion processes. Unfortunately, too many leaders implicitly approach the management of their enterprise with the random walk theory and the lack of an institutional goal or strategy."[1]

The management/director addiction to random walking is probably congenital. Genetics plays a big part insofar as a large proportion of outside directors come from specific strata of society. But chance is equally significant in that there are few, if any, academic apprenticeship or performance criteria for director selection. Nor are there any acceptable measures of individual director contribution or board worthiness. This is disappointing, at the least, since modern management is firmly based on

---

[1]Robert Kirk Mueller, "Boardspeak: Buzzwords in the Boardroom," *Directors and Boards,* Spring 1976, p. 20.

252

scientific analysis and measurement. This conviction is aptly expressed in Lord Kelvin's frequently quoted statement: "I often say that when you can measure what you are speaking about, and express it in numbers, you know something about it; but when you cannot measure it, when you cannot express it in numbers, your knowledge is of meager and unsatisfactory kind. It may be the beginning of knowledge, but you have scarcely in your thoughts advanced to the stage of science whatever the matter might be."[2]

Mueller, perhaps seeking to replace the "chanciness" of his boardroom random walk with a measure of Lord Kelvin's measurement and expression in numbers, devised a unique Board-Score-Board.[3] This was one of the first attempts at deciding what it is that directors should do and then measuring their performance on these norms. Mueller selected eleven norms: competence, ethics, ambassadorship, independence, preparedness, practice, committee activity, development, attendance, chairmanship, and special service. These attributes were then measured on a fail/pass/honors basis. While Mueller's director measurement device is still very subjective, it undoubtedly is a big step in the direction of numbers, measurement, evaluation, and science. Mueller emphasizes that we are long overdue in our director selection and acceptance process. Although it is difficult to examine peer performance, there is an overriding necessity for scientific management at the top of the management pyramid "if only to face up to the evaluation process internally rather than permit some hostile interrogator to take the initiative."[4]

The complexity of peer evaluation at the top rung in the management level is evident in an earlier measurement suggestion. Edward McSweeney, a consultant, devised "A Score Card for Rating Management," whose fifteen factors related to the chief executive's performance. While this proposed analysis did a fairly comprehensive breakdown and evaluation of the CEO's job, it completely ignored the director's role. In fact, one of the inferences was that outside directors are the only real safeguard the stockholders have against incompetent management. Yet this proposal provides absolutely no yardstick for measuring the caliber or performance of outside directors.

Earlier attempts at management audits were equally flawed. Probably the first large-scale venture in this area was the *Manual of Excellent Managements*, published by the American Institute of Management (AIM). The institute engaged panels of recognized experts to review periodically the managements of several hundred leading corporations. The panels used

[2]Stanley C. Vance, *Industrial Administration* (New York: McGraw-Hill Book Company, 1959), p. 5.

[3]Robert K. Mueller, "Are Directors Boardworthy?—A Report Card for Board Members," *Management Review*, American Management Associations, September 1976, pp. 14–24.

[4]Ibid., p. 14.

a modified Delphi technique, long before this method became academically popular. The institute developed the Management Audit Questionnaire, made up of 301 specific and pertinent questions, which was submitted to key corporate executives. The answers were then reviewed by the panel of experts, who grouped the questions on the basis of ten factors such as directorate analysis, executive evaluation, etc. Each of the ten factors was assigned a point value; when combined, the maximum values could total 10,000 points. Realistically, a minimum score of 7500 was acceptable for the excellence rating.

But even the semiscience of the AIM had a shaky analytical base premised on bias—its orientation was philosophically pro-outside director and vehemently anti-inside director. For example, one visibly tainted conclusion stated that it was a fundamental tenet of the institute that a majority of the members of any board should be drawn from outside the company. According to the AIM, this was the only way to get excellence in performance—"companies which are rated excellent in this category who do not fulfill this requirement, are excellent *despite* the condition."[5] Yet at that very time, during the early and mid-1950s, most of our superperforming firms—Standard Oil (N.J.), Bethlehem Steel, Du Pont, Dow, Monsanto, Deere, and several hundred others—had distinctly inside-type boards. It was blatantly wrong for the AIM to support such an unfounded preconception.

Perhaps the first meaningful study in the use of unstructured or untainted arithmetical analysis appeared in 1955, when 200 major manufacturing firms were compared on a twenty-five-year performance basis. The dependent variable was the inside-director/outside-director dichotomy. This study became the subject of a lengthy commentary in *Business Week*.[6] While the methodology of this study was rather simplistic, the conclusions showed that, contrary to the AIM's bias, firms with a majority of inside directors or officer-directors had distinctly superior track records as compared with those with a majority of outside or absentee directors.

Almost a decade after this first foray into the arithmetic of corporate directorate excellence, a second attempt was made.[7] This sample consisted of one hundred three outstanding corporations, grouped into twelve industry models plus two models based on company size. Eleven comparison factors were used—six growth norms and five productivity norms. Here again, ratio analysis showed that during the 1925–1963 test period,

---

[5]*Manual of Excellent Managements,* 1955 ed., American Institute of Management, p. 23.

[6]Stanley C. Vance, "Functional Control and Corporate Performance in Large-Scale Industrial Enterprise," University of Massachusetts, 1955. See also *Business Week,* November 25, 1955, pp. 128–132.

[7]Stanley C. Vance, *Boards of Directors: Structure and Performance* (Eugene, Oregon: University of Oregon Press, 1964).

inside-director-run firms were invariably better performers than their outside-director-run counterparts.

For the first time the relationship between board structure and board size was expressed in formula: $Yc = a + bX = 78.0 + 0.484X$; that is, the intercept value a indicated a hypothetical performance value 78 for a firm with no inside directors. For every percentage point of inside directors added, performance hypothetically increased by an average of 0.484 of 1 percent. Consequently, an all-inside-director board would have a performance level calculated at the base 78 plus 100 (0.484), or 126 percent of average. This is distinctly different from the 78 percent performance level of the all-outside-director board.

Although these early arithmetical comparisons on an inside-director/outside-director dichotomy were feasible a generation ago, today's conglomeration, the surge of new industries, the transnational trend, and foreign competition now make it difficult, if not impossible, to group companies by industries. Complicating even more is the increase of directorate dimensions assumed to be important. While classification by inside and outside labels was once feasible and universally accepted, today's directors can be categorized by backgrounds (academic, legal, financial), as representatives of vested groups (consumers, minorities), as public or independent directors, and as multinational directors, and there has even been an ingress of the worker as a director.

A subsequent study in 1968 sought to delineate directors individually on the basis of eight factors or directorate dimensions[8]:

1 Technical expertise
2 Management experience
3 Specific economic service
4 Broad economic sophistication
5 Image
6 Asset impact
7 Interlock
8 Owners' equity

Each of these eight directorate dimensions was carefully defined and assigned point values according to varying degrees for each factor. Then each member of a given board was measured on the basis of the degree to which he or she possessed each of the dimensions. More than a hundred directors and chief executives at forty-three major multinational corporations were visited and interviewed. Despite many differences of opinion, there seemed to be a general consensus: boards of large-scale publicly owned corporations were undergoing a substantial evolutionary change.

[8]Stanley C. Vance, *The Corporate Director* (Homewood, Ill.: Dow Jones-Irwin, Inc., 1968).

The once simplistic inside/outside structures were now being superseded by more intricate categorization (see "Board Types"):

1 Constitutional boards
2 Consultive boards
3 Collegial boards
4 Communal boards

Because the force of boardroom evolution had intensified during the past twenty years, additional boardroom dimensions needed to be considered. Two companion studies [9,10] sought to note the significance of five of the more prominent of these forces:

1 Multinational focus
2 Representativeness
3 Social responsibility
4 Public directors
5 Comanagement

Each of these factors has been discussed in previous sections. Their growing significance was tested in a sample of forty large corporations. This testing was somewhat ambitious and involved the rating, by a research team, of more than 600 directors on the basis of fifteen attributes. When feasible, these ratings were checked and corroborated with comparable ratings by corporate key executives of the respective firms. The individual ratings, per company, were then totaled to provide a composite, and admittedly somewhat crude, fifteen-dimensional boardroom profile.

Three separate tests were attempted. If a single yardstick were to be used to measure company performance, probably the most meaningful norm would be total return to investors over a period of time. This could be considered as a measure of investment productivity, and is the ultimate justification for shareowner investment. A second test related the directorate dimensions to return on stockholder capital (ROSC), and the third test compared these firms on their relative rankings—between 1956 and 1977—on the five factors listed in the "Fortune 500."

The several tests yielded almost identical conclusions: succinctly, there is no substitute for competent and dynamic internal management. Initially, these vital ingredients were supplied by owner-entrepreneurs, and even as the factor of owners' equity loses its significance, the related factors of technical expertise and managerial experience continue to dominate. The

---

[9]Stanley C. Vance, "Director Diversity: New Dimensions in the Boardroom," *Directors and Boards,* Spring 1977, pp. 40–50.
[10]Stanley C. Vance, "Corporate Governance: Assessing Corporate Performance by Boardroom Attributes," *Journal of Business Research,* June 1978, pp. 203–220.

vital necessity of these factors becomes evident when comparing the top bracket of performers with the bottom group. Whereas in the top group about one-fifth of the directorate dimensions consist of technical expertise and one-third of managerial experience, the poorest performers dedicate only one-tenth and one-sixteenth, respectively, to these dimensions.

As new dimensions become essential for modern directorate design, so analysis becomes more complicated, and recommending an optimal pattern becomes almost impossible. One reason for this is the tremendous variety in American business. For example, the Standard Industrial Classification Index lists more than a thousand readily identifiable and yet quite different kinds of business endeavors. Then, too, we have differences in scale of operation, product mix, geographical peculiarities, financial structure, technological status, and a host of other conditioning variables. We have extreme pluralism in our business sector, and while this pluralism creates many problems, it also affords our system maximum flexibility and adaptability.

Yet lack of absolute criteria does not mean status quo in leadership style. At a Conference Board symposium, John M. Fox, president of H. P. Hood and Sons, illustrated the diverse requirements of his three-phase career. In his first CEO experience at Minute Maid in 1945, " 'I didn't know my knee from my necktie. I used the board as a substitute and really a very cheap substitute, for all the consultants I couldn't afford. They helped me decide on such vital issues as getting the company launched with an organization structure and later in carrying out a major acquisition program. They held my hand through all kinds of growing pains.' "[11]

Leaving Minute Maid, Fox then went to United Fruit where, after the death of Samuel Zemurray—the last of UF's "banana barons"—he experienced something different. United Fruit was the target of a hostile takeover. Fox admits his limitations and his failure—UF was taken over by Eli Black.

His third experience was at H. P. Hood and Sons, a longtime family firm. Again, Fox was subjected to a new challenge—his job was to effect a transition from old-style entrepreneurship governance to more modern professional management. If John Fox's tripartite chief executive career were translated into the directorate dimensions just discussed, it would be obvious that all three experiences required different proportions of the various vital dimensions. The best advice in Fox's message is that CEOs and directors must adapt or find new posts. The corporate helmsman has no infallible chart and must still navigate by the stars.

In this context our corporate governance statesmen could be likened to the Assassins, the medieval sect of Muslim fanatics. It is said they ranked

---

[11]*The Board of Directors: New Challenges, New Directions,* The Conference Board, 1972, p. 24.

their faithful in several gradations. "Upon being promoted into the next highest order, initiates would be given a new, and presumably loftier, set of rules to live by. After years during which these strictures became second nature to them, the devout might even find a place in the ninth, or highest order. These few would wait with hushed reverence as the sect's leader welcomed them individually into the elect, whispering into the ear of each the final, ultimate wisdom. The message: 'There are no rules.' "[12]

DIRECTOR CERTIFICATION

Glossolalia is the gift of speaking in strange tongues. In some religious sects, it is assumed to be a special divine attribute bestowed upon the Lord's favored few. The "glossolaliator," who has never had any prior contact with a particular language, will suddenly use it fluently. Most of us do not accept this instant attainment of linguistic competence; yet we are willing to accept the idea that some individuals, though lacking specific and pertinent corporate governance grooming, will suddenly turn into perfectly knowledgeable corporate directors. And we generally assume that these neophyte directors will "glossolaliate" from day one, that is, speak in business and technical tongues never heard before.

The boardroom babel, where directors speak in many diverse tongues, needs a common language and a standard body of knowledge. How, for example, can inside directors or officer-directors communicate when their common language of business is sprinkled with various dialects— accounting, marketing, or production? Some progressive firms attempt to correct this provincialism by implementing a systematic executive rotational policy.

But the deficiency is more acute among outside directors. Coming from all sectors of society, many have not even mastered the business alphabet. Some justify this corporate governance illiteracy by stating that these individuals bring a fresh perspective to the board. What nonsense—no one would hire a plumber to perform surgery or a barber to build a bridge! Plumbers, surgeons, barbers, and bridge builders, in order to perform in their fields, must be licensed or certified. Both licensing and certification imply that a person has passed specified written and oral examinations, that he or she has paid prescribed fees and agrees to perform according to set standards. The state performs most licensing. Certification, although similar in most respects, generally initiates and rests with professional groups.

Surprisingly, the whole area of management, of which corporate governance is the ultimate level, has resisted both licensing and certification. In

---

[12]Walter Kiechel, "Playing by the Rules of the Corporate Strategy Game," *Fortune,* September 24, 1979, p. 118.

so doing, management's professional stature continues to be suspect. Serious objection to licensing is based on the fact that it would involve state and federal meddling in the setting of managerial standards and in performance evaluation and policing. Certification, although less objectionable, can also give arbitrary powers to small but politically potent groups of certifiers.

A number of years ago, the Society for Advancement of Management became concerned with the lack of universally accepted professional designations in the field of management. A special committee, assigned to study this void, found quite a number of professional designations in related business sectors, but none in general management. To emphasize management's backwardness, the committee, in a special report,[13] listed most of the principal business-related professional designations, grouping them according to Fayol's six managerial functions:

A. Administration:
  Certified Financial Planner (CFP)
  Certified Administrative Manager (CAM)
  Fellow of the Life Management Institute (FLMI)
B. External Relations, including sales, marketing, advertising, purchasing, public relations, governmental relations:
  Chartered Association Executive (CAE)
  Certified International Executive (CIE)
C. Finance
  Chartered Financial Analyst (CFA)
D. Intelligence, including accounting and information processing:
  Certified Public Accountant (CPA) or Chartered Accountant (CA)
  Chartered Industrial Accountant (CIA)
  Certified Public Secretary (CPS)
  Certificate in Data Processing (CDP)
  Certified Data Processing Auditor (CDPA)
E. Production and Transportation:
  Professional Engineer (PE) in industrial engineering
  Certified Member, American Society of Traffic and Transportation
  Certified Fleet Maintenance Manager (CFMM)
  Certified Shop Service Manager (CSSM)
F. Security or Risk Management
  Associate in Management Studies (AMS)
  Associate in Risk Management (ARM)
  Certified Director of Fleet Safety
  Chartered Life Underwriter (CLU)
  Chartered Property Casualty Underwriter (CPCU)
  Enrolled Pension Actuary

[13]"Report of the Professional Management Designation Committee," *Society for Advancement of Management,* March 5, 1981, p. 9.

Fellow of the Casualty Actuarial Society (FCAS)
Fellow of the Society of Actuaries (FSA)
Member, American Academy of Actuaries (MAAA)
(Many similar designations exist in the British Commonwealth, and a few in
other countries)

The report stresses that every one of these designations is granted on the basis of tests of knowledge—invariably being restricted to the specific vocabulary, concepts, theories, and problems of the subdiscipline. None of the competency tests probes, in depth, the managerial relationships and implications. Consequently, the Society for Advancement's special committee recommended some form of standardized education and testing. Then an authorized board could proceed with initiating a CPM—certified professional manager—or some comparable designation.

The lack of certified professional managers is paralleled by an equal lack of certified public or professional directors. Stanley Sporkin, the energetic and highly respected chief of enforcement for the SEC, "finds the idea of professional directors so attractive that he has even suggested there might be a school, perhaps attached to an existing university, where people could learn such things as how to serve on audit committees. 'There is a foreign service school that produces an elite corps for the State Department,' says Sporkin. 'So there could also be a school that would produce qualified directors.' "[14]

Some years earlier, several leading businesspeople implicitly echoed the same sentiments. Recognizing that very few institutional investors or their shareholders or beneficiaries were represented on boards, they proposed "establishment of a non-profit association or foundation that would provide directors to represent institutions and their shareholders. This organization, financed by the institutions, would employ—and itself pay, perhaps $100,000 a year each—a number of highly competent professional directors. Each would serve on several boards, representing all institutions and their shareholders."[15]

Directors of acceptable caliber and prestige, whose current pay—because of inflation—would top a quarter of a million dollars annually, would have to be certified. The idea of having institutional investors select, school, and use a pool of qualified and truly certified professional directors makes sense. It ensures corporate control's remaining in the hands of businesspeople, managers, and enterprisers. It would counter the current drift into control by politicians, presently in or out of office.

Some localized experiments in director education have been attempted.

[14]Lee Smith, "The Boardroom Is Becoming a Different Scene," *Fortune,* May 8, 1978, p. 170.
[15]Peter Vander Wicken, "Change Invades the Boardroom," *Fortune,* May 1972, p. 285.

For example, a decade ago, the National Rural Electric Cooperative Association established a certification program. It set up two summer schools: an eastern division at Gatlinburg, Tennessee, and a western division at Colorado Springs, Colorado. These, plus a Pre-Annual Meeting School, offered a reasonably complete set of special courses to participants with statewide or local sponsorship. Board members had to complete a minimum of fifteen points of credit to be eligible for the board member's certificate.

The most ambitious attempt at director schooling and certification was initiated under the auspices of the National Association of Corporate Directors (NACD). It was the brainchild of Stephen I. Cummings, founder and first president of NACD, who was assisted by NACD's current head, John M. Nash. Their proposed goal was to bestow the title certified corporate director (CCD) upon those who successfully completed NACD's program. The first offering, under the NACD Institute, was deaned in October 1980 by Stanley C. Vance, at St. Simons Island, Georgia. The second session was held in June 1981 at Williamsburg, Virginia.

The NACD Institute, earlier known as the Corporate Directors School, was set up as a one-week intensive program, providing the participants with knowledge of how boards are structured and how they function. Eminent directors, serving as instructors, covered topics such as Why a Board?, Evolution of the Board, Director Job Descriptions, Organizing Board Committees, Designing Director Information Systems, Identifying Conflicts of Interest, Evaluating D&O Liability Insurance, and most other pertinent topics.

The NACD recognizes that the title of certified corporate director will not, in itself, guarantee that a director will always make the right decision or take the proper course of action. Yet it is a logical response to the hackneyed, taken-for-granted view of director attributes. These faulty impressions picture the corporate director as a superhuman, if not a minor deity. "To state that a director candidate is an individual with integrity, judgment, enthusiasm, and diligence promotes little confidence in the minds of discerning shareholders, regulators, or even company executives. It is clear there must be a better solution. One solution: NACD Director Certification."[16]

SUNSHINE IN THE BOARDROOM

It was most fitting that 1976, the year of our bicentennial, was also the year for enacting the Government in Sunshine Act. This was a quantum stride in participatory governance, the issue over which the Revolutionary War was

---

[16]"NACD Announces Director Certification," *Directors Monthly,* April 1978, p. 3.

fought. Yet even though we won the war and freedom, we soon lost much of the right to govern ourselves. Regulatory agency bureaucrats usurped this right. Now the new Sunshine Act at least gave us the right to observe how these agencies operated. The Act mandated that forty-seven federal regulatory agencies must advertise when meetings are to be held, and must permit the general public to attend. This applies not only to the formal or regularly scheduled sessions, at which votes are taken, but also to all sessions where a majority of the board convenes to discuss official business. The label "sunshine" was taken from an opinion of Justice Louis Brandeis: " 'Publicity is justly commended as a remedy for social and industrial disease. Sunlight is said to be the best disinfectant and electric light the most efficient policeman.' "[17]

As expected, the proposal to let light into meetings created a furor. A Federal Home Loan Bank Board official quipped: " 'Sunshine can indeed be salutory; excessive exposure or inadequate protection against it can be harmful as well.' "[18] But a most compelling argument was the fact that forty-nine states then had their own versions of open-meeting laws. Governor Reuben Askew of Florida, which had the most stringent law, stated emphatically that Florida's laws had not led to unnecessary embarrassment of public employees, exacerbated bickering, or other problems assumed by opponents.

In a sense, the Sunshine Act supplements the Freedom of Information Act of 1966, which initially was a noble democratic gesture but generally useless. Subsequently, a series of amendments served to give the Freedom of Information Act more meaning so that Americans had the right to see a wide range of previously confidential government documents and files. This would apply even to dossiers on the citizen himself, compiled by federal law enforcement and securities agencies.

The Sunshine Act went several steps further, giving the citizen the right to observe the decision-making process in action. Yet the lawmakers, in their collective wisdom, recognized that there were situations warranting exceptions. So they provided for ten different kinds of secret sessions. These exclusions encompassed meetings for discussion of:

1 National defense or foreign policy
2 Agency personnel matters
3 Matters required to be kept secret by law
4 Trade secrets obtained on a confidential basis
5 Accusing someone of a crime

---

[17]Arlen J. Large, "Federal Agencies Fight Bill to Open Meetings to Scrutiny by Public," *The Wall Street Journal,* September 23, 1975, p. 1.
[18]Ibid.

6 Personal information that would be a clearly unwarranted invasion of privacy

7 Certain types of law enforcement investigatory records

8 Bank-examination records

9 Information about certain kinds of currency, commodities, and securities dealings considered privy for Federal Reserve purposes

10 An agency's participation in court proceedings

One of the strongest arguments against the Sunshine Act was the realistic comment that the commissioners and other board members would simply circumvent the law. Important issues would not be brought up at meetings until informal, out-of-meeting agreements had been reached. Cocktail parties, golf matches, luncheon get-togethers, and a variety of off-the-premises informal meetings would be substituted for board sessions. An ingenious device, called notation voting, was also suggested as a way to beat the law. Notation voting consists in proposals being circulated from commissioner to commissioner or member to member, each voting by initialing the document. Thus, there is no discussion to record or any formal and open vote to take. "The ICC uses that system now for most of the 1000 decisions it makes each month. The possibility that such gimmicks may be employed leads one Washington lobbyist for financial institutions to quip that under the new law, 'it will be government in the shade.' "[19]

At Tennessee Valley Authority (TVA), in the first year of open board meetings (1975), nearly half (47 percent) of its decisions were made informally, outside the board's public discussions. Of the 361 proposed actions for the first period, 169 (47 percent) were approved informally before the public meetings were held. Additionally, of the 138 purchase awards the board considered during this period, 105 of them (76 percent) were decided by informal actions outside the public meetings. In a subsequent twelve-month period (1978), on a national basis, out of 2177 meetings held by federal agencies, only 48 percent were fully open to the public.

So far this discussion has centered on public agencies, where there is irrefutable logic that the lawmakers are public servants and must answer to their employers—the public. Similarly, corporate directors are servants of the shareholders and should answer to them. Despite the increasing pressure from federal regulatory bodies, from the press, and from concerned citizens and shareholders, very little of what goes on in the boardroom is ever revealed. But as in the public sector, private enterprise governance will, undoubtedly, come under more intensive scrutiny.

[19]"Federal Agencies Move out of the Shadows," *Business Week,* March 14, 1977, p. 75.

In the past, the boardroom resembled a corporate *kiva*. Among the southwest Pueblo Indians, the kiva was a single aperture, below-ground mud hut where the males met, presumably for mystic religious rituals. Whatever took place in the kiva was a deep secret, never to be divulged to the uninitiated. Even while their squaws suspected that nothing of consequence went on in the kiva, the clever Indian braves, by hiding in the kiva sanctuary, got out of domestic duties—hoeing the fields, grinding the maize, or baby-sitting with the papoose.

For too long, boards of directors have been meeting in a kivalike secrecy, and in a sanctuary that is taboo for all but the initiated. Most boards continue along the kiva-meeting pattern. But this supersecrecy, under threat of punishment, goes beyond the Pueblo Indian analogy. There is the better-known Mafiosa *omerta,* and the lesser-known but equally effective German corporate governance *Schweigepflicht,* or obligation to silence. This is a legal prescription binding all board members from revealing headquarters and boardroom secrets. To what extent should our directors be protected by kivas, *Schweigepflicht,* Fifth Amendments, and Miranda-decision equivalents? Time and shareholder impatience will tell.

Meanwhile, before we propose for industry a Corporate Governance in Sunshine Act, we might learn from observing the record of the Government in Sunshine Act of 1976, and its older sibling, the Freedom of Information Act of 1966. For example, the Federal Trade Commission points out that most requests for information come from law firms or corporations seeking information pertinent to lawsuits in which they are presently involved. While this is a legitimate use of information, keep in mind that it is compiled and made available for individual and corporate profit-making purposes, through the taxpayer's generosity. Perhaps such service should carry a fee, at least sufficient to cover costs.

Other agencies claim that, by far, most requests are from authors and college students writing term papers. The government does the research and often does much of the writing, and charges only the cost of copying. If only a fraction of the millions of striving students recognize this readily available federal aid, bureaus will be inundated with requests. While more students might graduate with honors, taxpayers will also graduate—into higher tax payments.

CORPORATE CONSTITUENCIES

An organization is a group of people going in the same direction, for the same purpose, following a single leader. Obviously, there is no organization if there are no followers—these are the constituents. Corporations (as mentioned earlier) have stakeholders who consist of shareholders, managers, line and staff employees, customers, suppliers, distributors, and even the general public. But the most significant corporate constituency is the body of shareowners.

In this context, everyone is a corporate constituent because, directly or indirectly, everyone has investments in the business system. The most partisan of these constituents should be the 33 million or more investors who actually own shares of stock in their own names. Yet except for an occasional tempestuous annual meeting or an irate letter to the chairman of the board, stockholders are neither seen nor heard. Financial analysts explain this phenomenon by assuming that all shareowners are only interested in making immediate profits. Consequently, short-term speculation rather than long-term investment is the money motivator. Yet speculators do not make good constituents—their span of interest and loyalty can be very brief.

A few years ago Ralph Nader—and similar prophets—preached a new doctrine based upon consumers as corporate constituents. Unfortunately, the major thrust of this consumerism was adversarial. Since an organization with adversaries posing as constituents can never make meaningful progress, the result of this tactic was to substitute federal agencies—such as the Occupational Safety and Health Administration—for the would-be corporate consumer constituents.

Periodically, there are attempts at elevating company employees from the level of "hands" to that of constituents. Presumably, this has had some limited success in comanagement and works councils. Even in Communist Poland, during the early Solidarity days of the 1980s, one of the union's prime demands was for the workers to have the right to name their own managers. In a totalitarian environment, it would have been a big step for workers to become corporate constituents. In the United States, however, adversarial unionism continues as the basic union-management philosophy, and workers are only incidentally considered to be constituents.

This mutual antagonism (discussed in "Wa: The Japanese Way") breeds distrust, friction, waste, and even hate. Wa, on the contrary, translated as "a communality," premises a firm labor-management-public-government cooperation. It is built upon (1) consensus before action, (2) group loyalty, (3) confidence in community values, and (4) a sense of shared purpose. On the basis of these wa criteria, American organized labor is nowhere near the level of corporate constituency. People's capitalism, worker-owned companies, and ESOPs offer only a glimmer of hope.

The wa precepts, however, are not exclusively meant for worker-management relations; they should be just as applicable to directors and shareowners. Unfortunately, here, too, the wa attributes are equally lacking. Even when a board of directors authorizes a campaign to improve company-shareowner relations, there seldom is any real *wa* communality. For example, rarely does the board seek consensus before action. Like the Japanese *ringi* system, this seems too time-consuming.

As for the other three *wa* ingredients—group loyalty, confidence in community values, and a sense of shared purpose—some boards of directors and their corporations occasionally do embark upon shareowner constituency campaigns, but the net effect seems to be transitory or too little and too late. While many CEOs make audible sounds and friendly gestures toward their shareowners, particularly at annual meetings, something vital seems to be missing. Usually these CEOs give the impression that it would be nice if stockholders became an identifiable and helpful constituency, providing they did not become a bother to the board.

If boards of directors are to shape their shareowners into effective corporate constituencies, they must reread and reapply the basic principles requisite to effective organization. There are numerous listings of these principles, with varying designations and meanings. The following compromise code lists twelve vital principles[20] for boards of directors striving to imbue their shareowners with a corporate constituency zest and zeal:

1 Principle of causation. The basic reason for organization is the realization by human beings that the results of joint endeavor exceed the sum of the individual efforts.

2 Principle of conviction. The effectiveness of organization is closely correlated with the degree to which its members believe that the objectives of this specific organization are worth striving for, that the group venture has a very high probability of attaining its goals, and that the maximum rewards will be apportioned in an equitable manner to its members. Group action will be ineffective if the members (a) doubt the morality of the venture, (b) have misgivings as to the group's ability to reach its goals, (c) suspect the integrity or ability of their leadership, (d) do not get adequate personal satisfaction from the tangible and intangible rewards of the joint venture.

Among the other principles every board should enunciate are:

3 Principle of the objective
4 Principle of direction and control
5 Principle of standardization
6 Principle of authority
7 Principle of responsibility
8 Principle of division of labor
9 Principle of delegation
10 Principle of functionalization

[20]Vance, *Industrial Administration,* pp. 118–121.

11 Principle of structural unity
12 Principle of personification

The twelfth principle, although last, is far from being the least. The principle of personification states that, eventually, the group members should tend to regard the organization, of which they are a part, as a living organism endowed with human attributes. Such personification is intimately concerned with the factor of morale, which, in turn, is the basic ingredient in the efficient functioning of the organization. When shareowners feel and say "my company" or "our company," not only are they personifying, but they are also identifying with it. This combination of a farsighted leadership, a positively personified enterprise, and a dedicated corporate constituency would be hard to surpass.

It is understandable that some objections might be raised against these twelve principles—particularly against personification—as being utopian. Yet a small measure of this shareowner-as-constituent utopia might be achieved if shareholders could see the dollar advantages. Presently, most rules of the investment game are stacked in favor of the speculator. Consequently, immediate profits are more attractive than long-term rewards.

As a start in redressing long- and short-term advantages, would it be unreasonable to change the definition of "long-term," from the conventional six-month period accountants ascribe, to at least a year or even five? In accordance with this redefinition, tax rates on capital gains could then be adjusted to reward long-term holders of common stock. The new focus would be away from immediate bottom-line figures and toward long-term entrepreneurial endeavor. Along with this, there could be a scalar progression that would reduce capital gains taxes by 5 or 10 percentage points each year an investor resisted turning speculator.

A comparable thesis was advanced by Irving Kristol, Henry Luce Professor of Urban Values at New York University. Kristol advocated a simple plan for rewarding the investor at the expense of the speculator. Basically he proposed to give stock dividend bonuses pegged not to the size of holdings as of the dividend declaration day, but rather to the length of time the shares were held. For example, a five-year-old account might merit a 5 percent bonus; a ten-year holding, 10 percent.

In addition to tax breaks and stock dividend inducements, investors should also get voting and control advantages. This brings to mind the scaled voting proposal advocated by Alexander Hamilton for his plan for our first National Bank. Under Hamilton's plan, holders of between 1 and 10 shares would get 1 vote per share; owners of from 11 to 20 shares would get 1 vote for each additional 2 shares held. At 100 shares, this progression would allow the owner only 1 vote for each additional 10 shares. This scaling, unquestionably, would give more meaning to our present inequitable proxy system. The "little guys" currently recognize that their votes are meaningless—they feel disenfranchised, and the disenfranchised cannot be counted as constituents.

There are other possibilities for enkindling the constituency: would it be an infringement on voting rights to limit common stock voting solely to the actual owners, the holders in fee? In particular, as pension funds grow, there is a possibility that union leaders could demand and win the right for workers and pensioners to vote their proportionate pension fund portfolios.

If all other attempts at generating shareholder constituencies fail, there is the presently remote possibility of stockholder unionization. To date, the closest approximation has been stockholder protection committees which, occasionally, surface in times of company crisis. At a 1980 meeting of Southern Company, some restless stockholders, concerned with their utility's prolonged depressed performance, talked union. " 'We have labor unions and management unions in this country' stormed one stockholder. 'It's time for shareholder unions.' "[21] Some utility holder associations already exist in public utilities, but critics contend these are actually organized by the utilities to heighten public pressure on state regulators.

Meaningful grass-roots unionism among shareholders, at present, is nonexistent. The Campaign GM and corporate gadfly organizational attempts have left hardly a vestige. Lewis D. and John H. Gilbert's Corporate Democracy, Inc., though not a real union, has been the longest-lived attempt at stimulating a national shareowner constituency. Benjamin Javits, a New York lawyer, struggled for years to establish the concept of "ownerism"; he formed his own stockholder group and even wrote a book on the theme. Basically, Javits envisioned a strong working alliance between shareowners and management for advancing free enterprise. Among other attempts is the Federation of Women Shareholders in American Business, Incorporated, founded and headed by Wilma Soss, who is also a well-known corporate annual meeting gadfly. But as these and similar attempts have shown, unionization is probably not the proper route for the development of a dedicated corporate shareowner constituency.

Yet unless corporations, and particularly their boards of directors, find a model in which shareowners identify and feel part of a personified organization, control will continue to be usurped. On the other hand, if U.S. boards could somehow arouse even a modest part of the 30 million in-fee owners of common stock to become loyalists, concerned constituents, or even activist partisans, our corporations would pack a most

[21]Susan Harrigan, "Holders of Southern Co. May Be Planning to Form Association," *The Wall Street Journal,* May 29, 1980, p. 21.

powerful political clout. It would be the greatest of democratic political punches—serving in the best interests of enterprise, equity, productivity, and progress.

BOARDS AND PRODUCTIVITY

Productivity, or the rate of output per unit of input (generally measured in worker hours), is decidedly on the decline in the United States. Data in Table 9-1 (first column), compiled from a variety of sources, show that as the United States entered its industrial age, it had a very gradual productivity improvement. It was not until the early twentieth century when several merger waves, an avalanche of innovations and inventions, and the perturbations of World War I stimulated annual productivity gains to an average of about 2 percent. This climb plateaued for almost two decades after World War II at better than 3 percent annually. In their optimism, Americans even capitulated to organized labor at the collective bargaining table by guaranteeing a 3 percent annual productivity pay raise to many unionists. Yet since this concession, there have been almost no years when industry, as a whole, even came close to this 3 percent supposedly assured annual productivity increment. As noted, we have been in a progressive slide ever since the mid-1960s, with the early 1980s even recording a negative productivity. The last available corrected data show that U.S. productivity fell at a rate of 7.6 percent in the fourth quarter of 1981, the sharpest decline ever recorded.

Many reasons have been advanced for explaining this phenomenon. The most frequently blamed culprits are the uncontrolled influx into the labor market of masses of unskilled workers, particularly women, youths, and illegal immigrants; astronomical energy costs; sluggish capital investment;

TABLE 9-1 ANNUAL PRODUCTIVITY
GAINS, 1800–1981

Period	Average annual change, %	Average inside directors, %
1800–1855	0.5	20
1856–1890	1.1	30
1891–1920	2.0	45
1921–1947	2.4	55
1948–1966	3.2	60
1967–1973	2.1	50
1974–1978	1.1	45
1979–1981	−0.5	40

and suffocating federal and state regulations. Edward F. Denison, a Brookings Institution economist, has listed seventeen possible reasons for the sharp and sudden decline in productivity. Denison and others blame a drop in the capital-per-worker ratio, namely, the stock of invested capital facilitating worker productivity. Then there are intersectoral shifts such as the prior generations' move of farmers to factories and the more recent exodus from factories to services. Stagflation and deteriorating attitudes toward work itself, a by-product of the counterculture's antipathy in the late 1960s toward regimentation and orderliness, likewise, get blamed.

But the most perturbing accusation is that Americans have lost their sense of the work ethic and that they just do not want to work. *Forbes* countered this contention with this statement: "There's nothing seriously wrong with the American work ethic that couldn't be cured by sounder tax laws and a more enlightened and long-sighted corporate management. The American worker is taking the rap for a lot of things that his politicians and executives are doing wrong."[22] *Forbes* supports this view with data showing the United States is still the productivity leader—ahead of Japan by better than 30 percent, United Kingdom by 40 percent, France and West Germany by 11 percent. "What you get for Japan is some export-oriented industries with very high productivity. But when you get away from the biggest companies, the picture changes."[23]

This defense, however, should not lull us into complacency. When compared with their American counterparts, figures show that, on an annual basis, Japanese autoworkers and steelmakers have almost double output. While there are explanations for this, such as the longer workweek of the typical Japanese worker, the lighter impact of governmental control, and the refereeing by the Ministry of International Trade and Industry, there is also ample evidence to show our superiority is waning.

Another interesting thesis has been advanced by William Ouchi, professor at University of California at Los Angeles. Ouchi stresses that Japanese companies can more easily introduce technological innovations because, in effect, all Japanese workers belong to one union. When Japanese employees are threatened with technological unemployment, they can easily be transferred from one area to another. Late in summer 1981, CNA Insurance Companies sponsored a productivity conference where the differences in labor union structure were emphasized. A group of American experts visiting one tool plant in Japan were impressed with its 18 robot-controlled machining centers which replaced 72 machine tools. Only 10 employees were doing the work formerly done by 210 machinists. However, the surplus workers were not laid off—they were retrained and reassigned. But

---

[22]"The Myth of the Lazy American," *Forbes*, July 6, 1981, p. 11.
[23]Ibid.

in the United States, where several rival unions might be involved, such easy technological adjustment is impossible, and as a consequence, productivity slumps.

Most recently, the finger of blame has been pointed at our managers. "A report by the U.S. Chamber of Commerce Productivity Center pins the major blame for slowing efficiency on *stubborn management*. New techniques for sparking a team spirit among work forces have been largely ignored."[24] And almost everyone except the managers themselves admit that we have far too many managers. A Ford Motor Company executive, William J. Harahan, stresses that while at Ford there are twelve layers of organization from factory to company chairman, competitor Toyota has only seven layers. "The resolution of the problem is 80% a management responsibility and 20% production worker responsibility."[25]

Sloppy management can, of course, initiate from many factors. However, the bottom-line syndrome seems to be getting an ever-increasing share of blame for this sloppiness. The bottom-line approach exaggerates the current profit and loss summary and gives only minimal consideration to probable bottom-line figures five or ten years hence. "The horizon of the average American manager seems to be several years nearer than the horizons of most of his competitors in other industrial nations. While our competitors have been seeking to optimize market position and competitiveness over the longer term, we have been increasingly preoccupied with immediate results."[26]

But why put the ultimate responsibility on the lower-level managers? Theirs is but to do and not to reason why. Actually, for the greater part of our history, managers did little else but manage. Top decision making was the exclusive prerogative of the owner, whether an individual, family, or a syndicate of investors. It was only in the late 1920s, and thereafter, that company executives became acceptable as company directors. Note the unique correlation in Table 9-1; as the numbers of officer-directors increased, so did U.S. industrial productivity.

Unfortunately, this trend then shifted in the mid-1960s—if we were seeking a simplistic explanation, we might say it all began with Keith Funston. In 1965, Funston, president of the New York Stock Exchange (NYSE), single-handedly mandated that all new listings on the NYSE had to have at least two outside directors. This unilateral action disturbed the large segment of American industry which at that time had predominantly inside or officer-type boards. Significantly, most experts peg our productivity

---

[24]*U.S. News & World Report,* August 24, 1981, p. 54.

[25]"Japan's Edge in Auto Costs," *Business Week,* September 14, 1981, p. 97.

[26]Frank A. Weil, "Management's Drag on Productivity," *Business Week,* December 3, 1979, p. 14.

decline from the late 1960s, just a few years after the Funston foible. Though this inference may seem simplistic, it is no more simple than the elongated list of quasi and pseudo productivity-slump explanations which have been advanced by reputable scholars.

In the rationale for Funston's decision, a significant ingredient is too often overlooked. Funston did not issue his ruling simply because he abhorred officer-directors; after all, most outside directors are actually officer-directors in their own companies. There was, indeed, a more pressing reason. As a consequence of increased merging and tremendous expansion in the early 1960s, institutional investors came into ascendancy. With increased debt-to-equity ratios, pension plan pressures for increased earnings, and a complex of comparable reasons, many managements lost their independence. They were forced to maximize immediate results even to the detriment of longer-term aspirations. They could not gaze too far into the future—they had to concentrate on present profit performance. "Why has the American manager gotten into this frame of mind? Because the managers of the powerful institutional owners of his company's shares don't want a lot of explanations. They want results now. Five years from now won't do."[27]

Dominance by institutional investors is graphically shown in Table 9-2, which lists twenty large-scale public corporations, the number of institutional investors, and percentages of ownership. These data are published annually (late in December) in *Business Week*'s "Investment Outlook Scoreboard." Note that most of the companies in Table 9-2 were once classic family firms, and are still considered by many Americans to be in that ownership-control category. But, alas, even Ford Motor Company, with 43 percent institutional ownership, is no longer considered a crown jewel of the Ford family.

Along with this ownership trend, there has been a surge in outside directors and a fixation on net income—*here and now*—on price-earnings (P/E) ratios, yield, leveraging, and, of course, "plastic-money" mergers. Probably there has been a greater loss in productivity from inflationary stock-watered mergers than from all combined labor-associated causes. Of more than $80 billion directed into large-scale merging in 1981, virtually none went into research, development, new equipment, or facilities, whereas at least one-third went into watered stock, a lure used to entice an acquired firm.

Today one rarely associates synergy with big mergers. The word "synergy" is justifiably passé. It never was apparent in any productivity increase in the successor firm over the combined productivity of the premerged firms.

[27]Ibid.

TABLE 9-2 SAMPLE OF COMPANY COMMON STOCK
HELD BY INSTITUTIONS

Company	Percent stock held	Number of institutions
AT&T	50	1530
ALCOA	65	380
Bethlehem Steel	40	192
Du Pont	61	622
Deere	64	377
Exxon	42	1105
Eastman Kodak	55	942
Ford Motor	43	309
General Electric	49	1006
General Motors	32	869
Heinz	60	205
IBM	50	1530
Johnson & Johnson	61	574
Eli Lilly	66	645
Xerox	64	799
Median: 900 companies	37	106

Source: Business Week, "Investment Outlook Scoreboard,"
December 28, 1981, pp. 109–125.

Measuring productivity and attributing causality are tenuous things. Explanations of productivity fluctuations seem to be no better than the weather-by-sunspot theory. Even the Harris Upham (brokerage firm) hemline theory, showing that overall stock market prices rise and fall with changing lengths of women's skirts, makes as much sense as most productivity theory. Consequently, even with the imperfect data in Table 9-1, and using only the simplest approximation and trend-smoothing techniques, Figure 9-1 seems to show a remarkable relationship. Boardroom structure does have some meaning for industrial productivity: when officer-directors assumed more responsible roles in managing and controlling the affairs of our companies, our industrial system's productivity surged; when, however, an increasing number of firms began to reject officer-directors, productivity slumped.

Fortune, in an interesting commentary on "The Top 20 Stocks of the Decade," corroborates this thesis.[28] All but two or three of the twenty super-performers among the "Fortune 500" have strong officer/owner directorates. Moreover, insider ownership in the top twenty averages 9

[28]Gwen Kinkead, "The Top 20 Stocks of the Decade," Fortune, May 3, 1982, p. 299.

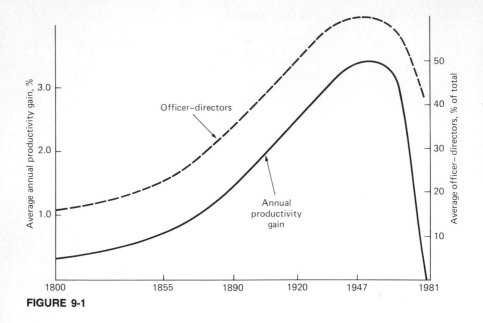

FIGURE 9-1

percent compared with less than 1 percent for the rest of the 500. "No quarrel with the conventional wisdom that executives will not dash their own cash."[29]

With a total of 186 directors, the twenty best performers had approximately 62 percent officers/owners serving as directors. This is the reverse ratio that typifies today's "oversight" boards.

In respect to profit and productivity, the top twenty, with average annual returns of 26.3 percent, outpaced the 8.5 percent average annual return of the rest of big business. And growth in earnings per share over the decade, at 27.1 percent, was more than double that of the "Fortune 500."

The author suggests that proponents of outside directors should test this interesting hypothesis. The author's studies, as mentioned earlier, support the contention that directors close to the scene, competent and dedicated, are far more effective than part-time directors of questionable interest, availability, or competency. Is this not the case in every system, even in totalitarian environments? When central planning agencies, staffed with politically safe personnel, are far removed physically and technically from the production scene, these absentee directors seldom generate productivity-gain records.

[29]Ibid., p. 300.

ENTELECHY: BORN AGAIN DIRECTORS

Corporate directors perform for a variety of reasons. As previously mentioned, Britain's Lord Boothby liked to accumulate directorships because of the "permanent hot bath" feeling they provided. Then there is the drum beater analogy where some bank directors believe their prime function is to "beat the business drum" and attract customers to their bank. Some directors seek seats to get privy information which is then translated into personal gain such as in arbitraging mergers. University presidents who serve on corporate boards often hope to attract gifts and endowments to their universities; their underling professors generally serve for supplemental income. A number of directors simply like the challenge of climbing to the corporate boardroom mountaintop. Pride, prestige, greed, and a host of other driving factors influence boardroom seating.

In spite of all the given reasons, the most gratifying would be that directors serve on boards because of their inner altruistic, humanistic, or moralistic impulses. If this were the case, then these enlightened directors would become their brothers' keepers, surrogates dedicated to protecting and enhancing shareholder and society's commonweal. They might even be called philosopher-directors, emulating Plato's paragon of the philosopher-kings.

Unfortunately, this is a lofty aspiration. There are no visible manifestations of angelic haloes or embryonic wings to differentiate boardroom saint from sinner. In fact, if compensation for boardroom services were to be used as the measure of director altruism (and saintliness), one would find very few saints in the lot. How many directors would be willing to turn over their outside-director earnings to their full-time employer or even to a favorite charity? Presently, the great majority of outside directors hold firmly to the "charity begins at home" notion.

Yet at one time boardroom service was called eleemosynary, that is, in the manner of almsgiving—a gift to the poor, the ailing, the less fortunate. It was charity in the good sense. Now, however, with some outside directorates paying in excess of $50,000 for sixty hours of endeavor (frequently less) per year, the mercenary has definitely superseded the eleemosynary. Moonlighting has become paramount; enlightenment, as a motivator, has been largely eclipsed. This is lamentable. As we know, other societies condemn capitalism for its unblinking focus on the big buck, on profits, the bottom line, debits versus credits. That, our critics contend, is the capital sin of capitalism.

Perhaps we should recall the ancient concept of entelechy, 2½ millennia old. The preeminent Greek philosopher Aristotle talked about entelechy, the highest order of motivation. The word "entelechy" derives from three little Greek words: εχω (I have) τελοσ (my goal or purpose) εν (within). By using this ancient blend, Aristotle coined a new word meaning: "I have my goal or purpose within me." Aristotle interpreted entelechy as the inner drive by which each person or thing is drawn to its fulfillment. Perfect entelechy is achieved when any being maximizes or utilizes its full potential, in other words, when potentiality becomes reality. Aristotle's motivation needs no goads or "carrots"; it initiates from the soul. It is a primordial and unfathomable force, crowning the scalar sequencing of, first, the protective needs, then the nutritive, followed by the sensitive and, ultimately, the rational needs.

Entelechy was no revelation to the Greeks of Aristotle's day—it was "old stuff." Common sense told the ancients that everybody works—first to survive, then to play the social animal game, and ultimately to commune with Zeus and Zoroaster. But even in Aristotle's time the great ideal was too frequently measured in prosaic common denominators—gold talents, drachmas, special favors, and inside dealings.

Some of today's behavioral scientists, in their writings about the hierarchy of needs, act as if they discovered the motivational wheel; yet almost weekly every church-going American receives the message of entelechy through various preachings. Sometimes sermons are most effectively delivered in nonecclesiastical form. Several years ago, the F. Jos. Lamb Company of Warren, Michigan, preached entelechy without knowing or saying so. In a two-page *Fortune* advertisement, "A two-story shack on a forty-story foundation," the company decried the waste of unutilized talent and substance.

In the ad, a business executive looks down from the eminence of his office (upon recent construction below), commenting to a friend: "Look at that building. They sank a forty-story foundation and then built a two-story shack on it." This, the executive philosophizes, is like so many people he knows—forty-story foundations and two-story lives. There are those who have natural skill and training sufficient to make significant contributions, and yet they are content to idle away their time and talent—that is building a shack on a skyscraper foundation.

The ad then lists other examples: those who have opportunities and potential to grow in their personal lives; those who have education and training for potential leadership; those who have a heritage of faith and idealism sufficient to serve as exemplars. Yet when these attributes are not self actualized, then that is building a shack on a skyscraper foundation.

Most American corporate boards have sturdy foundations with forty-story superstructure potential. This is a heritage of several generations of superior organization and workmanship, by a remarkably dynamic economic system. Yet far too many boards of directors are content to build two-story shacks on skyscraper foundations. This is the case when high-caliber directors either are perfunctory in their meeting attendance or do not take the time to study the issues. Boards also build two-story shacks when they seek easy consensus rather than hammered-out decisions. Even more serious boardroom architectural flaws follow from director myopia, when immediate bottom-line results completely obscure long-run benefits of risk taking, invention, and innovation.

There are a near-infinite number of ways to unwittingly reduce the scale of a potential boardroom skyscraper. Perhaps the quickest, surest, and most common way to throw together a miserable shack, rather than construct a lofty edifice, is to let board members ignore the firm's proprietors—the shareowners. Far too many corporations have come to consider their boardroom seats in a narrow proprietary way—as if these seats belonged to them and not to the stockholders. So many corporations equate their boardroom seats with seats on the stock exchange—to be bought and sold. *The Wall Street Journal,* in the summer of 1982, carried a candid advertisement by a major private university which offered positions as trustees on the university's board to "investors" who were willing to give a minimum of $1 million cash!

Perhaps it is time to initiate a corporate "urban renewal" program. The shacky two-story directorate structures must be demolished, and in their place must come a boardroom rebuilding, and a staffing with a new breed of director. Then and only then, when forty-story foundations are graced with forty-story structures, when corporate governance potentiality becomes organizational reality, can corporations and their dedicated directors say, "*Echo, telos, en:* I have done my best; I have reached my goal."

NAME INDEX

Abs, Herman Josef, 226, 227
Africanus, Servaeus, 193
Agee, William H., 187–191, 202
Agnelli, Giovanni, 31, 33
Allen, George E., 47
Araskog, Rand V., 41, 42
Archimedes, 251
Aristotle, 275
Ash, Roy L., 42, 43
Askew, Governor Reuben, 262

Beeghly, Charles M., 171
Bennett, Harry, 5
Berle, Adolf A., 45, 243
Black, William, 26
Blough, Roger, 76
Boothby, Lord, 46, 51, 52, 274
Boulis, J. Richard, 240
Bradshaw, Thornton, 45
Brandeis, Justice Louis, 262
Bressler, Richard M., 78
Brimmer, Andrew F., 107
Bronfman, Charles, 217
Bronfman, Edgar M., 217, 218
Brown, R. Manning, Jr., 184
Bryan, Charles E., 83, 221, 222
Buckley, William F., Jr., 97, 180–182

Bulow, Jeremy, 234
Bunker, Ellsworth, 48
Bunting, John R., 109, 110
Burnham, Donald C., 209
Butcher, Howard, III, 48, 166
Byrom, Fletcher L., 113

Catchings, Waddell, 48
Celler, Emmanuel, 100, 101, 143
Chafee, Senator John, 132, 133
Charpie, Robert A., 47, 77
Chiles, Senator Lawton, 122
Church, Senator Frank, 121
Cleary, Catherine B., 147
Coates, Francis G., 162
Connally, John B., 208
Connor, John T., 146
Conrad, Anthony L., 44
Conway, E. Virgil, 184
Cordiner, Ralph, 159, 160
Corn, Ira G., Jr., 90
Cronkite, Walter, 103
Crystal, Graef S., 79, 210
Cummings, Nate, 151
Cummins, Stephen I., 261
Cunningham, Mary, 187–191, 202

279

COMPANY INDEX

SUBJECT INDEX